Juridicum – Schriften zum Medien-, Informations- und Datenrecht

In der Schriftenreihe erscheinen Forschungsbeiträge zum Kommunikations- und Medienrecht in seiner vollen Breite, vom Äußerungs-, Urheber- und Kunsturheberrecht über das Daten- und Informationsrecht bis zu Fragen öffentlich-rechtlicher Medien- oder Intermediärsregulierung, einschließlich ihrer theoretischen Hintergründe. Erfasst sind insbesondere innovative akademische Qualifikationsschriften, aber auch Abhandlungen und Sammelbände von herausragendem wissenschaftlichen Wert.

Nina Dethloff · Katharina Kaesling ·
Louisa Specht-Riemenschneider
Editors

Families and New Media

Comparative Perspectives on Digital Transformations in Law and Society

Springer

Editors
Nina Dethloff
Institute for German, European, and International Family Law
University of Bonn
Bonn, Germany

Katharina Kaesling
Institute of International Law, Intellectual Property and Technology Law (IRGET)
University of Dresden (TU)
Dresden, Germany

Louisa Specht-Riemenschneider
Department of Law
University of Bonn
Bonn, Germany

ISSN 2662-9488 ISSN 2662-9496 (electronic)
Juridicum – Schriften zum Medien-, Informations- und Datenrecht
ISBN 978-3-658-39663-3 ISBN 978-3-658-39664-0 (eBook)
https://doi.org/10.1007/978-3-658-39664-0

This Springer imprint is published by the registered company Springer Fachmedien Wiesbaden GmbH, part of Springer Nature.
The registered company address is: Abraham-Lincoln-Str. 46, 65189 Wiesbaden, Germany

Editors' Introduction: Families and New Media

Communication structures and business models have changed globally, encompassing substantial opportunities and a new range of dangers for users of digital media. Both the potential and dangers apply especially to children's online participation as acting subjects and as objects of imagery. New media usage entails disclosure of various types of information; offers new ways of secluded one-on-one and group communication; and bears new risks of violations of privacy, emotional integrity, and sexual self-determination. While particularly vulnerable, children also benefit greatly from inclusion in online discourse, access to information, and online social opportunities. Rights to participation are to be reconciled with rights to protection. Children— as normative subjects and human beings—have rights to free expression and privacy; parental and societal efforts to protect children risk undermining these rights. Digital transformation affects numerous, if not all, areas of life. As the Committee on the Rights of the Child formulates in its General Comment No. 25 (2021) on children's rights in relation to the digital environment, "The digital environment is constantly evolving and expanding, encompassing information and communication technologies, including digital networks, content, services and applications, connected devices and environments, virtual and augmented reality, artificial intelligence, robotics, automated systems, algorithms and data analytics, biometrics and implant technology." This much-expected General Comment was adopted in Spring 2021, about one year after our international and interdisciplinary conference "Digital Transformation in Law & Society: Comparative Perspectives on Families and New Media", which took place at the Käte Hamburger Center "Law as Culture" in Bonn in February 2020. The conference, on which this volume is based, turned out to be one of the last opportunities for intensive as well as light-hearted personal exchange on site, before the Covid-19 pandemic manifested across the globe. While the challenges associated with this pandemic did not facilitate the work on this volume, conditions for families during Covid-19 times certainly highlighted the relevance of new media and technologies for sociality, education, and play. Children's rights in relation to the digital environment have only gained importance in the face of homeschooling, distance learning, and the substitution of much in-person contact with online meetings. Like a burning glass, pandemic conditions show the need to support children and their surroundings in dealing with opportunities and risks arising from the use of new media.

In response to these opportunities and risks, legal norms largely rely on the paradigm of adult supervision and guidance. In the European Union and elsewhere, parental consent is a precondition for the child's access to information society services. State laws generally impose not only a right, but also a duty on parents to care for their minor children as part of their parental responsibility. In the care and upbringing of a child, parents have to take into account the growing ability and growing need of their child for independent responsible action. However, new media practices and collectives shape childhood in ways that today's adults have not experienced themselves. The challenges brought about by the digital transformation in law and society raise fundamental questions as to the relationship between the state and families as social entities.

Applicable legal norms stem from a number of relevant legal areas and concern data and parental responsibility as well as (artistic) copyright; they include general, sector-specific, and child-centered approaches. Relevant legal sources come from many regulatory levels, such as international treaties, European Union law, and the laws of individual nation-states. Regulation within the field of families and new media is thus characterized by the interplay of various regulatory levels. In addition, state laws and policies collide with developing transnational codes, digital (youth) cultures, and other social norms. Online imagery, for example, gives both children and parents a new means of outward (self-)representation, touching on behavioral as well as responsibility dimensions of parent-child relationships. At the same time, children risk becoming pure objects of digital parental action strategies and practices, rather than partaking in accordance with their abilities. Conventional expectations of both parents and children, such as privacy in one's own home, are called into question. While privacy has never been as certain for children as for parents, as the latter could always invade children's privacy at home quite easily, digitally connected devices enable parents to monitor children's behavior with little effort and without the children even noticing. When using smart devices at home, third parties are invited into the family home and regularly receive data on various aspects of family life taking place within a seemingly protected space, suggesting that surveillance has become socially acceptable. Practices involving the disclosure of children's personal data, such as storytelling on social networks and the use of smart devices and toys at home, lead to a datafication of children. In order to better understand these paradigm shifts and further challenges for traditional conceptions of the roles of children, parents, the state, and new actors like online platforms, this volume brings together scholars from various backgrounds. The interplay of social and legal norms, regulatory needs, and existing legal policies and laws are analyzed with a focus on children's rights and agency. Perspectives from international legal scholars with specialization in data law, intellectual property law, and family law are complemented by viewpoints of scholars of sociology, political science, education, and media studies. The volume is divided into three parts, dealing with children's agency and rights in the digital world in part 1, with the risk of diminishing their role to that of an object (of imagery) in part 2, and the impact of data and digital economy regulation on children in part 3.

At the outset, *Nina Dethloff* outlines the manifold ways in which digital transformation has changed family lives and examines how, with the paradigm shift towards children as holders of rights, their evolving capacities are to be taken into account both in analogue and digital spheres. Digital parenting is then analyzed from a perspective of media and communication research by *Caja Thimm*, who distinguishes *media usage* within the family from the family as a *mediated object*. Defining digital parenting both with regard to the regulation and control of children's media use and with regard to the ways parents themselves incorporate digital media into their daily activities and parenting practices, *Thimm* focuses on parenting practices on social media. The ambivalences in children's and parents' perspectives on practices of digital parenting are subsequently exposed by *Nadia Kutscher*. Building on Kutscher's and social psychologist Sonia Livingstone's rights-based claims, *Katharina Kaesling* demonstrates the importance of a rights-based approach to children's digital participation from a legal point of view and with special regard to multi-level norm-setting, legal architecture, and fundamental principles of the European Union. She specifically addresses the implementation of the legal principle of the best interests of the child and the role of proportionality and coherence of measures limiting children's rights.

The second part examines digital parenting strategies, particularly in the context of the visualization of family life, in more detail. Parental action strategies regarding 'sharenting', i.e. the parental use of social media to share pictures of their children, are shown to be multifaceted communicative practices in *Ulla Autenrieth's* contribution. Based on data generated during a Swiss research project on the image-based presentation of familial occasions in participative online contexts, she describes not only the quantity and role of private photos in intra- and inter-familial communication, but also the parental weighing of risks. While she finds that sharenting should not be constructed as fundamentally irresponsible, family law courts' views on that matter may differ. Given that legal approaches to parental practices of sharenting diverge and are still being developed in many legal orders, *Paula Távora Vítor's* examination of Portuguese family court jurisprudence on that matter, which included a ban on sharenting as part of a court order on parental responsibility, is of particular interest from a comparative point of view. The responses of German courts to internet-related questions of parental responsibility in the context of copyright and civil law are analyzed by *Thomas Dreier.* In addition to a legal analysis, he evokes Niklas Luhmann's model of social subsystems to make sense of the law in its relationship to technology, the economy, and social norms of conduct. Applying Norbert Elias' process sociology, *Marta Bucholc* undertakes a systematic theorizing of digital parenting strategies in light of the changes for childhood, family, and parenthood associated with new media.

As developed in the first two parts, children's agency and participative rights are not always at the center of setting and interpreting norms. This is especially true for measures regulating the emerging fields of data and digital economy. Business models, cultural practices, and legal regulation of data collection and privacy mirror first and foremost the increasing economic importance and value of data, information, and other intangibles for companies, as *Olufunmilayo B. Arewa* finds. Their impact on children is illustrated with regard to the datafication of children in smart homes, the protection of children on video-sharing platforms, and children's position under data protection law. The societal implications of children's data being captured and transmitted in smart homes, often without much awareness by parents, are emphasized by *Victoria Nash*. She illustrates how the creation of a datafied 'algorithmic child' bears the risk that its perceived needs take precedence over the actual individual and self-claimed needs. With regard to the diverse audio-visual content accessible online, including sexually explicit, violent, and other potentially harmful videos, children are in particular need of protection. Legal responses to this regulatory need regarding the video-sharing platform economy are evaluated by *Louisa Specht-Riemenschneider*, *Alina Marko*, and *Sascha Wette*. Finally, shortcomings of the legal regimes and policies of children's informational privacy are described by *Ayelet Blecher-Prigat.* She identifies a divergence of children's rights to privacy, as formally recognized under the laws of various jurisdictions and international treaties, from the importance accorded to children's privacy in existing laws. To her, this is attributable not only to adult-centered theories on privacy and dated conceptions of the family and parent-child relationships, but also to a disconnect between research and legal policy. This interdisciplinary volume aspires to contribute to bridging this gap.

Contents

Editors and Contributors

About the Editors

Prof. Dr. Nina Dethloff, LL.M. (Georgetown) is Professor of Civil Law, Private International Law, Comparative Law, and European Private Law and Director of the Institute for German, European, and International Family Law at the University of Bonn, Germany. At present, she is a member of the German Science Council, the Executive Board of the Association of German Jurists, the Executive Council of the International Society of Family Law (ISFL), and the Coordinating Group of the Family Law in Europe: Academic Network (FL-EUR). She has been elected a member of the American Law Institute and the Academia Europaea, where she currently chairs the Law Section. She was Director at the Käte Hamburger Center for Advanced Study in the Humanities "Law as Culture" and has also recently served as a member of the Expert Commission for the 9th Family Report of the German Federal Government. Her research focus is on comparative family law, on which she has published extensively. Among her recent publications are: Familienrecht (Verlag C. H. Beck, 33rd edition 2022, 610 pages); Child Participation in Germany (in: Schrama/Freeman/Taylor/Bruning (eds.): International Handbook on Child Participation in Family Law, Intersentia, 2021) (with Daniela Schröder); Personal autonomy and legal recognition of sexual and gender diversity—The German perspective (in: Rogerson/Antokolskaia/Miles et al. (eds.): Family Law and Family Realities: 16th ISFL World Conference Book, Eleven International Publishing, 2019, pp. 9–17); and Child Brides on the Move: Legal Responses to Culture Clashes (in: International Journal of Law, Policy and the Family 32/2018, pp. 302–315).

JProf. Dr. Katharina Kaesling, LL.M. is Junior Professor of Civil Law, Intellectual Property, especially Patent Law, and Legal Issues of AI at the University of Dresden (TU), Germany. From 2017 to 2022, she was Research Coordinator at the Käte Hamburger Center for Advanced Study in the Humanities "Law as Culture" at the University of Bonn, Germany. She is a habilitation candidate at the Department of Law at the University of Bonn, Member of the North Rhine-Westphalian Academy of Sciences, Humanities and the Arts, and Member of the Board of ForTech, the Research Center for Legal Issues of New Technologies and Data Law (Forschungsstelle für Rechtsfragen neuer Technologien sowie Datenrecht). Her research areas include European and Comparative Private Law, Platform Regulation, Private International Law, Intellectual Property Law and Data Law. Her comparative law dissertation on German and French family law has won several awards, including the prize for the best dissertation of the law department of the University of Bonn. Her recent publications include: Article-by-Article Commentary on the management of systemic risks by very large online platforms (Articles 33, 34, 35, 37, 41, 42 and 43) and data access for authorities and researchers (Art 40), in: Hofmann/Raue: Digital Services Act: Gesetz über digitale Dienste, Nomos, 2023; Rainbow Families on Social Media: Diversity and Plurality as Matters of Platform Regulation, in: Dethloff/Kaesling (eds.): Between Sexuality, Gender and Reproduction: On the Pluralisation of Family Forms, Intersentia, 2023, pp. 227–252; Children's Digital Rights: Realizing the Potential of the CRC, in: Laufer-Ukeles/Marrus (eds.): Global Reflections on Children's Rights and the Law: 30 Years After the U.N. Convention on the Rights of the Child, Routledge, 2021, Chapter 14, pp. 183–196.

Prof. Dr. Louisa Specht-Riemenschneider is Professor of Law at the Rheinische Friedrich-Wilhelms-University of Bonn, Germany, serving as Chair for Civil Law, Law of the Data Economy, Data Protection, Digitalization and Artificial Intelligence and as Head of the Research Center for Legal Issues of New Technologies and Data Law (ForTech, Forschungsstelle für Rechtsfragen neuer Technologien sowie Datenrecht). In addition, she chairs the Council of Experts on Consumer Issues at the German Federal Ministry for the Environment, Nature Conservation, Nuclear Safety and Consumer Protection. Her research focuses primarily on copyright, the internet, data, and data protection law. Among her recent publications are: Data access rights – A comparative perspective (in: German Federal Ministry of Justice and Consumer Protection/Max Planck Institute for Innovation and Competition (eds.): Data Access, Consumer Interests and Public Welfare, Nomos, 2021, pp. 401–438); Verantwortung von Online-Plattformen—ein Plädoyer für funktionszentrierte Verkehrspflichten (2021) (with Franz Hofmann); and Stuck Half Way: The Limitation of Joint Control after Fashion

ID (C-40/17) (in: GRUR International, 69(2), 2020, pp. 159–163) (together with Ruben Schneider).

Contributors

Prof. Dr. Olufunmilayo B. Arewa Temple University, Philadelphia, USA

Prof. Dr. Ulla Autenrieth University of Applied Sciences of the Grisons, Chur, Switzerland

Prof. Dr. Ayelet Blecher-Prigat Academic College of Law and Science, School of Law, Hod HaSharon, Israel

Prof. Dr. Marta Bucholc University of Warsaw, Warsaw, Poland

Prof. Dr. Nina Dethloff, LL.M. (Georgetown) Institute for German, European, and International Family Law, University of Bonn, Bonn, Germany

Prof. Dr. Thomas Dreier, M.C.J. (New York University) Karlsruhe Institute of Technology (KIT), Karlsruhe, Germany

JProf. Dr. Katharina Kaesling, LL.M. Institute of International Law, Intellectual Property and Technology Law (IRGET), University of Dresden (TU), Dresden, Germany

Prof. Dr. Nadia Kutscher University of Cologne, Cologne, Germany

Alina Marko University of Bonn, Bonn, Germany

Prof. Dr. Victoria Nash Oxford Internet Institute (OII), University of Oxford, Oxford, UK

Prof. Dr. Louisa Specht-Riemenschneider University of Bonn, Bonn, Germany

Prof. Dr. Caja Thimm Institute for Language, Media and Music Studies, Department for Media Studies, University of Bonn, Bonn, Germany

Prof. Dr. Paula Távora Vítor Faculty of Law, IJ, University of Coimbra, Coimbra, Portugal

Sascha Wette University of Bonn, Bonn, Germany

Children as Social Subjects in the Digital World

Families and the Law: Taking Account of Children's Evolving Capacities in Analogue and Digital Contexts

Nina Dethloff

New media have a fundamental influence on families and their lives. Especially for children, the process of digital transformation encompasses both substantial potential as well as a new range of risks. It thus challenges existing normative orders. During the last century and in particular the past decades, the position of children in families, in society, and in law has changed considerably. This requires legislators to increasingly take the child's evolving capacities into account, both in analogue and digital contexts. After first taking a look at the dramatic impact of digitalization on families and their lives (1), the following contribution will address the shift in children's position in law (2) before exploring in depth how various legal frameworks take cognizance of children's evolving capacities in analogue and digital spheres (3).

1 Impact of Digital Transformation on Families and their Lives

In recent years, the internet has provided a variety of new methods of communication, information, documentation, and representation that allow different ways of digital participation. The process of digitalization has a tremendous impact on the analogue society at large and thus profoundly transformes lives, including those of families and their members. Parents and children use their access to the online world in a multitude of ways, for instance by engaging in self-representa-

N. Dethloff (✉)
Institute for German, European, and International Family Law,
University of Bonn, Bonn, Germany
e-mail: dethloff@uni-bonn.de

N. Dethloff et al. (eds.), *Families and New Media*, Juridicum – Schriften zum Medien-, Informations- und Datenrecht,
https://doi.org/10.1007/978-3-658-39664-0_1

tion or by staging their family on social media. Likewise, ways of 'doing family' online are developing through new communication tools such as direct messenger applications like WhatsApp that family members use to interact with each other and to organize their family life.[1] As a result, in the digital world, children have increasingly become objects of imagery, their pictures among other personal data shared with family, friends, or the world.[2]

The sharing and re-sharing may be done by their parents, third parties, or the children themselves.[3] Some parents (to be) share details of their unborn baby, for example by posting sonographs or videos of them visiting the hospital. Daily toddler bedtime routines from the children's bedroom, as well as pictures from the child's first day of school, weekend getaways, and family holidays are also documented online to a mostly unrestricted audience.[4] Potential dangers for children[5] include cyberbullying, digital kidnapping, or sexual harassment. Moreover, in the longterm, such practices of so-called 'sharenting' may eventually have a negative impact on the normal development of the child.[6] Not surprisingly, there are concerns about children's online privacy[7] and questions in regard to the scope of parental power of representation.[8] While with such sharenting performative ele-

---

[1] For details, see Thimm: Mediatized Families, in this volume.

[2] For an example on how the Portuguese legal system approaches this phenomenon, see Távora Vítor: Banning Children's Image Online, in this volume.

[3] For details from the German perspective, see Kutscher: Positionings, Challenges, and Ambivalences in Children's and Parents' Perspectives in Digitalized Familial Contexts, in this volume.

[4] For a discussion of audience restrictions in the framework of EU data protection and German art copyright law, see Kaesling: Persönlich, familiär oder öffentlich? in: Croon-Gestefeld/Korch/Kuschel/Sarel/Scholz (eds.): Das Private im Privatrecht, 2022, pp. 151–174.

[5] For an overview, see Slavtcheva-Petkova/Nash/Bulger: Evidence on the extent of harms experienced by children as a result of online risks, Information, Communication & Society, 18(1), 2015, pp. 48–62.

[6] See Autenrieth: The Case of "Sharenting", in this volume.

[7] Raised e.g. by Livingstone/Stoilova/Nandagiri: Children's data and privacy online, 2018, p. 20; Nottingham: 'Dad! Cut that Part Out!', in: Murray/Blue Swadener/Smith (eds.): The Routledge International Handbook of Young Children's Rights; Kaesling: Children's Digital Rights, in: Marrus/Laufer-Ukeles (eds.): Global Reflections on Children's Rights and the Law, 2021, pp. 183–196, at p. 190.

[8] See Blecher-Prigat: Lost Between Data and Family? in this volume; for a parental view on sharenting and the privacy rights of kids, see Ross/Livingstone: Sharenting, Popular Communication, 15(2), 2017, pp. 110–125; in regard to the German legal discussion, see e.g. Rake: Kinderrechte und Sorgerechtsbefugnisse bei elterlichen Foto-Postings in sozialen Medien, FamRZ (Zeitschrift für das gesamte Familienrecht), 2020, pp. 1064–1070,

ments dominate,[9] financial aspects have taken center stage with the emanation of influencer marketing,[10] leading some parents to commercialize all aspects of their kids' childhood.

But children are not only objects of imagery: They also take part as actors in the digital world.[11] From increasingly young ages, and for extended periods of time every day, they are using new media through smart phones and other internet connected devices.[12] Thus, studies have shown that there has been a substantial increase in the time and ways that even young children under the age of nine are using the internet, for example, by watching and sharing videos, playing online games, searching for information, doing their homework, and socializing within children's virtual worlds.[13] Generally, online-communication with peers, romantic partners, and even strangers plays an important role in adolescence—with the interaction itself and the content potentially providing benefits and posing risks for the teen.[14] This being said, around half of all 11–16 year olds have at one stage encountered one or more of ten frequent internet risks, such as cyberbullying, sexting, grooming, exposure to harmful or disturbing content, or fake

---

at p. 1070; regarding sharenting and the UNCRC Kaesling: Children's Digital Rights, in: Marrus/Laufer-Ukeles (eds.): Global Reflections on Children's Rights and the Law, 2021, pp. 183–196, at pp. 189–190.

[9] For an overview of this phenomenon, see Davidson-Wall: "Mum, seriously!"; Steinberg: Sharenting, Emory Law Journal, 66, 2017, pp. 839–884.

[10] Cf. Archer: How influencer 'mumpreneur' bloggers and 'everyday' mums frame presenting their children online, Media International Australia, 170(1), 2019, pp. 47–56.

[11] With regard to risks and chances of digital participation for children, see Kaesling: A Rights-based Approach to Children's Digital Participation, in this volume; Kaesling: Children's Digital Rights, in: Marrus/Laufer-Ukeles (eds.): Global Reflections on Children's Rights and the Law, 2021, pp. 183–196, at pp. 183–184; in particular with regard to civic learning and engagement Kaesling: The Making of Citizens, in: Neuberger/Friesike/Krzywdzinski/Eiermann (eds.): Proceedings of the Weizenbaum Conference, 2021, pp. 67–71.

[12] For smart homes, see Nash: The Rise of the Algorithmic Child, in this volume.

[13] For EU data on children's internet use, see Holloway/Green/Livingstone: Zero to eight, p. 4; European Commission: Towards a safer use of the internet for children in the EU; for US data, see e.g. Center for Cyber Safety and Education: Children's internet usage study; for a South African perspective, see Center for Justice and Crime Prevention: Global Kids Online.

[14] Cf. Subrahmanyam/Greenfield: Online Communication and Adolescent Relationships, Children and Electronic Media, 18(1), 2008, pp. 119–146.

news.[15] Children might also use social media platforms to express themselves, for instance by sharing grief and mourning.[16] Moreover, digital youth cultures have emerged like participating in (dance) challenges on mobile short video apps like TikTok.[17] Although most legislation requires children to be of a certain age or to obtain their parents' consent for commercial activities, young children increasingly also use the internet for commercial purposes.[18] At even younger ages, smart toys provide new opportunities,[19] both as educational tools and as means of surveillance.[20] The use of real-time apps connected to smart technologies (i.e. baby monitors or sensors), whether at home or in daycare centers, literally allows an infant's every move to be supervised and a child's 'normal' development to be monitored—all while collecting enormous amounts of sensitive data on children[21] without necessarily providing the needed amount of protection, as experiences have shown.[22]

While children are availing themselves of the enormous potentials of the internet, they may become perpetrators, for example, when sharing (personal) data and thereby violating others' privacy or copyrights. Here, parental control apps come into play, but these may also invade the child's or adolescent's sphere of privacy[23] much to their dismay.[24] With data being today's 'digital gold,' powerful

[15] Cf. European Commission: How the EU protects your children online.

[16] Cf. Thimm/Nehls: Sharing grief and mourning on Instagram, Communications, 42(3), 2017, pp. 327–349.

[17] Cf. Kennedy: TikTok celebrity, girls and the Coronavirus crisis, European Journal of Cultural Studies, 23(6), 2020, pp. 857–873.

[18] Cf. Valcke et al.: Long-term study of safe Internet use of young children, Computers & Education, 57, 2011, pp. 1292–1305, at p. 1293.

[19] See Keymolen/Van der Hof: A philosophical and legal exploration of smart toys and trust, Journal of Cyber Policy, 4(2), 2019, pp. 143–159.

[20] Cf. Keymolen/Van der Hof: A philosophical and legal exploration of smart toys and trust, Journal of Cyber Policy, 4(2), 2019, pp. 143–159; Holloway/Green: The Internet of toys, Communication Research and Practice, 2(4), 2016, pp. 1–14.

[21] Cf. Leaver: Born Digital? in: Hartley/Qu (eds.): Re-Orientation, pp. 149–160, at p. 154.

[22] E.g. cases of hacked baby monitors in the United States, see Ensenat: Smart Baby Monitors, CATH. U. J. L. & TECH, 26, 2017, pp. 72–99.

[23] For an overview in regard to the German discussion around tracking providing further references, see Bundesministerium für Familie, Senioren, Frauen und Jugend (BMFSFJ): Neunter Familienbericht, Drucksache 19/27200, pp. 214 et seq. at 5.6.4.

[24] For the view of children, see e.g. Kumar/Arup et al.: Safety vs. Surveillance.

economic players are likewise involved in the digital transformation of family lives.[25]

2 Paradigm Shift in Law: From Children as Objects to Persons with Rights

2.1 Historical Perspective

Against this background, the paradigm shift in law affecting both the analogue and the digital world will now be outlined. For centuries, children were seen as objects, first needed as workers in agriculture and factories, then increasingly as objects of love and care.[26] However, over the course of the last century, their protection and well-being have gradually moved into the focus.[27] This was reflected in law: Increasingly, protecting children as societies' most vulnerable members became imperative, and the concept of the children's welfare gained importance.[28] Moreover, Western legal systems that built on Roman law had long adhered to the concept of *patria potestas*.[29] Even though "the father's power" no longer gave him total legal rights over his children as in Roman law,[30] children remained under *parental authority*, with the father's authority gradually being extended to both parents as gender equality became more recognized. Meanwhile, the change in awareness has found its expression in the replacement of the

[25] In regard to 'big data' and data breaches affecting children in the United States, see Arewa: Data Collection, Privacy, and Children in the Digital Economy, in this volume.

[26] Cf. Dethloff/Maschwitz: Kinderrechte in Europa—wo stehen wir? FPR (Familie Partnerschaft Recht), 2012, pp. 190–194; Hart: From property to person status, American Psychologist, 46(1), 1991, pp. 53–59.

[27] For a US-American perspective, see Williams: Child Protection, Journal of Clinical Psychology, 12(3), 1983, pp. 236–243.

[28] For a UK perspective, see Sclater/Piper: "Social Exclusion and the Welfare of the Child", Journal of Law and Society, 28(3), 2001, pp. 409–429.

[29] A Roman concept meaning the power of a Roman male ascendant, normally father or grandfather (pater familias), over descendants. For details on the concept and reach of the *patria potestas*, see Honsell: Römisches Recht, § 65 p. 182.

[30] Ibid.

concept of parental *authority* by that of parental *responsibility,* which today prevails above all in European and supranational law.[31]

2.2 Recognition of Children's Rights

However, the recognition of independent rights of children, which they are entitled to regardless of their minority, is a more recent development. For the first time, the position of the child, as a subject and holder of rights, found internationally binding recognition in the comprehensive guarantees of the UN Convention on the Rights of the Child (CRC) of 1989.[32] It commits the 196 state parties, which currently include all Member States of the European Union and—with the exception of the United States—all UN Member States,[33] to actively promote the rights of the child. Art. 3 (1) of the CRC not only requires that the best interest of the child be a primary consideration in all state actions concerning children. It also grants numerous specific rights to all children, who according to Art. 1 CRC are all persons under the age of 18, unless under the law applicable to the child, majority is attained earlier,[34] and thus explicitly also to adolescents.[35] These include, among others, the child's right to life and development (Art. 6 CRC); to protection from violence, abuse, and neglect (Art. 19 CRC); and to be heard (Art. 12 CRC).

Notably, the rights of the CRC apply both to the analogue and digital world. This becomes particularly obvious with the right to access to information from the media in Art. 17 CRC, which encompasses all forms of media with a main focus on the digital environment.[36] Such a right is especially important as the

---

[31] See e.g. for Europe The Commission on European Family Law (CEFL): The CEFL Principles of European Family Law Regarding Parental Responsibilities and Council of Europe: Committee of Ministers Recommondation No. R (84) 4 (adopted by the Committee of Ministers on 28.2.1984 at the 367th meeting of the Ministers' Deputies) on Parental Responsibilities.

[32] United Nations Human Rights Office of the High Comissioner: Convention on the Rights of the Child.

[33] Cf. United Nations Treaty Collection.

[34] Ibid.

[35] For the focus on adolescents, see Committee on the Rights of the Child: General Comment No. 20.

[36] Ibid., at VIII. 47 p. 13.

internet became de facto youth's main access point to information through the use of mobile technology. It thus provides the ability to access important information, for example, in regard to health and counseling, which could potentially influence the quest for equality.[37] Moreover, Art. 13 CRC expressly states that the right to freedom of expression includes the freedom to seek, receive, and impart information and ideas of all kinds, regardless of frontiers, either orally, in writing or in print, in the form of art, or through any other media of the child's choice, which consequently includes digital and audiovisual media.[38] As adolescents use the digital sphere for leisure to socialize and play, as well as to learn and participate and engage in (political) opinions,[39] the right to leisure activities and participation in cultural life and the arts in Art. 31 CRC, as well as the right to education in Art. 28 CRC, must be seen in the light of the digital era[40] and can only be fully guaranteed by providing access to the internet.[41] The opportunities offered by digital participation are also associated with increased risks *inter alia* for the right to privacy of adolescents,[42] which is explicitly protected by Art. 16 CRC. According to this provision, children shall be subjected to neither arbitrary or unlawful interference with their privacy, family, home, or correspondence nor to unlawful attacks on their honor and reputation.

The adoption of the CRC has been the starting point for the widespread development of children's rights.[43] They are not only enshrined in the EU Charter of Fundamental Rights (Art. 24), but also embedded in many national legal systems. In some states, such as Norway[44] and Spain,[45] the CRC became domestic law

[37] Ibid.

[38] Ibid., p. 11.

[39] Ibid., p. 13.

[40] For Art. 31 as underlined by Committee on the Rights of the Child: General Comment No. 17 at VI. 45 p. 14; for Art. 28, see Committee on the Rights of the Child: General Comment No. 20 at VIII. 47 p. 13.

[41] More details on children's rights to participation in the digital world in Kaesling: Children's Digital Rights, in: Marrus/Laufer-Ukeles (eds.): Global Reflections on Children's Rights and the Law, 2021, pp. 183–196.

[42] See in detail UNICEF: Child Safety Online.

[43] For an overview, see Dethloff/Maschwitz: Kinderrechte in Europa—wo stehen wir? FPR (Familie Partnerschaft Recht), 2012, pp. 190–194.

[44] Cf. UNICEF: The UN Convention on the Rights of the Child: a study of legal implementation in 12 countries at 4.5.

[45] Ibid., 4.6.

immediately upon ratification; in Spain, it even prevails over other legislation and can be invoked directly before the Constitutional and Supreme Court.[46] In other countries, like Germany, corresponding legislation has been passed to implement the treaty gradually.[47] Elsewhere, the entire body of law was reviewed to determine whether it complied with the Convention, such as in Sweden, where it recently explicitly also became law.[48] Moreover, a number of current European constitutions not only require taking into account the special need for protection of children, but also explicitly contain individual children's rights or even detailed guarantees of such rights.[49]

2.3 Children, Parents, and the State

Despite this broad recognition of children's rights brought about by the worldwide adoption of the CRC, there remain considerable differences in national systems.[50] At the heart of this lies the fact that children, at least initially, are not able to *exercise* these rights themselves. It is therefore equally well established that it is primarily the right *and* obligation of parents to care for and educate their children. Parental rights are also explicitly guaranteed by the CRC in Art. 5, in Art. 2 of the additional protocol of the ECHR,[51] and many national

[46] Ibid.

[47] For a detailed overview on how the UNCRC is incorporated in different states, see McCall-Smith: 'To incorporate the CRC or not—is this really the question?' The International Journal of Human Rights, 23(3), 2019, pp. 425–441.

[48] Cf. Regeringskansliet: Regeringens proposition 2017/18:186.

[49] E.g. Art. 22bis of the Belgian Constitution (from February 17, 1994, as amended on December 29, 2008) enumerates individual rights of the child: The right of the child to respect for moral, physical, mental, and sexual integrity; the right of the child to express themself in all matters concerning them; and the right to have their views taken into account in a manner appropriate to their age; as well as the best interests of the child as a guiding principle of state action are mentioned. Art. 31 of the Italian Constitution (from December 27, 1947) stipulates that the Republic protects mothers, children, and the young by adopting necessary provisions.

[50] Resulting in fundamental differences with respect to important issues such as access to comprehensive healthcare for children, see Palm: Children's universal right to health care in the EU, Eurohealth, 23(4), 2017, pp. 3–6.

[51] Council of Europe: Protocol to the Convention for the Protection of Human Rights and Fundamental Freedoms.

constitutions.[52] Accordingly, in Germany, Art. 6 (2) 1st st. Grundgesetz (GG; German Basic Law) guarantees that the care and upbringing of children is the natural right of parents and a duty primarily incumbent upon them. It also provides in Art. 6 (2) GG that the state shall watch over parents' performance of this duty. However, as children's abilities slowly mature, their capacities to exercise their rights correspondingly increase. Consequently, Art. 5 CRC explicitly requires that state parties shall respect parents' responsibilities to give appropriate direction and guidance to the child in exercising their rights in a manner consistent with their evolving capacities.

Having said this, it is evident that the granting of parental rights and duties on the one hand and the recognition of children's rights on the other raise fundamental questions as to the role of the state: When is the state allowed *or* required to interfere in the upbringing of a child? As is the case in the German legal system, for instance, it is often not seen as the state's role to second guess parents' decisions about what they consider best for their children or define the optimum standard for a child's upbringing,[53] but rather to merely interfere when the welfare of the child is at risk.[54] Accordingly, here it is assumed that in general, parents get to decide how much supervision their children need and how far their scope of actions may be restricted.[55] Pursuant to well-established case law of the Federal Constitutional Court, this requires that a present or at least imminent danger to the child's development is to be anticipated, which, should it persist, would

[52] E.g. Art. 30 of the Italian Constitution; Art. 18 of the Constitution of the Republic of Poland (from April 4, 1997); Art. 36 of the Constitution of the Portuguese Republic (from April 2, 1976, as amended on August 12, 2005); Art. 42 of the Irish Constitution (from December 29, 1937).

[53] Pursuant to the German Constitutional Court's (Bundesverfassungsgericht, BVerfG) decision from January 29, 2010 (1 BvR 374/09), BVerfGK (Kammerentscheidungen des Bundesverfassungsgerichts) 16, 517.

[54] Due to Sec. 1666 German Civil Code (Bürgerliches Gesetzbuch, BGB); see also German Constitutional Court's (Bundesverfassungsgericht, BVerfG) decision from January 29, 2010 (1 BvR 374/09), BVerfGK (Kammerentscheidungen des Bundesverfassungsgerichts) 16, 517, above; in detail, see Coester: Kindeswohlgefährdung, NZFam (Neue Zeitschrift für Familienrecht), 2016, pp. 577–580, at p. 578.

[55] The requirements regarding the duty of supervision generally depend on the age, character, and comprehension of the child as well as on the concrete possibilities of supervision by the parents: The decisive factor is what reasonable parents should have done under the given circumstances, see Federal Supreme Court of Germany (Bundesgerichtshof, BGH), decision from April 11, 2013 (IX ZR 94/10), FamRZ (Zeitschrift für das gesamte Familienrecht), 2013, pp. 1121–1123.

likely lead to substantial damage to the physical, mental, or psychological well-being of the child.[56] If, however, such a danger exists, the state is not only entitled but obliged to intervene.

Even with the recently proposed introduction of children's rights into the German Constitution, this fundamental premise would not have changed: Since the adoption of the CRC, there has been an ongoing discussion in Germany about including specific children's rights into the Constitution.[57] On the one hand, it has been claimed that taking such a step would be unnecessary, as it is well established that the German Basic Law grants fundamental rights, such as those to life and liberty, the free development of personality, and the freedom of expression, to everybody—including children. Thus, all the rights already exist, and the establishment of specific children's rights is considered redundant.[58] On the other hand, it has been maintained that by incorporating children's rights into the German Basic Law, as repeatedly called for by the UN Committee on the Rights of the Child,[59] children's concerns would take on a whole new weight and always have to be taken into account. More importantly, recognizing rights of the child should not be left to interpretation by the Constitutional Court, but children should instead be explicitly entitled as bearers of their own fundamental rights.[60] Additionally, it would emphasize the rights of children in relation to the rights

[56] Most recently German Constitutional Court's (Bundesverfassungsgericht, BVerfG) decision from November 19, 2014 (1 BvR 1178/14), NJW (Neue Juristische Wochenschrift), 2015, pp. 223–229.

[57] E.g. after German reunification, the Joint Constitutional Commission discussed the demand for the inclusion of children's rights into the constitution, see Deutscher Bundestag: Bericht der gemeinsamen Verfassungskommission, BT-Dr. 12/6000 p. 55; for a detailed and comprehensive overview of the discussion in Germany, see Wapler: Kinderrechte ins Grundgesetz? in: Sachverständigenkommission 15. Kinder- und Jugendbericht (eds.): Materialien zum 15. Kinder- und Jugendbericht, 2017, pp. 45–97; on the legal policy discussion, see Kreß/Gerhardt: Kinderrechte gehören nun auch ins Grundgesetz, Zeitschrift für Rechtspolitik, 4(7), 2014, pp. 215–217.

[58] E.g. brought forward by members of the Christian Union (Christlich Demokratische Union Deutschlands (CDU) and Christlich-Soziale Union (CSU)), see Deutscher Bundestag: Kontroverse Debatte über Gesetzentwürfe zu Kinderrechten im Grundgesetz.

[59] Cf. UN Committee on the Rights of the Child: Concluding observations on the combined third and fourth periodic reports of Germany, CRC/C/DEU/CO/3–4.

[60] Cf. Hohmann-Dennhardt: Kinderrechte ins Grundgesetz—warum? FPR, 2012, pp. 185–187, at p. 187.

of their parents.[61] Yet the recently proposed compromise[62] in this debate was to merely add to Art. 6 (2) GG a subsection stating that the constitutional rights of children, including their right to develop into self-reliant individuals, shall be respected and protected. Additionally, it stipulated that the best interests of the child shall be given due consideration, and finally, that children's constitutional right to be heard shall be safeguarded. However, this addition to Art. 6 GG was not supposed to impact the legal relationship of parents and children, and in particular, not limit parental rights. It therefore specifically stated that the primary responsibility of parents shall remain unaffected.[63]

Nevertheless, with regard to children's *rights,* the question remains in what way their exercise is then initially left primarily with the parents. It also begs the question of how children's evolving capacities to exercise their rights are recognized by the law, as is required by Art. 5 CRC, which provides the basis for the relationship between children, their parents, and the state. This becomes particularly relevant in cases where a conflict exists between parents and children, which may occur no less with regard to matters in the digital than in the analogue sphere.

3 Legal Recognition of Children's Evolving Capacities

Art. 5 CRC aims at encouraging respect for children's evolving capacities to exercise their rights themselves, while at the same time balancing this with their need to be protected due to their relative lack of experience and maturity. The following section will consider *how* the evolving capacities of children are recognized in different normative orders.

[61] Ibid.

[62] Deutscher Bundestag: Entwurf eines Gesetzes zur Änderung des Grundgesetzes zur ausdrücklichen Verankerung der Kinderrechte, Drucksache 19/28138; see in detail Deutscher Bundestag: Sachstand: Kinderrechte ins Grundgesetz, Az. WD 3-3000-012/20.

[63] For the legal questions arising from this draft amendment, see von Landenberg-Roberg: Der Regierungsentwurf zur Verankerung von Kinderrechten im Grundgesetz, NZFam (Neue Zeitschrift für Familienrecht), 2021, pp. 145–148; the draft amendment was not pursued further due to the lack of necessary consensus for a constitutional amendment, cf. Tagesschau: Kinderrechte vorerst nicht im Grundgesetz; Küstner: Kinderrechte nicht im Grundgesetz; in its coalition agreement, the new German federal government has agreed to enshrine children's rights in the Basic Law.

3.1 Principle of Parental Responsibility Until Majority

The starting point in all legal systems is that generally a person only reaches full legal capacity upon majority, most often the age of 18.[64] Until then, parents are generally granted parental responsibility of their children.[65] As holders of parental responsibility, they have to provide the child with care, protection, and education.[66] This encompasses *inter alia* the right and duty to decide in personal as well as financial matters for their child. Moreover, the holders of parental responsibility act as legal representatives regarding the child's person and property.[67]

A number of jurisdictions, though, provide for the possibility that under certain circumstances, minors, even before attaining the general age of majority, are no longer considered to be under the care and control of their parents but instead take full or at least limited legal responsibility for themselves. Such a full or partial emancipation may result from a declaration of majority, be it by parental consent or more often by judicial decree, provided that the necessary conditions are fulfilled.[68] However, (partial) premature majority or emancipation may also be the consequence of a specific event or act, such as marriage,[69] parenthood,[70] or setting up of a business, be it offline or online, by a minor.[71] The reason for legally granting premature majority in those cases is twofold: For one, such acts may in and of themselves be considered as an expression of a certain maturity of the minor, or they may also legally require the fulfillment of certain conditions, such as reaching a certain age or maturity, parental consent, and/or court approval.

[64] 18 years is the age of majority in all European countries except for Scotland where it is 16 years, see European Union Agency for Fundamental Rights: Age of majority.

[65] For parental responsibility of parents and third parties, see CEFL: Principles of European Family Law Regarding Parental Responsibilities, Principle 3:8 and 3:9.

[66] Ibid., Principle 3:19.

[67] Ibid., Principle 3:24.

[68] E.g. in France, through a judicial decree from the age of 16 due to Art. 413-2 Code Civil (CC); see also the declaration of majority of teenage mothers through judicial decree from the age of 16 in the Netherlands pursuant to Art. 1:253 ha Dutch Civil Code (DCC), which is related to obtaining parental responsibility.

[69] Either fully e.g. in Bulgaria due to Art. 6 (4) Family Law Code or at least partially as in Denmark due to Sec. 1 (1) 2nd st. Guardianship Act.

[70] Due to Art. 11 (3) Family Act Serbia.

[71] For example, in Germany due to Sec. 112 (1) 1st st. German Civil Code (Bürgerliches Gesetzbuch, BGB); in the Netherlands through a judicial decree from the age of 16 due to Art. 1:235 Dutch Civil Code (DCC).

Moreover, following such events, certain legal acts may often become necessary, like those involved in setting up a household, acting as parents, or conducting the firm's business, which requires legal capacity.

Additionally, however, if minors are not emancipated before reaching majority but remain, as is the rule, under parental responsibility, their evolving capacities are commonly recognized in various legal realms, which may be relevant both in the analogue and the digital world.

3.2 Children's Autonomy: Different Legal Realms and Rules

3.2.1 Exercise of Parental Responsibility

First of all, this concerns the relationship of parent and child as determined by national family laws. Here, parents, as holders of parental responsibility, are increasingly required to take account of children's autonomy in accordance with their developing ability and need to act independently.[72] This relates to a variety of issues, such as how and to what extent children are supervised, both offline and online, in order to prevent that *they* are harmed or that they harm *others*. It also pertains to parental decisions about contact with third parties, friends, and peers. Thus, it is currently being widely discussed whether, for what purposes, and to what extent parents may use tracking or parental control apps to follow their children's on- and offline activities.[73] In German law, the parents' duty of supervision according to Sec. 1631 (1) Bürgerliches Gesetzbuch (BGB; German Civil Code) also applies to the digital sphere and requires that parents monitor the child's usage behavior when a smartphone is given to them or when they otherwise begin using the internet.[74] In principle, parents may utilize an application, such as a tracking app, to fulfil their duty of supervision. Also, the parents' right of access to their child pursuant to Sec. 1632 (2) BGB, which is equally part of parental custody, gives them the right and duty to monitor with whom the child has contact in order to protect them from damaging influences and ultimately

---

[72] See CEFL: Principles of European Family Law Regarding Parental Responsibilities, Principle 3:4.

[73] Regarding the moral debate, see Gabriels: 'I keep a close watch on this child of mine', Ethics and Information Technology, 18, 2016, pp. 175–184.

[74] Cf. Huber, in: MüKoBGB, § 1626 mn. 69.

prevent harm.[75] Even applications that preclude communication with certain partners from the outset may, under certain conditions, be covered by the parents' right of access. However, when exercising both the duty of supervision as well as the right of access, the persons with custody must, according to Sec. 1626 (2) 1st st. BGB, take into account the evolving capacity and the growing need of the child to act independently and responsibly. As a matter of principle, parents should therefore use parental control apps only after disclosure to the child and with their consent, considering the child's age as well as stage of development, and discuss matters of parental care with the child as far as it is appropriate with regard to their maturity.[76] Furthermore, the child's general right of personality, protected under Art. 2 (1) in conjunction with Art. 1 (1) GG, must be given due consideration. Therefore, parents' control must first be limited to the external circumstances of use and communication, i.e. the whether and how of communication as well as who the communication partners are.[77] Controlling the content of the communication may only take place if there is a justified suspicion that the child's welfare is endangered.[78]

3.2.2 Limited Legal Capacity

In order to introduce children to economic participation while taking into account their evolving capacities, virtually all jurisdictions grant minors at a certain age or degree of maturity some limited legal capacities before reaching majority. Thus, they recognize a limited or partial legal capacity to validly perform certain legal acts, in particular to contract without parental consent, for example, in cases of beneficial or minor transactions. This may concern only certain transactions, such as those covering so-called 'necessaries',[79] those that have been paid for with funds earned by the minor or given to them for free disposal,[80] as well as

[75] Cf. Dürbeck, in: Johannsen/Henrich/Althammer (eds.): Familienrecht, § 1632 mn. 13.

[76] Cf. Specht-Riemenschneider: Gutachten im Auftrag der Sachverständigenkommission für den Neunten Familienbericht der Bundesregierung, 2018, p. 26.

[77] Ibid.

[78] Ibid.

[79] E.g. in the United Kingdom through Sec. 3 (2), (3) Sale of Goods Act 1979, but without applicability in Scotland (repealed there by the Age of Legal Capacity (Scotland) Act 1991, Sec. 10 (2), sch. 2).

[80] As in Germany due to Sec. 110 German Civil Code (Bürgerliches Gesetzbuch, BGB).

transactions that are customarily performed independently by minors of that age[81] or that are not detrimental to the minor.[82]

Whether a limited capacity to validly conclude offline or online contracts is recognized widely depends upon reaching a certain age, with the age limits and corresponding capacities ranging considerably from one legal system to another. While in Germany minors from an age as young as seven are considered to have partial legal capacity—which merely allows them to enter into legally beneficial or at least neutral transactions[83] or validly conclude contracts which the minor directly fulfills with their pocket money[84]—age limits for a partial legal capacity are most commonly 14,[85] 15,[86] or 16.[87] Still other jurisdictions have set up several age limits in order to mirror the evolving capacities of children and adolescents. For instance, in Austria,[88] children from the ages of seven to fourteen are able to consent to contracts about minor matters of everyday life,[89] while from the age of fourteen on, as 'mature minors', they possess partial contractual capacity. This enables them to validly consent to providing services or to entering contracts regarding property left to their free disposal as well as income from their own earnings.[90]

In contrast, instead of establishing a fixed age or age levels for a limited legal capacity of minors, other jurisdictions use criteria such as the minor's capacity of judgment. Whether a minor is able to validly engage in certain transactions therefore depends upon their individual competence to conclude the respective contract. Thus, in Switzerland, minors who are capable of judgment can validly

---

[81] See, for instance, in the Netherlands pursuant to Art. 1:234 (3) DCC.

[82] In Austria, for example, due to Sec. 21 (2) 2nd st. in conjunction with Sec. 170 (1) Allgemeines bürgerliches Gesetzbuch (ABGB; Austrian Civil Code).

[83] Due to Sec. 107 German Civil Code (Bürgerliches Gesetzbuch, BGB).

[84] Pursuant to Sec. 110 German Civil Code (Bürgerliches Gesetzbuch, BGB).

[85] E.g. in Romania due to Art. 41 Civil Code; in Hungary due to Sec. 2:11 Civil Code.

[86] For instance, in Denmark pursuant to Sec. 42, 43 Guardianship Law.

[87] See, for example, in Latvia due to Art. 195 Civil Code and in Malta pursuant Art. 156 Civil Code.

[88] Almost identical Art. 66 Family Act Serbia.

[89] Cf. Sec. 170 (3) ABGB.

[90] Cf. Sec. 171 ABGB, 170 (2) ABGB.

conclude contracts concerning the disposal of their own earned income without parental consent.[91] The same is the case in Finland.[92]

While, if the prescribed conditions are fulfilled, minors can sometimes act autonomously, in other jurisdictions they can validly conclude contracts with parental consent and/or other authorization. Occasionally, minors may act autonomously, but parents have the right to rescind the contract retrospectively.

3.2.3 Criminal and Civil Liability

Also, in most legal systems, children are criminally responsible, in some from rather young ages and in others later, with the conditions as well as consequences varying considerably.[93] Adults and minors alike may be held liable for wrongful acts.[94] If their on- or offline activities inflict harm on others, they may have to pay damages for injuries,[95] be they bodily[96] or otherwise, for instance in severe cases of cybermobbing.[97] Additionally, parents may be liable for acts of their children, if they have not sufficiently supervised them, with the respective standard for proper supervision dependent upon the legal regimes and applicable laws.[98] Thus, for example, in German law, the scale of sufficient supervision is related to what reasonable parents must expect according to the age, character, and inclination of

---

[91] Pursuant to Art. 16, 19 (2), 323 1st st. Zivilgesetzbuch (ZGB; Swiss Civil Code).

[92] Due to Sec. 25 Guardianship Services Act.

[93] In the United Kingdom, children can be held liable for criminal offenses from the age of ten, Sec. 50 Children and Young Persons Act 1933, in the Netherlands from the age of 12 pursuant to Sec. 486 Code of Criminal Procedure; in Iceland, no person can be punished for an offense committed while under the age of 15, Art. 14 Penal Code.

[94] For a comparative overview of the liability of the child, see Martín-Casals (ed): Children in Tort Law, pp. 425 et seqq.

[95] For the scope of liability of the minor, see Martín-Casals (ed.): Children in Tort Law, pp. 439 et seqq.

[96] As in the case of a 16-year-old in London having to pay a compensation of £600 after he was found guilty of racially aggravated grievous bodily harm against a Singapore student, see BBC: Coronavirus: Boy sentenced for racist street attack.

[97] See e.g. Landgericht (LG; Regional Court) Memmingen, decision from February 3, 2015 (21 O 1761/13), BeckRS (Beck-Rechtsprechung) 2016, 2120, where in the case of massive insults to a classmate using a fake internet account on "Facebook", which required psychotherapeutic treatment, compensation for pain and suffering in the amount of 1500 € was granted.

[98] For an overview of parents' liability, see Martín-Casals (ed.): Children in Tort Law, pp. 441 et seqq.

the child. Parents must also take into account the growing personal responsibility of the child as well as specific circumstances, such as the local environment, the imminent danger of third parties, the predictability of the damaging behavior, and the reasonableness of a measure. They then are obliged to observe, instruct, and warn their children or impose prohibitions in order to avoid damages to third parties.[99] Again, all of this may apply to both offline acts, such as scratching cars,[100] and online acts, such as potential privacy violations that third parties may suffer through the child's use of direct messenger apps like WhatsApp.[101]

3.2.4 Decisionmaking Capacity in Personal Matters

Furthermore, decisions in some contexts are deemed to be so personal and linked to fundamental rights, like those related to religion, physical and mental integrity, or privacy, that minors are often granted at least some power to act despite not having reached majority.

Thus, with regard to religion, a prominent example is the freedom of choosing the religious denomination which was granted to children in Germany by the Law on the Religious Education of Children (RelKErzG) of 1921. According to Sec. 5 (1), when children have reached the age of 14, it is up to them to decide which religious denomination they wish to belong to. If the child has reached the age of twelve, they may not be brought up in a different denomination than before against their will. Comparable rules apply in Austria.[102] Elsewhere, age limits for minors to independently decide their confession are set somewhat higher at 15 or 16 years,[103] or require parental consent until the child has reached the age of

---

[99] See German Federal Supreme Court (Bundesgerichtshof, BGH), decision from November 15, 2012 (I ZR 74/12), GRUR (Gewerblicher Rechtsschutz und Urheberrecht), 2013, pp. 511–516; see also the analysis of the decision by Dreier: Projecting Images of Families into the Law, in this volume.

[100] For example, in a case in which a five-and-a-half-year-old child scratched 17 cars, the German Federal Supreme Court ruled that a supervisor must ensure that a child aged 5½ is checked at regular intervals of no more than 30 min, German Federal Supreme Court (Bundesgerichtshof, BGH), decision from March 24, 2009 (VI ZR 51/08), NJW (Neue Juristische Wochenschrift), 2009, pp. 1952–1954.

[101] Cf. Amtsgericht (AG; Local Court) Bad Hersfeld, decision from March 20, 2017 (F 111/17 EASO), ZD (Zeitschrift für Datenschutz), 2017, pp. 435–437.

[102] Pursuant to Sec. 5 Bundesgesetz über die religiöse Kindererziehung (federal law on the religious education of children) 1985.

[103] In Norway, due to Sec. 3 Norwegian Act relating to religious communities of 1969 (15 years); in Switzerland due to Art. 303 (3) ZGB (16 years).

majority.[104] In most European jurisdictions, changing religion is not regulated by law at all, though.

Moreover, the increasing maturity of adolescents is widely acknowledged in one way or another with regard to decisions about medical treatment or reproductive health, which may include seeking advice on or concluding contracts for medical treatment. In some countries, the decision making capacity depends *inter alia* on age, such as in Denmark[105] and Spain[106] where the minimum age at which children can consent to medical treatments without parental approval is 15 and 16, respectively. In other countries, there is no specific age requirement for consent, but the capacity depends upon the minor's maturity in the individual case, as is found in Germany,[107] Switzerland,[108] and Sweden.[109] Moreover, regarding medical decision making, it is not uncommon that minors, despite having reached the prerequisite age or maturity, are not yet granted *full* autonomy. Instead, it is often regarded as a co-responsibility of children and parents.[110] Here, the parents,

[104] In Finland, a child aged 15 or older has the right to choose their religious affiliation if the child's custodians give their written consent. The religious affiliation of a child aged 12 or older cannot be changed without the child's own consent due to Sec. 3 of the Finnish Religious Freedom Act, see Kurki-Suonio: CEFL: Parental Responsibilities—National Report Finland. In Denmark, a child would need parental consent for a change of religion or a withdrawal from a particular church or religion, see Lund-Andersen/Gyldenløve Jeppesen de Boer: CEFL: Parental Responsibilities—National Report Denmark.

[105] Cf. Sec. 17 (1) of the Health Act 2005, though the parents still need to be informed and included in the decisionmaking process, see Nys et al.: "Patient Rights in the EU—Denmark", European Ethical-Legal Papers N°2, p. 17.

[106] Due to Art. 9.4 Ley 41/2002, de 14 de noviembre, básica reguladora de la autonomía del paciente y de derechos y obligaciones en materia de información y documentación clínica; see also the Netherlands, there children from the age of 16 decide themselves about medical treatments according to Art. 7:447 (1) DCC, while between the age of 12 and 16 years, there is a co-responsibility with their parents, cf. Art. 7:450 (2) DCC.

[107] Cf. German Federal Supreme Court (Bundesgerichtshof, BGH), decision from December 5, 1958 (VI ZR 266/57), NJW (Neue Juristische Wochenschrift), 1959, p. 811.

[108] Based on Art. 305 (1) in conjunction with Art. 19c ZGB, in detail, see Büchler: Parental Decisions on their Children's Medical Treatment in Switzerland, in: Goold/Auckland/Herring (eds.): Medical Decision-Making on Behalf of Young Children—A Comparative Perspective, 2020, pp. 39–52.

[109] See in detail Leviner: Who has the final Word? in: Goold/Auckland/Herring (eds.): Medical Decision-Making on Behalf of Young Children—A Comparative Perspective, 2020, pp. 155–166.

[110] E.g. in the Netherlands, due to Art. 7:450 (2) DCC for children from 12 to 16 years.

with the child's consent, may be the decision makers, or conversely, the child may make decisions with parental consent. The degree of autonomy may also depend upon the consequences of the decision. However, this might go both ways: The more far reaching they are deemed, the greater the need for protection *or* self-determination may be assumed. This is also why it is often highly controversial to determine in which cases there is actually a single or co-responsibility.[111]

Furthermore, minors may also be granted some decision making capacity regarding the publication of their pictures, which may occur in print media as well as in the digital sphere, where they may be posted or shared by family, friends, or minors themselves on websites, social media, or in group chats. In Germany, concerning the publication of pictures, minors are, in the absence of a statutory provision, generally deemed to be able to validly consent if they possess the respective cognitive faculty.[112] This is normally presumed to be the case starting at age 14.[113] It is predominantly assumed that from then on, both the minor's as well as their parents' consent are required.[114] In other countries, such as Spain, minors may exercise the right to their own image themselves when they are sufficiently mature, with this right thus being excluded from parental representation.[115]

[111] For example, in Germany, the discussion about minors even over the age of 16 needing the consent of their parents to terminate an unwanted pregnancy is ongoing. As the decision has far reaching consequences for the minor and the expectant life, a co-responsibility is often seen as neccessary, see e.g. Lugani: Einwilligung in Schwangerschaftsabbruch durch Minderjährige, NJW (Neue Juristische Wochenschrift), 2020, pp. 1330–1332; also, in cases of non-medically indicated plastic surgery, a co-responsibility is desirable, see Spickhoff, in: MüKoBGB, § 107 mn. 14.

[112] Cf. Specht-Riemenschneider, in: Dreier/Schulze, KUG, § 22 mn. 26.

[113] See e.g. Landgericht (LG; Regional Court) Bielefeld, decision from September 18, 2007 (6 O 360/07), ZUM (Zeitschrift für Urheber- und Medienrecht), 2008, pp. 528–530.

[114] See e.g. Dasch: Die Einwilligung zum Eingriff in das Recht am eigenen Bild, p. 103; Götting: Persönlichkeitsrechte als Vermögensrechte, p. 154; Klass: Die zivilrechtliche Einwilligung als Instrument zur Disposition über Persönlichkeitsrechte, AfP (Zeitschrift für das gesamte Medienrecht), 2005, pp. 507–515, at p. 515; the German Federal Supreme Court has left this question unresolved, see German Federal Supreme Court (Bundesgerichtshof, BGH), decision from July 2, 1974 (VI ZR 121/73), GRUR (Gewerblicher Rechtsschutz und Urheberrecht), 1975, pp. 561–565.

[115] Cf. Art. 162 (1) Spanish Civil Code in conjunction with Art. 3 Act for Civil Protection of the Right to Honor, Privacy, and Image, see in detail Sanchez-Ventura: The Exercise of Minors' Rights of Personality on Social Media, 8 Int'l. J. Juris. Fam., 2017, pp. 29–60, at p. 51.

3.2.5 Consent to Use Data

Closely linked to the question of consent to the publication of pictures is the question around the consent to use data, which in addition to being relevant in analogue contexts is especially pertinent for the digital world where it is often a prerequisite for participating. Since 2018, EU data protection law (General Data Protection Regulation, GDPR) has established 16 as the age when, in relation to the provision of information society services directly to a child, the child's consent for disclosure of personal data, such as name or date of birth, is sufficient.[116] Up until that age, such processing of data is only lawful if the consent is given or authorized by the holder of parental responsibility.[117] The introduction of a specific minimum age has impacted the previously existing vast variety of national legislation, as it introduced a harmonized presumption of the capacity to consent, at least starting at age 16.[118] For example, neither German, French, nor British data protection law previously had fixed age limits on the ability of minors to consent to the processing of their data.[119] In German law, it was based on the capacity of the minor to understand the implications of the decision.[120] However, EU law still does leave some discretion for different national age limits as low as 13 years. A number of Member States have already made use of the opening clause in Art. 8 (1) 3rd st. GDPR and adopted a different age limit,[121] for example 13 years in Sweden,[122]14 years in Austria,[123] and 15 years in Greece.[124]

---

[116] Art. 8 (1) 1st st. General Data Protection Regulation (GDPR).

[117] Art. 8 (1) 2nd st. General Data Protection Regulation (GDPR).

[118] Dethloff/Kaesling: Datenmündigkeit Minderjähriger in Europa, in: Nolte/Fischer/Senftleben/Specht-Riemenschneider (eds.): Gestaltung der Informationsrechtsordnung, 2022, pp. 537–552 with further references; for a comprehensive overview of the conception of Art. 8 GDPR, see Macenaite/Kosta: Consent for processing children's personal data in the EU, Information & Communications Technology Law, 26(2), 2017, pp. 146–197; see also Kaesling: A Rights-based Approach to Children's Digital Participation, in this volume.

[119] Cf. Kampert, in: NK-DSGVO, Art. 8 mn. 2; for a rights-based analysis of children's consent, see Van der Hof: I Agree, or Do I, Wis. INT'l L.J., 34, 2016, pp. 409–442.

[120] Cf. Kampert, in: NK-DSGVO, Art. 8 mn. 2.

[121] For an overview, see European Commission: Commission Staff Working Document, Data protection as a pillar of citizens' empowerment and the EU's approach to the digital transition, 2020, p. 17; see also Dethloff/Kaesling: Datenmündigkeit Minderjähriger in Europa, in: Nolte/Fischer/Senftleben/Specht-Riemenschneider (eds.): Gestaltung der Informationsrechtsordnung, 2022, pp. 537–552.

[122] Due to Chap. 2, s. 4 of the Swedish Data Protection Act (Swe. lag (2018:218)).

[123] Pursuant to Art. 2 s. 4 (4) Datenschutzgesetz.

[124] Due to Art. 21 (1) of the Data Protection Act 2019 (Law 4624/2019).

While setting specific age limits, like the GDPR does, instead of individually assessing a minor's maturity may be particularly suitable for digital verification, the concrete design of these methods is the linchpin for a sufficient protective effect. Whereas in the analogue world a salesperson can easily check the age of a minor when signing a contract by asking for identification, this is problematic in the digital world due to data protection regulations. Currently, for example, several social network providers use a simple query of age. If entering a date of birth or ticking a box suffices, age limits can be easily circumvented, and the desired protection will not be achieved. Here, one could consider adapting the verification method to the potential consequences for the child. It thus might be justified that in order to use additional functions on social networks, such as purchasing add-ons in the app or sharing images, another method of verification comes into play, such as verification by submitting an identity card in person (post ident) or even by turning on one's webcam (video ident).[125] However, the implemented methods may not be disproportionate and must sufficiently take all interests into account. While there must be an adequate level of protection for children, no excessive demands may be placed in order to provide services this way.

3.3 Diversity of Regulations Regarding Minors' Evolving Capacities

A comparative overview of legal regulations regarding the increasing recognition of minors' autonomy has revealed that there are considerable differences regarding ways to regulate this in various on- and offline contexts. First, this diversity concerns the way in which children's evolving capacities are determined: One way is by setting specific age limits, with age serving as a proxy for maturity. This assumes that both cognitive capacity and the ability to act increase with age. With a view to legal certainty, individual differences are disregarded. Here, we find a wide range of different age limits below the age of 18 for specific issues. The alternative is to assess the capability of decision making on a case-by-case basis, thereby taking into account both the individual capacities of the respective minor as well as the specific transaction or decision in question. A case-by-case analysis often comes into play when issues concerning the minor's constitutional

[125] Tinnefeld/Conrad: Die selbstbestimmte Einwilligung im europäischen Recht, ZD (Zeitschrift für Datenschutz), 2018, pp. 391–398, at p. 393.

rights are at stake and the ensuing decision could have potentially serious consequences for the minor. All methods of determining the evolving capacities, be it age or maturity, similarly require some sort of verification of the conditions, either by a public authority, the contracting partner, or by other means—and may thus prove to be more or less suitable in different contexts. A case-specific assessment of the determination of maturity is almost only conceivable in an analogue context and often requires comparatively costly resources, such as the opinions of experts. Additionally, age may prove to be difficult to verify in online contexts.

The other vital difference regarding the legal recognition of minors' evolving capacities concerns the question of who gets to decide when minors are granted rights before reaching majority: The first option is that they may be given unbounded responsibility instead of their parents. This assumes that in specific areas, such as those that touch on fundamental rights, the minor is mature enough to decide themself. The other option is to provide for a co-responsibility of children and parents, which can take the form of requiring the child's consent to the parents' decision. Or parental consent might be necessary for the child's own decision to take legal effect.

4 Conclusion

New media have a fundamental impact on families and their lives. While the digital transformation is associated with tremendous new possibilities and chances for children, it also entails substantial risks to them. With regard to the position of children in law, there has been a significant paradigm shift, from children as objects to holders of rights, as prompted by the UNCRC. This shift has resulted in their recognition as autonomous subjects, which extends to the analogue as well as the digital world. Nonetheless, since children are initially not able to exercise rights themselves, this lies primarily with their parents. However, the law is required to take the child's evolving capacities into account, again both in analogue and digital contexts. Thus, minors may be emancipated before reaching majority. But, as has been shown, if children remain under parental responsibility until majority, as is the rule, their increasing abilities are commonly recognized in various legal realms. This concerns their relationship with their parents, as holders of parental responsibilities, as well as their relationship with third parties, with some regulations on the supranational level, like the EU's GDPR, and many others like family, contract, copyright, and privacy laws on the national level. While such legislation is generally applicable in both on- and offline contexts, provided that the respective specifics are considered, some areas of the law, like the right to privacy, are by nature more relevant in the digital sphere than others.

With regard to how the increasing recognition of minors' autonomy is regulated in various on- and offline contexts, one encounters remarkably diverse solutions. The determination of maturity, by setting an age or by individual assessment, as well as the degree of autonomy, be it full or co-responsibility, may vary fundamentally depending on the specific legal area, be it contracting, medical decision making, the publication of pictures or the disclosure of data. Thus, different legal realms may call for different solutions. Also, some may be more appropriate in the analogue or in the digital sphere. However, also concerning the same matters, the solutions may differ from one legal system to another with their respective legal cultures affecting the delicate process of balancing the degree of autonomy and the requisite amount of protection.

As a result, all of this may well spark some tension: On the one hand, a certain homogeneity of legal regulation regarding the digital sphere on the supranational level may seem desirable. Thus, the specifics of the digital world can call for certain ways to regulate matters, with regard to technological requirements, or due to both the special relevance of adolescents' digital participation as well as its particular perils. Also, with businesses or platforms operating on a European or global level, a degree of uniformity may appear beneficial. On the other hand, the necessary coherence between the respective normative orders of the digital and the analogue sphere must be retained. In consequence, this may exert a certain pressure towards harmonizing the provisions with regard to the legal recognition of the evolving capacities of minors within a specific legal field, like contract law. However, at the same time, attention must be paid towards the requisite coherence of norms *within* the respective national systems. It has to be kept in mind that different spheres of the law are interrelated, for instance, the legal capacities of minors vis-à-vis third parties may be reflected in the recognition of the growing capabilities of minors in the parent–child-relationship and vice versa. Resolving these points of tension is a challenging task that profits from a comparative perspective.

References

Archer, Catherine: How influencer 'mumpreneur' bloggers and 'everyday' mums frame presenting their children online, Media International Australia, 170(1), 2019, pp. 47–56.

Arewa, Olufunmilayo B.: Data Collection, Privacy, and Children in the Digital Economy, in this volume.

Autenrieth, Ulla: The Case of "Sharenting"—Parental Action Strategies in the Contested Field of Visualizing Children in Online Environments, in this volume.

BBC: Coronavirus: Boy sentenced for racist street attack, BBC News, January 27, 2021, www.bbc.com/news/uk-england-london-54048546; last accessed April 6, 2021.

Blecher-Prigat, Ayelet: Lost Between Data and Family? Shortcomings of Current Understandings of the Law, in this volume.

BMFSFJ: Neunter Familienbericht: Eltern sein in Deutschland—Ansprüche, Anforderungen und Angebote bei wachsender Vielfalt von Familien. Empfehlungen für eine wirksame Politik für Familien, 2021, Drucksache 19/27200.

Büchler, Andrea: Parental Decisions on their Children's Medical Treatment in Switzerland, in: Goold, Imogen/Auckland, Cressida/Herring, Jonathan (eds.): Medical Decision-Making on Behalf of Young Children—A Comparative Perspective, Oxford 2020, pp. 39–52.

CEFL (Commission on European Family Law): The CEFL Principles of European Family Law Regarding Parental Responsibilities, ceflonline.net/wp-content/uploads/Principles-PR-English.pdf; last accessed February 16, 2021.

Center for Cyber Safety and Education: Children's internet usage study, 2016, www.iamcybersafe.org/s/parent-research; last accessed February 16, 2021.

Center for Justice and Crime Prevention: Global Kids Online, A glimpse into South African children's internet use and online activities. South African Kids Online: Barriers, opportunities & risks. Technical Report, 2016, www.globalkidsonline.net/wp-content/uploads/2016/06/GKO_Country-Report_South-Africa_CJCP_upload.pdf; last accessed February 16, 2021.

Coester, Michael: Kindeswohlgefährdung: Anforderungen an die Gefährdung aus juristischer Sicht, NZFam (Neue Zeitschrift für Familienrecht), 2016, pp. 577–580.

Committee on the Rights of the Child: General Comment No. 20 on the implementation of the rights of the child during adolescence, 2016, https://www.refworld.org/docid/589dad3d4.html; last accessed April 15, 2021.

Committee on the Rights of the Child: General Comment No. 17 on the right of the child to rest, leisure, play, recreational activities, cultural life and the arts (Art. 31), 2013, https://www.refworld.org/docid/51ef9bcc4.html; last accessed April 15, 2021.

Council of Europe: Committee of Ministers Recommendation No. R (84) 4 (adopted by the Committee of Ministers on 28.2.1984 at the 367th meeting of the Ministers' Deputies) on Parental responsibilities, www.euromed-justiceii.eu/files/repository/20090707173539_Coe.Recommendation(84)4onParentalResponsabilities.pdf; last accessed February 16, 2021.

Council of Europe: Protocol to the Convention for the Protection of Human Rights and Fundamental Freedoms, www.coe.int/en/web/conventions/full-list/-/conventions/rms/090000168006377b; last accessed February 24, 2021.

Dasch, Norbert: Die Einwilligung zum Eingriff in das Recht am eigenen Bild, Munich 1990.

Davidson-Wall, Nadine: "Mum, seriously!": Sharenting the new social trend with no opt-out, Debating Communities and Social Networks OUA Conference, 2018, https://networkconference.netstudies.org/2018OUA/2018/04/22/mum-seriously-sharenting-the-new-social-trend-with-no-opt-out/; last accessed February 24, 2021.

Dethloff, Nina/Kaesling, Katharina: Datenmündigkeit Minderjähriger in Europa, in: Nolte/Fischer/Senftleben/Specht-Riemenschneider (eds.): Gestaltung der Informationsrechtsordnung, Festschrift für Thomas Dreier, Munich 2022, pp. 537–552.

Dethloff, Nina/Maschwitz, Alexandra: Kinderrechte in Europa—wo stehen wir? FPR (Familie Partnerschaft Recht), 2012, pp. 190–194.

Deutscher Bundestag: Bericht der gemeinsamen Verfassungskommission, Drucksache 12/6000.

Deutscher Bundestag: Entwurf eines Gesetzes zur Änderung des Grundgesetzes zur ausdrücklichen Verankerung der Kinderrechte, Drucksache 19/28138.

Deutscher Bundestag: Kontroverse Debatte über Gesetzentwürfe zu Kinderrechten im Grundgesetz, www.bundestag.de/dokumente/textarchiv/2019/kw23-de-kinderrechte-643308; last accessed February 24, 2021.

Deutscher Bundestag: Sachstand: Kinderrechte ins Grundgesetz—Zum Gesetzentwurf des Bundesministeriums der Justiz und für Verbraucherschutz aus November 2019 und seiner Diskussion, Az. WD 3-3000-012/20.

Dreier, Thomas: Projecting Images of Families into the Law—The Example of Internet-Related Cases Decided by the German Courts, in this volume.

Dürbeck, Werner, in: Johannsen, Kurt/Henrich, Dieter/Althammer, Christoph (eds): Familienrecht: Scheidung Unterhalt Verfahren—Kommentar, 7th ed., Munich 2020, § 1632.

Ensenat, Sarah: Smart Baby Monitors: The Modern Nanny or a Home Invader, CATH. U. J. L. & TECH, 26, 2017, pp. 72–99.

European Commission: Commission Staff Working Document, Data protection as a pillar of citizens' empowerment and the EU's approach to the digital transition—two years of application of the General Data Protection Regulation, COM 264 final, 2020.

European Commission: Towards a safer use of the internet for children in the EU—a parents' perspective, Flash EB Series 248, 2008, https://op.europa.eu/en/publication-detail/-/publication/4c7ece29-058c-44fe-9aa0-27d67cfc3029/language-en; last accessed June 28, 2021.

European Commission: How the EU protects your children online, 2019, https://european-commission.medium.com/how-the-eu-protects-your-children-online-b3f3c3a939fb; last accessed February 16, 2021.

European Union Agency for Fundamental Rights: Age of majority, http://fra.europa.eu/en/publication/2017/mapping-minimum-age-requirements/age-majority; last accessed February 20, 2021.

Gabriels, Katleen: 'I keep a close watch on this child of mine': a moral critique of other-tracking apps, Ethics and Information Technology, 18, 2016, pp. 175–184.

Götting, Horst-Peter: Persönlichkeitsrechte als Vermögensrechte, Tübingen 1995.

Hart, Stuart N.: From property to person status: Historical perspective on children's rights, American Psychologist, 46(1), 1991, pp. 53–59.

Hohmann-Dennhardt, Christine: Kinderrechte ins Grundgesetz—warum? FPR (Familie Partnerschaft Recht), 2012, pp. 185–187.

Holloway, Donelle/Green, Lelia: The Internet of toys, Communication Research and Practice, 2(4), 2016, pp. 1–14.

Holloway, Donell/Green, Lelia/Livingstone, Sonia: Zero to eight. Young children and their internet use, LSE, London: EU Kids Online, 2013.

Honsell, Heinrich: Römisches Recht, 8th ed., Heidelberg 2015.

Huber, Peter, in: Säcker, Franz Jürgen et al. (eds.): Münchener Kommentar zum Bürgerlichen Gesetzbuch (MüKoBGB), Vol. 10 Familienrecht II, 8th ed., Munich 2020, § 1626.
Kaesling, Katharina: A Rights-based Approach to Children's Digital Participation in the Multi-Level System of the European Union, in this volume.
Kaesling, Katharina: Children's Digital Rights: Realizing the Potential of the CRC, in: Marrus/Laufer-Ukeles (eds.): Global Reflections on Children's Rights and the Law, London/New York 2021, pp. 183–196.
Kaesling, Katharina: The Making of Citizens: Democracy and Children's Rights in Digital Spheres, in: Neuberger/Friesike/Krzywdzinski/Eiermann (eds.): Proceedings of the Weizenbaum Conference 2021 "Democracy in Flux: Order, Dynamics and Voices in Digital Public Spheres", 2021, pp. 67–71.
Kaesling, Katharina: Persönlich, familiär oder öffentlich? Grenzverschiebungen im Datenschutz- und Kunsturheberrecht am Beispiel des Teilens von Kinderbildern auf sozialen Netzwerken, in: Croon-Gestefeld/Korch/Kuschel/Sarel/Scholz (eds.): Das Private im Privatrecht, Baden-Baden 2022, pp. 151–174.
Kampert, David, in: Sydow, Gernot (ed.): Nomos Kommentar Europäische Datenschutzgrundverordnung (NK-DSGVO), 2nd ed., Baden-Baden 2018, Art. 8.
Kennedy, Melanie: 'If the rise of the TikTok dance and e-girl aesthetic has taught us anything, it's that teenage girls rule the internet right now': TikTok celebrity, girls and the Coronavirus crisis, European Journal of Cultural Studies, 23(6), 2020, pp. 857–873.
Keymolen, Esther/Van der Hof, Simone: Can I still trust you, my dear doll? A philosophical and legal exploration of smart toys and trust, Journal of Cyber Policy, 4(2), 2019, pp. 143–159.
Küstner, Kai: Kinderrechte nicht im Grundgesetz, Tagesschau, June 8, 2021, https://www.tagesschau.de/inland/kinderrechte-grundgesetz-117.html; last accessed June 28, 2021.
Kurki-Suonio, Kirsti: CEFL: Parental Responsibilities—National Report Finland, ceflonline.net/wp-content/uploads/Finland-Parental-Responsibilities.pdf; last accessed April 6, 2021.
Kutscher, Nadia: Positionings, Challenges, and Ambivalences in Children's and Parents' Perspectives in Digitalized Familial Contexts, in this volume.
Klass, Nadine: Die zivilrechtliche Einwilligung als Instrument zur Disposition über Persönlichkeitsrechte, AfP (Zeitschrift für das gesamte Medienrecht), 2005, pp. 507–515.
Kreß, Hartmut/Gerhardt, Rudolf: Kinderrechte gehören nun auch ins Grundgesetz: Die UN-Kinderrechtskonvention ist jetzt seit 25 Jahren in Kraft, Zeitschrift für Rechtspolitik, 4(7), 2014, pp. 215–217.
Kumar Ghosh, Arup et al.: Safety vs. Surveillance: What Children Have to Say about Mobile Apps for Parental Control, CHI April 21–26, Montréal, 2018, QC, Canada.
Landenberg-Roberg, Michael: Der Regierungsentwurf zur Verankerung von Kinderrechten im Grundgesetz, NZFam (Neue Zeitschrift für Familienrecht), 2021, pp. 145–148.
Leaver, Tama: Born Digital? Presence, Privacy, and Intimate Surveillance, in: Hartley, John/Qu, Weiguo (eds.): Re-Orientation: Translingual Transcultural Transmedia. Studies in narrative, language, identity, and knowledge, Shanghai 2015, pp. 149–160.
Leviner, Pernilla: Who has the Final Word? On Trust and Legal Uncertainty within the Swedish Healthcare System, in: Goold, Imogen/Auckland, Cressida/Herring, Jonathan (eds.): Medical Decision-Making on Behalf of Young Children—A Comparative Perspective, 2020, pp. 155–166.

Livingstone, Sonia/Stoilova, Mariya/Nandagiri, Rishita: Children's data and privacy online: Growing up in a digital age. An evidence review, London 2018.

Lugani, Katharina: Einwilligung in Schwangerschaftsabbruch durch Minderjährige, NJW (Neue Juristische Wochenschrift), 2020, pp. 1330–1332.

Lund-Andersen, Ingrid/Gyldenløve Jeppesen de Boer, Christina: CEFL: Parental Responsibilities—National Report Denmark, ceflonline.net/wp-content/uploads/Denmark-Parental-Responsibilities.pdf; last accessed April 6, 2021.

Macenaite, Milda/Kosta, Eleni: Consent for processing children's personal data in the EU: following in US footsteps? Information & Communications Technology Law, 26(2), 2017, pp. 146–197.

Martín-Casals, Miquel (ed.): Children in Tort Law—Part I: Children as Tortfeasors, Tort and Insurance Law Vol. 17, Vienna/NewYork 2006.

McCall-Smith, Kasay: 'To incorporate the CRC or not—is this really the question?', The International Journal of Human Rights, 23(3), 2019, pp. 425–441.

Nash, Victoria: The Rise of the Algorithmic Child: Protecting Children in Smart Homes, in this volume.

Nottingham, Emma: 'Dad! Cut that Part Out!' Children's Rights to Privacy in the Age of 'Generation Tagged': Sharenting, Digital Kidnapping and the Child Micro-Celebrity, in: Murray, Jane/Blue Swadener, Beth/Smith, Kylie (eds.): The Routledge International Handbook of Young Children's Rights, 2019, https://papers.ssrn.com/sol3/papers.cfm?abstract_id=3602712; last accessed April 14, 2021.

Nys, Herman et al.: "Patient Rights in the EU—Denmark", European Ethical-Legal Papers N°2, Leuven 2007, www.orpha.net/actor/EuropaNews/2007/doc/denmarkbk.pdf; last accessed April 8, 2021.

Palm, Willy: Children's universal right to health care in the EU: Compliance with the UNCRC, Eurohealth, 23(4), 2017, pp. 3–6.

Rake, Ulrich: Kinderrechte und Sorgerechtsbefugnisse bei elterlichen Foto-Postings in sozialen Medien, FamRZ (Zeitschrift für das gesamte Familienrecht), 2020, pp. 1064–1070.

Regeringskansliet: Regeringens proposition 2017/18:186, Inkorporering av FN:s konvention om barnets rättigheter, March 20, 2018, https://www.regeringen.se/rattsliga-dokument/proposition/2018/03/prop2.-201718186/; last accessed April 27, 2021.

Ross, Alicia/Livingstone, Sonia: Sharenting: Parent blogging and the boundaries of the digital self, Popular Communication, 15(2), 2017, pp. 110–125.

Sánchez-Ventura, Inés: The Exercise of Minors' Rights of Personality on Social Media: An Examination of the Spanish Legal Context, 8 Int'l J. Juris. Fam., 2017, pp. 29–60.

Sclater, Shelley Day/Piper, Christine: Social Exclusion and the Welfare of the Child, Journal of Law and Society, 28(3), 2001, pp. 409–429.

Slavtcheva-Petkova, Vera/Nash, Victoria Jane/Bulger, Monica: Evidence on the extent of harms experienced by children as a result of online risks: implications for policy and research, Information, Communication & Society, 18(1), 2015, pp. 48–62.

Specht-Riemenschneider, Louisa: Gutachten im Auftrag der Sachverständigenkommission für den Neunten Familienbericht der Bundesregierung 2018.

Specht-Riemenschneider, Louisa, in: Dreier, Thomas/Schulze, Gernot (eds.): Urheberrechtsgesetz, Verwertungsgesellschaftengesetz, Kunsturhebergesetz, Kommentar (Dreier/Schulze), 7th ed., Munich 2022, KUG, § 22.

Spickhoff, Andreas, in: Säcker, Franz Jürgen et al. (eds.): Münchener Kommentar zum Bürgerlichen Gesetzbuch (MüKoBGB), Vol. 1 Allgemeiner Teil, 9th ed., Munich 2021, § 107.

Steinberg, Stacey: Sharenting: Children's Privacy in the Age of Social Media, Emory Law Journal, 66, 2017, pp. 839–884.

Sveriges Riksdag: UN Convention on the Rights of the Child to become law in Sweden, June 18, 2018, www.riksdagen.se/en/news/2018/jun/18/un-convention-on-the-rights-of-the-child-to-become-law-in-sweden/; last accessed February 22, 2021.

Tagesschau: Kinderrechte vorerst nicht im Grundgesetz, Tageschau, June 7, 2021, https://www.tagesschau.de/inland/innenpolitik/kinderrechte-grundgesetz-113.html; last accessed June 30, 2021.

Távora Vítor, Paula: Banning Children's Image Online—A Portuguese Perspective, in this volume.

Thimm, Caja: Mediatized Families: Digital Parenting on Social Media, in this volume.

Thimm, Caja/Nehls, Patrick: Sharing grief and mourning on Instagram: Digital patterns of family memories, Communications, 42(3), 2017, pp. 327–349.

Tinnefeld, Marie-Theres/Conrad, Isabell: Die selbstbestimmte Einwilligung im europäischen Recht, ZD (Zeitschrift für Datenschutz), 2018, pp. 391–398.

UN Committee on the Rights of the Child (CRC): Concluding observations on the combined third and fourth periodic reports of Germany, CRC/C/DEU/CO/3–4, 2014, www.refworld.org/docid/52f8a2074.html; last accessed February 24, 2021.

UNICEF: Age Matters! Age-related barriers to service access and the realisation of rights for children, adolescents and youth, Final Report October 2016, agemattersnow.org/downloads/YPL_Age_Matters_Final_Report_Oct2016.pdf; last accessed March 30, 2021.

UNICEF: Child Safety Online, Global Challenges and Strategies, Technical report (Florence, Innocenti Research Centre), 2012, www.unicef-irc.org/publications/650-child-safety-online-global-challenges-and-strategies.html; last accessed February 24, 2021.

UNICEF: The UN Convention on the Rights of the Child: a study of legal implementation in 12 countries, 2012, www.unicef.org.uk/wp-content/uploads/2012/11/UNICEFUK_2012CRCimplementationreport-FINAL-PDF-version.pdf; last accessed February 24, 2021.

United Nations Human Rights Office of the High Commissioner: Convention on the Rights of the Child, www.ohchr.org/en/professionalinterest/pages/crc.aspx; last accessed February 24, 2021.

United Nations Treaty Collection, www.treaties.un.org/pages/ViewDetails.aspx?src=IND&mtdsg_no=IV-11&chapter=4&lang=en; last accessed February 24, 2021.

Valcke, Martin et al.: Long-term study of safe Internet use of young children, Computers & Education, 57, 2011, pp. 1292–1305.

Van der Hof, Simone: I Agree, or Do I: A Rights-Based Analysis of the Law on Children's Consent in the Digital World, Wis. INT'l L.J., 34, 2016, pp. 409–442.

Wapler, Friederike: Kinderrechte ins Grundgesetz? in: Sachverständigenkommission 15. Kinder- und Jugendbericht (eds.): Materialien zum 15. Kinder- und Jugendbericht, 2017, pp. 45–97, www.dji.de/fileadmin/user_upload/bibs2017/15_KJB_Wapler_b.pdf; last accessed February 23, 2021.

Williams, Gertrude: Child Protection: A Journey into History, Journal of Clinical Psychology, 12(3), 1983, pp. 236–243.

Prof. Dr. Nina Dethloff, LL.M. (Georgetown) is Professor of Civil Law, Private International Law, Comparative Law, and European Private Law and Director of the Institute for German, European, and International Family Law at the University of Bonn, Germany. At present, she is a member of the German Science Council, the Executive Board of the Association of German Jurists, the Executive Council of the International Society of Family Law (ISFL), and the Coordinating Group of the Family Law in Europe: Academic Network (FL-EUR). She has been elected a member of the American Law Institute and the Academia Europaea, where she currently chairs the Law Section. She was Director at the Käte Hamburger Center for Advanced Study in the Humanities "Law as Culture" and has also recently served as a member of the Expert Commission for the 9th Family Report of the German Federal Government. Her research focus is on comparative family law, on which she has published extensively. Among her recent publications are: Familienrecht (Verlag C. H. Beck, 33rd edition 2022, 610 p.); Child Participation in Germany (in: Schrama/Freeman/Taylor/Bruning (eds.): International Handbook on Child Participation in Family Law, Intersentia, 2021) (with Daniela Schröder); Personal autonomy and legal recognition of sexual and gender diversity—The German perspective (in: Rogerson/Antokolskaia/Miles et al. (eds.): Family Law and Family Realities: 16th ISFL World Conference Book, Eleven International Publishing, 2019, pp. 9–17); and Child Brides on the Move: Legal Responses to Culture Clashes (in: International Journal of Law, Policy and The Family 32/2018, pp. 302–315).

Mediatized Families: Digital Parenting on Social Media

Caja Thimm

1 Introduction: Digital Platforms, Digital Publics, and the Mediatized Family

The digital transformation is a structural change that affects all areas of society and does not leave the individual untouched. It is reflected in new economic sectors and business models, as well as in the way people communicate, learn, work, and live together. These massive transformation processes that are currently taking place in almost all areas of society have also influenced families around the globe. Particularly, various social media platforms play an important role—ranging from fast diffusion of news on Twitter, social networking on Facebook, photo sharing on Instagram, or self-broadcasting on YouTube or Tiktok—not to mention the various messenger services which have started to dominate interpersonal exchange. But it is not only the perspective of media usage which needs to be taken into account when reflecting on the changes families undergo in a digital society. It is also the decrease of barriers between privacy and publicity, which has categorically changed over the last years. Digital publics, whether they concern millions of followers of international film and pop stars or 'mini-publics' dedicated to smaller

For reasons of research ethics, no pictorial representations are used in this contribution. However, all references inthe text rely on existing images online.

C. Thimm (✉)
Institute for Language, Media and Music Studies, Department for Media Studies, University of Bonn, Bonn, Germany
e-mail: thimm@uni-bonn.de

N. Dethloff et al. (eds.), *Families and New Media*, Juridicum – Schriften zum Medien-, Informations- und Datenrecht,
https://doi.org/10.1007/978-3-658-39664-0_2

groups,[1] have created new spaces for communication and interpersonal interaction that have been used by many families for their personal stories.

While at first glance the idea of making family life public to others and sharing precious moments with close family or friends is not new,[2] the digitalization of the public sphere has impacted these sharing practices categorically. Today, public discourse is undergoing considerable structural change thanks to millions of people having access to digital platforms. While in pre-digital times established gatekeepers, such as the traditional media of television, radio, or print, were crucial for the public sphere or publicly accessible information, new forms of participation have developed through participatory digital media ('social media'), which in turn are changing the framework conditions of social processes of understanding and establishing new forms of the public sphere. The public sphere needs to be conceptualized as a dynamic: mutually conditioned and reinforcing co-production of individuals, institutions, and the state within converging media-technological networks, the growing relevance of which encompasses almost all areas of society. This development goes hand in hand with changes in the perspective on privacy and private data. As pointed out by Einspänner-Pflock, privacy is 'user-generated',[3] not only by means of using the respective privacy setting of the social media platform in question, but also by deciding what to publish and what not. With the absence of traditional gatekeeping functions on social media, there are factually no limits on the publication of data, notwithstanding legal constraints, for example, for child pornography or violence. But as is known, the abundance of hate speech, cyber mobbing, and fake and manipulated information[4] on the internet has proven that the digital public is hardly controllable and open for good use sensu freedom of expression as well as abusive and perturbing practices.

Due to the 'media logics',[5] which characterize the affordances of the various digital platforms, certain digital cultures and digital practices have developed,

---

[1] Cf. Thimm: Mediatization of Politics, in: Frame/Brachotte (eds.): Citizen Participation and Political Communication in a Digital World, pp. 167–183.

[2] Cf. Holloway/Green: Mediated memory making, Communications. The European Journal of Communication Research, 42(3), 2017, pp. 351–368.

[3] Cf. Einspänner-Pflock: Privatheit im Netz.

[4] Overview in Thimm: Hate Speech, Fake News, Filter Bubbles, in: Sander/von Gross/Hugger (eds.): Handbuch Medienpädagogik.

[5] Cf. Thimm: Media Technology and Media Logic(s), in: Thimm/Anastasiadis/Einspänner-Pflock (eds.): Media Logic(s) Revisited, pp. 111–132.

such as the story function on Instagram. 'Instastories' are short narratives which consist of photos and videos that have been taken with the story camera. Additional features are, for example, 'boomerangs'—short clips that play an animated shot repetitively in a loop. Initially developed by Snapchat and, due to its success, copycatted by Instagram and Facebook, it enables users to tell short stories of their own, with material produced with their private smartphones.

As will be explained below, such publication options for stories and photos have made Instagram one of the most-liked platforms for storytelling. But as more and more data is published online pertaining to children themselves, particularly personal photos, questions about data ownership and data control need to be answered. As Barassi points out, children need to be understood as "datafied citizens",[6] and critical questions about the relationship between the datafication of children, algorithmic inaccuracies, and data justice must be made. Benedetto/Ingrassia see the need for child protection, particularly during the Covid-19 pandemic.[7] Amidst such changing conditions, families, as groups of people, have to find their way, which is often accompanied by the rather worrisome activities of some users.

In the subsequent contribution, I will briefly outline some of the practices used by families which reflect on media change in reference to families and family life. The digital practices can be regarded from a range of perspectives:

- Societal impacts on the individual due to the digitization of society as a whole and specific services in particular. These impacts affect family members in their various roles, for example, as consumers, citizens, or members of the workforce. Societal impacts can be regarded under the exclusion/inclusion perspective, if, for example, grandparents are disconnected from family life through the digitalization of family interaction or need more support with daily needs due to digitization of certain services.
- Digital media and daily life of families: This perspective ranges from problematic media usage like excessive gaming by teens or long mobile phone screen times. This can result in family tensions, such as conflicting practices of parents and children, e.g. the perception of control needs by the parents (viewing restrictions, accessibility, physical control of the whereabouts of

[6] Barassi: Child as Datafied Citizen, in: Mascheroni/Ponte/Jorge (eds.): Digital Parenting, p. 169.

[7] Cf. Benedetto/Ingrassia: Digital Parenting.

teens, etc.). On the other hand, within family communication, messenger tools like WhatsApp have proven to enhance family cohesion and inner closeness.[8] Here, we see media usage as a source of conflict and of emotional closeness, better relationships, and more sharing by family members of all generations.

- Public family and the 'displaying of family': this perspective regards the publicity created by family members, particularly parents, about their family life. Some specific usages can be characterized as 'sharenting'.[9] Due to the media logics of social media platforms, particularly Facebook and Instagram, family life is broadcast to (sometimes) thousands of followers and has, at least for some families, even created business models like 'mummy blogs' or 'insta families'.[10]

When reflecting on this development from a media research perspective, four broad fields can be distinguished:

1. *Media usage* within families and by individual family members. This perspective can be related to all media—new or traditional—used within the family home.
2. *Digital media practices:* Platform practices and digital platform cultures which evoke new communication patterns, for example, specific age-related practices of children and parents or grandparents due to digital media.
3. *'Doing family':* Mediated construction of family and family identity based on digital practices by adults about family life.
4. *Consequences, digital literacy, education:* Platform practices rely on media literacy which is under constant pressure by the increasing speed of digital change.

In order to give an overview over some of these perspectives, the approach of 'doing family' on selected digital practices will be applied. As to illustrate one of the main practices of doing family, so-called 'sharenting' strategies will be highlighted using examples from Instagram.

[8] Cf. Aharony/Gazit: Importance of the Whatsapp family group, Aslib Journal of Information Management, 68(2), 2016, pp. 174–192.

[9] Cf. Blum-Ross/Livingstone: "Sharenting," parent blogging, The International Journal of Media and Culture, 15(2), 2017, pp. 110–125.

[10] Cf. Archer: Social media influencers, Public Relations Inquiry, 8(2), 2019, pp. 149–166.

2 'Doing Family' in the Digital Age

Father, mother, and child(ren)—in Western society this has long been the ideal image of the family. But the family, as a group, is not easily defined. As diversity in family constellations increases evermore, so does uncertainty about where the boundary of the concept of 'family' should be drawn. Nowadays, family definitions vary widely, and what people would characterize as family might not be reflected in research. Trost found a large variety of self-definitions: spousal, opposite-sex cohabitational, parent–child, and sibling relationships were most likely to be characterized as familial. However, many other relational forms, including friends or same-sex cohabitants, were considered by various percentages of the respondents as family as well.[11] More recently, social change affected the understanding of the family concept profoundly. More and more forms, such as patchwork families, single or separated parents, same-sex partnerships, and same-sex parents, are accepted and lived by society as forms of family. In addition, roles and tasks (for example, the classic image of the man as the breadwinner) within the family are being renegotiated.[12] Family is therefore no longer seen as "a supposedly self-evident group of people, natural or determined by family law",[13] but as a network of personal caring relationships between the individual members, which presents itself as a community through practices and interactions. Family, in that sense, focuses on the one hand on the processes in which family as a collective is permanently recreated in everyday and biographical actions ('doing family'), and on the other hand on the "concrete practices and creative achievements of the family members in order to make family liveable in everyday life".[14]

Parenting has never been easy. But the widespread usage of the internet, the adoption of smartphones by nearly all family members, and the rise of social media has introduced a new side to the challenges of parenthood.[15] According to a study by PWE Internet Research, a majority of parents in the United States (66%) with at least one child under the age of 18 say that parenting is harder

[11] Cf. Trost: Do We Mean the Same, Communication Research, 17(4), 1990, pp. 431–443.

[12] Cf. Autenrieth: ‚Digital Natives‘ präsentieren ihre Kinder, Studies in Communication Sciences, 14(2), 2014, pp. 99–107.

[13] Schlör: Doing Family und Social Media, Studies in Communication Sciences, 16(1), 2016, pp. 28, 29.

[14] Schier/Jurczyk: „Familie als Herstellungsleistung“, in: Frickel (ed.): soFid, p. 9.

[15] Cf. Duggan et al.: Parents and social media.

today than it was 20 years ago, with many in this group citing technology as a reason why.[16]

Digital media have not only changed within family communication, but have also influenced parent–child relationships and intergenerational contact. This has not been a sudden or abrupt development, but rather a continuous process of media adaption, media usage, and the constant flow of new technology. This kind of media driven social change is one of the core concepts of the 'mediatization approach', which is the theoretical backing of this paper. Mediatization describes the interconnection of human communication with media and the resulting social and cultural changes, or as Couldry/Hepp summarize:

> "Generally speaking, mediatization is a concept used to analyze critically the interrelation between changes in media and communications on the one hand, and changes in culture and society on the other".[17]

The authors see quantitative as well as qualitative aspects in mediatization processes, such as the increasing temporal, spatial, and social spread, or the specificity of certain media within socio-cultural change. Media have become so important because of how they are used in communicative behavior within society and help construct reality.

As argued elsewhere the mediatization of daily, ordinary experience as well as of non-daily, exceptional family events, such as the birth of a child, marriage, or death, equally constitute an individual family identity.[18] These experiences play a major role when considering how family life is perceived, what is remembered, and how a family chronicle is developed. Memories are shared both within the closer family circle as well as with friends or colleagues. Oftentimes, media help to document and store these experiences for future recall. Though this interdependence is not a newly emerging phenomenon restricted to digital media and the internet, the process of mediatization significantly changes the communication environments where family identity is negotiated and (re-)produced by introducing the digital public as a new actor in family dynamics. Whereas family

[16] Cf. Auxier/Anderson/Perrin/Turner: Parenting Children in the Age of Screens.

[17] Couldry/Hepp: Conceptualising mediatization, Communication Theory, 23(3), 2013, pp. 191, 197 (italics in original).

[18] Cf. Thimm/Nehls: Sharing grief and mourning on Instagram, Communications. The European Journal of Communication Research, 42(3), 2017, pp. 327–349.

interaction traditionally remained largely private, this has changed over the years as more and more family matters are disclosed online. And it is not only the younger generation that uses social media to digitally construct family identity. Parents are sharing baby pictures on Facebook, posting about their kids' achievements in school, and uploading vacation pictures on Pinterest or Instagram—all of which voluntarily open up family life to a larger audience.

The process of mediatization significantly changes the communication environments in all of society, and it is particularly the exchange with a global public on social media that has reshaped family communication.[19] Schlör underlines the role of mediatization and states that "families increasingly resort to media activities such as communication, information, entertainment and presentation practices as a form of doing family".[20] And particularly social media are regarded as "platforms which offer a broad variety of services to socialize, they support families in (re-)constructing both their self-concept and their public image through practices of inclusion and integration".[21]

But the new digital activities worry many parents. In the 2020 study about parenting in the digital age, PEW research revealed that parents with young children clearly express they are anxious about the effects of screen time: 71% of parents with a child under the age of 12 say they are at least somewhat concerned their child might spend too much time in front of screens, including 31% who are very worried about this. Until recently, Facebook had dominated the social media landscape among youth—but it is no longer the most popular online platform among teens, according to a PEW Research Center survey.[22] Most notably, smartphone ownership has become a nearly ubiquitous element of teen life: 95% of teens now report that they have a smartphone or access to one. These mobile connections are in turn fueling more-persistent online activities: 45% of teens now say they are online on a near-constant basis. Studies for Germany confirm similar usage cultures, with 93% of teens owning a smartphone.[23]

---

[19] Cf. Rose: Doing Family Photography.

[20] Schlör: Doing Family und Social Media, Studies in Communication Sciences, 16(1), 2016, p. 28.

[21] Pew: Parenting Children in the Age of Screens.

[22] Cf. Anderson/Jiang: Teens, Social Media & Technology.

[23] Cf. Medienpädagogischer Forschungsverbund Südwest (ed.): JIM-Studie 2020.

Mobile media are increasingly used in the family environment and are part of the social interactions between individual family members. More than a third of those surveyed in the German "Youth Media Study" claim that they feel the smartphone is very important for organizing everyday family life.[24] The advanced media skills of children and young people, who have grown up with daily media use and the resulting routine use of the smartphone, promotes—and in some cases makes possible—intergenerational communication. Technical communication media have become constitutive for many social contexts in the sense that they would not be possible in their present form without media.

The mobile phone transformed the relationship between those who are physically co-located and the 'absent presence', referring to relationships we hold with partners, children, and family who are not physically present in one space. Various studies have shown that increasing mobility and multilocality of families in everyday life is supported by certain apps and actually strengthens the family system. Especially in terms of family organization and expressions of belonging, shared digital spaces can do good for all generations. Schlör summarizes that discursive, presentational, and audio-visual communication practices facilitate participation in the everyday life of other family members.[25] Examples of such practices include requests to go to bed via WhatsApp and posting family photographs on SNS (social network services).

Whereas some may postulate that media influences are pulling individuals and families apart,[26] others contend that media has become an integral part of mainstream family life that can have positive as well as negative effects on family functioning. Procentese, Gatti, and Di Napoli point out that, regardless of effects, media do not always have to be in competition with family members for time or attention in the lives of adolescents.[27] Rodríguez-de-Dios/van Oosten/Igartua likewise underline that parents and adolescents are often engaging in media platforms together and use them to stay connected and structure family routines.[28]

---

[24] Cf. ibid., p. 49.

[25] Cf. Schlör: Doing Family und Social Media, Studies in Communication Sciences, 16(1), 2016, pp. 28–35.

[26] Cf. Turkle: Alone Together.

[27] Cf. Procentese/Gatti/Di Napoli: Families and Social Media Use, International Journal of Environmental Research and Public Health, 16(24), 2019, 5006, pp. 1–11.

[28] Cf. Rodríguez-de-Dios/van Oosten/Igartu: Relationship between parental mediation and adolescents' digital skills, Computers in Human Behavior 82, 2018, pp. 186–198.

3 Digital Parenting

The challenges described above have influenced parent–child relations as well as intergenerational relations in the family as a whole. Generational differences play a major role when considering digital practices applied in the family context. The widely discussed concept of 'digital parenting'[29] reflects parenting from two perspectives. For one, it refers to the regulation and control of children's media use, which many studies have shown to be of concern for parents of younger children. Secondly, it looks at the ways parents themselves incorporate digital media into their daily activities and parenting practices. Hence, digital parenting includes the incorporation of digital media into daily educational practices and the shift of childcare and care to the digital space.

3.1 Digital Parenting on Messenger Services

Messenger services like WhatsApp have become the most important among family communication means. The popularity of this messenger app is related to the increased spread of the smartphone. As a result, communication via WhatsApp is the most frequently used function on the smartphone, along with the exchange of text, image, video, and voice messages. As O'Hara, Harper, and Morris point out, WhatsApp is a relationship-oriented tool, on which togetherness and intimacy are enacted through small, continuous traces of narratives, of tellings and tidbits, noticings and thoughts as well as shared images.[30] The German Youth and Media Study found that 85% of girls and 78% of boys between 12 and 19 years regarded WhatsApp as their most important mobile app, followed by Instagram, with 53% of girls and 40% of boys listing it. 82% of the respondents also stated that they send messages on the messenger service daily.[31] With an average of 36 messages received per day, WhatsApp is an important platform for staying in touch with people, keeping up to date with news and current issues, and coordinating daily life. With one in two children now owning a smartphone in most Western countries, WhatsApp is also important for six to 13-year-olds. For half of the respond-

[29] Cf. Mascheroni/Ponte/Jorge: Introduction, in: Mascheroni/Ponte/Jorge (eds.): Digital Parenting, pp. 9–16.

[30] Cf. O'Hara et al.: Everday dwelling.

[31] Cf. Medienpädagogischer Forschungsverbund Südwest (ed.): JIM-Studie 2020.

ents in this user group, communication via WhatsApp was the most important smartphone application.[32] 47% of those surveyed in the 2018 KIM Study stated that they send WhatsApp messages daily. As children grow older, a growing subjective relevance of message exchange via smartphone can be observed. In addition, it is clear that messenger services are already used in early to middle childhood—the age group of six to seven-year-olds—to exchange messages with friends and family members. While 59% of those surveyed use WhatsApp to communicate with people in the household, only 39% of those surveyed use the messenger service to communicate with relatives outside the household. As Nouwens, Griggio, and Mackay confirm, WhatsApp is the most popular messenger system for families.[33] Their research title "WhatsApp is for family; Messenger is for friends" sums up the digital practices with many families. The smartphone is thus "seminal to keeping the family together".[34] Digital parenting therefore encompasses the inclusion of digital media in daily educational practices and the shift of childcare to the digital space, including WhatsApp.

Different types of messages are important for communication between family members. For example, text, picture, voice, and video messages are all sent on WhatsApp, particularly to routinely stay in touch with distant family members. But communication via WhatsApp is susceptible to misunderstandings and misinterpretations due to the lack of para- and non-verbal signals. Compared to face-to-face communication, family WhatsApp chats are also a more polite form of communication. The request to lock the front door when leaving the house is a politely formulated appeal to the other family members—but it is not necessary due to the daily routine of locking the door.

3.2 Sharenting

One of the more problematic and highly contested activities of digital parenting is the fact that parents share their parental experiences, joy, and challenges in the digital public. This practice has been labeled 'sharenting' and has received wide attention in research of various disciplines. Sharenting is defined as a parent's use of social media to discuss their children's lives by sharing text posts,

---

[32] Cf. Medienpädagogischer Forschungsverbund Südwest (ed.): KIM-Studie 2018, p. 18.

[33] Cf. Nouwens/Griggio/Mackay: "WhatsApp is for family", in: CHI'17, pp.727–735.

[34] Pink et al.: Digital Ethnography, p. 101.

photographs, and videos that convey personal information about their children.[35] Studies have shown that more than 50% of parents, especially mothers, who use social media, also post details about their children.[36] For Germany, the miniKIM study from 2014 revealed that 41% of parents who use social media share information—mostly in the form of pictures—about their children.[37] Although sharenting refers to social media platforms, parents have sought advice, information, and exchange with other parents well before the introduction of these participatory media. The transition from being a couple to their new role as parents confronts adults with major changes on an emotional, social, and life-practical level. The increased social isolation that parents sometimes experience after the birth of their child can be eased by SNS,[38] and some of them are socially and digitally (re)constructed.

Sharenting is linked to a diverse set of digital practices. Widely known are photo sharing on social media, particularly Facebook and Instagram, and blogs. On the other hand, SNS is a well-liked way to compare yourself with other parents and to present yourself as a good parent. Through sharing, they prove to family, friends, and/or the public that they are up to their task as parents.[39] Sharenting also creates recognition and confirmation for parents. By sharing images of babies and children on SNS, parents hope for, and often receive, positive feedback in the form of likes and comments from friends and subscribers. This also leads to contributions with children generating greater attention (likes and comments), thus further encouraging parents.[40]

Much of the parental activities has been attributed to their desire to be seen as a good parent in the eyes of the society.[41] For example, it has become relatively

---

[35] Cf. Haley: Sharenting and the (Potential) Right, Indiana Law Journal, 95(3), 2020, pp. 1005–1020.

[36] Cf. Brosch: When the Child is Born into the Internet, The New Educational Review, 43(1), 2016, pp. 225–235.

[37] Cf. Medienpädagogischer Forschungsverband Südwest (ed.): miniKIM 2014, p. 30.

[38] Cf. Le Moignan et al.: Has Instagram Fundamentally Altered, in: CHI'17, pp. 4935, 4938.

[39] Cf. Brosch: When the Child is Born into the Internet, The New Educational Review, 43(1), 2016, pp. 225, 233.

[40] Cf. Le Moignan et al.: Has Instagram Fundamentally Altered, in: CHI'17, pp. 4935, 4938.

[41] Cf. Damkjaer: Sharenting = Good Parenting? in: Mascheroni/Ponte/Jorge (eds.): Digital Parenting, pp. 209–218.

common for the parents-to-be to create 'digital shadows'[42] for their children even before they are born.

One specific digital practice are so-called 'mummy blogs'. These are mostly concerned with sharing experiences and giving advice, as well as marketing children's products. Blogging mothers of young children are not only sharing their experiences, but they are also negotiating their identities as mothers and thereby creating a sense of belonging. And as not to forget the financial side of these bloggers: More and more mummy bloggers are making money by becoming 'mummy influencers'.[43] While most mummy influencers feed into the 'good mother' images, there are also some 'confession blogs' which talk about the "bad" or "slummy" mummy, blogs that share stories of boredom, frustration, and maternal deficiency while relishing the subversive status of the "bad" mother.[44]

Sharenting needs to be analyzed as a complex digital practice. While many parents seek support or advice, some research points to the trend of 'oversharing'.[45] Sharenting has become increasingly controversial as parents have to balance their right to share and children's privacy interest. For one, parents' main aim can be to involve their family members and close friends in their child's upbringing. For example, research by Blum-Ross and Livingston suggests that 56% of mothers and 34% of fathers of infants and toddlers (up to four years) use social media to share information about parenting topics.[46] All of the above indicates that present-day parents are increasingly seeing social media and sharenting 'as a ubiquitous part of their parenting experience'. At the same time, however, sharenting has also gained quite a negative public image, and much of the public discussion related to sharenting emphasizes a variety of potential problems that such a practice might induce.

---

[42] Cf. Leaver: Researching the ends of identity, Social Media + Society, 1(1), 2015, p. 1.

[43] Cf. Archer: Social media influencers, Public Relations Inquiry, 8(2), 2019, pp. 149–166.

[44] Cf. Orton-Johnson: Mummy Blogs, Social Media + Society, April-June 2017, 2017, pp. 1–10.

[45] Cf. Wagner/Gasche: Sharenting: Making Decisions, in: Multikonferenz Wirtschaftsinformatik 2018, pp. 977–988.

[46] Cf. Blum-Ross/Livingston: "Sharenting," parent blogging, The International Journal of Media and Culture, 15(2), 2017, pp. 110–125.

3.3 Visualization and Privacy

Family pictures have always been shared and shown to others in order to create favorable memories,[47] whether it concerned snapshots from home or the presentation of slides from vacations. Especially the common viewing of photo albums invites one to remember, but also to communicate about the pictures themselves.[48] Photos are not taken to capture them for posterity, but rather to use them to exchange information with others for the moment and to communicate with them on the basis of images.[49] With the ephemeral use of images, photo sharing is "the prerequisite for visual communication by means of photographic representations or for the subsequent communication with them".[50]

There are various possibilities of visual sharing, which are influenced by different factors.[51] Typical photographic practices and motifs for families are manyfold. These include celebrations, such as birthdays or Christmas; life-cycle milestones like weddings, births, baptisms, graduations, and the documentation of achievements and status symbols like buying a new car or house. As further highlights in family life, and as a break with everyday life, there are also pictures of vacations and journeys in family photo albums.[52] Particularly in the first year after birth, a large number of pictures are taken. In addition to milestones (first steps, first smile, first tooth, etc.), many everyday moments with the child are also documented. Taking pictures of family members, especially of (small) children, is an important part of family life for most families.[53] Interestingly, these pictorial practices are not (yet) changed by the process of mediatization, as pointed out by Le Moignan et al.[54] They emphasize the positive sides of family snapshots, such as the capacity

[47] Cf. Pauweis: Communicating Desired Pasts, Journal of Visual Literacy, 22(2), 2002, pp. 161–174.

[48] Reißmann: Mediatisierung visuell.

[49] Cf. Autenrieth: Family photography in a networked age, in: Mascheroni/Ponte/Jorge (eds.): Digital Parenting, pp. 219, 221.

[50] Lobinger/Schreiber: Photo Sharing, in: Lobinger (ed.): Handbuch Visuelle Kommunikationsforschung, pp. 1, 4.

[51] Cf. Schreiber: Showing/Sharing: Analysing Visual Communication, Media and Communication, 5(4), 2017, pp. 37–50.

[52] Cf. Reißmann: Mediatisierung visuell, pp. 129 f.

[53] Cf. Rose: Doing Family Photography.

[54] Cf. Le Moignan et al.: Has Instagram Fundamentally Altered, in: CHI'17, pp. 4935–4947.

for social media to elicit responses from close family members which can confirm that 'good parenting' is taking place. The sharing of digital snapshots can also be used to gain support from weaker-tie networks, in addition to immediate friends and family. Research indicates that such online sharing can be a positive source of support, as well as a way to gather information, especially for new parents. It seems, however, that with visualization, and the resulting increase in the number of images, more trivial moments (casual snapshots of everyday life) are captured by the families. But family photos are not only used for private pleasure and shared memories within the family; they are also shared with friends, acquaintances, and even strangers. The exchange of images enables a feeling of mutual participation in the lives of the others.[55] Pictures, as material objects, can be used as personalized gifts (such as portraits in a picture frame) to strengthen the social relationship among each other. However, pictures are not only artifacts or objects, but also serve as a means of communication. They are a form of social action.[56]

When families consciously decide to present themselves on social media platforms, parents and children alike are displayed. Although most SNS have an age rating of 13 years or older, children can also use the platforms if their legal representatives maintain the account. Parents are "the gatekeeper of personal information of their children, they are the ones to decide whether and how many pictures they contribute to SNS".[57] As guardians, parents are responsible for protecting their children's privacy on the web. However, families—young parents in particular—are often criticized for sharing too much private information online (oversharing) and especially for exploiting their children. For example, ultrasound images of their unborn child are already being shared online, and every milestone in the baby's life is publicly documented.[58] Children thus have an online identity and biography before they can decide to take this step themselves. In her study on sharenting on Facebook, Damkjaer found different approaches to sharenting.[59]

[55] Cf. Kneidinger: Social Media als digitales Fotoalbum, in: Lobinger/Geise (eds.): Visualisierung—Mediatisierung, pp. 146, 161.

[56] Cf. Lobinger: Praktiken des Bildhandelns, in: Lobinger/Geise (eds.): Visualisierung—Mediatisierung, pp. 37–58.

[57] Wagner/Gasche: Sharenting: Making Decisions, in: Multikonferenz Wirtschaftsinformatik 2018, pp. 977, 978.

[58] Cf. Autenrieth: Die Visualisierung von Kindheit, in: Hoffmann/Krotz/ Reißmann (eds.): Mediatisierung und Mediensozialisation, pp. 137, 143.

[59] Cf. Damkjaer: Sharenting = Good Parenting? in: Mascheroni/Ponte/Jorge (eds.): Digital Parenting, pp. 209–218.

In the family-oriented use, information is shared on Facebook "to create and perform a family narrative and identity, to mark and celebrate intergenerational ties and to confirm family values such as tradition, the cyclic nature of everyday life and being part of a lineage".[60] In this sense, the SNS is used like a public photo album, presenting biographical highlights such as the announcement of birth and milestones to friends and acquaintances. At the same time, the presentation of the family also reinforces family identity and is as such a form of doing family. In her interview-based study on the motivations behind Instagram storytelling about family pastimes, Shannon came to the conclusion that posted family leisure images and narratives were intended to communicate "non-normative definitions of family, clarify family identity, help individuals feel a sense of belonging within their social network and community and resist the typical idealization of family life and offer authentic representations of family leisure".[61]

It is noticeable, however, that some families rarely react to the comments of friends, while others engage in lively exchanges. Here, sharenting is more a one-way presentation of the family, while in contrast other parents rely on dialogue and exchange with like-minded people to form a support network: "This approach is generally marked by continuous projection, reporting, self-monitoring, information retrieval and, not least, self-identity production through sharenting, often in close interaction with peers".[62]

Although parents are not ignorant to problems which come along with such display practices of their children, many warnings have been issued. Just to name one of the most prominent institutions, UNICEF points to various risks in its report on "The State of The World's Children: Children in a Digital World" and stresses:

> "[Sharenting] can create potentially serious results in an economy where individuals' online histories may increasingly outweigh their credit histories in the eyes of retailers, insurers and service providers. Parents' lack of awareness can cause damage to a child's well-being when these digital assets depict a child without clothing, as they can be misused by child sex offenders. It can also harm child well-being in the longer term by interfering with children's ability to self-actualize, create their own identity and find employment."[63]

---

[60] Ibid., p. 213.

[61] Shannon: #Family: Exploring the Display of Family, Leisure Sciences, 2019, pp. 1, 2.

[62] Damkjaer: Sharenting=Good Parenting? in: Mascheroni/Ponte/Jorge (eds.): Digital Parenting, pp. 209, 215.

[63] UNICEF (eds.): The State of the World's Children 2017, p. 92.

Especially inappropriate photos, such as nude or shaming photos, which expose children as a means of education in situations that are embarrassing for them, can have negative effects on the children's psyche. Besides bullying (both online and offline), there is an additional risk that the publicly provided images may be downloaded, partially edited, and distributed on pornographic or pedophilic sites.[64] In their interview-based study, Kutscher and Bouillon found that children and parents have different ideas about which photos should be shared.[65] In general, however, children would reveal fewer pictures than their parents. For this reason, attention is repeatedly drawn to this problem in the media and on parents' advice pages (see, for example, the German initiative #deinkindauchnicht, https://deinkindauchnicht.org). As Ouvrein and Verswijvel noted, young people do not reject parental sharing in principle, but they do demand that certain limits be set on what types of images are shared, how often, and with whom.[66]

Despite all criticism of sharenting by parents, it should be noted that they themselves are sometimes overwhelmed by the media logics and the challenges of media use. They are also often under pressure from outside. "Parents' approaches to communication technologies do not spring from rational, intentional decision making, but rather from the competing demands of social, work and family life, self-realization and the desire to be good parents".[67] The conflict between presenting and communicating the "good parenting" of parents and protecting one's own child from the abuse of their images leads to new strategies and an adaptation of image practices. Families and parents are well aware of the risks of children's images on SNS, and react to them differently. One strategy is generally to share fewer images, or only do so on special occasions such as birth announcements. Another approach is to limit the audience and addressees for the pictures, as well as to accept fewer friends/subscribers on SNS in general. Above all, inappropriate photos, such as nude or shaming pictures, should be deleted, which is advised by many scholars. For example, parents set their Facebook or Instagram profiles to 'private' from the outset to limit the public visibility

---

[64] Cf. Kutscher/Bouillon: Kinder. Bilder. Rechte, p. 11.

[65] See also Kutscher: Positionings, Challenges, and Ambivalences in Children's and Parents' Perspectives in Digitalized Familial Contexts, in this volume.

[66] Cf. Ouvrein/Verswijvel: Sharenting: Parental adoration or public humiliation? Children and Youth Services Review, 99, 2019, pp. 319–327.

[67] Damkjaer: Sharenting = Good Parenting? in: Mascheroni/Ponte/Jorge (eds.): Digital Parenting, pp. 209, 210.

of posts. Others refrain completely from presenting pictures on certain SNS and share family and children's pictures with friends and relatives via other more secure channels. However, parents still wish to show their children while maintaining their anonymity. In order to protect the children's identity, a new pictorial practice has arisen: no longer showing their faces. This can be done either through strategic pictorial compositions (the child from behind, far away, or only detail shots of the body) or by masking of the face (disguise or subsequent digital processing). These 'anti-sharenting' photos on SNS also lead to new pictorial aesthetics and new visualization practices. Sharenting is hence a digital practice that stages the family on social media as its core subject.

Image-centered platforms such as Instagram are therefore particularly well suited for not only practicing 'doing family', but also displaying it. "Opportunities to share digital images (i.e., family photos) on SNSs have magnified the ability of photography, as a modern tool of choice, to inscribe meanings about family and construct one's identity, and convey it to others".[68] Doing family, so it seems, is primarily represented in the form of displaying family. But displaying needs to be reflected critically, as elaborated above.

4 Family Narratives and Child Protection on Instagram

One of the most frequented platforms for family communication is Instagram. A simple search for the German hashtag #familie yielded more than 7.5 million posts; the English equivalent #family totals more than 380 million posts—not even taking into account the many composita, ad-hoc creations, or related hashtags like #baby, #photooftheday, #instagram, #familytime, #kids, #cute, #smile, #beautiful, and many more. With successive posts about the daily routines and highlights, many Instagram profiles of families follow quite similar patterns. Even if the narration sometimes takes place mainly via the photo or mainly via the caption, the photo and the caption still form a unit, and the post on Instagram is the result of the combination of these two elements.

Most images, which can be found under the many family related hashtags, report about the daily life of the families; show the furnishing of the houses/flats; and depict (house) animals, meals, and especially family members. Vacations,

[68] Shannon: #Family: Exploring the Display of Family, Leisure Sciences, 2019, pp. 1, 4.

family celebrations, holidays, pregnancies, and even just landscapes and surroundings are often photographed and shared. In general, the photos show the beautiful moments and highlights in life and special snapshots from everyday life.[69] However, Le Moignan et al. also found that, unlike analog photo albums, Instagram shows more trivial images that report on everyday life.[70] Due to the limitlessness of the digital space, many families present their children for years in a row. At the same time, the photos display perfect and happy families presented 'on stage'. Finch explains this need as founded well before the ages of SNS, with a desire for recognition by others and a positive reaction to their doing family practices.[71] With the combination of images and text in the contributions, Instagram provides the perfect tools for displaying family: they show their unity and community as a family on a visual level and also tell about their activities in the caption. Through likes, shares, and comments, they receive direct feedback from others and thus confirm their family identity.

Many photos "tell" a lot about the values and lives of the family, but particularly in combination with the caption, it becomes clear that these photos talk about a family-oriented topic. As split images, the textual elaborations, often just a list of hashtags, have the function of contextualizing the visual narration on the family's everyday life or the thoughts on a topic. The operators of Instagram—hashtags, links and emojis—are specifically used to make digital storytelling more interactive.

But posting on Instagram is not meant to be just a declaration or display—it is intended to evoke reactions from the digital public or specific communities. Consequently, the public display of the photographs needs to be regarded in relation to the accompanying text passages. Just depicting the family is usually not sufficient for the parents; in order to feel like a successful 'Instafamily', feedback from others external to the family unit, who observe the activities, can reinforce or validate the practices that they observe. To evoke such reactions, accompanying text passages often address the public directly. Others use a whole list of hashtags as part of 'hashtag storytelling'[72] in order to attract attention.

---

[69] Cf. Le Moignan et al.: Has Instagram Fundamentally Altered, in: CHI'17, pp. 4935–4947.

[70] Cf. ibid.

[71] Cf. Finch: Displaying Families, Sociology, 41(1), 2007, pp. 65–81.

[72] Cf. Thimm/Nehls: Sharing grief and mourning on Instagram, Communications. The European Journal of Communication Research, 42(3), 2017, pp. 327–349.

With regard to sharenting practices, families differ greatly in their awareness of the problems connected with the use of the children's photographs. Some families generally do not show the children's faces, e.g. by taking photos from behind or from the side. Other families openly show their children and sometimes publish photos of them in which they are only sparsely clothed. In a few years, one might assume, these pictures could possibly make the children themselves uncomfortable. More and more parents have started to use stickers, a tool supplied by Instagram that was developed to decorate and highlight elements of the uploaded content. But in this case, the parents do not use the stickers to highlight objects, but to cover parts of the children's bodies. If, for example, the children look straight into the camera, their faces, especially eyes and nose, are covered by such stickers. If the parents post nude pictures, they cover the respective body parts. In this way, they grant their children a certain degree of privacy. But the audience has started to be critical of these depictions. Some families adopted the practice of so-called "anti-sharing", as described by Autenrieth.[73] As Instagram has a 'no nudity' policy, nude pictures are often deleted. But in many cases, photos of nude children tagged with family issues stayed undetected, and it is more than ever the responsibility of parents to be aware of the risks they are taking.

5 Summary: Digital Families, Mediatization, and Legal Challenges

Families are always in a process of community building through common practices and activities. Digital doing family practices increasingly takes place in and with the media, and are influenced and changed by mediatization processes. At the same time, through the use of the media, families influence and change digital cultures. An example of doing family practices influenced by mediatization is the production and display of family photographs. In the course of the technical development, such as integrating cameras into smartphones, it is becoming increasingly easy to take, edit, and share photos. With the exponential growth of images in everyday life, they are therefore not only used as a medium of memory, but as a means of communication,[74] resulting in an increasing visualization of family lives.

[73] Autenrieth: Family photography in a networked age, in: Mascheroni/Ponte/Jorge (eds.): Digital Parenting, pp. 219–231.

[74] Cf. Van House: Personal photography, Visual Studies, 26(2), 2011, pp. 125–134.

Media usage by and about families is characterized by a variety of motives, goals, and practices. From the perspective of media and communication research, two main lines of thought can be distinguished: *media usage* within the family, and the family as a *mediated object*. For both perspectives, the definition of 'family' is up for personal expansions and configurations—some see close friends as 'family', while others regard only the nucleus as 'family'.

Media usage studies often focus on the conflicts arising from the generational gap in media usage and media cultures, but more and more studies are dedicated to the productive side of media usage, which is designed to organize, help, interact, and connect family members.

The second perspective concerns the family as an object and topic in the mediated public. Concepts such as 'digital parenting' refer to the perspective of media usage by parents in order to connect with other family members, of which sharenting is a specific strategy. Through the representation of family ties and family cohesion, family images contribute to the construction of the reality of the family. Sharing the images with others therefore serves on the one hand to reassure the family about itself, and on the other hand to demonstrate social recognition and family affiliation to others. While some follower responses have highlighted concerns over the children's well-being, a vast majority overtly signal their love, support, and even envy toward such parenting. Photos cannot only be shown to selected friends and acquaintances, but can also be made available to a broad, sometimes anonymous public. As a consequence, families have to deal with balancing the need for social recognition, exchange, and identity formation with the limitations of privacy and data protection. As Steinberg explains from a legal perspective, parents who show pictures of their children on social networks are in conflict with the desire to both protect children's rights and present family practices and activities to others.[75]

With the increasing digitalization of society, mediatization takes over many more contexts and daily practices. Every new platform that is adopted by parents for doing family practices enhances the responsibility of exposing their children. And as Steinberg points out: "Parents should consider the objects of their disclosure, their children, as autonomous persons entitled to protection not only from physical harm (such as the harm posed by pedophiles and identity thieves), but also from more intangible harms such as those that may come from inviting the

[75] Cf. Steinberg: Sharenting: Children's Privacy, Emory Law Journal, 66(4), 2017, pp. 839–884.

world into their children's lives without first obtaining informed consent".[76] It seems that this principle has not yet reached many parents sufficiently. It looks as if media research, legal studies, and family psychology need to put more emphasis on this issue.

References

Aharony, Noa/Gazit, Tali: The importance of the Whatsapp family group: an exploratory analysis, Aslib Journal of Information Management, 68(2), 2016, pp. 174–192.

Anderson, Monica/Jiang, Jingjing: Teens, Social Media & Technology 2018, Washington, D.C 2018.

Archer, Catherine: Social media influencers, post-feminism and neoliberalism: How mum bloggers' 'playbour' is reshaping public relations, Public Relations Inquiry, 8(2), 2019, pp. 149–166.

Autenrieth, Ulla: Die ‚Digital Natives' präsentieren ihre Kinder—Eine Analyse der zunehmenden (Selbst-)Visualisierung von Familie und Kindheit in Onlineumgebungen, Studies in Communication Sciences, 14(2), 2014, pp. 99–107.

Autenrieth, Ulla: Die Visualisierung von Kindheit und Familie im Social Web als Forschungsfeld einer mediatisierten Gesellschaft, in: Hoffmann, Dagmar/Krotz, Friedrich/ Reißmann, Wolfgang (eds.): Mediatisierung und Mediensozialisation. Prozesse—Räume—Praktiken, Wiesbaden 2017, pp. 137–151.

Autenrieth, Ulla: Family photography in a networked age. Anti-sharenting as a reaction to risk assessment and behaviour adaption, in: Mascheroni, Giovanna/Ponte, Cristina/ Jorge, Ana (eds.): Digital Parenting. The Challenges for Families in the Digital Age, Göteborg 2018, pp. 219–231.

Auxier, Brooke/Anderson, Monica/Perrin, Andrew/Turner, Erica: Parenting Children in the Age of Screens, Washington, D.C. 2020.

Barassi, Veronica: The Child as Datafied Citizen. Critical Questions on Data Justice in Family Life, in: Mascheroni, Giovanna/Ponte, Cristina/Jorge, Ana (eds.): Digital Parenting. The Challenges for Families in the Digital Age, Göteborg 2018, pp. 169–177.

Benedetto, Loredana/Ingrassia, Massimo: Digital Parenting: Raising and Protecting Children in Media World, 2020.

Blum-Ross, Alicia/Livingstone, Sonia: "Sharenting," parent blogging, and the boundaries of the digital self, Popular Communication. The International Journal of Media and Culture, 15(2), 2017, pp. 110–125.

Brosch, Anna: When the Child is Born into the Internet: Sharenting as a Growing Trend among Parents on Facebook, The New Educational Review, 43(1), 2016, pp. 225–235.

Couldry, Nick/Hepp, Andreas: Conceptualising mediatization: Contexts, traditions, arguments, Communication Theory, 23(3), 2013, pp. 191–202.

[76] Ibid., p. 878.

Damkjaer, Maja Sonne: Sharenting = Good Parenting? Four Parental Approaches to Sharenting on Facebook, in: Mascheroni, Giovanna/Ponte, Cristina/Jorge, Ana (eds.): Digital Parenting. The Challenges for Families in the Digital Age, Göteborg 2018, pp. 209–218.

Duggan, Maeve/Lenhart, Amanda/Lampe, Cliff/Ellison, Nicole B.: Parents and social media, Washington, D.C. 2015.

Einspänner-Pflock, Jessica: Privatheit im Netz. Konstruktions- und Gestaltungsstrategien von Online-Privatheit bei Jugendlichen, Wiesbaden 2017.

Finch, Janet: Displaying Families, Sociology, 41(1), 2007, pp. 65–81.

Haley, Keltie: Sharenting and the (Potential) Right to Be Forgotten, Indiana Law Journal, 95(3), 2020, pp. 1005–1020.

Holloway, Donell/Green, Lelia: Mediated memory making: The virtual family photograph album, Communications. The European Journal of Communication Research, 42(3), 2017, pp. 351–368.

Kneidinger, Bernadette: Social Media als digitales Fotoalbum multilokaler Familien. Die Bedeutung visueller Kommunikation in intergenerationalen Beziehungen, in: Lobinger, Katharina/Geise, Stephanie (eds.): Visualisierung—Mediatisierung. Bildliche Kommunikation und bildliches Handeln in mediatisierten Gesellschaften, Cologne 2015, pp. 146–163.

Kutscher, Nadia/Bouillon, Ramona: Kinder. Bilder. Rechte. Persönlichkeitsrechte von Kindern im Kontext der digitalen Mediennutzung in der Familie, Berlin 2018.

Kutscher, Nadia: Positionings, Challenges, and Ambivalences in Children's and Parents' Perspectives in Digitalized Familial Contexts, in this volume.

Le Moignan, Effie/Lawson, Shaun/Rowland, Duncan A./Mahoney, Jamie/Briggs, Pamela: Has Instagram Fundamentally Altered the 'Family Snapshot'? in: CHI'17: Proceedings of the 2017 CHI Conference on Human Factors in Computing Systems, Denver/CO 2017, pp. 4935–4947.

Leaver, Tama: Researching the ends of identity: Birth and death on social media, Social Media + Society, 1(1).2015, pp. 1–2.

Lobinger, Katharina: Praktiken des Bildhandelns in mediatisierten Gesellschaften—eine Systematisierung, in: Lobinger, Katharina/Geise, Stephanie (eds.): Visualisierung–Mediatisierung. Bildliche Kommunikation und bildliches Handeln in mediatisierten Gesellschaften, Cologne 2015, pp. 37–58.

Lobinger, Katharina/Schreiber, Maria: Photo Sharing. Visuelle Praktiken des Mit-Teilens, in: Lobinger, Katharina (ed.): Handbuch Visuelle Kommunikationsforschung, Wiesbaden 2017, pp. 1–22.

Mascheroni, Giovanna/Ponte, Cristina/Jorge, Ana: Introduction, in: Mascheroni, Giovanna/Ponte, Cristina/Jorge, Ana (eds.): Digital Parenting. The Challenges for Families in the Digital Age, Göteborg 2018, pp. 9–16.

Media impact (eds.): Studie zur digitalen Familienkommunikation—Key Findings, Berlin 2017.

Medienpädagogischer Forschungsverbund Südwest (ed.): JIM-Studie 2018: Jugend, Information, Medien. Basisuntersuchung zum Medienumgang 12- bis 19-Jähriger, Stuttgart 2018.

Medienpädagogischer Forschungsverbund Südwest (ed.): JIM-Studie 2020: Jugend, Information, Medien. Basisuntersuchung zum Medienumgang 12- bis 19-Jähriger, Stuttgart 2020.

Medienpädagogischer Forschungsverbund Südwest (ed.): KIM-Studie 2018: Kindheit, Internet, Medien. Basisuntersuchung zum Medienumgang 6- bis 13-Jähriger, Stuttgart 2018.

Medienpädagogischer Forschungsverband Südwest (ed.): miniKIM 2014: Kleinkinder und Medien. Basisuntersuchung zum Medienumgang 2- bis 5-Jähriger in Deutschland, Stuttgart 2015.

Nouwens, Midas/Griggio, Carla F./Mackay, Wendy E.: "WhatsApp is for family; Messenger is for friends": Communication Places in App Ecosystems, in: CHI'17: Proceedings of the 2017 CHI Conference on Human Factors in Computing Systems, Denver/CO 2017, pp.727–735.

Orton-Johnson, Kate: Mummy Blogs and Representations of Motherhood: "Bad Mummies" and Their Readers, Social Media + Society, April-June 2017, 2017, pp. 1–10.

Ouvrein, Gaëlle/Verswijvel, Karen: Sharenting: Parental adoration or public humiliation? A focus group study on adolescents' experiences with sharenting against the background of their own impression management, Children and Youth Services Review, 99, 2019, pp. 319–327.

O'Hara, Kenton/Massimi, Michael/Harper, Richard/Rubens, Simon/Morris, Jessica: Everyday Dwelling with WhatsApp, in: CSCW'14, February 15–19, 2014, Proceedings of the 17th ACM conference on Computer supported cooperative work & social computing, https://doi.org/10.1145/2531602.2531679.

Pauweis, Luc: Communicating Desired Pasts. On the Digital (Re)construction of Private Histories: What is Really at Stake? Journal of Visual Literacy, 22(2), 2002, pp. 161–174.

Pew Research Center: Parenting Children in the Age of Screens, 2020, https://www.pewresearch.org/internet/2020/07/28/parenting-children-in-the-age-of-screens/; last accessed May 19, 2021.

Pink, Sarah/Horst, Heather A./Postill, John/Hjorth, Larissa/Lewis, Tania/Tacchi, Jo: Digital Ethnography. Principles and Practice, Los Angeles/London 2016.

Procentese, Fortuna/Gatti, Flora/Di Napoli, Immacolata: Families and Social Media Use: The Role of Parents' Perceptions about Social Media Impact on Family Systems in the Relationship between Family Collective Efficacy and Open Communication, International Journal of Environmental Research and Public Health, 16(24), 2019, 5006, pp. 1–11.

Reißmann, Wolfgang: Mediatisierung visuell. Kommunikationstheoretische Überlegungen und eine Studie zum Wandel privater Bildpraxis, Baden-Baden 2015.

Rodríguez-de-Dios, Isabel/van Oosten, Johanna M.F./Igartua, Juan-José: A study of the relationship between parental mediation and adolescents' digital skills, online risks and online opportunities, Computers in Human Behavior 82, 2018, pp. 186–198.

Rose, Gillian: Doing Family Photography. The Domestic, The Public and The Politics of Sentiment, Surrey/Burlington 2010.

Schier, Michaela/Jurczyk, Karin: „Familie als Herstellungsleistung" in Zeiten der Entgrenzung, in: Frickel, Sybille (ed.): soFid—Sozialwissenschaftlicher Fachinformationsdienst. Familienforschung, 2008/1, pp. 9–18.

Schlör, Katrin: Doing Family und Social Media. (Re-)Konstruktionspraktiken von Familie im Spannungsfeld von Vergemeinschaftung und Abgrenzung, Studies in Communication Sciences, 16(1), 2016, pp. 28–35.

Schreiber, Maria: Showing/Sharing: Analysing Visual Communication from a Praxeological Perspective, Media and Communication, 5(4), 2017, pp. 37–50.

Shannon, Charlene S.: #Family: Exploring the Display of Family and Family Leisure on Facebook and Instagram, Leisure Sciences, 2019, pp. 1–17.

Steinberg, Stacey B.: Sharenting: Children's Privacy in the Age of Social Media, Emory Law Journal, 66(4), 2017, pp. 839–884.

Thimm, Caja: Hate Speech, Fake News, Filter Bubbles & demokratische Öffentlichkeit, to appear in: Sander, Uwe/von Gross, Friederike/Hugger, Kai-Uwe (eds.): Handbuch Medienpädagogik, 2nd Ed., Wiesbaden i.pr. 2021.

Thimm, Caja: Media Technology and Media Logic(s): The Media Grammar Approach, in: Thimm, Caja/Anastasiadis, Mario/Einspänner-Pflock, Jessica (eds.): Media Logic(s) Revisited. Modelling the Interplay between Media Institutions, Media Technology and Societal Change, Cham 2018, pp. 111–132.

Thimm, Caja: The Mediatization of Politics and the Digital Public Sphere: The Dynamics of Mini-Publics, in: Frame, Alex/Brachotte, Gilles (eds.): Citizen Participation and Political Communication in a Digital World, New York 2016, pp. 167–183.

Thimm, Caja/Nehls, Patrick: Sharing grief and mourning on Instagram: Digital patterns of family memories, Communications. The European Journal of Communication Research, 42(3), 2017, pp. 327–349.

Trost, Jan: Do We Mean the Same by the Concept of Family? Communication Research, 17(4), 1990, pp. 431–443.

Turkle, Sherry: Alone Together. Why We Expect More from Technology and Less from Each Other, New York 2011.

UNICEF (ed.): The State of the World's Children 2017. Children in a Digital World, New York 2017.

Van House, Nancy A.: Personal photography, digital technologies and the uses of the visual, Visual Studies, 26(2), 2011, pp. 125–134.

Wagner, Amina/Gasche, Lisa Alina: Sharenting: Making Decisions about Other's Privacy on Social Networking Sites, in: Multikonferenz Wirtschaftsinformatik 2018, Lüneburg 2018, pp. 977–988.

Prof. Dr. Caja Thimm is a tenured professor at the University of Bonn, Germany, and the Head of the Department for Media Studies. She is the spokesperson of the research network "Digital Society and Democracy" and member of the NRW Academy of Science. She has done extensive research on social media, digital technologies, and e-democracy. Her most recent book is on "The machine—friend or foe? Humans and technology in the digital age." (Spinger, 2019).

Positionings, Challenges, and Ambivalences in Children's and Parents' Perspectives in Digitalized Familial Contexts

Nadia Kutscher

1 Sharenting—Personal Rights of Children and Parental Responsibility

Digital media use has long been part of families' everyday lives. Various studies[1] show that digital media is not only a component of the everyday lives of children and parents, but also raises new questions—or, rather, old questions in a new context. Everyday practices in families combine with digital practices with media, sometimes changing their form and reach and interlocking with other contexts and effects. In parent blogs, Instagram posts, and YouTube channels, families document their everyday lives in a plethora of ways. In the process, a great deal of information about children, young people, and adults, as well as pictures and videos of them, are published and shared with others via social networks or apps such as Facebook, WhatsApp, Instagram, YouTube, and Snapchat. Many parents post pictures to let relatives and friends participate in their family life or in their child(ren)'s development. Some make a living from this and reach a large public audience.

[1] Cf. Wagner et al.: Zwischen Anspruch und Alltagsbewältigung; Medienpädagogischer Forschungsverbund Südwest: miniKIM 2012; Grobbin: Online–Medien im Kindesalter; Kammerl et al.: EXIF—Exzessive Internetnutzung in Familien.

N. Kutscher (✉)
University of Cologne, Cologne, Germany
e-mail: nadia.kutscher@uni-koeln.de

N. Dethloff et al. (eds.), *Families and New Media*, Juridicum – Schriften zum Medien-, Informations- und Datenrecht,
https://doi.org/10.1007/978-3-658-39664-0_3

In recent years, the so-called practice of "sharenting"—a mix of the terms "sharing" and "parenting" used to describe the habitual use of social media to share news, images, etc. of one's child(ren)[2]—has increasingly come to the fore. With sharenting, the practice of (mostly parents) taking photographs of family members,[3] which has long been part of "doing family", conjoins with the digital social network practice of posting and sharing. Photos are habitually taken in families even when the children do not feel comfortable with it, often hinting that they will later be happy when these pictures are available. The spread of smartphones with camera functions has allowed for everyday life to be pictorially documented to an unprecedented extent and masses of pictures to be shared with others via messaging services and social networks. This is therefore a "perfectly normal thing". Thus, pictures, videos, and other information about children—starting from an early age—are being spread among family members, friends, acquaintances, and (via social media sites) strangers.

This practice is embedded in everyday familial contexts, based on the assumption that parents, as adults responsible for children, do care for their rights; know their children; and due to experience and being informed, are able to estimate media-related acting and its consequences better than children. The miniKIM study shows that many parents of two to five-year-old children are members of social networks and share their children's data.[4] In "The State of the World's Children: Children in a Digital World 2017", UNICEF warns that parents are potentially distributing information about their children to a mass audience, which could damage the child's reputation and thus expose him or her to economic and sexual exploitation, as well as impair his or her ability to develop an identity or find work.[5]

A closer look at what is understood as "sharing" reveals a wide range of data types and contexts in which such data is used[6]:

- unproblematic images that can be downloaded by third parties, modified, and distributed in pedophile forums
- embarrassing information for children

---

[2] Collins English Dictionary.

[3] Cf. Rose: Doing Family Photography; Brake: Der Bildungsort Familie, pp. 54 ff.

[4] Cf. Medienpädagogischer Forschungsverbund Südwest: miniKIM 2012 and 2014.

[5] Cf. UNICEF: The State of The World's Children.

[6] Cf. Steinberg: Sharenting, pp. 847 et seq.

- information that makes children identifiable in other contexts (e.g., unwanted access to private information for distant acquaintances, data brokers who consider children to be the addressees of advertisements, or surveillance actors)
- inappropriate photos (e.g., nude photos)
- sharing information (sometimes unknowingly) in not clearly defined circles via social media
- sensitive data (e.g., health information) about the child in the context of parent blogs or network activities (e.g., information and exchanges on specific diseases or political commitment)
- public shaming photos as a means of education to put children under pressure through public presentation on conflict issues.

"Children have no control over the dissemination of their personal information by their parents".[7] This quote by legal scholar Stacey Steinberg refers to a fundamental—and usually everyday—constellation in families, which in turn is based on the assumption that parents, as guardians, are aware of children's rights, know their children well, and are able to assess them. It also draws on the recurring idea that adults are better able to assess media-related actions and their consequences than children due to a head start in experience and information. In the context of digital media practices today, however, it is becoming increasingly clear that—on closer inspection—this does not necessarily raise new questions. Moreover, everyday practices in families under the conditions of data aggregation and algorithmization in the context of digitization raise far-reaching questions as well as risks for the future of children.

For example, Steinberg argues that sharenting has so far not been debated enough in the areas of children's education and conflict negotiation between children's and parental rights.[8] The focus is often on how children use digital media and expose themselves to risky situations, or how third parties can become dangerous to children online. Only recently has the focus shifted to the consequences that parents' actions in the context of digital media can have for their children. The focus is often on well-intentioned, everyday family media practices that, unknowingly or at least not sufficiently reflected, can have far-reaching impacts on children's well-being. In many contexts, parents act as guardians of their children's online identities to protect them from danger. Many parents expect, for

[7] Ibid., p. 846.

[8] Cf. ibid., p. 842.

example, that daycare centers, schools, or other public institutions ask for permission before putting their child(ren)'s image online. They also critically discuss what it means when commercial providers publish personal information about children. Parents control their children's access to digital media or services in different ways to protect them. At the same time, according to Steinberg, parents not only protect their children in this context, but also disclose their children's data. Children are usually dependent on their parents' decision-making power in this respect. There is, in fact, no "opt-out" option for children as long as their parents decide.[9] At the same time, there is often an "Interfamilial Privacy Divide"[10] if a child and its parents have different interests in sharing private data. This poses difficult questions and and risks with unforeseeable consequences for the future of children under the conditions of data aggregation and algorithmization.[11]

2 The Study

With this background, an empirical research was conducted,[12] that aimed to reconstruct familial practices when dealing with photos and children's data in everyday, digitalized life.[13] In 37 semi-structured and media-based interviews with 12 families (including 21 children) from four federal states in Germany, children, parents, and in some cases whole families were asked about topics including: the role of digital media in their family's everyday life, styles of media education in their family, how they handle data (especially photos of oneself and others), how children participate in decisions about sharenting (taking pictures and sharing), their knowledge about the right to protect one's image and the desire for participation, knowledge and notions of parents about digital media, privacy, and children's rights. Participating children, of whom 9 were male and 12 were female, were 6 to 15 years old. The families were chosen by contrasting samplings with regard to experiences in media use, educational background, income, Goldthorpe/Erikson/Portocarero class schemes, migration background, and family structures.

[9] Cf. ibid., pp. 842 et seq.

[10] Ibid., p. 856.

[11] Cf. UNICEF: The State of The World's Children, p. 92.

[12] Funded by and in cooperation with the Children's Charity of Germany (Deutsches Kinderhilfswerk e.V.).

[13] Cf. Kutscher/Bouillon: Kinder. Bilder. Rechte.

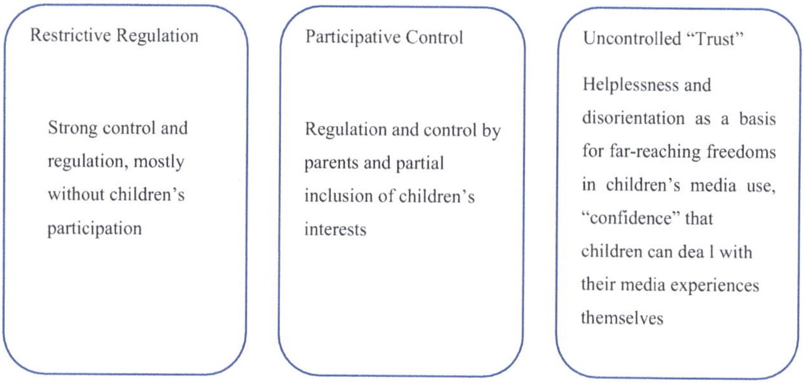

Fig. 1 Types of Media Education

The types of media education in the families ranged from restrictive and over-controlling to uncontrolled (cf. Fig. 1).

3 Contradictory Parental Practices of Data Protection

Similar to the types of media education, the practices of parents in terms of data protection varied and turned out to be quite contradictory. Also, digitally savvy parents showed a kind of 'metadata pragmatism', stating, for example, "I have nothing to hide" or "[w]e are all objects of surveillance". In some cases, they even talked about the advantages of metadata-based personalization of services. Despite an approximate awareness of data collection and processing of social networking services and apps, parents expressed (almost) no knowledge or ideas about opportunities of action regarding how to protect their own or their children's data in this context. In two of the families, the parents shared that parental privacy settings were determined with the children's support, as the parents did not know what to do and their children were more informed so they showed them which settings and services to disable or install.

Several parents reported difficulties regarding their child's ability to communicate with others via messaging apps. Although their child was younger than 16, they allowed him or her to use WhatsApp, knowing that this could raise questions of appropriateness. While letting the child use an age-inappropriate app—and thus giving some early autonomy to the child—they decided to make the child hand over his or her smartphone every evening and let them search all communication (messages, threads, etc.) to exercise parental control and protection, whereby the child's privacy sphere thus becomes violated. Some parents told about controlling their children's usage of services, such as games or YouTube, by using apps that close applications once the parentally permitted time of use has run out.

The reported practices show that parents' intention to protect their children's data is thwarted by a lack of knowledge, as well as by uncertainty, naivety, resignation, and pragmatism.

4 Children's and Parents' Criteria for Sharing or Protecting Photos

In the interviews, children were shown seven exemplary children's photos, which they were asked to describe and classify. The pictures differed in terms of the motifs and the recognizability of the children's faces. In four pictures, the children's faces could be recognized, and in three, the faces could not be recognized due to pixilation or the shot's angle. The interviewers asked the children what they thought of the pictures, and how they would rate them if they themselves were depicted in them. Moreover, the children were asked, along with questions about their knowledge of their personal rights, to indicate to what extent their own photos may be shown or shared. This was followed by questions about their knowledge of data protection on the internet, as well as their existing knowledge of data processing in the context of digital services.

During those interviews, the children named different criteria regarding the disclosure of photos to others. Their consent to share or to protect photos of themselves related to the extent of their *participation* in parental decisions on the disclosure of the photos (which ones and to whom), their *relation to potential addressees* in regard to trust towards potential recipients, the *degrees of publicness of the presentation context,* the *content* of the pictures with regard to positive or negative connotation and the potential of recognition or shaming, and their fear of sanctions regarding the depicted situation—in relation to their wanted or unwanted recognizability. The criteria unfold against the backdrop of the children's own experiences and perceptions:

A 11-year old interviewee differentiates between different ranges of public:

> Y1: Okay, who would be allowed to see such a picture of you?
> L1m(11): Actually, everybody.
> Y1: Okay, who is everybody?
> L1m(11): Well, all my friends and my family.
> Y1: Okay, and would it be okay to put this on the internet, for example?
> L1m(11): No, I wouldn't put it on the internet.
> Y1: Okay, why not?
> L1m(11): Because I wouldn't want the whole world to see this
> (line 670 ff.)

Another 7-year old girl also shows in her argumentation that trust and relationship plays a role in who should be allowed to see a picture of her:

> F3w(7): Well, I would not take strangers, only, well, people whom I have met before perhaps, or whom I know already, or people who helped me (line 628 ff.)

In general, the children expressed diverging positionings towards the same pictures, which resulted in each photo receiving various ratings.

In their interviews, parents were asked also about their sharing practices in relation to the content of the shared photos, the children's participation in this practice, the parents' reasons for the children's participation (whether or not it took place), and the addressees of the shared photos. The criteria from the parents' perspective for sharing or protecting pictures were rather unanimous: Those who shared pictures said that they do it with photos of their children which are regarded as particularly "cute" or "funny". One mother described which pictures of her daughter she takes and shares:

> H3w: When they look cute or sleep or I don't know what, when something is funny, well, then... and yeah when she is lying on the couch once again absolutely flabby, driveling, dead or halloween when she is made up funnily in such situations [...] goes directly to the family WhatsApp group (line 220 ff.).

Photos worth protecting were described as those where the content could potentially negatively impact the children's (future) life and those found to be revealing, such as naked or swimsuit pictures. In both cases, the parent's perspective usually guides the action, even when contrary to the children's wishes. One child interviewee expressed her annoyance about her mother's sharing of pictures she does not want to be shared. Some of the children stated that they did not know if, when, and with whom their parents shared pictures of them; others reported that their parents took and shared pictures of them despite their protest. Some interviewees found that they had no right, as the parents were the ones who were in charge.

> F3w(7): Actually, they need not ask me because they are my parents, and they rule me. Yes, they rule me. (line 796 ff.)

Nonetheless, most of the children expressed that they want to be involved in decisions about taking and sharing photos.

> F1m(10): But if they take a whole photo, then they should ask first. (line 1313 f.)

Among them were both, children who have so far not perceived having any say in their parents' decisions, as well as children who had already explicitly expressed to their parents that they wanted to be involved. Primarily younger children stated that they did not want to be involved or would leave it to their parents to decide. Some also only want to be involved in certain situations, especially when it is a matter of being recognizable, when pictures are perceived as "embarrassing", or when pictures are perceived as disadvantageous. Even if they are not included in parental decisions, children sometimes have very precise ideas about how they would like to be represented, but not necessarily a precise idea of how they should be involved. At the same time, children who already had profiles on social media and had discussed what to share with their peers did not view themselves as empowered to act vis-à-vis their parents.

Parents reported that they increasingly involve their children in decisions about taking and sharing photos according to their ability to protest, especially connected to rising age. Whereas there was a broad range of reports about children's (non-)participation, in some of the families, the children did not participate because the parents presupposed consent and assumed that the children would make it known if they did not agree. Some parents expressed the opinion that the children had—due to their age—no right and no capability to decide; some children stated that the parents consulted with them before they shared or that the children were granted participation after sharing and that they participated in an "ex-post" intervention.

> Y1w: And are you allowed to decide what pictures are being shared?
> I1w(11): No, but my mother mostly asks me if this is okay, and then I say "yes".
> Y1w: Ah, okay. You mean when she uploads it, right?
> I1w(11): Well, mostly, she uploads it first, and then I see it. Well, mhm, mhm but these are not pictures of me that are embarrassing. (line 718 ff.)

In some separate interviews with children and with parents, divergencies between reported and factual practices became apparent. Some of the parents reported that they never would publish or share pictures of their children wearing swimwear or barely clothed, but contrary to that, some of the children said that their parents shared such pictures on their Facebook account. When reviewing the family's Facebook profile, there were photos of the family (with children) in swimsuits. All parents differentiated between Facebook as a "public space", where data should be protected more, and WhatsApp as a "private space", where data sharing was viewed as uncritical. As their difference criterion here—reconstructed from the interview data—is the controllability of the target group for the shared children's data, issues such as data protection in regard to metadata analyses are not considered.

5 Spectrum of Strategies Dealing with the Areas of Conflict Between Autonomy and Protection, Responsibility, and Participation

Regarding the strategies reconstructed from the interview data, the fundamental children's rights dilemma between autonomy rights and protective rights, as well as the question of responsibility and participation, become clear at numerous points (cf. Fig. 2).

Children's *autonomy* is given space—in very different forms—by on the one hand side parental permission to use social media or a range of permits which implies giving freedoms, allowing or conducting risky practices or setting no rules at all, and on the other hand side by the children finding ways to use digital media in secrecy or developing creative strategies of expanding media time. In one family, the siblings added together the daily permitted time for each child and used it up jointly, thus extending the time available. In terms of protecting children, parents introduce restrictions regarding time and areas or content of media use, or limit the presentation of their children on social media (sometimes only rhetorically when posting pictures of their children, nevertheless). The children's role in supporting themselves and their data *protection* is that they develop strategies to get information about and to control parental sharenting, for example, by searching the parent's smartphone for posted pictures or teaching the parents about data protection by helping them with settings on their digital device. Here, the *distribution of responsibility* within the family also reveals a broad range—from controlling children's access to media use and content to shifting responsibility to the children. One mother of a 10-year-old girl said that she didn't oversee

	Children's Autonomy	Children's Protection	Familial Distribution of Responsibility	Children's Participation
Parents	• Permission of early social media use • Freedoms of use within a certain frame • No rules	• Restrictions in media use • (Rhetoric) limitations of children's presentation in media	• (Technical) control of children's media and content • Shifting responsibility to children	• Decision on the children's place when dealing with data production and sharing • Consulting the children • Age differentiation
Children	• Secret use when forbidden • Creative strategies of expanding media time	• Control of parental sharenting • Teaching the parents	• Responsible use • Taking over responsibility for data protection in the family	• Idea of no right to participation and acceptance of parental power • More or less successful demanding of participation • Protest

Fig. 2 Children's and Parents' Strategies in Dealing with Autonomy, Responsibility, Protection, and Participation

the child's media use at all; her daughter is allowed to go on the internet without any control, and she trusts that her child would come to her if there were any problems. In some families, children or parents reported that the children get or take responsibility for data protection in regard to digital media, also for the parents' devices. As for *children's participation* in decisions about media use and sharenting, the parental practices range from no participation to regularly consulting with the children when deciding what to share. In many cases, this was connected to age: The older the children were, the more involvement they were granted in such decisions. From the children's perspective, some of the younger ones not only assumed a parental decision-making power, but also demanded participation by protesting parental practices with which they did not consent. The children's demands for participation were sometimes more and sometimes less successful depending on what the parents allowed. But even in negotiation-oriented families, parental decision-making power was mostly undisputed when it came to digital media.

6 Discussion

The results show that "normal" (generational) regimes and everyday practices in families and society in combination with even adults feeling overwhelmed in the context of digital media can lead to a lack of consideration of children's rights by parents. In general, childhood concepts and generational orders, as well as the parents' available knowledge of data protection issues and the resulting consequences for the protection or participation and respect for children's autonomy, are shaping frameworks. In the contexts studied, attention to children's rights in media education is clearly absent in some families' everyday lives. In many cases, children are hardly involved in decision-making or are denied the ability to make decisions. On the other hand, they are attributed extensive responsibility and freedom of action in areas where parents do not view themselves as having the power to act.

In the context of respecting children's rights in digitalized, everyday familial life, the question arises as to how parental responsibility for children's upbringing is expressed in media education practices, especially in the form of reduced participation and inadequate protection of children. This, in turn, raises the question of whether, in the context of digital media use, it can be assumed that parents can always know what is best for their children. It is also questionable whether parental decision-making power is always in the best interests of children, given the fact that children express themselves significantly more "data-sensitively" than their parents on various points. On the other hand, it is questionable whether parents have the "right" to violate their children's privacy in order to protect them. Furthermore, the possibility of demanding certain rights, especially in the context of digitization—for example, when it comes to the future consequences of algorithmically-evaluated metadata from parental sharing practices for children—requires appropriate information about the processes, contexts, and consequences of such data collection and exploitation. This lack of information is a problem for both parents and children: How can parents take responsibility for their children's data when they have only rudimentary knowledge about data use? How can children judge what is too public for them if they cannot assess the public dimension of Facebook, for example? Is protection by intervening in privacy legitimate? What would be an adequate level of information to be able to give factual "informed consent"[14]? And how do we deal with the fact that children, at different points in their biographies, consider certain data or photos to be problematic or protected in different ways?

The questions addressed here point out that an effective consideration of children's rights in digitized, everyday life requires both protective and autonomous spaces at various levels. In addition to the subjective empowerment of children and parents in dealing with data—as far as this is comprehensible and feasible for the individual—children and parents need support from public educational and upbringing institutions such as day-care centers, schools, family education institutes, educational counselling services, and other relevant actors. It also becomes clear that, if their views are to be taken seriously, children should in many places be involved more systematically in decisions that affect them and their data or rights to their own image. Beyond that, however, it is also clear that in view of the contexts of data use and the availability of children's data in the digital space—over the production of which they largely have no say—a structural framework is necessary that enables the protection of children's rights, and—as these issues do not only affect children's but basic civil rights—also of adult's digital civil rights, through political control such as debate and law-based control. More participation of children is obviously already possible at a rather early age. With regard to the distribution of responsibility, an individualization of responsibility like "more media competence for parents" can only be part of a bigger solution to protect children's rights in digitalized contexts.

References

Brake, Anna: Der Bildungsort Familie. Methodische Grundlagen der Untersuchung, in: Büchner, Peter/Brake, Anna (eds.): Bildungsort Familie. Transmission von Bildung und Kultur im Alltag von Mehrgenerationenfamilien, Wiesbaden 2006, pp. 49–79.

Collins English Dictionary, https://www.collinsdictionary.com/dictionary/English; last accessed April 20, 2021.

Grobbin, Alexander: Online-Medien im Kindesalter. Ergebnisse aus dem DJI-Projekt: "Digitale Medien: Beratungs-, Handlungs- und Regulierungsbedarf aus Elternperspektive", 2016, http://www.dji.de/fileadmin/user_upload/wwwkinderseiten/1161/Grobbin_Onlinemedien%20im%20Kindesalter.pdf; last accessed September 22, 2018.

Kammerl, Rudolf/Hirschhauser, Lena/Rosenkranz, Moritz/Schwinge, Christiane/Hein, Sandra/Wartberg, Lutz/Petersen, Kay Uwe: EXIF—Exzessive Internetnutzung in Familien,

[14] Cf. Reamer: Social Work in a Digital Age.

2012, https://www.bmfsfj.de/blob/jump/93708/exif-exzessive-internetnutzung-in-familien-data.pdf; last accessed February 18, 2020.

Kutscher, Nadia/Bouillon, Ramona: Kinder. Bilder. Rechte Persönlichkeitsrechte von Kindern im Kontext der digitalen Mediennutzung in der Familie, 2018. https://www.dkhw.de/fileadmin/Redaktion/1_Unsere_Arbeit/1_Schwerpunkte/6_Medienkompetenz/6.13._Studie_Kinder_Bilder_Rechte/DKHW_Schriftenreihe_4_KinderBilderRechte.pdf; last accessed November 2, 2021.

Medienpädagogischer Forschungsverbund Südwest: miniKIM 2012. Kleinkinder und Medien, https://www.mpfs.de/studien/minikim-studie/2012/; last accessed February 18, 2020.

Medienpädagogischer Forschungsverbund Südwest: miniKIM 2014. Kleinkinder und Medien, https://www.mpfs.de/studien/minikim-studie/2014/; last accessed February 18, 2020.

Reamer, Frederic G.: Social Work in a Digital Age: Ethical and Risk Management Challenges, Social Work, 58(2), 2013, pp. 163–172.

Rose, Gillian: Doing Family Photography: The Domestic, the Public and the Politics of Sentiment, Farnham 2010.

Steinberg, Stacey: Sharenting: Children's Privacy in the Age of Social Media (March 8, 2016), University of Florida Levin College of Law Research Paper No. 16–41, 2016, https://ssrn.com/abstract=2711442; last accessed July 13, 2020.

UNICEF: The State of The World's Children: Children in a Digital World 2017, https://www.unicef.org/publications/files/SOWC_2017_ENG_WEB.pdf; last accessed September 20, 2020.

Wagner, Ulrike/Gebel, Christa/Lampert, Claudia (eds.): Zwischen Anspruch und Alltagsbewältigung: Medienerziehung in der Familie, Schriftenreihe Medienforschung der LfM, Band 72, Berlin 2013.

Prof. Dr. Nadia Kutscher is an educational scientist. She is Professor at the Department of Special Education and Rehabilitation at the Faculty of Human Sciences at the University of Cologne, Germany, and has published extensively on questions of digital media in the context of childhood, youth, and family, as well as on social work and refugees'* lives, ethical issues of social work, children's rights, and welfare state policies. Among her recent publications are: Educational participation of young refugees in the context of digitalized settings (in: Information, Communication and Society, 25, 2022, Special Issue 'Constructing Young Selves', in press) (with Michi S. Fujii, Jana Hüttmann, Niko Engfer, and Henrike Friedrichs-Liesenkötter); Handbuch Soziale Arbeit und Digitalisierung (ed. with Thomas Ley, Udo Seelmeyer, Friederike Siller, Angela Tillmann, Isabel Zorn, Beltz/Juventa, 2020); Ethische Dimensionen des Einsatzes von algorithmenbasierten Entscheidungen und Scoring in pädagogischen und sozialpolitischen Kontexten (in: Gapski/Packard (eds.): Super-Scoring? Datengetriebene Sozialtechnologien als neue Bildungsherausforderung, kopaed, 2021, pp. 177–190).

A Rights-Based Approach to Children's Digital Participation in the Multi-Level System of the European Union

Katharina Kaesling

1 Rights-based Approaches Against Risk-based Narratives

At the young ages of six and seven, 40% of children in Germany used the internet in 2019. This percentage only increases with age, with 71% of those aged eight to nine, 85% of those aged ten to eleven, and 97% of those aged 12 to 18 being active internet users.[1] This is not surprising given that a considerable part of sociality has shifted from analogue to digital means, such as communication via social networks and smartphone apps.

Communication in the digital age encompasses not only messaging services, but also content creation on social media for the public or a selected audience. Social networking sites have become such an integral part of young people's everyday lives that it is practically out of the question for young people to reject this form of communication.[2] Children's main focus with online activities is actually communicating within existing relationships, i.e. the reinforcement of

[1] Statista: Internetnutzung von Kindern und Jugendlichen nach Altersgruppen in Deutschland.

[2] Neumann-Braun/Autenrieth: Soziale Beziehungen im Web 2.0 und deren Visualisierung, p. 21.

K. Kaesling (✉)
Institute of International Law, Intellectual Property and Technology Law (IRGET), University of Dresden (TU), Dresden, Germany
e-mail: katharina.kaesling@coleurope.eu

N. Dethloff et al. (eds.), *Families and New Media*, Juridicum – Schriften zum Medien-, Informations- und Datenrecht,
https://doi.org/10.1007/978-3-658-39664-0_4

relationships with peers.[3] Creating and maintaining social capital is one of the social benefits of children's online activities.[4] Taking part in online sociality can also prevent isolation of children.[5] A large part of children's identity practices and experimentation takes place online.[6] In addition, it can further young people's engagement with public life.[7] Digital spheres offer specific opportunities for (civic) engagement and participation[8] as well as for creativity.[9] Not all of these benefits are the focus of adults who decide about children's participation, such

---

[3] Autenrieth et al.: Gebrauch und Bedeutung von Social Network Sites im Alltag junger Menschen, in: Neumann-Braun (ed.): Freundschaft und Gemeinschaft im Social Web, p. 31, p. 51; Subrahmanyam/Greenfield: Online Communication and Adolescent Relationships, The Future of Children, 18, 2008, pp. 119–120; Moravscik: Negotiating the Single European Act, International Organization, 45(1), 1991, pp. 651–688.

[4] Cf. Ellison et al.: The Benefits of Facebook "Friends", Journal of computer-mediated communication, 12(4), 2007, pp. 1134–1161.

[5] Marwick et al.: Youth, Privacy and Reputation—Literature Review, pp. 10 f., 61 f.; Giroux: Racial Injustice and Disposable Youth, International Journal of Qualitative Studies in Education, 16, 2003, p. 553 (examining the social costs of repressive policies regarding young people, including those that increase surveillance of youth).

[6] For everyday identity practices of young adults: Kleinen-von Königslöw/Förster: Multimedia theme repertoires in the everyday identity practices of young adults, Communications, 41(4) 2016, pp. 375–398; Schulz: Mediatisierte Sozialisation im Jugendalter, pp. 28–52; Valkenburg/Peter: Adolescents' Identity Experiments on the Internet, Communication Research, 35(2), 2008, pp. 208–231.

[7] Carpini: Gen.com: Youth, Civic Engagement, and the New Information Environment, Political Communication, 17(4), 2000, pp. 341–349; Montgomery/Gottlieb-Robles: Youth as E-Citizens. The Internet's Contribution to Civic Engagement, in: Buckingham/Willett (eds.): Digital Generations, pp. 131 ff.

[8] Margetts: Tiny Acts of Digital Democracy; "tiny acts of participation" such as "following, liking, tweeting, retweeting, sharing text or images relating to a political issue, or signing up to a digital campaign" should be regarded as the categorical difference "that social media have brought to the democratic landscape", Margetts: Rethinking Democracy with Social Media, The Political Quarterly, 19(21), 2019, p. 108; see also Picone/Kleut et al.: Small acts of engagement, New Media & Society, 21(9), 2019, pp. 2010–2028; Shah et al.: Information and Expression in a Digital Age, Communication Research, 32(5), 2005, pp. 531–565; Kenski/Stroud: Connections Between Internet Use and Political Efficacy, Knowledge, and Participation, Journal of Broadcasting & Electronic Media, 50(2), 2006, pp. 173–192; see also Lane: In Search of the Expressive Citizen, Public Opinion Quarterly, 84, Special Issue 2020, pp. 257–283.

[9] Kaesling: The Making of Citizens, in: Neuberger/Friesike/Krzywdzinski/Eiermann (eds.): Proceedings of the Weizenbaum Conference 2021, p. 69; Kaesling/Knapp: Massenkreativität in sozialen Netzwerken, MMR (Multi Media und Recht), 23(12), 2020, pp. 816–821.

as lawmakers and parents.[10] Parents especially associate more risks than benefits with their children's use of mobile technology, including addiction, neglect of other activities, cognitive absorption, decrease in physical activities, impairment of physical health and cognitive development, decrease in personal interaction, and impairment of social skills.[11] These rather concrete concerns are accompanied by further, vague parental concerns.[12]

Children's digital participation also concerns smart toys, enabling toy-child interaction, often with the use of "Artificial Intelligence" functions. Such toys can make enhanced learning experiences possible.[13] In doing so, they generally record information and transmit it offsite,[14] oftentimes creating cross-border data streams. Toymakers increasingly record more data,[15] leading to a 'datafication' of children.[16] In connection with internet-connected toys,[17] data hacking and other encroachments upon privacy and security have occurred,[18] most prominently with regard to Mattel's 'Hello Barbie'[19] and VTech[20] hacks.[21] Mattel's talking 'Hello Barbie' doll recorded human's speech when interacting and transmitted it to its partner ToyTalk, which then used it to improve its speech recognition

10 For the use of mobile technology, see Bergert et al.: Missing Out on Life, International Conference on Wirtschaftsinformatik.

11 Ibid.

12 Ibid.

13 Zaman/Castro/Miranda: Internet of Toys, Intercom: Revista Brasileira de Ciências da Comunicação, 41, 2018, pp. 216 f.

14 Peyton: A Litigator's Guide to the Internet of Things, Richmond Journal of Law and Technology, 22(3), 2016, p. 5.

15 See Maple: Security and privacy in the internet of things, Journal of Cyber Policy, 2(2), 2017, p. 174; Jones: Your New Best Frenemy, Engaging Science, Technology, and Society, 2, 2016, pp. 242–246; Peterson: Toymakers are tracking more data about kids—leaving them exposed to hackers.

16 Nash: The Rise of the Algorithmic Child, in this volume; Holloway/Green: The Internet of Toys, Communication Research and Practice, 2(4), 2016, pp. 506–519.

17 Ibid.

18 Cf. Singer: Uncovering security flaws in digital education products for schoolchildren.

19 Gibbs: Hackers can hijack Wi-Fi Hello Barbie to spy on your children.

20 Gilbert: VTech Takes Learning Lodge Website Offline After Hack; Finkle/Wagstaff: VTech hack exposes ID theft risk in connecting kids to Internet.

21 See Keymolen/Van der Hof: Can I still trust you, my dear doll? Journal of Cyber Policy, 4(2), 2019, pp. 143–159.

technology.[22] Parents could also listen to their children's conversations. In such a way, connected toys can be used as surveillance mechanisms by parents and third parties, with parental consent or by hacking.[23] Children are often unaware that their data is being processed, contrary to general principles of data protection law[24] and family law,[25] which generally foresee their involvement according to their abilities.[26] At present, it is hard to tell what ramifications this data collection will have for children. Both the potential and the risks associated with emerging digital spheres are only just beginning to be better understood and outlined.[27]

The magnitude of known risks as well as the uncertainty regarding further risks, both at present and in the future, has led to a risk-based narrative.[28] This is firstly true for coverage in popular media about children's participation in connected activities.[29] Furthermore, risks pertaining to children's use of online communication tools have also been found to be 'grossly overstated' in scholarly literature.[30] Children's need for protection is thus emphasized, while the benefits associated with them partaking in digital communication, sociality, and play tend to be undervalued.

Children's rights have been employed to balance that narrative and formulate their needs in an increasingly digitalized world from an educational and

---

[22] ToyTalk: Privacy Policy.

[23] Chaudron et al.: Kaleidoscope on the Internet of Toys.

[24] Turner: Connected Toys, p. 3.

[25] Cf. e.g. Sec. 1626 (2) of the German Civil Code (Bürgerliches Gesetzbuch, BGB): In caring for and raising the child, the parents shall take into account the child's growing ability and need to act independently and responsibly. They discuss issues of parental care with the child, as far as is appropriate according to the child's stage of development, and strive for agreement.

[26] Cf. Dethloff: Families and the Law: Taking Account of Children's Evolving Capacities, in this volume.

[27] See Arewa: Data Collection, Privacy, and Children in the Digital Economy, in this volume.

[28] See generally Palfrey et al.: Enhancing Child Safety and Online Technologies; Stone: Now Parents Can Hire a Hall Monitor for the Web; regarding networking platforms Autenrieth et al.: Gebrauch und Bedeutung von Social Network Sites im Alltag junger Menschen, in: Neumann-Braun (ed.): Freundschaft und Gemeinschaft im Social Web, p. 31.

[29] See ibid.; Leamy: On parenting: The danger of giving your child 'smart toys'; Venkataramakrishnan: Cyber risks take the fun out of connected toys; for the German media see e.g. Hönicke: Smartphone erst ab 14?.

[30] Holmes: Myths and Missed Opportunities, Information, Communication & Society, 12(8), 2009, pp. 1174, 1185.

socio-psychological perspective.[31] Social psychologist Sonia Livingstone in particular has promoted the idea of basing children's claims on their fundamental rights, namely those provided for in the United Nations Convention of the Rights of the Child (UNCRC).[32] This chapter aims to demonstrate the impact of a rights-based approach from a juridic point of view and with special regard to specificities of European Union (EU) legal architecture, principles, and multi-level norm-setting.

2 Children's Rights in the EU and Transnational Digital Spheres

Children's rights are enshrined in various instruments at multiple regulatory levels. Around the world—albeit not in the United States—children's rights are guaranteed by the UNCRC. The UNCRC has had a lasting effect on our understanding of children's rights and their individual agency,[33] and it has proven to be a "touchstone for children's rights throughout the world".[34] As an instrument of public international law, its incorporation into internal national legal systems varies according to the respective legal order. In 47 countries, it is complemented by the Council of Europe's European Convention of Human Rights. European

[31] Livingstone: Children's digital rights: a priority, Intermedia, 42(4/5), 2014, pp. 20–24; Kutscher/Bouillon: Kinder. Bilder. Rechte.; Kutscher: Positionings, Challenges, and Ambivalences in Children's and Parents' Perspectives in Digitalized Familial Contexts, in this volume.

[32] Livingstone: Reframing media effects, Journal of Children and Media, 10(1), 2016, pp. 4–12; Third/Livingstone/Lansdown: Recognizing children's rights in relation to digital technologies, in: Wagner/Kettemann/Vieth (eds.): Research Handbook on Human Rights and Digital Technology, 2019, pp. 376–410; Livingstone/Bulger: A global research agenda for children's rights in the digital age, Journal of Children and Media, 8(4), 2014, pp. 317–335.

[33] Cf. Dethloff/Maschwitz: Kinderrechte in Europa, FPR (Familie Partnerschaft Recht), 18(5), 2012, pp. 190–194; Dethloff: Families and the Law: Taking Account of Children's Evolving Capacities, in this volume; Khazova: How to ensure a wider implementation of the CRC, in: Marrus/Laufer-Ukeles (eds.): Global Reflections on Children's Rights and the Law, p. 4.

[34] Fortin: Children's Rights and the Developing Law, p. 49; Kilkelly/Lundy: Children's rights in action, Child and Family Law Quarterly, 18(3), 2006, p. 311.

children's rights law is largely based on the UNCRC.[35] Within the EU and the scope of application of EU law, the EU Charter of Fundamental Rights applies. Some national constitutions also provide for specific children's rights,[36] while others do not formulate fundamental rights for children specifically.[37]

When the Lisbon Treaty took effect in 2009, the European Community became the European Union, and the protection of children's rights was included in the general objectives in Art. 3 of the Treaty on European Union (TEU). The Charter of Fundamental Rights (hereafter EU Charter) was attributed the same legal status as the Treaties.[38] The EU Charter's influence on the Court of Justice of the European Union (CJEU), however, even predates its entry into force.[39] Once proclaimed by the EU Parliament, Council, and Commission in 2000,[40] the Advocate Generals already began relying upon the EU Charter.[41] Before the existence of an EU fundamental rights catalogue, the CJEU drew on the shared constitutional traditions of the Member States, determined by means of evaluative

[35] European Union Agency for Fundamental Rights and Council of Europe: Handbook on European law relating to the rights of the child, p. 26.

[36] Ireland (Art. 42A of the Irish Constitution), Serbia (Art. 65 of the Serbian Constitution), Poland (Art. 72 of the Polish Constitution), Belgium (Art. 22 of the Belgian Constitution), Italy (Art. 31 of the Italian Constitution).

[37] E.g. Germany, where a recent bill providing for the introduction of specific children's rights in the German Basic Law (Grundgesetz) did not pass, see Deutscher Bundestag: Entwurf eines Gesetzes zur Änderung des Grundgesetzes zur ausdrücklichen Verankerung der Kinderrechte, Bundestag Printed Matter (BT-Drucksache) 19/28138; Dethloff: Families and the Law: Taking Account of Children's Evolving Capacities, in this volume.

[38] The Treaty on European Union (TEU) and the Treaty on the Functioning of the European Union (TFEU).

[39] Kokott/Sobotta: The Charter of Fundamental Rights of the European Union after Lisbon, p. 94.

[40] OJ Official Journal of the European Union, C 364, December 18, 2000, p. 1–22.

[41] Cf. Opinion of AG Alber, February 1, 2001, Case C-340/99, TNT Traco, ECLI:EU:C:2001:74, para. 94; Opinion of AG Tizzano, February 8, 2001, Case C-173/99, BECTU, ECLI:EU:C:2001:81, para. 28; Opinion of AG Leger, July 10, 2001, Case C-353/99, Council v. Hautala, ECLI:EU:C:2001:392, para. 82, 83; Opinion of AG Mischo, September 20, 2001, Joined cases C-20/00 and C-64/00, Booker Aquaculture and Hydro Seafood, ECLI:EU:C:2001:469, para. 126; Opinion of AG Poiares Maduro, June 29, 2004, Case C-181/03, P Nardone, ECLI:EU:C:2004:397, para. 51; Opinion of AG Kokott, October 14, 2004, joined Cases C-387/02, C-391/02 and C-403/02 Berlusconi and Others, ECLI:EU:C:2004:624, para. 83.

comparative law,[42] as well as on international treaties common to the Member States, such as the European Convention on Human Rights (ECHR).[43] Hence, the EU Charter does not stand incoherently alongside the other instruments for the protection of children's rights.

The EU Charter holds not only great symbolic value[44] and consequence for the constitutional architecture of the Union, but also for the protection of children's rights.[45] Various rights of the EU Charter are of particular relevance for children, such as Art. 7, which safeguards private and family life as well as home and communications, the right to receive free education under Art. 14 and the prohibition of discrimination on grounds of age under Art. 21. General fundamental rights of the EU Charter extend to children as well.[46] Moreover, the changes brought about by the EU Charter gave visibility to children's rights.[47] Building on the UNCRC,[48] Art. 24 of the EU Charter specifically addresses and recognizes children's rights at the EU level. According to Art. 24 (1), children shall have the right to such protection and care as is necessary for their well-being (Sentence 1). They may express their views freely (Sentence 2), and these views shall be taken into consideration on matters which concern them in accordance with their age and maturity (Sentence 3). Art. 24 (2) mirrors Art. 3 of the UNCRC. According to these provisions, the child's best interests must be a primary consideration in all actions concerning children. This principle of the best interest of the child and the principle of child participation are related to the understanding of children as autonomous rights holders. The recognition of children as such rights holders

---

[42] Kokott/Sobotta: The Charter of Fundamental Rights of the European Union after Lisbon, p. 95 ("wertende Rechtsvergleichung").

[43] See CJEU, decision from November 22, 2005 (C-144/04), Mangold, ECLI:EU:C:2005:709, para. 74.

[44] Pernice: Treaty of Lisbon and Fundamental Rights, in: Griller/Ziller (eds.): The Lisbon Treaty, pp. 235 ff.

[45] Stalford: The CRC in Litigation Under EU Law, in: Liefaard/Doek (eds.): Litigating the Rights of the Child, pp. 211–230.

[46] Fundamental right to liberty recognized in Art. 6 of the Charter as possessed by 'everyone', and, consequently, also by a 'child', CJEU, decision from March 28, 2012 (C-92/12), PPU Health Service Executive, ECLI:EU:C:2013:548, para. 111.

[47] Stalford/Drywood: Using the CRC to Inform EU Law and Policy-Making, in: Invernizzi (ed.): The Human Rights of Children, p. 206.

[48] Kisunaite/Delicati: Towards a fully-fledged European Union child rights strategy, in: Marrus/Laufer-Ukeles (eds.): Global Reflections on Children's Rights and the Law, p. 17.

with individual agency is one of the key accomplishments of the UNCRC.[49] Its significance not only unfolds in analogue contexts,[50] but is also a fundament for the UNCRC's potential in digital contexts.[51]

As an international human rights instrument, the UNCRC is part of the general principles of EU law, thus binding the EU when setting, interpreting, and applying law.[52] The EU has pledged to implement children's rights in line with the UNCRC,[53] and the EU Commission has reaffirmed this commitment in key EU legal and policy documents.[54] Legal acts, such as the EU Citizenship Directive[55] or the General Data Protection Regulation (GDPR),[56] contain references to children's well-being and protection.[57] But the EU is still far away from realizing its potential as a children's rights actor.[58] While the EU may not have the competence to set legal norms in a number of areas, more and more aspects of children's lives are regulated at the supranational level, as online activities are transnational in nature. TikTok and Facebook, for example, are active in over 150 countries, with the short video application TikTok popular among young people in particular.[59] The protection of minors on video platforms is one of the areas the EU has

[49] Dethloff/Maschwitz: Kinderrechte in Europa, FPR (Familie Partnerschaft Recht), 18(5), 2012, pp. 190–194; Freeman: The Value and Values of Children's Rights, in: Invernizzi/Williams (eds.): The Human Rights of Children, p. 7.

[50] For its relevance in the digital context, see Graziani: Les enfants et internet, Journal du droit des jeunes, 7, 2012, pp. 36–45.

[51] Kaesling: Children's Digital Rights, in: Marrus/Laufer-Ukeles (eds.): Global Reflections on Children's Rights and the Law, pp. 185–186.

[52] Stalford/Drywood: Using the CRC to Inform EU Law and Policy-Making, in: Invernizzi (ed.): The Human Rights of Children, p. 200.

[53] Iusmen: How are Children's Rights (Mis)Interpreted in Practice? in: Rhodes (ed.): Narrative Policy Analysis, p. 100.

[54] Ibid. p. 97.

[55] Directive 2004/38/EU.

[56] Regulation (EU) 2016/679 of the European Parliament and of the Council of 27 April 2016 on the protection of natural persons with regard to the processing of personal data and on the free movement of such data (General Data Protection Regulation).

[57] See e.g. Recital 24 of the EU Citizenship Directive; Recital 38 of the General Data Protection Regulation.

[58] Kisunaite/Delicati: Towards a fully-fledged European Union child rights strategy, in: Marrus/Laufer-Ukeles (eds.): Global Reflections on Children's Rights and the Law, p. 17.

[59] Worldpopulationreview.com: Facebook Users by Country 2021; Statista: TikTok—Statistics & Facts.

regulated in its Audiovisual Media Services Directive (EU AVMSD).[60] So far, the EU's instruments have focused on children's rights to protection rather than on their rights to participation.[61] A rights-based approach in the EU can counteract one-sided, risk-based narratives of children's digital activities already at the norm-setting stage. Both reactive and proactive policies require careful evaluations of both their objectives and the strategies for their realization with regard to affected fundamental rights.[62]

3 Balancing Rights to Participation and Protection

Regarding the participation of children in online contexts, a number of fundamental rights are relevant,[63] including the right to education,[64] freedom of expression,[65] children's privacy,[66] and their right to play.[67] Children's rights are often

[60] Directive 2010/13/EU of the European Parliament and of the Council of 10 March 2010 on the coordination of certain provisions laid down by law, regulation or administrative action in Member States concerning the provision of audiovisual media services (Audiovisual Media Services Directive), Official Journal of the European Union, L 95/1, April 15, 2010; see specifically Art. 28b (1) (a) of the EU AVMSD; see also Specht-Riemenschneider/Marko/Wette: Protection of Minors on Video Sharing Platforms, in this volume.

[61] For GDPR and Children's autonomy, see European Council speaking out against the COM Proposal of data autonomy at 13 years old, The European Parliament and the Council of the European Union: Position (EU) No 6/2016 of the Council at first reading with a view to the adoption of a Regulation of the European Parliament and of the Council on the protection of natural persons with regard to the processing of personal data and on the free movement of such data, and repealing Directive 95/46/EC (General Data Protection Regulation).

[62] O'Neill/Staksrud/McLaughlin: Towards a better internet for children, p. 18.

[63] For the range of children's digital rights, see Kaesling: Children's Digital Rights, in: Marrus/Laufer-Ukeles (eds.): Global Reflections on Children's Rights and the Law, pp. 183 ff.

[64] See Art. 28 of the UNCRC, Art. 2 of the first additional protocol to the ECHR, Art. 14 (1) of the EU Charter.

[65] Art. 13 of the UNCRC, Art. 10 (1) of the ECHR, Art. 11 (1) of the EU Charter, Art. 5 of the German Basic Law.

[66] Art. 16 of the UNCRC, Art. 8 of the ECHR, Art. 7 of the EU Charter, Art. 2 (1) and Art. 1 (1) of the German Basic Law.

[67] Art. 31 of the UNCRC, Art. 2 (1), Art. 1 (1) of the German Basic Law; see Lester: Children's right to play, in: Ruck/Peterson-Badali/Freeman (eds.): Handbook of Children's Rights, pp. 312 ff.

divided into three categories: rights to provision, protection, and participation.[68] Children's protective and participative rights must be balanced. Following a rights-based approach means closely looking at regulatory measures as limitations of children's rights, which need to be justified. A risk-based narrative cannot cancel out children's claims. Even in light of danger to their safety, children have a right to privacy.[69]

The EU AVMSD, for example, contains measures "to protect minors from harmful content" (Recital 4) on video sharing platforms.[70] While the specific risks children encounter on such platforms are mentioned, there is no reference to specific benefits from their participation. Much like the accessibility of audiovisual content for elderly people and those with impairments was stated in Recital 22 to further their integration in the social and cultural life of the EU, the situation of children should have also been included. Participatory children's rights have, however, not found their way into the recited motives of the AVMSD, despite shaping the limits of such restrictions on children's participatory rights.

In addition to the freedom of expression (Art. 13 of the UNCRC), children's right to engage in play and recreational activities as well as to participate freely in cultural life and the arts (Art. 31 of the UNCRC) is limited. In the context of children's access to information and material from a diversity of national and international sources, Art. 17 of the UNCRC in lit. (e) also refers to the development of appropriate guidelines for the protection of the child from information and material injurious to their well-being, but not without mentioning that Art. 13 and 18 of the UNCRC must be borne in mind. A rights-based approach to children's activities online highlights the interplay between protection and participation. Children's freedom of expression, for example, may be limited by protective measures, which in turn even increase the benefits of children's online activities.

Given the risk-based narrative, which is susceptible to influence both norm-setting and judicial review, it is important to highlight these links and make the balancing of rights. As part of the judicial review, such balancing involves weighing each interest and considering all circumstances of the case in order to

---

[68] Critical Quennerstedt: Children, But Not Really Humans? The International Journal of Children's Rights, 18, 2010, pp. 619–635.

[69] See Shmueli/Blecher-Prigat: Privacy for Children, Columbia Human Rights Law Review, 42, 2011, pp. 4, 759, 762; Palfrey/Gasser: Born Digital, p. 61; Blecher-Prigat: Lost Between Data and Family? in this volume.

[70] See for measures under Art. 28b Abs. 3 of the AVMD and the German implementation, Dreyer/Bernzen, in: Erdemir (ed.): Das neue Jugendschutzgesetz, § 5 Rn. 96 f.

determine whether a fair balance was struck between interests in the particular case at hand.[71] The balancing of children's protective and participative rights is, of course, directly linked to the implementation of the principle of the best interests of the child.[72] From the point of view of legal psychology, the best interests of the child are ensured if the child's needs are in harmony with their living conditions and family situation,[73] so that age-appropriate personality development is possible.[74]

4 Implementing the Legal Principle of the Best Interest of the Child

The core principle of the best interests of the child (Art. 3 of the UNCRC, Art. 24 (2) of the EU Charter) shall ensure the full and effective enjoyment of all UNCRC rights.[75] It contains a fundamental interpretative legal principle, a substantive right, and a rule of procedure.[76] The principle of the best interests of the child influences the interpretation of legal norms: "If a legal provision is open to more than one interpretation, the interpretation which most effectively serves the child's best interests should be chosen."[77]

As holders of the substantive right, children have a right to have their best interests assessed and taken into account as a primary consideration.[78] This applies not only when determinations concerning an individual child are made,

[71] See CJEU, decision from June 12, 2003 (C-112/00), Schmidberger, ECLI:EU:C:2003:333, para 77, with regard to balancing a fundamental right and an economic freedom; with regard to the balance between the child's liberty under Art. 6 of the EU Charter as well as its needs for protection see CJEU, decision from March 28, 2012 (C-92/12), PPU Health Service Executive, ECLI:EU:C:2013:548, para. 111.

[72] Rosas: Balancing Fundamental Rights in EU Law, Cambridge Yearbook of European Legal Studies, Vol. 16, p. 351.

[73] Kemper, in: Schulze, Sec. 1666 mn. 2.

[74] Dettenborn: Kindeswohl und Kindeswille: psychologische und rechtliche Aspekte, p. 51.

[75] For Art. 3 of the UNCRC, see Committee on the Rights of the Child: General Comment No. 14 at IV. 25 p. 8.

[76] Ibid., I. 5 p. 4.

[77] Ibid., I. 6 p. 4.

[78] Ibid., I. 5 p. 3.

but also when decisions affect groups of children or children in general.[79] Procedurally, the principle of the best interests of the child includes the evaluation of the impact of these decisions on the children concerned.[80] In addition, the justification of a decision must show that the right has been explicitly taken into account by explaining "what has been considered to be in the child's best interests, based on which criteria and how the child's interests have been weighed against other considerations, be they broad issues of policy or individual cases".[81] In order to satisfy these requirements, trans-sectorial analyses can be necessary. In particular, regulatory measures from different legal areas, such as data protection, platform regulation, youth media protection, contract law, and family law, may have to be considered collectively in order to understand the impact of the legal situation on children. This may also include measures that do not target children specifically, but that might affect children differently than adults.

5 Proportionality and Coherence of Measures in the EU

The principle of proportionality plays an exceptional role in protecting children's rights, specifically in the EU. It not only limits restrictions on children's rights to the necessary amount, but also assures a certain coherence of measures in this multi-level system. The principle of proportionality does not only govern the balance of principles and rights, but also the balance of EU and Member State responsibilities and interests.[82]

With Art. 7 of the Treaty on the Functioning of the European Union (TFEU), a general, cross-cutting clause[83] at the beginning of the operative part outlining EU policies is dedicated solely to coherence, hereby stressing the importance of the principle of coherence in primary law.[84] According to that provision, the EU

[79] Ibid.

[80] Ibid., I 6 c p. 4.

[81] Ibid., I 6 p. 4.

[82] Sauter: Proportionality in EU Law, Cambridge Yearbook of European Legal Studies, Vol. 15, 2013, p. 466; cf. also Trstenjak/Beysen: Das Prinzip der Verhältnismäßigkeit in der Unionsrechtsordnung, Europarecht, 47, 2012, p. 265.

[83] Lippert: Das Kohärenzerfordernis des EuGH, Europarecht, 47, 2012, p. 90 (in German "*Querschnittsklausel*").

[84] Ibid.

shall ensure consistency between its policies and activities, taking all of its objectives into account and abiding to the principle of conferral of powers. The legal principle of coherence even extends beyond Art. 7 of the TFEU.[85] It is a general principle of lawmaking,[86] applicable to all EU law.[87] Additionally, coherence is an expression of the principle of proportionality.[88] While coherence as part of the proportionality test is not the coherence requirement of Art. 7 of the TFEU, it is based on the same theoretical background.[89]

The proportionality test is applied in different contexts and thus takes on meaning beyond the compatibility of national measures in purely national contexts. Much like the proportionality test in purely national contexts, the legality of EU restrictions on children's rights is reviewed with regard to the principle of proportionality in Sect. 5.1, while aspects of proportionality and multi-level coherence in the EU will be discussed in Sect. 5.2.

5.1 Justification of EU Limitations to Children's Rights

At EU level, the principle of proportionality is enshrined in Art. 52 (1) 2nd st. of the EU Charter and corresponds to a general principle of EU law.[90] Under Art. 52 (1), any limitation on the exercise of the rights and freedoms recognized by this Charter must be provided for by law and respect the essence of those rights and freedoms. Subject to the principle of proportionality, limitations are only legal if they are necessary and genuinely meet objectives of general interest acknowledged by the EU or the need to protect the rights and freedoms of others.

---

[85] See CJEU, decision from April 26, 2012 (RX-II C-334/12), Arango Jaramillo and Others v EIB, ECLI:EU:C:2013:134, para. 50.

[86] In German: *Rechtsgestaltungsprinzip*.

[87] Blanke, in: Calliess/Ruffert (eds.): EUV/EGV, Art. 3 EUV mn. 6; Schorkopf, in: Grabitz/Hilf/Nettesheim (eds.): EUV/AEUV, Art. 7 AEUV mn. 1 ff.

[88] On the argumentive figure "in a consistent and systematic manner" as a part of the European fundamental freedoms, Schorkopf: Wahrhaftigkeit im Recht der Grundfreiheiten, DÖV (Die öffentliche Verwaltung), 2010, p.260; CJEU, decision from September 8, 2010 (C-46/08), Carmen Media, ECLI:EU:C:2010:505, para 55, 64 f.; CJEU, decision from March 3, 2011 (C-161/09), Kakavetsos, ECLI:EU:C:2011:110, para 42, 47 ff.

[89] Schorkopf, in: Grabitz/Hilf/Nettesheim (eds.): EUV/AEUV, Art. 7 AEUV mn. 12.

[90] Jarass, in: Jarass (ed.): EU-Grundrechte-Charta, Art. 52 GRCh mn. 23, 34, 39 f.

The CJEU has long held—even before the Treaty of Lisbon[91]—that restrictions may be imposed on the exercise of fundamental rights, but only if they correspond to objectives of general interest and do not constitute a disproportionate and intolerable interference in relation to the aim pursued.[92] The proportionality test generally[93] includes an evaluation of objectives, suitability, and necessity.[94]

In that context, a focus on children's rights sheds light on specific consequences for children. Regulations for the Digital Single Market, such as the Directive on copyright and related rights in the Digital Single Market (DSM Directive),[95] are not aimed at children particularly. Children's experience online, especially on online platforms, differ from those of adults. They encounter certain particular risks, such as grooming, and rely to a greater extent on online communication to maintain social connections. The reach of filtering and monitoring obligations of these platforms, such as those following from the DSM Directive, the E-Commerce Directive,[96] and the planned Digital Services Act,[97] therefore

---

[91] For EEC law, see Tridimas: Principle of Proportionality, in: Schütze/Tridimas (eds.): Oxford Principles of European Union Law.

[92] CJEU, decision from September 9, 2004 (C-184/02), Spain/Parliament, ECLI:EU:C:2004:497, para. 52; CJEU, decision from December 6, 2005 (C-453/03), Fratelli, ECLI:EU:C:2005:741, para. 87; CJEU, decision from June 15, 2006 (C-28/05), Dokter, ECLI:EU:C:2006:408, para. 75; CJEU, decision from September 9, 2008 (C-120/06), Montecchio, ECLI:EU:C:2008:476, para. 183.

[93] Though not always consistently applied, see Sauter: Proportionality in EU Law, Cambridge Yearbook of European Legal Studies, Vol. 15, 2013, p. 466.

[94] Harbo: The Function of the Proportionality Principle in EU Law, European Law Journal, 16(2), 2010, p. 164; as, for example: CJEU, decision from May 13, 1986 (C-170/84), Bilka, ECLI:EU:C:1986:204, para. 36 ("appropriate with a view to achieving the objectives pursued and are necessary to that end"); CJEU, decision from March 11, 1987 (C-279/84), Rau and others, ECLI:EU:C:1987:119, para. 34; CJEU, decision from February 15, 2016 (C-601/15), J. N., ECLI:EU:C:2016:84, para. 54; CJEU, decision from September 14, 2017 (C-18/16), K. v Staatssecretaris van Veiligheid en Justitie, ECLI:EU:C:2017:680, para. 37; CJEU, decision from January 25, 2018 (C-473/16), Bevándorlási, para. 56.

[95] Directive (EU) 2019/790 of the European Parliament and of the Council of 17 April 2019 on copyright and related rights in the Digital Single Market and amending Directives 96/9/EC and 2001/29/EC (Text with EEA relevance).

[96] Directive 2000/31/EC of the European Parliament and of the Council of 8 June 2000 on certain legal aspects of information society services, in particular electronic commerce, in the Internal Market ('Directive on electronic commerce').

[97] See European Commission: Proposal for a Regulation on a Single Market for Digital Services (Digital Services Act) and amending Directive 2000/31/EC.

needs to be evaluated with regard to children's distinct situation online. In cases where children are concerned, the balancing of rights with a view to monitoring obligations on platforms might have a different outcome than in situations involving only adult users and platform operators.[98]

The special effect on children can also stem from an interplay with other legal instruments aimed at children specifically. For video sharing platforms, for example, the EU lawmaker has introduced specific protective measures for children with the AVMSD.[99] With regard to EU legislation, the coherence requirement in Art. 7 of the TFEU applies directly. First of all, the EU itself is obliged to maintain stringency and systemic justice in its measures.[100] Beyond that, it is the interplay between national and EU measures that characterizes the protection of children's rights in the EU. Such protection in the context of audiovisual media, for example, is complemented by German national provisions in the Interstate Treaty on the Protection of Minors in the Media,[101] the Protection of Minors Act,[102] and the Network Enforcement Act.[103]

[98] Thanks to Louisa Specht-Riemenschneider, who introduced that idea at our conference "Families and New Media" in February 2020 with regard to general monitoring obligations in the E-Commerce-Directive and possible exceptions.

[99] Directive (EU) 2018/1808 of the European Parliament and of the Council of 14 November 2018 amending Directive 2010/13/EU on the coordination of certain provisions laid down by law, regulation or administrative action in member states concerning the provision of audiovisual media services (Audiovisual Media Services Directive) regarding changing market conditions; see Specht Riemenschneider/Marko/Wette: Protection of Minors on Video Sharing Platforms, in this volume.

[100] Ruffert, in: Calliess/Ruffert (eds.): EUV/EGV, Art. 7 AEUV mn. 4; Schröder, in: Pechstein/Nowak/Häde (eds.): Frankfurter Kommentar zu EUV/GRC/AEUV, Art. 7 AEUV mn. 5.

[101] Jugendmedienschutz-Staatsvertrag (JMStV), Interstate Treaty on the Modernized Media Regulation (Staatsvertrag zur Modernisierung der Medienordnung in Deutschland; MoModStV) dated April 14, 2020, enacted November 7, 2020.

[102] Jugendschutzgesetz (JuSchG), Second Law amending the Protection of Minors Act (Zweites Gesetz zur Änderung des Jugendschutzgesetzes); adopted March 26, 2021; announced April 9, 2021; entered into force May 1, 2021.

[103] Netzwerkdurchsetzungsgesetz (NetzDG).

5.2 Limits to Member State Limitations to Children's Rights

In addition to the supranational level of EU law, legal norms are set at the level of the Member States. Further regulatory levels existing in Member States, such as the German states *(Länder),* are only relevant within each Member State.[104] Member States may not rely on provisions, practices, or situations of its internal legal order in order to justify non-compliance with its obligations under EU law.[105] A coherence of measures must be ensured at the Member State level, i.e. in Germany at the federal level.[106]

Competences not conferred on the EU by the Treaties remain with EU countries (Art. 4 and 5 of the TEU). The use of these competences is governed by the principles of subsidiarity and proportionality, designed to limit the powers of the EU vis-à-vis Member States.[107] The negative presumption of competence in favor of the Member States has now been explicitly laid down in Art. 4 (1) and Art. 5 (2) 2nd st. of the TEU.[108] Residual competences remain with the Member States. Member States must, however, also respect EU law even when they exercise powers falling within their exclusive competences.[109] In that context, coherence serves as a constraint on the national legislator's room for maneuver.[110]

---

[104] CJEU, decision from September 8, 2010 (C-46/08), Carmen Media, ECLI:EU:C:2010:505, para. 69–70.

[105] Ibid. para. 69; CJEU, decision from September 13, 2001 (C-417/99), Commission v Spain, ECLI:EU:C:2001:445, para. 37.

[106] CJEU, decision from September 8, 2010 (C-46/08), Carmen Media, ECLI:EU:C:2010:505, para. 70.

[107] Konstadinides: The Competences of the Union, in: Schütze/Tridimas (eds.): Oxford Principles of European Union Law.

[108] Previously be derived from Art. 5 (1) of the EC Treaty.

[109] CJEU, decision from June 16, 2011 (C-10/10), Commission v. Austria, ECLI:EU:C:2011:399, para. 23 ff.; CJEU, decision from October 28, 2010 (C-72/09), Établissements Rimbaud, ECLI:EU:C:2010:645, para. 23 ff.; CJEU, decision from July 1, 2010 (C-233/09), Dijkman and Dijkman-Lavaleije, ECLI:EU:C:2010:397, para. 20 ff.; CJEU, decision from September 17, 2009 (C-182/08), Glaxo Wellcome, para. 34 ff.; Regarding the competence of the Member States in the field of education, CJEU, decision from September 11, 2007, Schwarz and Gootjes-Schwarz, ECLI:EU:C:2007:492, para. 70; Regarding the competence of the Member States of their social security systems, CJEU, decision from May 16, 2006 (C-372/04), Watts, ECLI:EU:C:2006:325, para. 92.

[110] See CJEU, decision from July 21, 2011 (C-159/10), Fuchs and Köhler, ECLI:EU:C:2011:508, para. 84 ff. (civil service law); CJEU, decision from January

In *Zenatti,* the CJEU already invoked the idea of coherence when directing the national court to verify whether "the national legislation is genuinely directed to realising the objectives which are capable of justifying it and whether the restrictions which it imposes do not appear disproportionate in the light of those objectives".[111] Relying on *Zenatti,* the Court went on to specify in *Gambelli* that national restrictions in the general interest must also be suitable for achieving those objectives, inasmuch as they must serve to reach the objectives "in a consistent and systematic manner".[112] If this requirement is not fulfilled, the CJEU finds the concerned Member State's restrictions are not suitable.[113] Coherence is thus used as a criterion for proportionality, to be assessed as part of the first of the three steps, which examines the suitability of the measure.[114] Some authors, however, do not see coherence as part of proportionality, but as a separate barrier that imposes additional requirements on a regulation of the Member States.[115] National measures must first be tested for individual proportionality and subsequently for coherence with other measures. Notwithstanding the classification,

---

12, 2010 (C-341/08), Domnica Petersen v. Appointment Committee for Dentists for the District of Westphalia-Lippe, ECLI:EU:C:2010:4, para. 53 ff. (maximum age limit for contract dentists); CJEU, decision from December 16, 2010 (C-137/09), Josemans, ECLI:EU:C:2010:774, para. 69 ff. (access to coffee shops).

[111] CJEU, decision from October 21, 1999 (C-67/98), Zenatti, ECLI:EU:C:1999:514, para. 37.

[112] CJEU, decision from November 6, 2003 (C-243/01), Gambelli, ECLI:EU:C:2003:597, para. 67 ("in a consistent and systematic manner").

[113] See CJEU, decision from September 8, 2010 (C-46/08), Carmen Media, ECLI:EU:C:2010:505, para. 110; CJEU, decision from July 21, 2011 (C-159/10), Fuchs and Köhler, ECLI:EU:C:2011:508, para. 85; CJEU, decision from October 20, 2011 (C-123/10), Brachner, ECLI:EU:C:2011:675, para. 71; CJEU, decision from July 5, 2017 (C-190/16), Fries, ECLI:EU:C:2017:513, para. 48; CJEU, decision from September 8, 2010 (C-316/07), Markus Stoß and Others, ECLI:EU:C:2010:504, para. 107; CJEU, decision from March 6, 2007 (C-338/04), Placanica, ECLI:EU:C:2007:133, para 49; Jarass, in: Jarass (ed.): EU-Grundrechte-Charta, Art. 52 GRCh mn.38; Trstenjak/Beysen: Das Prinzip der Verhältnismäßigkeit in der Unionsrechtsordnung, Europarecht, 47, 2012, p. 265.

[114] Frenz: Kohärente und systematische nationale Normgebung, Europarecht, 47(3), 2012, p. 349; Kämmerer: Interprofessionelle Zusammenarbeit und europarechtliche Kohärenz, Deutsches Steuerrecht, 53 (Appendix 13), 2015, p. 36; Kirschner: Grundfreiheiten und nationale Gestaltungsspielräume, pp. 179 ff.

[115] Lippert: Das Kohärenzerfordernis des EuGHs, Europarecht, 47, 2012, p. 90; Schuster: Das Kohärenzprinzip in der Europäischen Union, p. 104.

the coherence test entails a comprehensive evaluation of the legislator's overall concept, including all measures in the relevant regulatory area.[116] Derogations do not necessarily impair coherence.[117] Several measures must, however, be coordinated and consistent with one another.[118] For example, various national regulations relating to gambling, player protection, prevention of addiction, and prevention of crime were considered together.[119]

The development of the criterion of consistency is intertwined with CJEU jurisprudence on the justification of the encroachment on the freedom to provide services by the ban on organizing and brokering games of chance.[120] This strand of case law is also related to the concurrence of national competences for regulation and cross-border elements due to the use of the internet. In *Carmen Media,* a company based in Gibraltar took action against the rejection of its application by the State of Schleswig–Holstein to be allowed to offer sports betting online.[121] Member States enjoy discretion in setting the objectives of their policy.[122] It is also not necessary, with a view to the criterion of proportionality, that "a restrictive measure decreed by the authorities of one Member State should correspond to a view shared by all the Member States concerning the means of protecting the legitimate interest at issue".[123]

Member State discretion extends to the level of protection sought.[124] Particularly in areas where cultural or moral values are rooted in national traditions, Member States are largely free to determine the level of protection they wish

---

[116] Schuster: Das Kohärenzprinzip in der Europäischen Union, p. 104.

[117] CJEU, decision from July 21, 2011 (C-159/10), Fuchs and Köhler, ECLI:EU:C:2011:508, para. 87 ff.

[118] Jarass, in: Jarass (ed.): EU-Grundrechte-Charta, Art. 52 GRCh mn. 38.

[119] Lippert: Das Kohärenzerfordernis des EuGH, Europarecht, 47, 2012, p. 99.

[120] CJEU, decision from November 6, 2003 (C-243/01), Gambelli, ECLI:EU:C:2003:597, para. 67; CJEU, decision from September 8, 2010 (C-46/08), Carmen Media, ECLI:EU:C:2010:505, para. 64 ff.; CJEU, decision from September 8, 2010 (C-316/07), Markus Stoß and Others, ECLI:EU:C:2010:504, para. 107; CJEU, decision from March 6, 2007 (C-338/04), Placanica and Others, ECLI:EU:C:2007:133, para. 52 and 53.

[121] CJEU, decision from September 8, 2010 (C-46/08), Carmen Media, ECLI:EU:C:2010:505.

[122] Ibid., para. 104.

[123] Ibid.; citing by analogy, CJEU, decision from September 9, 2008 (C-518/06), Commission v. Italy, ECLI:EU:C:2008:477, para. 83 and 84.

[124] CJEU, decision from September 8, 2009 (C-42/07), Liga Portuguesa de Futebol Profissional and Bwin International, ECLI:EU:C:2009:519, para. 58.

to provide.[125] This applies beyond gambling, health policy,[126] and prohibitions under criminal law.[127] Especially with regard to family law and a harmonization or unification in Europe, the rootedness of the law in the national cultural context is emphasized.[128] With family law, general contract law, and tort law in Member State hands, the level of protection and autonomy of minors is largely determined by Member States.

It is essential for the application of the coherence requirement that all relevant measures across legal areas are identified. The principle of coherence applies only insofar as an interrelation or (systemic[129]) connection between regulated subject matters exists.[130] The rights-based approach to children's participation online facilitates the application of the principle of coherence, as it can help identify all legal areas relevant for children's participation. Regarding multiple aspects of children's activities online, Member State competences are touched upon. Joining a social network and posting user-generated content, for example, might trigger the application of general contract law including the child's (limited) legal capacity to contract, tort law, and penal law, including special provisions from copyright law.

With the level of protection being determined by Member States, national limits on children's autonomy do not only vary in accordance with the subject matter and associated risks, but also from Member State to Member State. While it is the national lawmakers' prerogative to assess the risks and determine minimum age requirements for children accordingly, they must still be consistent with one another. With regard to the focus on risks in online environments rather than on the potential of children's participation online, this coherence can be assured by contrasting state limitations on children's participation in analogue and digital

---

[125] Frenz: Kohärente und systematische nationale Normgebung, Europarecht, 47(3), 2012, p. 346.

[126] For example, CJEU, decision from March 10, 2009 (C-169/07), Hartlauer, ECLI:EU:C:2009:141, para. 55; CJEU, decision from July 17, 2008 (C-500/06), Corporación Dermoestética, ECLI:EU:C:2008:421, para. 39 f.

[127] CJEU, decision from December 16, 2010 (C-137/09), Josemans, ECLI:EU:C:2010:774, para. 70.

[128] De Oliveira: Um direito da família europeu? Revista de Legislação e de Jurisprudência, ano133, n.º 3913 e 3914, set. 2000, pp. 105–110; but see Antokolskaia: Family law and national culture, Utrecht Law Review, 4(2), 2008, pp. 25 ff.

[129] Kämmerer: Interprofessionelle Zusammenarbeit und europarechtliche Kohärenz, Deutsches Steuerrecht, 53 (Appendix 13), 2015, p. 33.

[130] Dieterich: Systemgerechtigkeit und Kohärenz, pp. 98 ff.

sectors. For example, the capacity to contract is determined irrespectively of the (technological) means used. Even though situations encountered by children are arguably comparable among Member States, the growing recognition of children's autonomy with increasing development and age differs from Member State to Member State.

The preconditions for contractual capacity of children, for instance, are subject to diverse national regulations.[131] The majority of Member States foresee age-based gradations of children's contractual autonomy.[132] In German law, for example, minors below the age of seven are legally incompetent.[133] Between the ages of seven and 18, the persons have limited legal capacity,[134] meaning that their acts are only legally effective if they are purely legally advantageous or if the holder of parental responsibility consents.[135] Similar to the German law, advantages for the child often lead to an earlier autonomy.[136] Minors with a commercial enterprise or professional activity are accorded more autonomy within related fields.[137] Routine daily transactions are also privileged in many legal orders,[138]

---

[131] See Dethloff: Families and the Law: Taking Account of Children's Evolving Capacities, in this volume.

[132] Lithuania: Art. 2.7 and Art. 2.8 of the Civil Code Lithuania; Bulgaria: Art. 4 of the Bulgarian Persons and Family Act; see Mladenova, in: Rieck/Lettmaier (eds.): Ausländisches Familienrecht, Bulgarien, mn. 2; for an overview on age of majority, limited or partial legal capacity, see Mankowski, in: Staudinger: Kommentar zum Bürgerlichen Gesetzbuch, Annex to Art. 7 EGBGB.

[133] Due to Sec. 104 of the German Civil Code.

[134] Sec. 2, Sec.106 of the German Civil Code.

[135] Sec. 107, Sec. 108 (1), (3) of the German Civil Code.

[136] See for Greece Art. 129, 133 ff. of the Greek Civil Code; for Malta: Smehyl, in: Rieck/Lettmaier (eds.): Ausländisches Familienrecht, Malta, mn. 2 with further references; for Ireland: Blaser, in: Rieck/Lettmaier (eds.): Ausländisches Familienrecht, Irland, mn. 2; see for Switzerland: Art. 19 1st, 2nd st. of the Swiss Civil Law Code (ZGB; Zivilgesetzbuch) for gratuitous advantageous transactions; Italy: Enßlin, in: Rieck/Lettmaier (eds.): Ausländisches Familienrecht, Italien, mn. 2 for advantageous transactions corresponding to the to the age-appropriate development and will; Estonia: Sec. 11 and Sec. 12 of the Civil Code Estonia.

[137] Malta: Art. 156 of the Civil Code Malta for professional activities; Croatia: Art. 85 of the Croatian Family Act; as well as explanations from Majstorović/Hoško, in: Bergmann/Ferid: Internationales Ehe- und Kindschaftsrecht, Kroatien, III. A. 5.; Germany: Sec. 112, 113 of the German Civil Code (full legal capacity in related fields).

[138] For Belgium see Heitmüller, in: Rieck/Lettmaier (eds.): Ausländisches Familienrecht, Belgien mn. 2 (recognition of autonomy regarding routine daily transactions by customary

as are transactions of minors using their own (pocket) money.[139] The cognitive faculty of children is largely drawn from their age. In a number of circumstances, however, the development of the individual child in question is decisive.[140] The legal effectivity of acts then presupposes the individual maturity of the acting child.[141] Declarations made by persons lacking capacity are null and void under the legal orders of other Member States,[142] unless the legal representative consents.[143] However, the protection of minors can also be realized by giving rights to rescind[144] or withdraw from[145] the contract and to have the contract declared invalid by court order.[146]

While both prerequisites for contractual capacity and legal consequences of its limitation or lack of it vary, common points could already be identified in this

---

law); Finland Sec. 24 of the Guardianship Act; Art. 14 § 2 of the Polish Civil Code; Art. 1263 No. 1 of the Civil Code Spain, (Código Civil, CC).

[139] Estonia Sec. 11 of the General Part of the Estonian Civil Code; Germany Sec. 110 of the German Civil Code; Denmark: Autonomy regarding income from professional activity under Sec. 42 of the Guardianship Act.

[140] For the rescission of the contract in Portugal e.g., see Art. 123, 127 of the Civil Code Portugal (Código Civil; CC).

[141] Sec. 31, 33, 34 of the Civil Code Czech Republic; Italy: Enßlin, in: Rieck/Lettmaier (eds.): Ausländisches Familienrecht, Italien, mn. 2; Sec. 11 of the Estonian Civil Code; for Slovakia see Sec. 9 of the Civil Code Slovakia.

[142] Art. 3 of the Bulgarian Persons and Family Act; Denmark Sec. 1 (2) of the Guardianship Act; Art. 130 of the Greek Civil Code; Art. 1.84 of the Lithuanian Civil Code; Sec. 170 (1) of the Civil Code Austria (Allgemeines bürgerliches Gesetzbuch; ABGB); Art. 14 of the Polish Civil Code (recognition of autonomy regarding routine daily transactions in Art. 14 § 2 of the Polish Civil Code); Art. 123 of the Civil Code Portugal; Chapter 9 s. 1 of the Children and Parents Code of Sweden; Art. 1263 No. 1 of the Civil Code Spain; Sec. 2, 9 of the Hungarian Civil Code.

[143] Art. 4 (2) of the Bulgarian Persons and Family Act; Art. 197 of the Civil Code Latvia (otherwise no liability); Art. 17 of the Polish Civil Code; Art. 41 (2) of the Romanian Civil Code; Sec. 2:12 of the Civil Code Hungary.

[144] Denmark Sec. 44 of the Guardianship Act; Chapter 9 s. 6 of the Children and Parents Code of Sweden; Art. 125, 123, 127 of the Civil Code Portugal.

[145] Sec. 11 (6) of the Estonian Civil Code.

[146] Art. 192 of the Civil Code Malta; see also Art. 1.88 (1) of the Civil Code Lithuania; Art. 46 (2) of the Romanian Civil Code.

short comparative overview,[147] begging the question whether national legal cultures would really prohibit European harmonization.

6 Interplay of EU and National Legal Norms

Due to the increasing importance of the Digital Single Market,[148] more and more subject matters also fall under the competence of the EU. The relationship between EU and Member States is based on the principle of loyalty (Art. 4 (3) of the TEU), which applies to all areas of EU activity. The EU thus generally offers limited answers to more general questions, i.e. sectorial approaches, that are then complemented by national legal norms.[149] Specific effects on children can result from the interaction of norms from different areas or from norms of different levels.

6.1 Interplay of EU and National Law in the Same Legal Area: The Example of Art. 8 (1) of the GDPR

A prime example for the interplay of EU and national law in the same legal area is the protection of children's data. The EU's GDPR contains a number of specific provisions on the protection of children's data. Art. 8 of the GDPR provides the conditions applicable to a child's consent in relation to the offer of information society services directly to a child. At least from the age of 16, minors are able to give their own effective consent to the processing of their data in accordance

---

147 See also Dethloff: Families and the Law: Taking Account of Children's Evolving Capacities, in this volume.

148 Cf. the legislative agenda including proposals for both the Digital Markets Act (COM/2020/842 final) and for the Digital Services Act (COM/2020/825 final), the proposal for a revised directive on the Security of Network and Information Systems (COM/2020/823 final), Proposal for an ePrivacy Regulation (COM/2017/010 final.
- 2017/03 (COD)) and Presidency Compromise Proposal 12,336/18; European Commission's "Digital Compass" strategy (COM(2021) 118 final).

149 Ackermann: Sektorielles EU-Recht und allgemeine Privatrechtssystematik, ZEuP (Zeitschrift für Europäisches Privatrecht), 26(4), 2018, p. 767.

with Art. 8 of the GDPR.[150] Art. 8 of the GDPR thus standardizes specific requirements for consent pursuant to Art. 6 (1) (a) of the GDPR for personal data of minors.[151] Lowering the age of consent to not less than 13 years of age is possible by national regulation.[152] If the minor has not yet reached the relevant age limit, consent may be given either directly by the parents or guardian or, with their consent, by the minor themself.[153]

The provision of Art. 8 of the GDPR is complemented by Art. 12 of the GDPR, according to which particularly clear and simple language must be used in cases where information is addressed to children.[154] The use of such child-friendly language reflects the GDPR's recognition of the heightened need for protection of children.[155] Art. 17 (1) (f) of the GDPR also provides for a separate right to delete data that was collected on the basis of Art. 8 of the GDPR,[156] even if the processing of the data was lawful.[157] It allows protected persons to request the deletion of content they have disclosed on the basis of consent under Art. 8 of the GDPR, even once they have reached adulthood. Data protection authorities

---

[150] Kampert, in: Sydow (ed.): Europäische Datenschutzgrundverordnung, Art. 8 DSGVO mn. 1; Roßnagel: Der Datenschutz von Kindern in der DS-GVO, ZD (Zeitschrift für Datenschutz), 10, 2020, p. 89.

[151] Schulz, in: Gola (ed.): Datenschutzgrundverordnung, Art. 8 mn. 1; Spindler/Dalby, in: Spindler/Schuster (eds.): Recht der elektronischen Medien, Art. 8 DSGVO mn. 3; Tinnefeld/Conrad: Die selbstbestimmte Einwilligung im europäischen Recht, ZD (Zeitschrift für Datenschutz), 9, 2018, p. 393.

[152] Kampert, in: Sydow (ed.): Europäische Datenschutzgrundverordnung, Art. 8 DSGVO mn. 1; Spindler/Dalby, in: Spindler/Schuster (eds.): Recht der elektronischen Medien, Art. 8 DSGVO mn. 3.

[153] Spindler/Dalby, in: Spindler/Schuster (eds.): Recht der elektronischen Medien, Art. 8 DSGVO mn. 3; Peuker, in: Sydow (ed.): Europäische Datenschutzgrundverordnung, Art. 17 DSGVO mn. 28; Heckmann/Paschke, in: Ehmann/Selmayr (eds.): Datenschutz-Grundverordnung, Art. 8 DSGVO mn. 26; Taeger, in: Taeger/Gabel (eds.): DS-GVO/BDSG, Art. 8 DSGVO mn. 24; Gola/Schulz: DS-GVO—Neue Vorgaben für den Datenschutz bei Kindern? ZD (Zeitschrift für Datenschutz), 3, 2013, p. 478.

[154] Franck, in: Gola (ed.): Datenschutzgrundverordnung, Art. 12 DSGVO mn. 17; Roßnagel: Der Datenschutz von Kindern in der DS-GVO, ZD (Zeitschrift für Datenschutz), 10, 2020, p. 89.

[155] Greve, in: Sydow (ed.): Europäische Datenschutzgrundverordnung, Art. 12 DSGVO mn. 17.

[156] Peuker, in: Sydow (ed.): Europäische Datenschutzgrundverordnung, Art. 17 DSGVO mn. 28.

[157] Ibid., mn. 29.

have a duty to inform and educate under Art. 57 (1) (b) of the GDPR,[158] which particularly benefits children's informed consent under Art. 8 of the GDPR.[159]

Although the GDPR as Regulation is directly applicable in all Member States, Member States still have room to maneuver when it comes to the definition of data minors. This is remarkable, as the GDPR aims to level out differences in the degree of protection of the rights and freedoms of natural persons in connection with the processing of personal data in Member States according to its Recital 9. While the purpose of the GDPR's predecessor, the Data Protection Directive, was to achieve comprehensive harmonization,[160] the GDPR was also intended to reduce obstacles to the free movement of data in the internal market through a unification of law (cf. Art. 1 of the GDPR). Due to the introduction of the opening clause in Art. 8 (1) 3rd st. of the GDPR, only a partial harmonization of children's autonomy has been achieved. The harmonization effect relates on the one hand to the autonomy of 16 to 18-year-olds under data protection law and on the other to the protection of children up to the age of 12. For minors between the ages of 13 and 16, harmonization has also been achieved, but merely to the extent that the child's ability to consent is only to be considered on a blanket basis, namely by setting a rigid age limit. The opening clause does not allow for the possibility of reverting to a flexible model of age assessment based on capacity of insight. Member States have made use of this opening clause, leading to a diversity of national regulations on the child's consent in the scope of application of Art. 8 of the GDPR.[161] It is private international law that designates the applicable legal order.[162]

[158] Nguyen, in: Gola (ed.): Datenschutz-Grundverordnung, Art. 57 DSGVO mn. 12; Ziebarth, in: Sydow (ed.): Europäische Datenschutzgrundverordnung, Art. 57 DSGVO mn. 16.

[159] Cf. Ziebarth, in: Sydow (ed.): Europäische Datenschutzgrundverordnung, Art. 57 DSGVO mn. 20.

[160] CJEU, decision from November 6, 2003 (C-101/01), Lindqvist, ECLI:EU:C:2003:596, mn. 95 ff.

[161] Dethloff/Kaesling: Datenmündigkeit Minderjähriger in Europa, in: Fischer et al. (eds.): Gestaltung der Informationsordnung, München 2022, p. 537, p. 541.

[162] Wolff, in: Schantz/Wolff (eds.): Das neue Datenschutzrecht, Grundprinzipien, mn. 482; Heckmann/Paschke, in: Ehmann/Selmayr (eds.): Datenschutz-Grundverordnung, Art. 8 DSGVO mn. 4; Persano: GDPR and children rights in the EU Data Protection Law, European Journal of Privacy Law & Technologies, Special issue, 2020, p. 32, p. 34, pp. 37 f.; Talley: Major Flaws in Minor Laws, Indina Int'l & Comp. Law Review, 30(1), 2019, p. 153.

Furthermore, Art. 8 of the GDPR has a rather limited scope of application. It only covers data processing in connection with information society services.[163] In order to define the term 'information society', Art. 4 No. 25 of the GDPR refers to the definition in Art. 1 No. 1 (b) of the Directive 2015/1535.[164] Services provided via the internet are included.[165] It is necessary that the offer is made directly to the child, e.g. by a child-friendly design.[166] For reasons of expediency, so-called dual-use offers should be included, as well as offers to the general public.[167] It is also a prerequisite that consent is involved as an element of justification for the collection of data.[168]

Even within the scope of application of Art. 8 of the GDPR, national laws come into play regarding the question of the persons giving or authorizing consent. Art. 8 of the GDPR refers to the holder of parental responsibility. The law on parental responsibility remains part of Member States' competences.[169] Beyond the scope of application, national law generally determines the conditions

[163] Kampert, in: Sydow (ed.): Europäische Datenschutzgrundverordnung, Art. 8 DSGVO mn. 8.

[164] Spindler/Dalby, in: Spindler/Schuster (eds.): Recht der elektronischen Medien, Art. 8 DSGVO mn. 4; Heckmann/Paschke, in: Ehmann/Selmayr (eds.): Datenschutz-Grundverordnung, Art. 8 DSGVO mn. 17; Wolff, in: Schantz/Wolff (eds.): Das neue Datenschutzrecht, mn. 479; Peuker, in: Sydow (ed.): Europäische Datenschutzgrundverordnung, Art. 17 DSGVO mn. 28; Gola/Schulz: DS-GVO—Neue Vorgaben für den Datenschutz bei Kindern? ZD (Zeitschrift für Datenschutz), 3, 2013, p. 475, p. 477.

[165] Spindler/Dalby, in: Spindler/Schuster (eds.): Recht der elektronischen Medien, Art. 8 DSGVO mn. 4.

[166] Ibid. mn.6; Wolff, in: Schantz/Wolff (eds.): Das neue Datenschutzrecht, mn. 480; Kampert, in: Sydow (ed.): Europäische Datenschutzgrundverordnung, Art. 8 DSGVO mn. 8; Joachim: Besonders schutzbedürftige Personengruppen, ZD (Zeitschrift für Datenschutz), 7, 2017, pp. 414, 416.

[167] Spindler/Dalby, in: Spindler/Schuster (eds.): Recht der elektronischen Medien, Art. 8 DSGVO mn. 6; Wolff, in: Schantz/Wolff (eds.): Das neue Datenschutzrecht, mn. 481; critical Heckmann/Paschke, in: Ehmann/Selmayr (eds.): Datenschutz-Grundverordnung, Art. 8 DSGVO mn. 20.

[168] Fenelon: GDPR series: children and parental consent, Privacy & Data Protection, 17(8), 2017, pp. 3–5; Persano: GDPR and children rights in the EU Data Protection Law, European Journal of Privacy Law & Technologies, Special Issue, 2020, p. 32, p. 34.

[169] For an overview of rules on parental responsibility, see Boele-Woelki et al.: Principles of European Family Law Regarding Parental Responsibilities.

for the child's consent.[170] In German law, this means that the ability to give consent in the individual case is decisive, as was already the case under the German Federal Data Protection Act *(Bundesdatenschutzgesetz, BDSG)* before the GDPR entered into force.[171] It cannot be deduced from this EU Regulation that national orders must assume a capacity to consent starting at the age of 16,[172] but once this age threshold is reached, it is generally presumed that the necessary capacity for understanding exists.[173]

6.2 Interplay of EU Law and National Law Across Legal Areas: The Example of Art. 8 of the GDPR and National Contract Law

Finally, Art. 8 (3) of the GDPR explicitly states that it shall not affect the general contract law of Member States, such as the rules on the validity, formation, or effect of a contract in relation to a child. General contract law, as part of Member States' competences, is thus not affected by the provision on the effectiveness of consent under data protection law.[174] But what influence do Member State rules on contractual legal autonomy have on data autonomy within the scope of application of Art. 8 of the GDPR? As per Art. 6 (1) (b) of the GDPR, data processing is lawful insofar as it is necessary for the performance of a contract to which the data subject is party or in order to take steps at the request of the data subject prior to entering into a contract. Read together, the national rules on contractual capacity

[170] Fenelon: GDPR series: children and parental consent, Privacy & Data Protection, 17(8), 2017, pp. 3–5.

[171] Klement, in: Simitis/Hornung/Spiecker (eds.): Datenschutzrecht, Art. 8 DSGVO mn. 10; Wolff, in: Schantz/Wolff (eds.): Das neue Datenschutzrecht, Grundprinzipien, mn. 486.

[172] Kampert, in: Sydow (ed.): Europäische Datenschutzgrundverordnung, Art. 8 DSGVO mn. 8.; but see Klement, in: Simitis/Hornung/Spiecker (eds.): Datenschutzrecht, Art. 8 DSGVO mn. 12.

[173] Heckmann/Paschke, in: Ehmann/Selmayr (eds.): Datenschutz-Grundverordnung, Art. 8 DSGVO mn. 9.

[174] Spindler/Dalby, in: Spindler/Schuster (eds.): Recht der elektronischen Medien, Art. 8 DSGVO mn. 14; Heckmann/Paschke, in: Ehmann/Selmayr (eds.): Datenschutz-Grundverordnung, Art. 8 DSGVO mn. 7, 39; Taeger, in: Taeger/Gabel (eds.): DS-GVO/BDSG, Art. 8 DSGVO mn. 46; Buchner/Kühling, in: Kühling/Buchner (eds.): DS-GVO BDSG, Art. 8 DSGVO mn. 29; Persano: GDPR and children rights in the EU Data Protection Law, European Journal of Privacy Law & Technologies, Special issue, 2020, p. 32, p. 39.

thus determine children's data autonomy in the context of the respective contract. GDPR contains no indications, specifically with regard to children, that the application of Art. 6 (1) (b) of the GDPR should be excluded.[175] If the applicable rules on contractual legal capacity are followed, parental consent under data protection law is not required if the person with limited legal capacity can effectively conclude it without parental consent.[176] The data processing based on the contract does not have to meet the additional requirements of Art. 8 (1) of the GDPR.[177]

For the purposes of the contract, the permission for data processing lies within the conclusion of the contract (Art. 6 (1) (1) (b) of the GDPR).[178] Broad national rules, e.g. regarding contractual capacity when spending pocket money,[179] thus entail further consequences regarding the processing of data and associated risks, even though national rules on the necessary age or individual development do not address the children's capacity to understand the significance of decisions regarding their data. Hence, EU law extends national rules on general contractual capacity to data protection law. This leads to a hybridization of these norms.[180] National contract law becomes EU data protection law through the GDPR.

[175] Spindler/Dalby, in: Spindler/Schuster (eds.): Recht der elektronischen Medien, Art. 8 DSGVO mn.15; Frenzel, in: Paal/Pauly (eds.): DS-GVO BDSG, Art. 8 DSGVO mn. 16.

[176] Taeger, in: Taeger/Gabel (eds.): DS-GVO/BDSG, Art. 8 DSGVO mn. 46, 52; Gola/Schulz: DS-GVO—Neue Vorgaben für den Datenschutz bei Kindern? ZD (Zeitschrift für Datenschutz), 3, 2013, p. 475, p. 480; Schulz, in: Gola (ed.): Datenschutz-Grundverordnung, Art. 8 DSGVO mn. 23, 24; Frenzel, in: Paal/Pauly (eds.): DS-GVO BDSG, Art. 8 DSGVO mn. 16; Wolff, in: Schantz/Wolff (eds.): Das neue Datenschutzrecht, Grundprinzipien, mn. 486; Nebel/Richter: Datenschutz bei Internetdiensten nach der DS-GVO, ZD (Zeitschrift für Datenschutz), 2, 2012, p. 407, p. 411; Persano: GDPR and children rights in the EU Date Protection Law, European Journal of Privacy Law & Technologie Special Issue, 2020, p. 32, p. 34 f.; Jandt/Roßnagel: Social Networks für Kinder und Jugendliche, MMR (Multimedia und Recht), 14, 2011, p. 637, p. 640; probably also Talley: Major Flaws in Minor Laws, Indina Int'l & Comp. Law Review, 30(1), 2019, p. 150; to the contrary, Spindler/Dalby, in: Spindler/Schuster (eds.): Recht der elektronischen Medien, Art. 8 DSGVO mn. 15; Frenzel, in; Paal/Pauly (eds.): DS-GVO BDSG, Art. 8 DSGVO mn. 16.

[177] Gola/Schulz: DS-GVO—Neue Vorgaben für den Datenschutz bei Kindern? ZD (Zeitschrift für Datenschutz), 3, 2013, p. 475, p. 480; Schulz, in: Gola (ed.): Datenschutz-Grundverordnung, Art. 8 DSGVO mn. 23.

[178] Schulz, in: Gola (ed.): Datenschutz-Grundverordnung, Art. 8 DSGVO mn. 22 f.

[179] See supra under Sect. 5.2.

[180] See Dethloff: Zusammenspiel der Rechtsquellen aus privatrechtlicher Sicht, in: Paulus et al. (eds.): Internationales, nationales und privates Recht: Hybridisierung der Rechtsordnungen?: Immunität, pp. 47–86.

While Art. 8 (1) 3rd st. of the GDPR is a testament to the national diversity and political power of the Member States despite the common goal of an EU digital market,[181] Art. 8 (3) does not, in fact, respect national legal traditions and law. Rather, EU law extends the proxies used for children's capacity to conclude contracts, mainly individual development or attainment of a certain age, to another legal area where Member States do not necessarily use the same proxies. For example, German general contract law confers legal capacity to contract based on the attainment of a certain age, while the capacity to decide on the processing of data is determined in accordance with the individual development and ability to understand the significance of that particular decision. Under the German Federal Data Protection Act (BDSG), such an understanding was generally assumed at 14 years or older, and each individual case had to be considered. The individual age limit could also be higher.[182] The extension of contractual capacity into data autonomy in the framework of the GDPR bridges the gap between rules for the analogue and digital worlds, with rules on contractual capacity of minors being developed with regard to analogue contexts and Art. 8 of the GDPR applying to specific digital contexts. The interplay of EU law and national law across legal areas makes an approach based on the specific effects on the exercise of children's rights all the more important.

7 Conclusions

Against risk-based narratives, which one-sidedly further the protection of children in digital spheres, a rights-based approach to children's digital participation underscores vital points for their digital participation in the multi-level system of the European Union. The European Union's role as a children's rights actor has gained considerable importance with regard to digital and therefore commonly transnational contexts as well as in the EU's legislative agenda with regard to the digital single market. Children's rights, as established in the EU Charter, the ECHR, and the UNCRC, contain both protective and participative dimensions that need to be balanced. Currently, the benefits of children's digital participation

[181] See Dethloff/Kaesling: Datenmündigkeit Minderjähriger in Europa, in: Fischer et al. (eds.): Gestaltung der Informationsordnung, München 2022, p. 537, p. 550–552.

[182] Schulz, in: Gola (ed.): Datenschutz-Grundverordnung, Art. 8 DSGVO mn. 10; Gola/ Schulz: DS-GVO—Neue Vorgaben für den Datenschutz bei Kindern? ZD (Zeitschrift für Datenschutz), 3, 2013, p. 475, p. 468.

are not yet adequately reflected in legislative motives, regulations, and directives. The balancing of children's protective and participative rights is directly linked to the implementation of the principle of the best interests of the child, which contains an interpretative legal principle, a substantive right, and a rule of procedure. Children's best interests must be the primary consideration, also amid a large number of stakeholders. The principle of the best interests of the child requires a specific evaluation of the impact of these decisions on the children concerned and a justification demonstrating that the best interests of the child has been expressly taken into account when weighing interests. Depending on the issue and measure at hand, trans-sectorial analyses can be needed in order to carry out that impact assessment and give a suitable justification.

Children's digital participation can be affected by a number of different instruments from various, partly overlapping legal areas, such as contract law, family law, private international law, platform regulation, and media law (including youth protection). As a result of sector-specific approaches and corresponding specializations of legal scholars analyzing the legal instruments, effects of such tools are rarely evaluated comprehensively. Instruments can also stem from various levels of norm-setting, such as the EU and Member State level. A rights-based approach emphasizes the need for integrative analyses, firstly, with regard to measures from different legal areas and secondly, with regard to those from different regulatory levels.

The principle of proportionality does not only govern the justification of EU limitations to children's rights, but also the balance of EU and Member State responsibilities and interests. National limits on children's participation and autonomy may vary, but coherence serves as a constraint on national legislators' room to maneuver when exercising their competences. Specifically, Member States need to ensure coherence of all national measures in the relevant regulatory area. The rights-based approach to children's participation online facilitates the application of the principle of coherence, as it can help identify all legal areas relevant for children's participation in that specific context. As the example of children's data autonomy shows, the interplay of EU and national law can not only take the shape of (partial) EU harmonization and supplement national law,[183] but also lead to hybridization, e.g. when EU law extends national rules on general contractual capacity to data protection law. In these cases, the rights-based, integrative approach becomes all the more important for the protection of children's rights to digital participation in the European Union.

---

[183] See supra Sect. 6.1.

References

Ackermann, Thomas: Sektorielles EU-Recht und allgemeine Privatrechtssystematik, ZEuP (Zeitschrift für europäisches Privatrecht), 26(4), 2018, pp. 741–781.

Antokolskaia, Masha: Family law and national culture: Arguing against the cultural constraints argument, Utrecht Law Review, 4, 2008, pp. 25–34.

Arewa, Olufunmilayo B.: Data Collection, Privacy, and Children in the Digital Economy, in this volume.

Autenrieth, Ulla/Bänziger, Andreas/Rohde, Wiebke/Schmidt, Jan: Gebrauch und Bedeutung von Social Network Sites im Alltag junger Menschen. Ein Ländervergleich zwischen Deutschland und der Schweiz, in: Neumann-Braun, Klaus (ed.): Freundschaft und Gemeinschaft im Social Web. Bildbezogenes Handeln und Peergroup-Kommunikation auf Facebook & Co, Baden-Baden 2011, pp. 31–54.

Bergert, Cora/Köster, Antonia/Krasnova, Hanna/Turel, Ofir: Missing Out on Life: Parental Perceptions of Children's Mobile Technology Use, Proceedings of the 15th International Conference on Wirtschaftsinformatik, March 8–11, Potsdam, 2020.

Blanke, Herman J., in: Calliess, Christian/Ruffert, Matthias (eds.): EUV/EGV, Munich, 3rd ed. 2007, Art. 3 EUV.

Blaser, T., in: Rieck, Jürgen/Lettmaier, Saskia (eds.): Ausländisches Familienrecht, Munich, 21st ed. 2021, Ireland.

Blecher-Prigat, Ayelet: Lost Between Data and Family? Shortcomings of Current Understandings of the Law, in this volume.

Boele-Woelki, Katharina/Ferrand, Frédérique/González-Beilfuss, Cristina/Jänterä-Jareborg, Maarit/Lowe, Nigel/Martiny, Dieter/Pintens, Walter: Principles of European Family Law Regarding Parental Responsibilities, Cambridge 2007.

Buchner, Benedikt/Kühling, Jürgen, in: Kühling, Jürgen/Buchner, Benedikt (eds.): DS-GVO BDSG, Munich, 3rd ed. 2020, Art. 8 DSGVO.

Carpini, Michael X. Delli: Gen.com: Youth, Civic Engagement, and the New Information Environment, Political Communication, 17(4), 2000, pp. 341–349.

Chaudron, Stèphane/Di Gioia, Rosanna/Gemo, Monica/Holloway, Donell/Marsh, Jackie/Mascheroni, Giovanna/Peter, Jochen/Yamada-Rice, Dylan: Kaleidoscope on the Internet of Toys—Safety, security, privacy and societal insights, 2017.

Committee on the Rights of the Child: General comment No. 25 on children's rights in relation to the digital environment, 2021, CRC/C/GC/25.

Cullingford, Cedric: Children and Society—Children's Attitudes to Politics and Power, London 1992.

De Oliveira, Guilherme: Um direito da família europeu? Play it again… Europe!, Revista de Legislação e de Jurisprudência, ano133, n.º 3913 e 3914, set. 2000, pp. 105–110.

Dethloff, Nina: Families and the Law: Taking Account of Children's Evolving Capacities in Analogue and Digital Contexts, in this volume.

Dethloff, Nina: Zusammenspiel der Rechtsquellen aus privatrechtlicher Sicht, in: Paulus, Andreas et al. (eds.): Internationales, nationales und privates Recht: Hybridisierung der Rechtsordnungen?: Immunität, Heidelberg 2014, pp. 47–86.

Dethloff, Nina/Kaesling, Katharina: Datenmündigkeit Minderjähriger in Europa, in: Fischer, Veronika/Nolte, Georg/Senftleben, Martin/Specht-Riemenschneider, Louisa (eds.):

Gestaltung der Informationsordnung—Festschrift für Thomas Dreier, München 2022, pp. 537–552.

Dethloff, Nina/Maschwitz, Alexandra: Kinderrechte in Europa—wo stehen wir? FPR (Familie Partnerschaft Recht), 18(5), 2012, pp. 190–194.

Dettenborn, Harry: Kindeswohl und Kindeswille: psychologische und rechtliche Aspekte, Munich 2017.

Deutscher Bundestag: Entwurf eines Gesetzes zur Änderung des Grundgesetzes zur ausdrücklichen Verankerung der Kinderrechte, Bundestag Printed Matter (BT- Drucksache) 19/28138.

Dieterich, Peter: Systemgerechtigkeit und Kohärenz, Berlin 2014.

Dittler, Ullrich/Hoyer, Michael (eds.): Social Network—Die Revolution der Kommunikation: Kundenkommunikation, Facebook-Freundschaften, digitale Demokratie und virtuelle Shitstorms unter medienpsychologischer und mediensoziologischer Perspektiven, Munich 2014.

Dreyer/Bernzen, in: Erdemir (ed.): Das neue Jugendschutzgesetz, Baden-Baden 2021, § 5.

Ellison, Nicolle B./Steinfield, Charles/Lampe, Cliff: The benefits of Facebook "Friends": Social capital and college students' use of online social network sites, Journal of Computer-mediated Communication, 12(4), 2007, pp. 1143–1168.

Enßlin, R., in: Rieck, Jürgen/Lettmaier, Saskia (eds.): Ausländisches Familienrecht, Munich, 21st ed. 2021, Italien.

European Commission: Proposal for a REGULATION OF THE EUROPEAN PARLIAMENT AND OF THE COUNCIL on a Single Market for Digital Services (Digital Services Act) and amending Directive 2000/31/EC, December 15, 2020, https://eur-lex.europa.eu/legal-content/EN/TXT/HTML/?uri=CELEX:52020PC0825&from=en; last accessed September 21, 2021.

European Union Agency for Fundamental Rights and Council of Europe: Handbook on European law relating to the rights of the child, 2015, https://www.echr.coe.int/Documents/Handbook_rights_child_ENG.PDF; last accessed August 19, 2021.

Fenelon, James: GDPR series: children and parental consent, Privacy & Data Protection, 17(8), 2017, pp. 3–5.

Finkle, Jim/Wagstaff, Jeremy: VTech hack exposes ID theft risk in connecting kids to Internet, Reuters, December 6, 2015, https://www.reuters.com/article/us-vtech-cyberattack-kids-analysis-idUSKBN0TP0FQ20151206; last accessed October 6, 2021.

Fortin, Jane: Children's Rights and the Developing Law, Cambridge 2009.

Franck, Lorenz, in: Gola, Peter (ed.): Datenschutzgrundverordung, Munich, 2nd ed. 2018, Art. 8 DSGVO.

Freeman, Michael: The Value and Values of Children's Rights, in: Invernizzi, Antonella/Williams, Jane (eds.): The Human Rights of Children: From Visions to Implementation, London 2016.

Frenz: Kohärente und systematische nationale Normgebung—nicht nur im Glücksspielrecht, Europarecht, 47(3), 2012, pp. 346–354.

Frenzel, Eike M., in: Paal, Boris/Pauly, Daniel A. (eds.): DS-GVO BDSG, Munich, 3rd ed. 2021, Art. 8 DSGVO.

Gibbs, Samuel: Hackers can hijack Wi-Fi Hello Barbie to spy on your children, The Guardian, November 26, 2021, https://www.theguardian.com/technology/2015/nov/26/hackers-can-hijack-wi-fi-hello-barbie-to-spy-on-your-children; last accessed October 6, 2021.

Gilbert, David: VTech Takes Learning Lodge Website Offline After Hack Reveals Details of Over 200,000 Children, International Business Times, November 30, 2015, https://www.ibtimes.com/vtech-takes-learning-lodge-website-offline-after-hack-reveals-details-over-200000-2203642; last accessed October 6, 2021.

Giroux, Henry A.: Racial Injustice and Disposable Youth in the Age of Zero Tolerance, Injustice and Disposable Youth in the Age of Zero Tolerance, International Journal of Qualitative Studies in Education, 16, 2003, pp. 553–565.

Gola, Peter/Schulz, Sebastian: DS-GVO—Neue Vorgaben für den Datenschutz bei Kindern? Überlegungen zur einwilligungsbasierten Verarbeitung von personenbezogenen Daten Minderjähriger, ZD (Zeitschrift für Datenschutz), 3, 2013, pp. 475–481.

Gottlieb-Robles, Barbara/Montgomery, Kathryn: Youth as E-Citizens. The Internet's Contribution to Civic Engagement, in: Buckingham, David/Willett, Rebekah (eds.): Digital Generations. Children, Young People and the Media, London 2006, pp. 131–148.

Graziani, Laurène: Les enfants et internet: La participation des jeunes à travers les réseaux sociaux, Journal du droit des jeunes, 7, 2012, pp. 36–45.

Greve, Holger, in: Sydow, Gernot (ed.): Europäische Datenschutzgrundverordnung, Baden-Baden, 2nd ed. 2018, Art. 12 DSGVO.

Harbo, Tor-Inge: The Function of the Proportionality Principle in EU Law, European Law Journal, 16(2), 2010, pp. 158–185.

Heckmann, Dirk/Paschke, Anne, in: Ehmann, Eugen/Selmayr, Martin (eds.): Datenschutz-Grundverordnung, Munich, 2nd ed. 2018, Artikel 8 DSGVO.

Heitmüller, M., in: Rieck, Jürgen/Lettmaier, Saskia (eds.): Ausländisches Familienrecht, Munich, 21st ed. 2021, Belgien.

Helwig, Charles C./Turiel, Elliot: Civil liberties, autonomy, and democracy: Children's perspective, International Journal of Law and Psychiatry, 25(3), 2002, pp. 253–270.

Hönicke, Christian: Smartphone erst ab 14? Ja unbedingt, Tagesspiegel, February 15, 2019, https://www.tagesspiegel.de/gesellschaft/kinderschutz-smartphone-erst-ab-14-ja-unbedingt/23991512.html; last accessed September 21, 2021.

Holloway, Donnell/Green, Leila: The Internet of Toys, Communication Research and Practice, 2(4), 2016, pp. 506–513.

Holmes, John: Myths and Missed Opportunities: Young People's Not So Risky Use of Online Communication, Information, Communication & Society, 12(8), 2008, pp. 1174–1196.

Iusmen, Ingi: How are Children's Rights (Mis)Interpreted in Practice? The European Commission, Children's Rights and Policy Narratives, in: Rhodes, Roderick Arthur William (ed.): Narrative Policy Analysis, 2018, pp. 97–120.

Jandt, Silke/Roßnagel, Alexander: Social Networks für Kinder und Jugendliche—Besteht ein ausreichender Datenschutz? MMR (Multimedia und Recht), 14, 2011, pp. 637–642.

Jarass, Hans D., in: Jarass, Hans D. (ed.): EU-Grundrechte-Charta, Munich, 4th ed. 2021, Art. 52 Grundrechte-Charta.

Joachim, Katharina: Besonders schutzbedürftige Personengruppen, ZD (Zeitschrift für Datenschutz), 7, 2017, pp. 414–418.

Jones, Meg Leta: Your New Best Frenemy: Hello Barbie and Privacy Without Screens, Engaging Science, Technology, and Society, 2, 2016, pp. 242–246.

Kämmerer, Jörn Axel: Interprofessionelle Zusammenarbeit und europarechtliche Kohärenz, Deutsches Steuerrecht, 53 (Appendix 13), 2015, pp. 33–44.

Kaesling, Katharina: Children's Digital Rights: Realizing the Potential of the CRC, in: Laufer-Ukeles, Pamela/Marrus, Ellen (eds.): Children's Rights and Interests: 30 Years After the U.N. Convention on the Rights of the Child, London/New York 2021a, pp. 183–196.

Kaesling, Katharina/Knapp, Jacob: "Massenkreativität" in sozialen Netzwerken, MMR (Multi Media und Recht), 23(12), 2020, pp. 816–821.

Kaesling, Katharina: The Making of Citizens: Democracy and Children's Rights in Digital Spheres, in: Neuberger, Christoph/Friesike, Sascha/Krzywdzinski, Martin/Eiermann, Karin-Irene (eds.): Proceedings of the Weizenbaum Conference 2021b "Democracy in Flux: Order, Dynamics and Voices in Digital Public Spheres", 2021b, pp. 67–71.

Kampert, David, in: Sydow, Gernot (ed.): Europäische Datenschutzgrundverordnung, Baden-Baden, 2nd ed. 2018, Art. 8 DSGVO.

Kemper, Rainer, in: Schulze, Reiner (ed.): Bürgerliches Gesetzbuch (BGB), Baden-Baden, 10th ed. 2019, Sec. 1666 BGB.

Kenski, Kate/Stroud, Natalie Jomini: Connections Between Internet Use and Political Efficacy, Knowledge, and Participation, Journal of Broadcasting & Electronic Media, 50(2), 2006, pp. 173–192.

Khazova, Olga: How to ensure a wider implementation of the CRC, in: Marrus, Ellen/Laufer-Ukeles, Pamela (eds.): Global Reflections on Children's Rights and the Law: 30 Years after the Convention on the Rights of the Child, London/New York 2021, pp. 4–15.

Kilkelly, Ursula/Lundy, Laura: Children's rights in action: Using the UN Convention on the Rights of the Child as an auditing tool, Child and Family Law Quarterly, 18(3), 2006, pp. 311–350.

Kirschner, Julia: Grundfreiheiten und nationale Gestaltungsspielräume, Munich 2013.

Kisunaite, Aida/Delicati, Simone: Towards a fully-fledged European Union child rights strategy, in: Marrus, Ellen/Laufer-Ukeles, Pamela (eds.): Global Reflections on Children's Rights and the Law—30 years after the Convention on the Rights of the Child, London/New York 2021.

Kleinen-von Königslöw, Katharina/Förster, Kati: Multi-media theme repertoires in the everyday identity practices of young adults, Communications, 41(4), 2016, pp. 375–398.

Klement, Jan Henrik, in: Simitis, Spiros/Hornung, Gerrit/Spiecker, Indra (eds.): Datenschutzrecht, Munich 1st ed. 2019, Art. 8 DSGVO.

Kokott, Juliane/Sobotta, Christoph: The Charter of Fundamental Rights of the European Union after Lisbon, Revista Romana de Drept European 2012, 5, 2012, pp. 93–112, https://cadmus.eui.eu/bitstream/handle/1814/15208/AEL_WP_2010_06.pdf?sequence=3&isAllowed=y; last accessed September 21, 2021.

Konstadinides, Theodore: The Competences of the Union, in: Schütze, Robert/Tridimas, Takis (eds.): Oxford Principles of European Union Law: The European Union Legal Order: Volume I, 2018, https://doi.org/10.1093/oso/9780199533770.003.0008.

Kutscher, Nadia/Bouillon, Romana: Kinder. Bilder. Rechte. Persönlichkeitsrechte von Kindern im Kontext der digitalen Mediennutzung in der Familie, Berlin 2018.

Kutscher, Nadia: Positionings, Challenges, and Ambivalences in Children's and Parents' Perspectives in Digitalized Familial Contexts, in this volume.

Lane, Daniel S.: In Search of the Expressive Citizen: Citizenship Norms and Youth Political Expression on Social Media, Public Opinion Quarterly, 84, Special Issue, 2020, pp. 257–283.

Leamy, Elisabeth: On parenting: The danger of giving your child 'smart toys', Washington Post, September 29, 2017, https://www.washingtonpost.com/lifestyle/on-parenting/giving-your-child-internet-connected-smart-toys-could-be-dumb/2017/09/29/a168218a-a241-11e7-8cfe-d5b912fabc99_story.html; last accessed September 21, 2021.

Lester, Stuart: Children's right to play—From the Margins to the Middle, in: Ruck, Martin D./Peterson-Badali, Michele/Freeman, Michael: Handbook of Children's Rights: Global and Multidisciplinary Perspectives, New York 2017, pp. 312 ff.

Lippert, André: Das Kohärenzerfordernis des EuGH—Eine Darstellung am Beispiel der Rechtsprechung zum deutschen Glücksspielmonopol, Europarecht, 47, 2012, pp. 90–99.

Livingstone, Sonia/Bulger, Monica E.: A global research agenda for children's rights in the digital age, Journal of Children and Media, 8(4), 2014, pp. 317–335.

Livingstone, Sonia: Children's digital rights: a priority, Intermedia, 42(4/5), 2014, pp. 20–24.

Livingstone, Sonia: Reframing media effects in terms of children's rights in the digital age, Journal of Children and Media, 10(1), 2016, pp. 4–12.

Majstorović, Irena/Hoško, Dubravka, in: Bergmann, Alexander/Ferid, Murad: Internationales Ehe- und Kindschaftsrecht, Frankfurt a. M./Berlin 2019, Kroatien.

Mankowski, Peter, in: Staudinger, Julius: Kommentar zum Bürgerlichen Gesetzbuch, Berlin, 14th ed. 2019, Art. 7 EGBGB.

Maple, Carsten: Security and privacy in the internet of things, Journal of Cyber Policy, 2(2), 2017, pp. 155–184.

Margetts, Helen: Rethinking Democracy with Social Media, The Political Quarterly, 19(21), 2019, pp. 107–123.

Margetts, Helen: Tiny Acts of Digital Democracy: The Good, the Bad, and the Ugly, Weizenbaum Conference 2021.

Marwick, Alice E. et al.: Youth, Privacy and Reputation—Literature Review, Harvard University Public Law Working Paper No. 10–29, 2010.

Mladenova, K., in: Rieck, Jürgen/Lettmaier, Saskia (eds.): Ausländisches Familienrecht, Munich, 21st ed. 2021, Bulgarien.

Moravscik, Andrew: Negotiating the Single European Act. National Interests and Conventional Statecraft in the European Community, International Organization, 45(1), 1991, pp. 651-688.

Nash, Victoria: The Rise of the Algorithmic Child: Protecting Children in Smart Homes, in this volume.

Nebel, Maxi/Richter, Philipp: Datenschutz bei Internetdiensten nach der DS-GVO—Vergleich der deutschen Rechtslage mit dem Kommissionsentwurf, ZD (Zeitschrift für Datenschutz), 2, 2012, pp. 407–413.

Neumann-Braun, Klaus/Autenrieth, Ulla P.: Soziale Beziehungen im Web 2.0 und deren Visualisierung, in: Neumann-Braun, Klaus (ed.): Freundschaft und Gemeinschaft im Social Web. Bildbezogenes Handeln und Peergroup-Kommunikation auf Facebook & Co, Baden-Baden 2011, pp. 9–30.

Neumann-Braun, Klaus: Freundschaft und Gemeinschaft im Social Web. Bildbezogenes Handeln und Peergroup-Kommunikation auf Facebook & Co, Baden-Baden 2011.

Nguyen, Alexander, in: Gola, Peter (ed.): Datenschutzgrundverordung, Munich, 2nd ed. 2018, Art. 57 DSGVO.

O'Neill, Brian/Staksrud, Elisabeth/McLaughlin, Sharon: Towards a better internet for children: Policy pillars, players and paradoxes, NORDICOM, 2013, https://www.diva-portal.org/smash/get/diva2:1534762/FULLTEXT01.pdf; last accessed September 21, 2021.

Palfrey, John et al.: Enhancing Child Safety and Online Technologies: Research Advisory Board Report for the Internet Safety Technical Task Force, 2008, Berkman Center for Internet & Society, http://cyber.law.harvard.edu/pubrelease/isttf/; last accessed September 21, 2021.

Palfrey, John/Gasser, Urs: Born Digital: Understanding the First Generation of Digital Natives 71, New York 2008.

Patti, Salvatore/Cubeddu, M. Giovanna: Introduzione al diritto della famiglia in Europa, Milan 2008.

Pernice, Ingolf: Treaty of Lisbon and Fundamental Rights, in: Griller, Stefan/Ziller, Jaques (eds.): The Lisbon Treaty. EU Constitutionalism without a Constitutional Treaty? Vienna/ New York 2008, pp. 235–254.

Persano, Federcia: GDPR and children rights in the EU Data Protection Law, European Journal of Privacy Law & Technologies, Special issue, 2020, p. 32 ff.

Peterson, Andrea: Toymakers are tracking more data about kids—leaving them exposed to hackers, Washington Post, November 30, 2015, https://www.washingtonpost.com/news/the-switch/wp/2015/11/30/toymakers-are-tracking-more-data-about-kids-leaving-them-exposed-to-hackers/; last accessed September 21, 2021.

Peuker, Enrico, in: Sydow, Gernot (ed.): Europäische Datenschutzgrundverordnung, Baden-Baden, 2nd ed. 2018, Art. 17 DSGVO.

Peyton, Antigone: A Litigator's Guide to the Internet of Things, Richmond Journal of Law and Technology, 22(3), 2016, Article 4, available at: https://scholarship.richmond.edu/jolt/vol22/iss3/4; last accessed September 21, 2021.

Picone, Ike/Kleut, Jelena et al.: Small acts of engagement: Reconnecting productive audience practices with everyday agency, New Media & Society, 21(9), 2019, pp. 2010–2028.

Quennerstedt, Ann: Children, But Not Really Humans? Critical Reflections on the Hampering Effect of the "3 p's", The International Journal of Children's Rights, 18, 2010, pp. 619–635.

Rosas, Allan: Balancing Fundamental Rights in EU Law, Cambridge Yearbook of European Legal Studies, Vol. 16, 2014, pp. 347–360.

Roßnagel, Alexander: Der Datenschutz von Kindern in der DS-GVO, ZD (Zeitschrift für Datenschutz), 10, 2020, pp. 88–92.

Ruffert, Matthias, in: Calliess, Christian/Ruffert, Matthias (eds.): EUV/EGV, Munich, 3rd ed. 2007, Art. 7 AEUV.

Sauter, Wolf: Proportionality in EU Law: A Balancing Act? Cambridge Yearbook of European Legal Studies, Vol. 15, 2013, pp. 439–466.

Schorkopf, Frank, in: Grabitz, Eberhard/Hilf, Meinhard/Nettesheim, Martin (eds.): Das Recht der Europäischen Union: EUV/AEUV, Munich, 73rd ed. 2021, Art. 7 AEUV.

Schorkopf, Frank: Wahrhaftigkeit im Recht der Grundfreiheiten—Zu Maßstab und Rechtsfolgen der Glücksspielurteile des Europäischen Gerichtshofs, (DÖV) Die öffentliche Verwaltung, 64, 2011, pp. 260 ff.

Schröder, Rainer, in: Pechstein, Matthias/Nowak, Carsten/Häde, Ulrich (eds.): Frankfurter Kommentar zu EUV/GRC/AEUV, Tübingen 2017, Art. 7 AEUV.

Schulz, Iren: Mediatisierte Sozialisation im Jugendalter—Kommunikative Praktiken und Beziehungsnetze im Wandel, Berlin 2010.

Schulz, Sebastian, in: Gola, Peter (ed.): Datenschutzgrundverordung, Munich, 2nd ed. 2018, Art. 8 DSGVO.

Schuster, Ulrike: Das Kohärenzprinzip in der Europäischen Union, Baden-Baden 2017.

Shah, Dhavan/Jaeho, Cho/Eveland, William/Kwak, Nojin: Information and Expression in a Digital Age: Modeling Internet Effects on Civic Participation, Communication Research, 32(5), 2005, pp. 531–565.

Shmueli, Benjamin/Blecher-Prigat, Ayelet: Privacy for Children, Columbia Human Rights Law Review, 42, 2011, pp. 758–795.

Singer, Natasha: Uncovering security flaws in digital education products for schoolchildren, New York Times, February 8, 2015, https://www.nytimes.com/2015/02/09/technology/uncovering-security-flaws-in-digital-education-products-for-schoolchildren.html; last accessed September 21, 2021.

Smehyl, S., in: Rieck, Jürgen/Lettmaier, Saskia (eds.): Ausländisches Familienrecht, Munich, 21st ed. 2021, Malta.

Specht-Riemenschneider, Louisa/Marko, Alina/Wette, Sascha: Protection of Minors on Video Sharing Platforms, in this volume.

Spindler, Gerald/Dalby, Lukas, in: Spindler, Gerald/Schuster, Fabian (eds.): Recht der elektronischen Medien, Munich, 4th ed. 2019, Art. 8 DSGVO.

Stalford, Helen: The CRC in Litigation Under EU Law, in: Liefaard, Ton/Doek, Jaap E. (eds.): Litigating the Rights of the Child, 2015, pp. 211–230.

Stalford, Helen/Drywood, Eleanor: Using the CRC to Inform EU Law and Policy-Making, in: Invernizzi, Antonio/Williams, Jane (eds.): The Human Rights of Children from Visions to Implementation, London 2011.

Statista: Internetnutzung von Kindern und Jugendlichen nach Altersgruppen in Deutschland 2019, June 18, 2020, https://de.statista.com/statistik/daten/studie/298170/umfrage/internetnutzung-von-kindern-und-jugendlichen-in-deutschland/; last accessed September 21, 2021.

Statista: TikTok—Statistics & Facts, May 5, 2021, https://www.statista.com/topics/6077/tiktok/; last accessed September 21, 2021.

Stone, Brad: Now Parents Can Hire a Hall Monitor for the Web, New York Times, July 4, 2010, http://www.nytimes.com/2010/07/04/technology/04ping.html; last accessed September 21, 2021.

Subrahmanyam, Kaveri/Greenfield, Patricia: Online Communication and Adolescent Relationships, The Future of Children, 18, 2008, pp. 119–120.

Taeger, Jürgen, in: Taeger, Jürgen/Gabel, Detlev (eds.): DS-GVO/BDSG, Munich, 3rd ed. 2019, Art. 8 DSGVO.

Tagesspiegel: Regierungsberaterin fordert Smartphone-Verbot für Kinder unter 14, Tagesspiegel, February 15, 2019, https://www.tagesspiegel.de/gesellschaft/panorama/schutz-vor-pornografie-regierungsberaterin-fordert-smartphone-verbot-fuer-kinder-unter-14/23990654.html; last accessed September 21, 2021.

Talley, Virginia A. M.: Major Flaws in Minor Laws, Indina Int'l & Comp. Law Review, 30(1), 2019, p. 150.

The European Parliament and the Council of the European Union: Position (EU) No 6/2016 of the Council at first reading with a view to the adoption of a Regulation of the European Parliament and of the Council on the protection of natural persons with regard to the processing of personal data and on the free movement of such data, and repealing Directive 95/46/EC (General Data Protection Regulation), May 3, 2016, https://eur-lex.europa.eu/legal-content/EN/TXT/HTML/?uri=CELEX:52016AG0006(01)&from=EN; last accessed September 21, 2021.

Thimm, Caya: Digitale Werteordnung: Kommentieren, kritisieren, debattieren im Netz, Forschung und Lehre, 12, 2017, pp. 1062–1063.

Third, Amanda/Livingstone, Sonia/Lansdown, Gerison: Recognizing children's rights in relation to digital technologies: Challenges of voice and evidence, principle and practice, in: Wagner, Ben/Kettemann, Matthias C./Vieth, Kilian (eds.): Research Handbook on Human Rights and Digital Technology, Cheltenham 2019, pp. 376–410.

Tinnefeld, Marie-Theres/Conrad, Isabell: Die selbstbestimmte Einwilligung im europäischen Recht, ZD (Zeitschrift für Datenschutz), 9, 2018, pp. 391–398.

ToyTalk: Privacy Policy, https://www.toytalk.com/legal/privacy/, archived at https://perma.cc/Z8K8-2DRS; last accessed September 21, 2021.

Tridimas, Takis: Principle of Proportionality, in: Schütze, Robert/Tridimas, Takis: Principle of Proportionality, in: Oxford Principles of European Union Law: The European Union Legal Order: Volume 1.

Trstenjak, Verica/Beysen, Erwin: Das Prinzip der Verhältnismäßigkeit in der Unionsrechtsordnung, Europarecht, 47, 2012, pp. 265–284.

Turner, Sarah: Connected Toys—What Device Documentation Explains about Privacy and Security, 2020.

Valkenburg, Patty M./Peter, Jochen: Adolescents' Identity Experiments on the Internet: Consequences for Social Competence and Self-Concept Unity, Communication Research, 35(2), 2008, pp. 208–231.

Keymolen, Esther/Van der Hof, Simone: Can I still trust you, my dear doll? A philosophical and legal exploration of smart toys and trust, Journal of Cyber Policy, 4(2), 2019, pp. 143–159.

Venkataramakrishnan, Siddharth: Cyber risks take the fun out of connected toys, Financial Times, November 25, 2020, https://www.ft.com/content/c653e977-435f-4553-8401-9fa9b0faf632; last accessed September 21, 2021.

Wolff, Heimrich A., in: Schantz, Peter/Wolff, Heinrich A. (eds.): Das neue Datenschutzrecht, Munich 2017.

Worldpopulationreview.com: Facebook Users by Country 2021, https://worldpopulationreview.com/country-rankings/facebook-users-by-country; last accessed September 21, 2021.

Zaman, Bieke/Castro, Theresa Sofia/Miranda, Fernanda Chocron: Internet of Toys: advantages, risks and challenges of a consumption scenario that is intriguing parents and researchers, Intercom: Revista Brasileira de Ciências da Comunicação, 41, 2018, pp. 213–219.

Ziebarth, Wolfgang, in: Sydow, Gernot (ed.): Europäische Datenschutzgrundverordnung, Baden-Baden, 2nd ed. 2018, Art. 57 DSGVO.

JProf. Dr. Katharina Kaesling, LL.M. is Junior Professor of Civil Law, Intellectual Property, especially Patent Law, and Legal Issues of AI at the University of Dresden (TU), Germany. From 2017 to 2022, she was Research Coordinator at the Käte Hamburger Center for Advanced Study in the Humanities "Law as Culture" at the University of Bonn, Germany. She is a habilitation candidate at the Department of Law at the University of Bonn, Member of the North Rhine-Westphalian Academy of Sciences, Humanities and the Arts, and Member of the Board of ForTech, the Research Center for Legal Issues of New Technologies and Data Law (Forschungsstelle für Rechtsfragen neuer Technologien sowie Datenrecht). Her research areas include European and Comparative Private Law, Platform Regulation, Private International Law, Intellectual Property Law and Data Law. Her comparative law dissertation on German and French family law has won several awards, including the prize for the best dissertation of the law department of the University of Bonn. Her recent publications include: Article-by-Article Commentary on the management of systemic risks by very large online platforms (Articles 33, 34, 35, 37, 41, 42 and 43) and data access for authorities and researchers (Art 40), in: Hofmann/Raue: Digital Services Act: Gesetz über digitale Dienste, Nomos, 2023; Rainbow Families on Social Media: Diversity and Plurality as Matters of Platform Regulation, in: Dethloff/Kaesling (eds.): Between Sexuality, Gender and Reproduction: On the Pluralisation of Family Forms, Intersentia, 2023, pp. 227–252; Children's Digital Rights: Realizing the Potential of the CRC, in: Laufer-Ukeles/Marrus (eds.): Global Reflections on Children's Rights and the Law: 30 Years After the U.N. Convention on the Rights of the Child, Routledge, 2021, Chapter 14, pp. 183–196.

Children as Objects (of Imagery)?

The Case of "Sharenting"—Parental Action Strategies in the Contested Field of Visualizing Children in Online Environments

Ulla Autenrieth

1 Introduction

The discussion about the presence of children's photos on social networks flares up again and again. At the center of this is the question of whether and which photos and videos parents may or should not show of their children on platforms such as Facebook, Instagram, and YouTube. The discussions are supported by campaigns and actions that point to a violation of rights on the part of children by their parents. One campaign that received much media attention in German-speaking countries was a photo series by blogger Toyah Diebel. On a website created especially for this purpose, 'deinkindauchnicht.org', she posted photos showing her and the actor Wilson Gonzalez Ochsenknecht. In all of the photos, they pose specifically as to reference subjects in classic children's photos on social network platforms—they sit naked on the toilet, eat porridge, breastfeed, or suck a pacifier while surrounded by packages labeled 'advertising'. Through the contextual break of adults being depicted in contrived and dramatized child poses, as well as through the resulting irritation, Diebel aims to draw attention to what she sees as the wrong and dangerous photographic practices of parents.[1]

[1] Cf. Zobel: Kinderfotos auf Instagram.

U. Autenrieth (✉)
University of Applied Sciences of the Grisons, Chur, Switzerland
e-mail: ulla.autenrieth@fhgr.ch

N. Dethloff et al. (eds.), *Families and New Media*, Juridicum – Schriften zum Medien-, Informations- und Datenrecht,
https://doi.org/10.1007/978-3-658-39664-0_5

Similar advocacy campaigns for children's image rights have also been launched by institutions such as the Deutsches Kinderhilfswerk (German Children's Fund), which sponsored the campaign 'Kinder haben Rechte' (Children Have Rights). In the course of this initiative, an image campaign was also developed, featuring photos of children in various situations that were accompanied by the tagline "Dear mom, dear dad, think before you post!".[2]

While drawing attention to the rights of children is appropriate and essential, it is equally important not to categorically condemn parents and their everyday photography practices. Nonetheless, well-meaning campaigns can leave such an impression. What is problematic about this is the perspective that corresponding campaigns report on seemingly objective misconduct on the part of the parents. However, the parents themselves do not have their say. The general assumption conveyed, on the other hand, is that when parents post their children's photos online, they are acting irresponsibly and out of purely narcissistic motives. The relevance of contexts and differentiation of content are often left out of the equation.

In the following, the parents' perspective will be shown. What are their motives and action strategies with regard to sharing children's photos on social media platforms like Facebook, WhatsApp, and Instagram? What considerations guide their actions? The analysis draws upon 34 focus interviews conducted with parents as part of "Picturing Family in the Social Web. A comparative analysis of the growing image-based presentation of familial occasions in participative online contexts using the example of the parenthood of the so-called digital natives", a project which was sponsored by the Swiss National Science Foundation and ran from 2014 to 2017.[3]

2 Theoretical Background

The term 'sharenting' was coined to describe the sharing of children's photos by parents in online environments. It is an amalgam of the words 'sharing' and 'parenting'. However, it is important to distinguish between a denotative and a connotative level in the meaning. On a denotative level, 'sharenting' stands as a

[2] Cf. Krempl: Kinderhilfswerk: Fotos vom Nachwuchs nicht unüberlegt posten.

[3] For more information, see www.netzbilder.net.

"shorthand term denoting when parents share information about themselves and their children online", or as a way to express "sharing representations of one's parenting or children online".[4] While this first scholarly definition is descriptive in nature—without making a judgement about the actions—the term already has a clearly negative connotation in everyday linguistic use. On a connotative level, definitions from popular online dictionaries illustrate how the term is widely understood and used. Sharenting is described here as "[...] the overuse of social media by parents to share content based on their children. It is related to the concept of 'too much information'".[5] Or, in another variant, sharenting stands for "[u]sing social media to share news and images of children [...]. It carries the connotation that parents are spending too much time showing the world how happy and fulfilled their children are rather than conducting actual parenting. The term also suggests that parents are oversharing".[6] As the use of terms such as "too much information", "spending too much time", or "oversharing" clearly demonstrates, the concept of sharenting is usually used in everyday life with a distinctly negative connotation.

The fact that the birth of children leads to an increase in the importance of photos and photography in parents' lives was documented even before the emergence of social media. Rose[7] describes how mothers, in particular, take on the task of family photo management and send up-to-date pictures of their children to more distant relatives at Christmas, for example. As such, the role that the distribution of children's photos plays within the contact network of families and their social environment also already becomes apparent. With the advent of online platforms, this is now happening in new contexts and extended personal networks, allowing for a greater public audience. Even in online environments, mothers are more likely to share photos of their children.[8] This allows them to interact with

[4] Blum-Ross/Livingstone: "Sharenting," parent blogging, and the boundaries of the digital self, Popular Communication, 15(2), 2017, pp. 110–125.

[5] Woods: Too much information?

[6] See Cyber Definitions: Sharenting.

[7] Rose: Doing family photography.

[8] See Brosch: When the child is born into the Internet, The New Educational Review, 43(1), 2016, pp. 225–235; Harding: Motherhood Reimag(in)ed, Photographies, 9(1), 2016, pp. 109–125; Kumar/Schoenebeck: The modern day baby book, in: Proceedings of the CSCW'15, pp. 1302–1312.

other parents, and it is an important factor in maintaining and building new social relationships, as well as in creating a sense of pride and joy in their own parenting achievements.[9] Sharing photos and exchanging views on aspects of child-rearing on social media allows new relationships to be formed with 'peers' that can fill some need for emotional support, especially for young mothers.[10] In this, mothers are aware of potential risks and seek ways to deal with them.[11] Of particular importance is the aspect of privacy protection of children[12] and the perception of their needs and wishes with regard to posting pictures.[13] Potential stereotypical portrayals of children and the resulting social implications are seen as potentially problematic.[14] At the same time, mothers are confronted with increased social pressure as a result of posting photos of their children and families. On the one hand, they have to deal with the occasionally strong rejection of sharenting[15]; on the other, they are subject to public criticism of their appearance and of decisions made in matters of child-rearing.[16]

---

[9] Cf. Lazard: 'I'm not showing off, I'm just trying to have a connection'; Lazard et al.: Sharenting. Pride, affect and the day-to-day politics of digital mothering, Social and Personality Psychology Compass, 13(4), 2019.

[10] Cf. Bizarri: Vergemeinschaftung und Mutterschaft, Studies in Communication Sciences, 16(2), 2016, pp. 163–173.

[11] Cf. Chalklen/Anderson: Mothering on Facebook, Social Media + Society, 3(2), 2017, pp. 1–10; Ammari/Kumar/Lampe/Schoenebeck: Managing Children's Online Identities, in: Proceedings of the 33rd Annual ACM Conference on Human Factors in Computing Systems, pp. 1895–1904.

[12] Cf. Blum-Ross/Livingstone: "Sharenting," parent blogging, and the boundaries of the digital self, Popular Communication, 15(2), 2017, pp. 110–125.

[13] Cf. Autenrieth: Die Visualisierung von Kindheit und Familie im Social Web, in: Hoffman/Krotz/Reissmann (eds.): Mediatisierung und Mediensozialisation, pp. 137–151; Autenrieth/Bizarri/Lützel: Kinderbilder im Social Web.

[14] Cf. Choi/Lewallen: "Say Instagram, kids!", Howard Journal of Communications, 29(2), 2017, pp. 144–164.

[15] Cf. Kneidinger: Social Media als digitales Fotoalbum multilokaler Familien, in: Lobinger/Geise (eds.): Visualisierung—Mediatisierung, pp. 146–162.

[16] Cf. Autenrieth: (Vor-)Bilder, in: Grittmann et al. (eds.): Körperbilder—Körperpraktiken, pp. 51–75; Johnson: Maternal Devices, Social Media and the Self-Management of Pregnancy, Societies, 4, 2014, pp. 330–350.

3 Methodological Approach—Researching Sharenting

The presented data were generated during the research project "Picturing Family in the Social Web. A comparative analysis of the growing image-based presentation of familial occasions in participative online contexts using the example of the parenthood of the so-called Digital Natives", which was carried out from 2014 to 2017. A total of 34 focused interviews were conducted with two different approaches: individual and couple interviews. In total, 40 parents were interviewed.

In a first focus group, individual interviews (n = 28) took place with young parents between the ages of 20 and 35 who regularly share pictures and/or videos on social media platforms and via mobile apps. In addition to a guided interview about family photo practices, an online ethnography of respondents' profiles was conducted. For this purpose, research profiles were created on the relevant platforms, and a friend request was sent with the participants' consent, which they then accepted.

In addition, there was a second focus group in which couples (n = 6) were interviewed in their homes. These were also conducted with 20–35-year-old parents who regularly post visual artifacts of their children (photos and videos) on social network sites and via mobile apps. In addition to a guideline-based interview and online ethnography, these 'home-ethnography' style surveys also documented the use of photos in private everyday family life, as well as focused more on the negotiations regarding posting practices between parents.

4 Results—Parental Action Strategies and Sharenting as a Communicative Practice

4.1 The Quantity and Role of Private Photos in Intra- and Inter-Familial Communication

The interviews confirmed that photographic activities within families increase significantly with the birth of a child. Parents' stated desire was to preserve the many 'special moments' and record milestones of their child's development. Owning 'good' photographs was often described as being personally important. The birth of a child was often considered to have the similar photographic significance as one's own wedding. Thus, professional baby or family photos were often commissioned and shot during pregnancy and/or shortly after birth, and for everyday familial life, photographic demands also increased. In some cases, people even specifically invested in new camera equipment in order to obtain higher-quality pictures and not just rely on their cell phone cameras. Regarding the storage and archiving of photos, four different focal points of use could be differentiated.

4.1.1 Visuals as Archives of Possibilities (and Guilt)

The increase in photographic activities is accompanied by the question of how to store and archive images. As photo technology has developed, material costs have increasingly become irrelevant, and the number of snapshots has thus risen. Interviewed families explained how they frequently captured scenes from everyday life, especially in the first months and years of their children's lives. In contrast to analog image practices, however, they did not just take individual shots of the corresponding scenes, but entire photo series, which allows them to catch the right moment and, if necessary, select the best shot. This further led to an enormous increase in the number of photos. Over time, some families accumulated many thousands of pictures, and these were often distributed over various devices. Besides a possible digital camera, parents rely most often on their cell phones, which are usually within a hand's reach and capable of storing large quantities of photos. Some parents manage to store the photos in a central place, such as on the family laptop (see Fig. 1). There, pictures are stored in the hope that one day they will be sorted and made visible again in different ways, such as in chronologically sorted photo albums. In many cases, however, these well-filled picture folders are a source of great dissatisfaction. The large mass of pictures is often contrasted by parents' limited free time. Thus, on the one hand, the created archives are seen as having great potential for the creation of an intra-family culture of remembrance, but on the other, they are also a constant source of bad conscience, since sorting and structuring the steady stream of new photos is difficult to surmount. In turn, the created data folders form both an archive of possibilities and feelings of inadequacy.

4.1.2 Visuals as Communication Material

Children's pictures play a major role in communication with parents' close social environment. With the widespread establishment of smartphones and messenger apps such as WhatsApp, sending photos and videos has become increasingly popular compared to sending just text messages. In particular, contacts who live far away can thus be more involved in their distant family's everyday life. Especially with new families, when the children are still small and quickly master

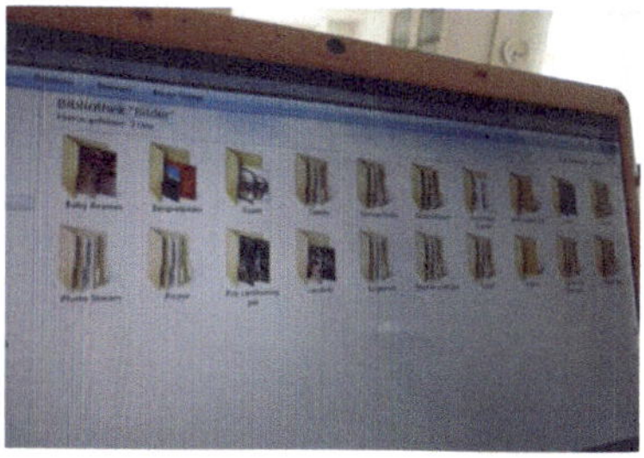

Fig. 1 Family laptop with image folders

many developmental steps, there is a great need among parents to share these moments. Mothers in particular, who still spend more time at home with young children, often alone, expressed that they appreciate the opportunity to talk to others about their children's development and share special moments. When fathers work outside the home, many mothers take advantage of the opportunity to share their children's daily lives with them throughout the day via snapshots and short videos:

> "I send him [the father] pictures of Sophie when, for example, she's dressed funny or something like that, which he just can't see during the day because he's at work." Elena

In addition to the parents among themselves, contact with the extended family is strongly characterized by the exchange of photos. In the context of family chats and groups (see Fig. 2), everyday pictures and special moments of the children are also frequently shared:

> "There [on WhatsApp] we have a lot of photos of her, where we kind of just want to show something briefly, or so, look here, new hairstyle, how she laughs, or what nonsense she does. We almost never have pictures of ourselves, so if we do, then only about her, because, of course, they [family and friends] want to know that, too. And they always want to see what new things she can do." Luisa

As revealed in the interviews, the birth of grandchildren is often the occasion for some grandparents to engage more deeply with digital and networked technologies and to acquire a smartphone consequently.

In addition, communication within parental peer groups is also strongly influenced by visual artifacts. Longtime friends want to be kept up to date on the children's development.

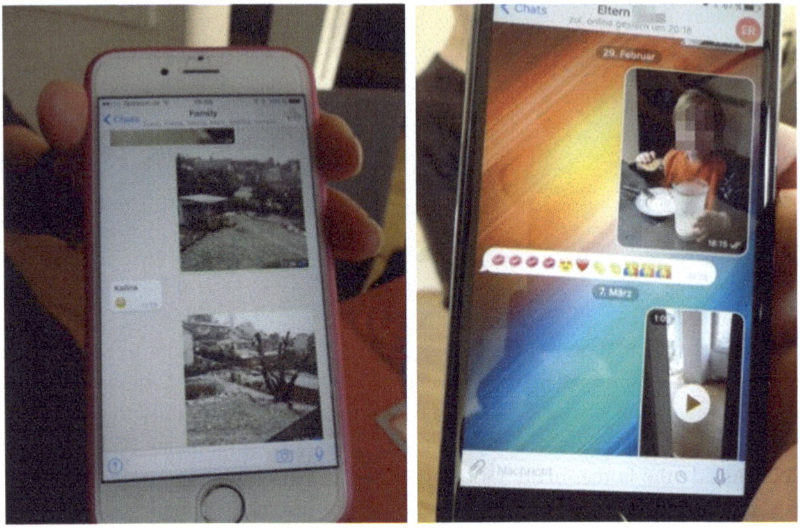

Fig. 2 Photos and videos in parental WhatsApp groups

Ben: "Yes, exactly. Then we have a baby group, where all the parents from our church congregation who have recently had a baby come together to solve baby problems or if someone has something urgent to ask: 'Hey, it's like this with me right now. Was it maybe like this with somebody else? How did you guys handle that? What did you guys do? How did you guys deal with it?' And stuff like that."

I: "And what role do photos play in the group?"

Ben: "Well, for example, when Ina got something new to eat, we just took a picture and sent it."

New contacts, for example from pregnancy classes and parenting groups, become an important place for social exchange. There is a correspondingly pronounced need to give the immediate environment, consisting of family and friends, a direct insight into one's own family life via visual artifacts.

4.1.3 Visuals as Personal Public Relation Material

In addition to the use of children's images in communicating with a direct and clearly defined audience, especially via messenger apps, photos are also sometimes shared with a more dispersed environment in the form of loose contacts.[17]

[17] Cf. Schmidt: Das neue Netz.

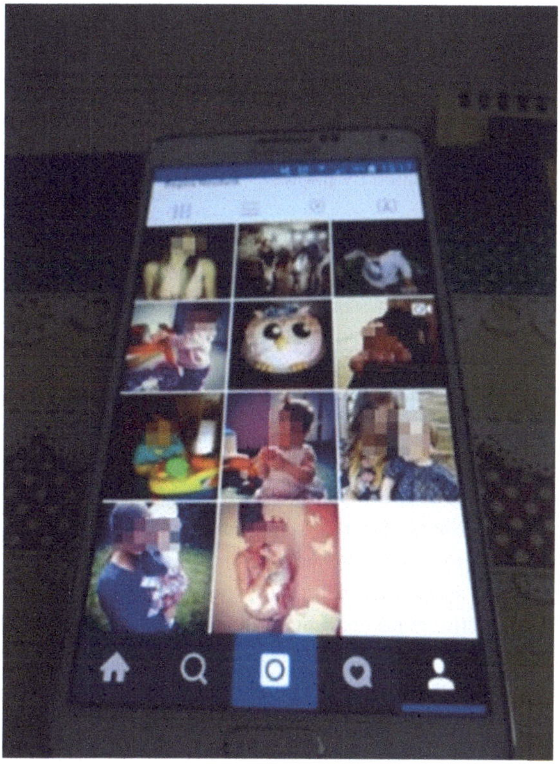

Fig. 3 Images on parental social media profiles

This happens via the parents' social media channels (see Fig. 3). Depending on the virtual presence and the respective preferences of the parents, children's and family photos are shared here with a significantly larger and thus less controllable audience. As a result, this form of using children's images is the most heavily criticized. Critics point out that children's privacy rights are affected here. Nevertheless, the interviews show that parents do not take the decision to share photos of their children lightly. There are sometimes intense negotiations, both between parents and within families and circles of friends, about whether and under what conditions photos of children can and should be shared and in what environments. In order to meet the various demands and attitudes, parents display a great deal of creativity (see Sect. 4.2.3). Posting a photo of a child does not necessarily mean that the child is completely and visibly depicted. Children are often only shown in sections, from behind or from a far distance, in order to protect their personal rights. Overall, a rather restrictive attitude was revealed with regard to sharing photos on public platforms and profiles. Thus, mainly only selected individual images were posted online. The focus is usually on special moments and events. For example, the birth of a child, or a greeting from a vacation or a special moment, is often communicated by photo.

4.1.4 Analog 'Museums'

Overall, photography has meanwhile become a largely digitized practice. Pictures are mostly taken with cell phones or digital cameras. They are then stored in digital archives or communicated via digital channels. But families still have a great need to own and show individual photos as objects. It is not uncommon for professional photographers to be hired for this purpose. Thus, in addition to classic wedding photography and family portraits, photo sessions for pregnant moms and newborns have now successfully established themselves in the canon of professional photography. The involvement of a professional photographer is associated with the desire for special images that stand out from the mass of daily snapshots. Accordingly, these pictures are deliberately and purposefully staged in a private environment like one's own home. Equally prominently presented are selected self-made pictures of the children, which are perceived as very well done. Such photo displays, some of which have the appearance of a museum, are primarily used to remind oneself of positive moments in family life, as well as to represent the family to guests (Fig. 4).

Fig. 4 Gallery of selected family and children's photos

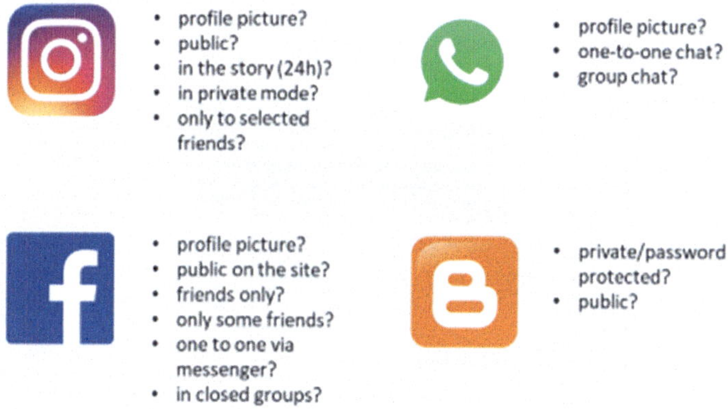

Fig. 5 Platforms and possible options

4.2 Sharenting as a Communicative and Multifaceted Practice

4.2.1 Distinction of Platforms

With regard to the sharing of children's photos via digital platforms, there are many complex and differentiated options for action. Accordingly, there are many considerations to address and decisions to be made on the part of parents (cf. Fig. 5). Exemplary questions include: Is it a tendentially public platform, such as Instagram or a messenger app like WhatsApp? Is the photo used as a public profile picture or shared with a small number of acquaintances in a private group? Is the profile, if in private mode, viewable only to direct contacts, or is it publicly visible? Each platform offers a range of different visibility, sharing, and privacy options.

Depending on the chosen platform, available settings, and number of contacts, parents can gauge if and what kind of photos and information they share:

> "On Facebook, everyone is just kind of present, and you also accept a lot more friend requests, and on Instagram [in private mode, author's note] it's just more limited. I have 20, you [interviewed mother, author's note] maybe have 40 contacts. That's a bit of a smaller circle, and you wouldn't want to follow everyone or allow everyone to follow you. And because of that, of course, there's a bit more, yes, I can share a bit more there." Sven

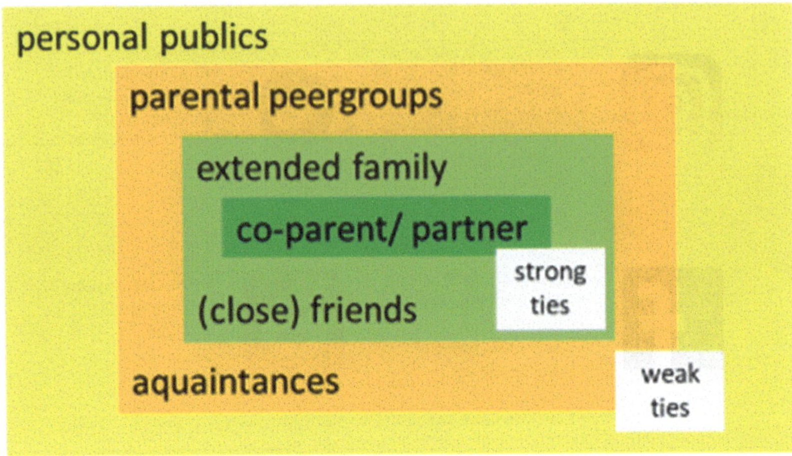

Fig. 6 Distinction of strong ties and weak ties

Accordingly, it is important to always consider the context of action, i.e. the platform chosen and the settings selected, in relation to shared children's photos and the intentions and possible risks associated with them. It makes a big difference whether one uses a photo as a public profile picture or shares it with 20 contacts on a private profile. Even the chosen platform alone is not telling in terms of an assessment of the context of action. For example, a profile picture on WhatsApp is visible to anyone who knows the corresponding phone number and has an account there themselves. This can be a considerable number of potential contacts. In contrast, a photo on a private Instagram profile may be visible to only 10 people.

4.2.2 Distinction of Audiences

In addition to the differentiation of platforms and the options available on them, parents surveyed strongly considered an image's potential target audience. Depending on the assessment of the strength of the relationship, different photos are shared. Following Granovetter,[18] close contacts, such as life partners, family, and friends (so-called "strong ties"), can be distinguished from more distant acquaintances and online contacts (so-called "weak ties") (see Fig. 6).

[18] Granovetter: The Strength of Weak Ties, American Journal of Sociology, 78, 1973, pp. 1360–1380.

Closer contacts are given more extensive insights and access to more images in direct exchanges via messenger apps or in private groups. In contrast, content is only shared sporadically and more restrictively with more distant contacts and within personal public spheres.[19]

4.2.3 Distinction of Contents and Modes of Presentation

Furthermore, it should be noted that images differ in terms of how depicted children are portrayed. With regard to showing and simultaneously not showing children in pictures, a number of typical handling strategies can be observed.[20] Frequently observed are pictures of masked or disguised children, as well as of children who are only shown from behind, from a great distance, or only in sections. If the child's face can be seen from the front, the face may be made unrecognizable by adding emojis or drawing over it (see Fig. 7).

Overall, parents show a great deal of creativity when dealing with children's photos in online environments. Their own need for exchange with their social environment is balanced against children's personal rights, their right to their own image, and their right to privacy. Parents try to meet these different needs by adapting their photographic practices. Accordingly, the image of a child and sharenting—as a parental practice—must be viewed in a differentiated way. What is shown, or rather not shown, in the process? The formal presence of a child in an image on an online platform does not necessarily say anything about the degree of intimacy or about parent's problematic image practices.

5 Conclusion

This paper shows that sharenting is not a phenomenon that can be generalized. Rather, it is dependent upon platforms and channels, differentiated by audiences, and aesthetically diverse. Family pictures and photos of children in online contexts have a variety of communicative functions. They serve as a means of participation in parental relationships, bridge distances between and integrate extended nuclear family members as well as close friends, and offer a visual reference point and object of negotiation in the context of parental peer relationships. In

[19] See Schmidt: Das neue Netz.

[20] For a typology of anti-sharenting, see Autenrieth: Family photography in a networked age, in: Mascheroni/Ponte/Jorge (eds.): Digital Parenting, pp. 219–231.

Fig. 7 Creative modes of presentation

this context, the presented findings reveal that parents are not indifferent or dismissive of their children's privacy rights, even when they share photos of them on social media platforms.

Parents are faced with a multitude of possible actions and thus decisions. Accordingly, when considering sharenting as a medical practice, specific attitudes and presentation contexts must be considered in addition to the platform. Furthermore, parents clearly differentiate between varying audiences and recipient groups of the images. Likewise, regarding the specific ways in which the photos are presented and edited, both a great creative potential and a need to protect the personal rights of children are revealed. There is a clear differentiation between close contacts ("strong ties") and more distant acquaintances ("weak ties"), with a corresponding adaptation of the shared content in terms of quantity and presentation modes (see Fig. 8). While close contacts receive many images from different contexts, only very specifically selected photos are shared on more public platforms.

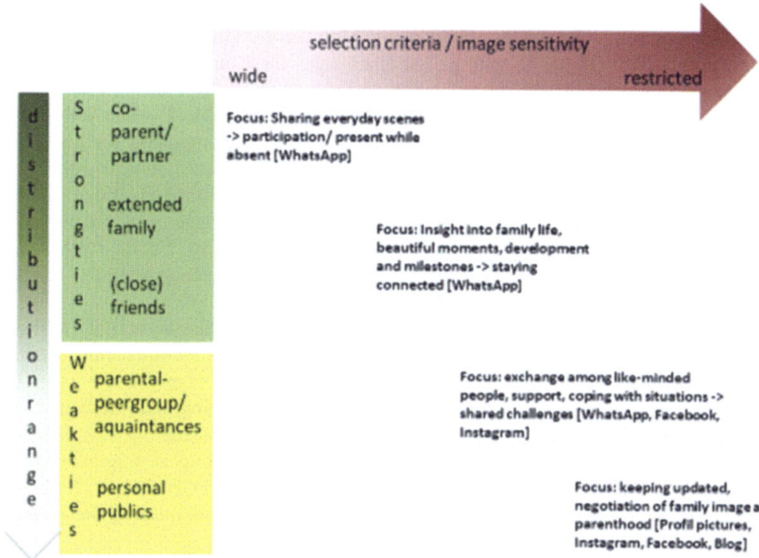

Fig. 8 Framework—Sharenting as a communicative practice

Accordingly, sharing children's photos in networked online environments should not be constructed as fundamentally irresponsible; as we have seen in the course of our interviews parents who share pictures of their children predominantly do so under weighing of potential risks. This article shows how multifaceted the phenomenon of sharenting is and how important it is to look at the particular example together with its specific contexts of action.

References

Ammari, Tawfig/Kumar, Priya/Lampe, Cliff/Schoenebeck, Sarita: Managing Children's Online Identities: How Parents Decide What to Disclose About Their Children Online, in: Proceedings of the 33rd Annual ACM Conference on Human Factors in Computing Systems, 2015, pp. 1895–1904.

Autenrieth, Ulla: Die Visualisierung von Kindheit und Familie im Social Web als Forschungsfeld einer mediatisierten Gesellschaft, in: Hoffman, Dagmar/Krotz, Friedrich/Reissmann, Wolfgang (eds.): Mediatisierung und Mediensozialisation: Prozesse—Räume—Praktiken, Wiesbaden 2017, pp. 137–151.

Autenrieth, Ulla: Family photography in a networked age. Anti-sharenting as a reaction to risk assessment and behaviour adaption, in: Mascheroni, Giovanna/Ponte, Christina/ Jorge, Ana (eds.): Digital Parenting. The Challenges for Families in the Digital Age, Göteborg 2018, pp. 219–231.

Autenrieth, Ulla: (Vor-)Bilder: Von Gisele Bündchen zur 'Average Mom'—Die Selbstdisziplinierungsspirale um den 'After-Baby-Body' unter den Bedingungen bildzentrierter Kommunikation in vernetzten Umgebungen, in: Grittmann, Elke/ Lobinger, Katharina/ Neverla, Irene/Pater, Monika (eds.): Körperbilder—Körperpraktiken. Visualisierung und Vergeschlechtlichung von Körpern in Medienkulturen, Cologne 2018, pp. 51–75.

Autenrieth, Ulla/Bizarri, Sarah/Lützel, Nadja: Kinderbilder im Social Web. Eine empirische Studie zur internetbasierten Bildpräsenz und Bildnutzung von unter 12-Jährigen, Baden-Baden 2017.

Bizarri, Sarah: Vergemeinschaftung und Mutterschaft im Zeitalter des vernetzten Individuums. Zum Stellenwert digital gestützter sozialer Vernetzung im Familienalltag, Studies in Communication Sciences, 16(2), 2016, pp. 163–173.

Blum-Ross, Alicia/Livingstone, Sonia: "Sharenting," parent blogging, and the boundaries of the digital self, Popular Communication, 15(2), 2017, pp. 110–125.

Brosch, Anna: When the child is born into the Internet: Sharenting as a growing trend among parents on Facebook, The New Educational Review, 43(1), 2016, pp. 225–235.

Chalklen, Charlotte/Anderson, Heather: Mothering on Facebook: Exploring the privacy/ openness paradox, Social Media + Society, 3(2), 2017, pp. 1–10.

Choi, Grace Yiseul/Lewallen, Jennifer: "Say Instagram, kids!": Examining sharenting and children's digital representations on Instagram, Howard Journal of Communications, 29(2), 2017, pp. 144–164.

Cyber Definitions: Sharenting, https://www.cyberdefinitions.com/definitions/SHARENTING.html; last accessed November 30, 2021.

Granovetter, Mark: The Strength of Weak Ties, American Journal of Sociology, 78, 1973, pp. 1360–1380.

Harding, Lindsey: Motherhood Reimag(in)ed: A study of domestic photography in the digital age, Photographies, 9(1), 2016, pp. 109–125.

Johnson, Sophia Alice: Maternal Devices, Social Media and the Self-Management of Pregnancy, Mothering and Child Health. Societies, 4, 2014, pp. 330–350.

Kneidinger, Bernadette: Social Media als digitales Fotoalbum multilokaler Familien. Die Bedeutung Visueller Kommunikation in intergenerationalen Beziehungen, in: Lobinger, Katharina/Geise, Stephanie (eds.): Visualisierung—Mediatisierung. Bildliche Kommunikation und bildliches Handeln in mediatisierten Gesellschaften, Cologne 2015, pp. 146–162.

Krempl, Stefan: Kinderhilfswerk: Fotos vom Nachwuchs nicht unüberlegt posten, 2017, https://www.heise.de/newsticker/meldung/Kinderhilfswerk-Fotos-vom-Nachwuchs-nicht-unueberlegt-posten-3886442.html; last accessed May 18, 2021.

Kumar, Priya/Schoenebeck, Sarita: The modern day baby book: Enacting good mothering and stewarding privacy on Facebook, in: Proceedings of the 18th ACM Conference on Computer Supported Cooperative Work and Social Computing (CSCW'15), 2015, pp. 1302–1312.

Lazard, Lisa: 'I'm not showing off, I'm just trying to have a connection': An analysis of mother pride and care in family photos on social media, presented at the Psychology of Women Section conference (BPS), Windsor/UK, July 12–14, 2017.

Lazard, Lisa/Capdevila, Rose/Dann, Charlotte/Locke, Abigail/Roper, Sandra: Sharenting. Pride, affect and the day-to-day politics of digital mothering, Social and Personality Psychology Compass, 13(4), 2019.

Rose, Gillian: Doing family photography: The domestic, the public and the politics of sentiment, London 2010.

Schmidt, Jan: Das neue Netz. Merkmale, Praktiken und Folgen des Web 2.0, Cologne 2011.

Woods, Lindsay: Too much information? Lindsay Woods on 'sharenting', Irish Examiner, 2018, https://www.irishexaminer.com/lifestyle/arid-30876986.html; last accessed November 30, 2021.

Zobel, Hanna: Kinderfotos auf Instagram: Was wäre, wenn Erwachsene wie Kinder dargestellt würden? Spiegel online, 2019, https://www.spiegel.de/netzwelt/web/kinderfotos-auf-instagram-toyah-diebel-zeigt-wie-eltern-ihre-kinder-im-netz-blossstellen-a-9d467c0c-0b43-42ce-b382-839fa9b65bce; last accessed May 18, 2021.

Prof. Dr. Ulla Autenrieth is a social scientist and head of research at the Institute for Multimedia Production of the University of Applied Sciences of the Grisons, Switzerland. Her research interests are visual communication, media literacy, social media and young audiences.

Banning Children's Image Online—a Portuguese Perspective

Paula Távora Vítor

1 Introduction

The questions raised by the reality of parents sharing photos and personal data of their children online, particularly in social networks, are now widespread. In today's globalized world, the issues posed by the use of social networks (its risks, dangers, but also advantages) are fundamentally the same. And, at least in the European context, there are common backgrounds in terms of legal culture[1] and of the protection of human rights afforded by international organizations and their instruments, the way parental responsibilities and children as subjects of their own rights are regarded—most notably that which has been provided by the United Nations Convention on the Rights of the Child (UNCRC) and the European Convention on Human Rights (ECHR).

However, the way each country and each legal system puts the same legal principles into practice may differ particularly in the field of family relations and personal rights. Therefore, even though the goal of addressing a specifically Portuguese perspective might seem difficult to achieve, an analysis of our courts' case law may provide us with a more accurate picture of the *law in action.*

[1] One that is not limited to continental European legal culture; cf. Wieacker: Foundations of European Legal Culture, The American Journal of Comparative Law, 38(1), 1990, pp. 6 and 20 ff.

P. T. Vítor (✉)
Faculty of Law, IJ, University of Coimbra, Coimbra, Portugal
e-mail: paulavit@fd.uc.pt

N. Dethloff et al. (eds.), *Families and New Media*, Juridicum – Schriften zum Medien-, Informations- und Datenrecht,
https://doi.org/10.1007/978-3-658-39664-0_6

2 The Public Display of the Child's Image—then and Now

2.1 *Then* – the Lisbon Court of Appeal Decision from October 19, 1977, or "My Face is on a Billboard!"

In order to fully understand our starting point, it is helpful to take a retrospective look at the first instances of Portuguese courts considering the public display of the child's image and how the best interest of the child was (or was not) addressed.

In 1977, the Lisbon Court of Appeal[2] had to decide a case that dealt with the use of a child's photo in a political propaganda billboard. The story began when, during a school festivity, which was attended by several people, a group of children was photographed in the school's courtyard. Six years later, the Portuguese Communist Party accessed those photos and used one in a propaganda billboard with the following motto: "The sun will shine on everyone". The mother of one child, as his legal representative, filed a petition, thereby suing the Portuguese Communist Party. She argued that since no authorization had been given to publicly display her child's image, his personality rights had been violated. According to her, this could result in severe consequences for her son—someone who was quite apart from the Communist Party's ideologies. She demanded the destruction of the billboards as well as compensation for moral damages. The Lisbon Court of Appeal ruled that such use of her child's photo in the billboard did not require any kind of consent, given the public context (a courtyard during school festivities) in which the photo had been taken. It considered that since the parent (the mother) had authorized the child's participation in the event, and since she knew there would be photographic coverage, no additional consent was needed. The decision's legal basis rested in Article 79, no. 2 of the Civil Code which, at that time (as it does today), dismissed the need for consent in several cases: (i) whenever justified by the notorious nature of the portrayed person, their activity, or the demands of police, justice, scientific, or cultural goals, (ii) as well as whenever the reproduction of the image is in the context of public locations, of facts of public interest or of facts that occur openly. Additionally, as far as the

[2] Decision of the Lisbon Court of Appeal from October 19, 1977 (proc. 0,012,348), Colectânea de Jurisprudência, 1977, pp. 1015 ff. and on www.dgsi.pt.

Court could tell, the child had been portrayed within a group of other children, and the photo was not recent. Therefore, it was difficult to recognize the identities of those portrayed. The Court found that no relevant moral damages should be considered, as, in their opinion, a 13-year-old child had neither "the dignity and the conscience of the facts that cause a moral damage" nor a political conscience, whereby his honor, reputation, and good name could not be affected.

At first glance, it is a surprising reasoning; however, we must bear in mind the socio-historical and legal context of this case.

The decision was rendered in October 1977, only three years after the Revolution of April of 1974, which had overthrown a dictatorship that had lasted for almost 50 years. In the previous year, the Constitution of 1976, a new constitution, had been approved. The Portuguese Constitution enshrines a catalog of fundamental rights and freedoms, including personality rights—among which the right to one's own likeness and image as well as the right to privacy[3]—and political freedoms.[4] In 1977, the Civil Code was also reformed and adapted to the new Constitution.[5] While it was approved in a month's time, many of the principles that had been included in the Constitution were already in force. Furthermore, the rules of the Civil Code that protect those rights—the right to one's own likeness and image and the right to privacy (Articles 79 and 80 of the Civil Code)—were not subject to any update and remain the ones in force today.

This framework reveals that legal grounds for protecting the child's right *not to have* his/her image used in such a public way (and associated with a political view) could already be found in the Portuguese legal system. However, by that time, the political discourse was at the center of social concerns. The guarantee of social political fundamental rights as the *freedom of expression* was a major issue and thus protecting these kinds of personal rights—and those of a child for that matter—did not seem as paramount.

Therefore, this verdict was (i) that a third party—an organization not connected to the child in any way—was authorized to use the child's image for its own political purposes; (ii) that such authorization was independent of explicit parental consent (much less of the child him/herself), a dismissal of consent which the Court grounded in an evaluation of the "public nature" of an event that

[3] Article 26 of the Portuguese Constitution; cf. Canotilho/Moreira: Constituição da República Portuguesa Anotada, pp. 467, 468; Miranda/Medeiros: Constituição Portuguesa Anotada, pp. 450 ff.

[4] Canotilho: Direito Constitucional, pp. 393, 394, 396.

[5] Decree-Law no. 496/77 from November 25.

could easily be contested; (iii) that the child, as a subject of his own rights, is to be more than ignored (the child is expressly diminished as a holder of rights that might be affected by the use of his/her own likeness); and that (iv) the role of the parent (a single widowed mother) in this instance was to act as a representative of the child in the procedure, exercising her duty to protect the right of the child (included in the then-named "paternal power"). She pled to the Courts (the state) for the protection of her child from an organization, but it was not granted.

2.2 *Now*—the Évora Court of Appeal Decision from June 25, 2015, or *"My Parents Keep Posting My Pictures on Instagram!"*

Since 1977 and the Lisbon Court of Appeal's decision, the Portuguese framework has undergone profound changes, both from a social and legal point of view.

At present, the technical possibilities to display a child's image (or anyone's image) are far more powerful and uncontrollable than a billboard. Indeed, the most recent surveys show that about half of the Portuguese population is currently using social networks in a fairly active way.[6] And since these channels are so easily available to every private citizen, they, and especially those inside another user's inner circle, have access to more and more sensitive information. In our case, the child's parents are the ones who are more likely to exhibit their image and share their personal data online.[7] Hence, "sharenting"—a combination of "sharing" and "parenting" that encompasses the ways through which parents distribute pictures, videos, or other information about their children online, par-

[6] Portugal has around 10 million (10,238,000) inhabitants, and recent surveys show that at least 5 million are currently using social media networks. *Facebook* is still the most widespread social media network (95% of those surveyed). *Whatsapp* and *Instagram* are also conquering a considerable share, and the popularity of Instagram is particularly relevant for our case, since its normal way of functioning implies sharing images. Additionally, it must also be mentioned that Portuguese users of social media networks are fairly active. 95.6% of Facebook users visit it at least once a week, and 56% post at least once a week, including, of course, personal content, photos of themselves, of their families (namely children), friends, and acquaintances; cf. Marktest: Os Portugueses e as Redes Sociais 2019.

[7] Shmueli/Blecher-Prigat: Privacy for Children, Columbia Human Rights Law Review, 42, 2011, pp. 792–793.

ticularly in social networks[8]—is one of the biggest present challenges when it comes to exposure of the child.

From a legal point of view, the judicial system, under the Constitution of 1976, particularly family law, has not ceased to evolve according to the developments of the theory of fundamental rights[9] and the challenges of new realities. As far as the rights of the child and the exposure of the child's image are concerned, two legal landmarks have since taken place: In 1990, the Portuguese state ratified the United Nations Convention on the Rights of the Child (UNCRC),[10] and in 2018, the General Data Protection Regulation (GDPR) entered into force in all European Union Member States. Moreover, the role of courts as gatekeepers of constitutional principles and fundamental rights, particularly those of vulnerable subjects, grew stronger.[11]

When addressing the issue of *children's images online* and *sharenting,* we find ourselves at the crossroads of how Portuguese law and courts understand several issues: (i) the *role of social networks,* particularly in the *context of family;* (ii) how this role connects with the *child's personality rights,* namely the right to privacy and the right to one's own likeness; (iii) the understanding of the *child as a subject of his/her own rights* (rather than an object of the parents' powers) and a *holder of a special interest* that is at the center of the legal discourse, which has implications both in the way we perceive the *capacity of the child to consent* regarding his/her own personality rights on the one hand, and the *exercise of*

[8] Cf. Blecher-Prigat: Children's Right to Privacy, in: Dwyer (ed.): The Oxford Handbook of Children and the Law, p. 373.

[9] For these developments in Portuguese legal literature, see, among others, de Andrade: Os direitos fundamentais na Constituição Portuguesa de 1976, in particular pp. 59 ff.; Novais: Direitos fundamentais nas relações entre particulares; Pinto: Direitos de personalidade e direitos fundamentais, in particular pp. 279 ff. and 299 ff.; Moniz: Os direitos fundamentais e a sua circunstância; Correia: Direitos fundamentais e relações jurídicas privadas, Revista de Legislação e Jurisprudência, Ano 146, no. 4001, Nov-Dec 2016, pp. 88–96; Ribeiro: Os direitos de personalidade como direitos fundamentais, in: Oliveira/Crorie (eds.): Pessoa, direito e direitos, 2014/2015, pp. 271–282; Neto: Direitos (fundamentais) de personalidade?, in: Oliveira/Crorie (eds.): Pessoa, direito e direitos, 2014/2015, pp. 295–313.

[10] Approved by the Parliament (Resolution no. 20/90) and ratified by the President (Decree no. 49/90 of 12/09).

[11] This trend can be observed, namely, by consulting the statistics of the Constitutional Court and the growing number of action filed each year, see Tribunal Constitucional Portugal: Estatisticas (from 1983 until 2019) and PORDATA: Tribunal Constitucional—processos entrados findos e pendentes (from 1993 until 2010).

parental responsibilities, on the other;[12] and finally, (iv) the *role of public entities* (namely courts) in controlling and ultimately limiting parental responsibilities.

The core of my analysis is the 2015 landmark decision by the Évora Court of Appeal,[13] and it focuses on the regulation of parents exercising responsibility over their child(ren). This is not the sole decision that concerns itself with the exposure of family life in social networks.[14] It is also neither the only one about the image of a child online[15] nor the only one in which issues raised by *sharenting* are addressed. Actually, both the Coimbra[16] and Lisbon[17] Courts of Appeal have rendered verdicts on two situations in which one of the parents identifies *sharenting* as a negative feature of the other's parental behavior in claims related to the exercise of parental responsibilities; furthermore, in 2017, the Coimbra Court of Appeal considered a case in which parents included "banning sharenting" as part of their parental responsibilities divorce agreement.[18] The decision

[12] Other decisions have dealt with the public use of the child's image in view of its effects in the development of the child's personality. The Guimarães Court of Appeal (decision from March 2, 2010, proc. 453/08.9TBPTL.G1, on www.dgsi.pt) decided the "little baker girl" case, which dealt with the use of the child's image in advertising and the need for consent. This case discusses the limits of subjective enjoyment of the child and the objective implications of the lack of consent provided by the parents in order to determine the civil liability of the corporation that used the image.

[13] Évora Court of Appeal, decision from June 25, 2015 (proc. no. 789/13.7TMSTB-B.E1), on www.dgsi.pt.

[14] In 2014, the Coimbra Court of Appeal (decision from January 14, 2014, proc. no. 194/11.0T6AVR.C1, on www.dgsi.pt) discussed a high-profile case in which the grandparents thoroughly expressed their claim to have contact with the child, namely on social media networks.

[15] In 2014, in a case regarding the attribution of the custody of the child to her grandparents, the Lisbon Court of Appeal considered their highly permissive education as to the use of social media networks by the adolescent girl and the dangers associated as one of the problems raised (decision from April 29, 2014, proc. 2454/13.6TBVFX.L1-1, on www.dgsi.pt).

[16] In 2017, in a parental responsibilities claim, one of the issues raised against the defendant (the mother) was that she had posted pictures of her child wearing women's underwear on social media networks (Coimbra Court of Appeal, decision from June 6, 2017, proc. no. 34/16.3T8FIG-A.C1, on www.dgsi.pt).

[17] In a parental responsibilities claim, one of the issues raised against the defendant (the mother) was the fact that she had posted pictures of her child bathing (Lisbon Court of Appeal, decision from September 20, 2018, proc. 835/17.5T8SXL-2, on www.dgsi.pt).

[18] The decision of the Coimbra Court of Appeal from April 4, 2017 (proc. no. 94/16.7T8PNH-A.C1), on www.dgsi.pt, mentions a parental agreement in which the parents commit not to post photos of the child's face on social media networks.

of the Évora Court of Appeal from June 25, 2015,[19] however, is the one that *directly* addresses *sharenting,* a decision in which the Court decides and imposes a regime—a ban—on the parents.

This decision stemmed from the appeal of a verdict of the first instance Court of Setúbal on the provisional regulation of the exercise of parental responsibilities in a case in which a child's parents could not reach an agreement. Social reports evaluating the family environment concluded that there was a high level of conflict between the parents that had impacted the child's life, but no other details of their lives were mentioned in the decision. The Setúbal Court determined a standard regime of exercise of parental responsibilities[20] (regarding residence, duties to inform, contact, and child support obligations), except for the last order, which addresses *sharenting* directly in the following terms: "parents shall refrain from publishing photos or personal data that render their child identifiable on social network websites".

Subsequently, the mother (plaintiff) decided to appeal to the Évora Court of Appeal (second instance court). She claimed that the issue of misusing the child's photos or personal data on social network platforms had never been raised and that the decision had not been grounded on any evidence. The public prosecutor,[21] however, argued in favor of the first instance court's decision, and the Évora Court of Appeal ultimately decided to reject the appeal, thereby confirming the previous decision.

The Court held that there was no need for a specific factual ground for such a court order, since it is a duty of the parents—one as natural as the duties to take care of the health of, support, and educate the child—to protect the rights of the child, namely to their own image or likeness and to privacy (Art. 79 and 80 of the Civil Code). Additionally, it was expressly highlighted that children are not commodities or objects that belong to parents, but rather subjects of their own rights, and that parents must not only protect their children but also promote and respect

[19] Évora Court of Appeal, decision from June 25, 2015 (proc. no. 789/13.7TMSTB-B.E1), on www.dgsi.pt.

[20] The exercise of parental responsibilities regarding matters of particular relevance belongs to both parents; the child resides with one parent and the other has contact rights. The latter had to pay maintenance and had the right to be informed about relevant events in the child's life.

[21] The statute of the public prosecutor's office identifies one of the functions to be the representative of minors ("incompetents") (Art. 4, no. 1, al. b) of Law no. 68/2019, from August 27) and to assume the defense and the promotion of the rights and interests of children and adolescents (Art. 4, no. 1, i) Law no. 68/2019, August 27).

their rights. The Court concluded by declaring that this is the way that parental responsibilities must be understood—as rights and duties that must fulfill the *best interest of the child* and foster the child's harmonious development. But it likewise stressed that not only *parents* must act towards this objective. The Court of Évora identifies the institutions and the *state* as *partners* in this mission.

The central argument reinforcing the measure is the fact that exposing the child on social networks poses *serious risks* to the *child's safety,* namely risks of sexual exploitation and sexual violence, even though it can be argued that such dangers are sometimes overestimated.[22] In order to justify such concerns, this reasoning summons an *array* of international instruments, such as the United Nations Convention on the Rights of the Child (UNCRC),[23] the International Labour Organization's Worst Forms of Child Labour Convention,[24] several Council of Europe instruments, the European Convention on Human Rights,[25] the European Social Charter,[26] the Lanzarote Convention on the Protection of Children against Sexual Exploitation and Sexual Abuse,[27] and the European Parliament and Council's Directive 2011/93/EU from December 13, 2011, on Combating the Sexual Abuse and Sexual Exploitation of Children and Child Pornography.

All these documents are mentioned in order to justify the existence of a "serious and real danger" that stems from publishing children's photos and personal data on social networks. The Évora Court of Appeal adopts three *premises* to ground a *presumption* of "real danger": (i) that such publication may seriously and permanently expose the *privacy* and the *safety* of children, (ii) that the

[22] For instance, there is evidence "that children value their privacy and engage in protective strategies but the disclosure forms part of a trade-off that teens engage in", Livingstone/Stoilova/Nandagirim: Children's data and privacy online, p. 22; additionally, it may be mentioned that there are already "excellent online safety and privacy-enhancing tools (…) for parents and teens to better safeguard their online privacy", Thierer: Kids, Privacy, Free Speech & The Internet, p. 10, and that, as the European Parliament resolution from November 20, 2012, on protecting children in the digital world (2012/2068(INI)) stresses, there is the "need for an educational alliance among families, school, civil society and interested parties, including those involved in media and audiovisual services, in order to guarantee a balanced and proactive dynamic between the digital world and minors".

[23] Article 34 of the UNCRC.

[24] Article 3, B) of the Worst Forms of Child Labour Convention.

[25] Article 5 of the European Convention on Human Rights.

[26] Article 17 of the European Social Charter.

[27] Article 30 of the Directive 2011/93/EU.

exponential growth of social networks allows *predators* to gather information and target children as victims of their crimes, and (iii) that young people may be *lured into situations of sexual exploitation* due to their lack of experience.

Therefore, the measure and the court order were justified primarily by the need to protect the *safety* of the child, which is to prevail over the *freedom of expression* and the *prohibition of state interference in the private life of citizens*, in this case the mother.

Two issues are raised in the appeal (lack of legal and factual grounds for the decision), but our analysis must go further:

This decision was made in the context of regulating the exercise of parental responsibilities—a complex of both powers and duties that parents will exercise on behalf of their minor child, and according to their best interest, in order not only to protect them, but also to promote their autonomy. Indeed, Portuguese law recognizes the *evolving nature of the child's capacity* and supports that, according to the child's maturity, their opinion should be taken into account in family matters and their autonomy must be recognized in the organization of their own lives (Article 1887 of the Civil Code).[28] Parents are therefore responsible for protecting the child's safety and *sharenting* may put it at stake. Parents exercising their *freedom of expression* by posting the child's data certainly create a *risk* in the child's sphere. The Court assumed that the regulation of these matters was a similar decision to those concerning education or support obligations, and this way, it ensures that parental responsibilities are properly exercised in accordance with the best interest of the child and not that of the parents.

In order to fully understand this decision, it is necessary to mention that the current regime of the exercise of parental responsibilities, which, inspired by the Principles of European Family Law Regarding Parental Responsibilities by the Commission of European Family Law (CEFL),[29] was extensively reformed in 2008,[30] revolves around two concepts. When parents do not lead a common life[31]—be it marriage or a *de facto* union—the rules on the exercise of parental

---

[28] This guiding principle of the UNCRC has had legal recognition in Portuguese law even before the ratification of this Convention in 1990. It has been introduced by the Reform of the Civil Code of 1977 (Decree-law no. 496/77 from November 25).

[29] CEFL: Principles of European Family Law Regarding Parental Responsibilities.

[30] Law no. 61/2008 from October 31.

[31] See Article 1906 of the Civil Code. This includes divorced couples, separated couples, couples whose marriage has been annulled or declared void, and those who never led a common life.

responsibilities draw a distinction between *matters of particular relevance,* in which the rule is the joint exercise of parental responsibilities, and *daily life decisions,* which are decided by the parent whom the child is with at the moment (be it the resident or non-resident parent).

When it comes to *sharenting,* the fact that it may be part of a *routine* could lead us to classify it as a daily life decision. However, it may have severe implications in terms of the child's (fundamental) personality rights—one of the criteria that may be used to identify "matters of particular relevance".[32]

Thus, the Court has decided to create a "precautionary rule" (risk-based),[33] an obligation to refrain from sharing such content (a decision beyond the possibility of the parents to agree otherwise).

It is interesting to note that the Évora Court has created a *blind rule:* There is consideration of neither *levels of exposure* nor the *kind of social networks* that are at stake.[34] It is also important to realize that *safety issues* were the basis of the decision—as far as I know, even in the absence of a factual red flag regarding this matter. While it is true that the child was identified as a *subject of his/her own rights,*[35] the problem—*per se* relevant—of *exposing the child's image* was not highlighted autonomously.[36] The option of the Court has been to rely on a

[32] In Principle 3:12(2) of the CEFL's Principles of European Family Law Regarding Parental Responsibilities, important decisions are identified as those that concern "matters such as education, medical treatment, the child's residence, or the administration of his or her property" and that those decisions "should be taken jointly". Guilherme de Oliveira admits that it may be discussed what a "matter of particular relevance" is and considers that changing residence to a different country, an invasive surgical procedure, or religious education are good examples, de Oliveira: Manual de Direito da Família, p. 343. This means that not every act within the aforementioned categories is a "matter of particular relevance" and that a criterion should be identified. As far as we understand it, when a decision may have severe implications in terms of the personality (fundamental) rights of the child, it should be considered a "matter of particular relevance".

[33] About the general procedural means to protect personality rights and requirements, Marques: Alguns aspectos processuais da tutela da personalidade humana no novo Código de Processo Civil de 2013.

[34] For instance, does it include social media networks such as WhatsApp (whose nature is debatable) in very restrictive groups such as family groups?

[35] For the child as a subject of his or her own rights in Portuguese law, see Martins: Responsabilidades parentais no séc. XXI, Lex Familiae—Revista Portuguesa de Direito da Família, Ano 5, no. 10, 2008, pp. 30 ff.

[36] And this could eventually lead to damages to the child and even be a ground to claim compensation. Civil liability in the relations between parents and children as a way to protect the child's personality rights is admitted by legal literature. See Pinheiro: A tutela da

precautionary principle regarding the protection of the child's data and to impose a *ban*, instead of a tailored measure,[37] probably more suited to meet the requirements of *proportionality* that the restriction of rights encompasses.[38,39]

The reference to the child as a *subject of its own rights* has consequences that should be considered and that assume a different shape depending on the age of the child.

The analysis of this case according to the age of the child presents an unexpected twist. Indeed, the version that was published on the official website refers to a child born in 2003, making the girl twelve -years-old at the time of the decision. The same happened with the decision of the Court of Setúbal (first instance). However, this could be a typing error, since in the analysis of the first instance court, documents suggest that the child was born in 2013—whereby the child would be a two-year-old girl who still attends nursery school.[40]

In the case of a two-year-old child, the presence of a toddler's image in social networks is dependent on the adults' (the parents') actions. If we were dealing

---

personalidade da criança, Scientia Juridica, Tomo LXIV, no. 338, Maio-Agosto 2015, p. 254.

[37] One must bear in mind the European Parliament resolution from November 20, 2012, on protecting children in the digital world (2012/2068(INI)), that stresses that, "while acknowledging the many dangers that minors face in the digital world, we should also continue to embrace the many opportunities that the digital world brings in growing a knowledge-based society".

[38] Indeed, some consider that along with dangers, there are many benefits to sharenting, namely creating a "positive social media presence to help counteract some of the negative behaviors they might themselves engage in as teenagers", or offering children "positive networks by inviting supportive family members and friends into their daily lives", Steinberg: Sharenting, Emory Law Journal, 66, 2017, p. 855. In the Portuguese context, Rossana Cruz argues that, in abstract, there are no benefits or an interest of the child in having his or her image exhibited online, Cruz: A divulgação da imagem do menor, pp. 289, 290.

[39] Mafalda Miranda Barbosa, when analyzing the decision of the Évora Court of Appeal, concludes that the *abstract and prospective perspective* adopted has led to an excessive solution, Barbosa: Podem os pais publicar fotografias dos filhos menores nas redes sociais?, Ab Instantia, Ano III, no. 5, 2015, p. 339.

[40] Indeed, the social security report from December 31, 2014 presented to court identifies the date of birth of the child as March 29, 2013. The same happens in the written appeal statement of the father's attorney (REFª: 15,873,326). And the written appeal statement of the mother's attorney (REFª: 15,870,161) mentions a "baby" and expenses with nursery and kindergarten.

with a pre-teen, then it must be borne in mind that social networks are an essential part of their socialization process.[41] And the decision is solely focused on *sharenting*. It addresses neither the duties regarding the control of the photos uploaded by the child, for instance, nor her capacity to freely limit the right to her own's likeness by participating herself in social networks or authorizing her parents to do so.[42] In this case, it should be mentioned that, under Portuguese law, even though there is not a system of levels in terms of capacity[43] and a person only reaches majority at 18, the theory of evolving autonomy is expressed by the law (Article 1878 of the Civil Code)[44], which is relevant for this purpose.

Finally, there is another option that should be highlighted: the fact that the Court decided to set aside the *prohibition of state interference* in the private life of citizens. The interference is assumed *motu proprio,* since the Court decided on a question that had not been specifically raised by any of the parents.

This initiative is coherent with the present growing trend of public entities intervening in order to protect the child, and it is allowed on a procedural level since the regulation of parental responsibilities is a non-contentious proceeding, which allows the judge to decide beyond the scope of the action. It must also be stressed that the public prosecutor's office, as the ultimate representative of the child, plays a pivotal role in this context, promoting this regime, in the absence of agreement between the parents.

[41] Thierer: Kids, Privacy, Free Speech & The Internet, p.7 and The Lancet Child & Adolescent Health: Growing up in a digital world, p. 79.

[42] Thus, it should be admitted the capacity to consent of a twelve-year-old girl, ibid., p. 335.

[43] As, for example, the Brazilian system. See articles 3, 4 and 5 of the Brazilian Civil Code. A system of levels has been proposed in Portuguese legal literature by Rosa Martins, cf. Martins: Menoridade, pp. 134 ff.

[44] Additionally, there are several cases of "anticipation of majority". For instance, 16-year-old children may decide their religion (Article 1886 of the Civil Code) and 12-year-old children have to consent to their adoption (Article 1981 (1) a) of the Civil Code), cf. de Oliveira: O acesso dos menores a cuidados de saúde, in: de Oliveira (ed.): Temas de Direito da Medicina, pp. 276 ff. In terms of the relevance that is granted to the right of the child to freely express the views in all matters affecting her or him, it is particularly relevant to stress that, regardless of age, the child has the right to be heard in any judicial and administrative proceedings (Article 5 of Law no. 141/2015, September 8). Finally, it should be mentioned that the rules of execution of the GDPR in Portugal have established age 13 as the minimum age for consent for the processing of personal data (Article 16 of Law no. 58/2019, from August 8).

2.3 *Now*—the *Super Nanny* Case, or "My Tantrum is on TV!"

More recently, Portuguese courts have been confronted with a very public case that can also provide us with precious insights into the Portuguese courts' approach to the use of the child's image, even though the challenges raised by social media are not at the case's core. The *Super Nanny* Case has been the object of several decisions, including ones of the Lisbon Court of Appeal,[45] the Portuguese Supreme Court,[46] and the Portuguese Constitutional Court.[47]

In this case, the public prosecutor's office intervened as representative of several children featured in the reality show *Super Nanny,* a television show about parents struggling with their children's behavior who receive child-rearing instructions from a professional nanny. The public prosecutor requested that broadcasting the show be prohibited—not only on television, but also on *social networks* and streaming services—so as to guarantee that the show's content would not be publicly available, since it violated the *personality rights* of the children. The television network that owned the show's rights argued, in turn, that it acted under a "participation agreement", signed by the children's parents, which allowed their children's image to be broadcast and thus also limited the latter's privacy.

Among the several issues raised by this case—some very relevant that concern the demands to participate in public shows and copyright—it is possible to understand the current position of Portuguese courts regarding the *image of the children*, the *role of parents,* and the *role of public institutions* as far as their protection is concerned.

This case deals with the use of these children's images *not* by the *parents*, but by a *third party,* a television network, authorized by the parents. It was claimed that the right to one's own likeness may be lawfully limited when there is *consent*—consent that had been provided by the parents (Article 79, no. 1 of the Civil Code) and that also covered the right to privacy (Article 80 of the Civil Code).

---

[45] Lisbon Court of Appeal, decision from December 11, 2018 (proc. no. 336/18.4T8OER.L1-6), on www.dgsi.pt.

[46] Supreme Court, decision from May 30, 2019 (proc. no. 336/18.4T8OER.L1.S1), on www.dgsi.pt.

[47] Constitutional Court, decision no. 262/2020 (proc. no. 958/2019), on http://www.european-rights.eu/public/sentenze/PORTOGALLO-Tribunal_constitucional_13.05.2020_262.2020_.pdf.

The Lisbon Court of Appeal, however, opposed such claims by clearly adopting the *theory of the evolving capacity of the child,* expressly stating that as far as the limitation of the *right to one's own likeness* is concerned, whenever children have sufficient competencies and maturity so as to evaluate the consequences of their consent, they should decide rather than being represented by their parents.[48] It has thus embraced a case-by-case approach, choosing not to specify any age limits, in conformity with the legal standards established in Article 1887 of the Civil Code, even if this solution still leaves an open question: Is parental consent still needed when the limitation of rights is severe as to contend with the education they provide?

The following step, however, is not traditionally embedded in Portuguese family law. According to the Lisbon Court of Appeal, whenever the child does not exhibit sufficient competencies and maturity so as to evaluate the consequences of consent, the parents should not decide autonomously. Instead, it is proposed that they obtain *approval* from the public prosecutor's office for their *project of consent* (with the possibility of appealing to the Court).[49] The role of the public prosecutor's office is stressed throughout the decision: It is stated that in the cases in which there is a conflict between the best interest of the child—risks to the free development of the child's personality and risks of being bullied have been identified—and the interests of the parents, the public prosecutor's office assumes the role of the child's representative (Article 1881, no. 2, of the Civil Code and Article 23 of the Civil Procedure Code).

The Portuguese Supreme Court has confirmed the Lisbon Court of Appeal's decision, namely to ban the show's broadcasting without prior authorization by the Commissions of Protection of Children and Adolescents in Danger[50], as required by the law.[51] Nonetheless, it is interesting to point out the differences in

[48] de Carvalho: Teoria Geral do Direito Civil, pp. 205 ff.; de Sousa: O Direito Geral de Personalidade, p. 412, footnote 1040; Trabuco: Dos contratos relativos ao direito à imagem, O Direito, Ano 133, Abril-Junho 2001, p. 435.

[49] This position is supported by legal literature. Pinto: A Limitação Voluntária do Direito à Reserva sobre a Intimidade da Vida Privada, in: de Figueiredo Dias et al. (eds.): Estudos em Homenagem a Cunha Rodrigues, Vol. II, p. 545.

[50] These commissions are non-judiciary official institutions that promote the rights of the Child and Adolescent and prevent or terminate situations that may endanger their security, health, upbringing, education and full development (Article 12, no. 1 of Law no. 147/99, from September 1).

[51] Law no. 105/2009, from September 14.

the path chosen. Central to the Portuguese Supreme Court's argument has been the value of *human dignity*.[52] It has stressed that human dignity is put at stake when people—children, in particular—are objectified and used as an instrument towards an end. It concludes with the same idea of irrelevance of the consent given in this context to allow for restrictions to personality rights, for being contrary to the *ordre public*. The Portuguese Supreme Court answered the question of the Lisbon Court of Appeal regarding the capacity of the child to consent. Indeed, it states that, even when the child is naturally competent to consent, parents must still intervene, by exercising their parental responsibilities, when the decision interferes with the former's education.

Finally, the decision of the Portuguese Constitutional Court ascertained the constitutional conformity of the legal demand of authorization provided by the Commissions of Protection of Children and Adolescents in Danger for children to participate in television shows.[53] It does not focus directly on the right to the child's own likeness—the decision to protect the child is rather focused on the perspective of child labor and its exceptions[54]—but sets a position regarding the right of parents to educate their children (Article 36, no. 5 of the Portuguese Constitution). The Portuguese Constitutional Court admits that the interests of parents are not always the best interest of the child, and that the (proportional[55])

---

[52] One of the main references of the Portuguese Supreme Court has been the *Super Nanny* case in Germany, which was decided by the Verwaltungsgericht (VG; Administrative Court) of Hannover, decision from July 8, 2014 (proc. no. 7 A 4679/12), on http://www.rechtsprechung.niedersachsen.juris.de/jportal/portal/page/bsndprod.psml?doc.id=MWRE140002695&st=null&doctyp=juris-r&showdoccase=1&paramfromHL=true#focuspoint.

In the past, Portuguese legal literature analyzed the intersection between "reality shows" and fundamental freedoms and the value of "human dignity". Gomes Canotilho and Jónatas Machado have concluded that such shows have to respect "human dignity" and "personality rights", as well as protect "childhood and youth", Canotilho/Machado: "Reality Shows" e Liberdade de Programação, p. 104.

[53] Law no. 105/2009, from September 14.

[54] Particularly relevant is the analysis of the supposed violation of the principle of separation of functions, which confronts the limits of the intervention of the Commissions of Protection of Children and Adolescents in Danger when deciding in matters of fundamental rights and the role of the courts. Portuguese Constitutional Court, decision no. 262/2020 (proc. no. 958/2019), 12–17.

[55] This criterion is stressed by Rui Medeiros and expressly mentioned by the Portuguese Constitutional Court, cf. Medeiros: Anotação ao artigo 69.º, in: Miranda/Medeiros (eds.): Constituição Portuguesa Anotada, p. 998.

intervention of public entities is allowed whenever there is a "serious risk"[56] that parents do not fulfill this best interest.[57]

3 Final Remarks

The analysis of these three important cases—in particular the Évora Court of Appeal's 2015 case—may serve as indicators that allow us to start sketching a Portuguese perspective on the public display of the child's image, especially on social media, that is embedded in the inherent tension between what is *private* and what is *public* in several senses.

First and foremost, the central position of *children* and their *personality rights* (including the right to one's own likeness) and the need to *protect* them is a clear feature of the present scenario. The traditional *protectors* of children's rights are still the *parents*, who, when exercising parental responsibilities must determine the *best interest of the child* and act accordingly. However, sometimes new realities—including new channels of expression provided by *social media networks*—create challenges to parents, who may not be able to correctly deal with them on their own.

These recent cases point towards a more *active intervention* by *public entities* (courts and public prosecutors offices) when the protection of children (and the promotion of their autonomy) is at stake.

This intervention by *public entities* in the protection of children's rights is not new. In cases of *conflict of interest,* there has traditionally been a compression of the parents' rights and powers and the child's representation has been assumed by a public prosecutor's office.[58] In case of *danger* to the child, Commissions of Protection of Children and Adolescents in Danger could act with the agreement of the parents, and ultimately the court would intervene.[59] Nevertheless, the deci-

[56] Portuguese Constitutional Court, decision no. 262/2020 (proc. no. 958/2019), 21.

[57] The Portuguese Constitutional Court argues there is a "public interest" to intervene because of the "danger" associated to the participation in a television show—a "danger" that, according to the Court, is pointed out by the International Labour Organization Convention no. 138 (Minimum Age Convention, 1973) and by the Council Directive 94/33/EC from June 22, 1994, on the protection of young people at work, that demands the aforementioned authorization by a third party.

[58] Vide supra.

[59] Articles 9 and 11 of Law no. 147/99, from September 1.

sions we analyzed led us further. The case of the Évora Court of Appeal shows us that *public entities* (courts and also public prosecutors) can intervene *before* any actual conflict, before any actual *danger*. We are facing an upsurge of *precautionary interventions* that interfere with *family life* based on the concept of *risk*. Underlying this approach may be the assumption that social media networks are much too dangerous instruments for (some) parents to deal with alone[60], and the idea that protecting the child *against* the parents perceives the family as a scenario of "conflict of interests" even before one actually emerges.

Fundamental rights—and (fundamental) personality rights included—were first conceived as a shield of individuals against the state.[61] At the present, it seems that the state is using this shield to protect individuals against other individuals[62] within one of their most private spheres—family—based on the recognition that these are especially *valuable* and especially *vulnerable* individuals. Hence, there is tension between *public* and *private*, and *protection* and *autonomy*, that must be addressed.

Hopefully, we will not forget that these concerns indeed stem from the idea that children *are subjects of their own rights* and that the use of social media networks is a central component of their social life, and of youth culture, all of which means we need also to ensure that they exercise their rights to *participation* in a safe, but also free way.

References

Andrade, José Carlos Vieira de: Os direitos fundamentais na Constituição Portuguesa de 1976, 6th ed., Coimbra 2019.

Barbosa, Ana Mafalda Castanheira Neves de Miranda: Podem os pais publicar fotografias dos filhos menores nas redes sociais?, Ab Instantia, Ano III, no. 5, 2015, pp. 313–339.

Blecher-Prigat, Ayelet: Children's Right to Privacy, in: Dwyer, James G. (ed.): The Oxford Handbook of Children and the Law, Oxford 2020, pp. 363–387.

---

[60] Indeed, "an intergenerational gap exists in digital knowledge and literacy" and parents (and teachers) "need training to teach digital skills and online safety to children", The Lancet Child & Adolescent Health: Growing up in a digital world.

[61] Novais: Direitos fundamentais nas relações entre particulares, pp. 150 ff.

[62] Vieira de Andrade identifies as an asymmetrical relation, equivalent to a relation within the state administration, the relation between parents and their minor children when conceptualizing "freedoms and liberties" in the context of private relations, cf. de Andrade: Os direitos fundamentais na Constituição Portuguesa de 1976, p. 243, footnote 571.

Canotilho, José Joaquim Gomes: Direito Constitucional e Teoria da Constituição, 7th ed., Coimbra 2003.
Canotilho, José Joaquim Gomes/Machado, Jónatas Eduardo Mendes: "Reality Shows" e Liberdade de Programação, Coimbra 2003.
Canotilho, José Joaquim Gomes/Moreira, Vital: Constituição da República Portuguesa Anotada, Vol. I, Coimbra 2007.
Carvalho, Orlando de: Teoria Geral do Direito Civil, 3rd ed., Coimbra 2012.
CEFL (Commission on European Family Law): Principles of European Family Law Regarding Parental Responsibilities, http://ceflonline.net/wp-content/uploads/Principles-PR-English.pdf; last accessed April 14, 2021.
Correia, Fernando Alves: Direitos fundamentais e relações jurídicas privadas: sinopse doutrinária e jurisprudencial, Revista de Legislação e de Jurisprudência, Ano 146, no. 4001, 2016, pp. 88–96.
Cruz, Rossana Martingo: A divulgação da imagem do filho menor nas redes sociais e o superior interesse da criança, in: Neto, Luísa/Ribeiro, Fernanda (eds.): Direito e Informação na Sociedade em Rede: Atas, Porto 2016, pp. 279–293, http://hdl.handle.net/1822/47936; last accessed April 14, 2021.
Livingstone, Sonia/ Stoilova, Mariya/Nandagirim, Rishita: Children's data and privacy online. Growing up in a digital age—An evidence review, London 2019, https://www.lse.ac.uk/media-and-communications/assets/documents/research/projects/childrens-privacy-online/Evidence-review.pdf; last accessed April 14, 2021.
Marktest: Os Portugueses e as Redes Sociais 2019, https://www.marktest.com/wap/private/images/Logos/Folheto_Portugueses_Redes_Sociais_2019.pdf; last accessed April 14, 2021.
Marques, João Paulo Fernandes Remédio: Alguns aspectos processuais da tutela da personalidade humana no novo Código de Processo Civil of 2013, http://www.cej.mj.pt/cej/recursos/ebooks/ProcessoCivil/Reforma_do_processo_civil.pdf; last accessed April 14, 2021.
Martins, Rosa: Menoridade, (In)capacidade e Cuidado Parental, Coimbra 2008.
Martins, Rosa: Responsabilidades parentais no séc. XXI: A tensão entre o direito de participação da criança e a função educativa dos pais, Lex Familiae—Revista Portuguesa de Direito da Família, Ano 5, no. 10, 2008, pp. 25–40.
Miranda, Jorge/Medeiros, Rui: Constituição Portuguesa Anotada, Vol. I, 2nd ed., Lisbon 2017.
Moniz, Ana Raquel Gonçalves: Os direitos fundamentais e a sua circunstância: crise e vinculação axiológica entre o Estado, a sociedade e a comunidade global, Coimbra 2017.
Neto, Luísa: Direitos (fundamentais) de personalidade?, in: Oliveira, Nuno Manuel Pinto/Crorie, Benedita Mac (eds.): Pessoa, direito e direitos, 2014/2015, Braga 2016, http://www.jusgov.uminho.pt/wp-content/uploads/2017/10/Pessoa_Direito_Direitos.pdf; last accessed April 14, 2021.
Novais, Jorges Reis: Direitos fundamentais nas relações entre particulares: do dever de protecção à proibição do défice, Coimbra 2018.
Oliveira, Guilherme de: Manual de Direito da Família, 2nd ed., Coimbra 2021.
Oliveira, Guilherme de: O acesso dos menores a cuidados de saúde, in: de Oliveira, Guilherme (ed.): Temas de Direito da Medicina, Coimbra 1999.
Pinheiro, Jorge Duarte: A tutela da personalidade da criança na relação com os pais, Scientia Juridica, Tomo LXIV, no. 338, Maio-Agosto 2015, pp. 249–266.

Pinto, Paulo Mota: A Limitação Voluntária do Direito à Reserva sobre a Intimidade da Vida Privada, in: de Figueiredo Dias, Jorge et al. (eds.): Estudos em Homenagem a Cunha Rodrigues, Vol. II, Coimbra 2001, pp. 527–558.
Pinto, Paulo Mota: Direitos de personalidade e direitos fundamentais: estudos, Coimbra 2018.
PORDATA: Tribunal Constitucional—processos entrados, findos e pendentes. https://www.pordata.pt/Portugal/Tribunal+Constitucional+processos+entrados++findos+e+pendentes-873; last accessed April 14, 2021.
Ribeiro, J. Sousa: Os direitos de personalidade como direitos fundamentais, in: Oliveira, Nuno Manuel Pinto/Crorie, Benedita Mac (eds.): Pessoa, direito e direitos, 2014/2015, Braga 2016, http://www.jusgov.uminho.pt/wp-content/uploads/2017/10/Pessoa_Direito_Direitos.pdf; last accessed April 14, 2021.
Shmueli, Benjamin/Blecher-Prigat, Ayelet: "Privacy for Children", Columbia Human Rights Law Review, 42, 2011, pp. 759–795.
Sousa, Rabindranath Valentino Aleixo Capelo de: O Direito Geral de Personalidade, Coimbra 2011.
Steinberg, Stacey B.: Sharenting: Children's Privacy in the Age of Social Media, Emory Law Journal, 66, 2017, pp. 839–884.
The Lancet Child & Adolescent Health: Growing up in a digital world: benefits and risks, 2018, https://www.thelancet.com/journals/lanchi/article/PIIS2352-4642(18)30002-6/fulltext; last accessed April 14, 2021.
Thierer, Adam: Kids, Privacy, Free Speech & The Internet: Finding The Right Balance, Mercatus Center, George Mason University, no. 11–32, August 2011, https://www.mercatus.org/system/files/Kids_Privacy_Free_Speech_and_the_Internet_Thierer_WP32.pdf; last accessed April 14, 2021.
Trabuco, Cláudia: Dos contratos relativos ao direito à imagem, O Direito, Ano 133, Abril-Junho 2001, p. 389–459.
Tribunal Constitutional Portugal: Estatisticas, http://www.tribunalconstitucional.pt/tc/tribunal estatisticas.html; last accessed April 14, 2021.
Wieacker, Franz: Foundations of European Legal Culture, The American Journal of Comparative Law, 38(1), 1990, pp. 1–29.

Prof. Dr. Paula Távora Vítor is Professor at Faculty of Law of the University of Coimbra, President of the Direction Board of Centro de Direito da Família (Family Law Center) and researcher of the Family Law Center and of the University of Coimbra Institute for Legal Research (IJ | UCILeR), Portugal. She is a member of the Coordinating Group of Family Law in Europe: Academic Network (FL-EUR) and of the Executive Council of the International Society of Family Law (ISFL). She is also member of the Editorial Board of Lex Familiae—Revista Portuguesa de Direito da Família and of the open-access peer-reviewed Journal Family&Law. Paula Távora Vítor is author of monographs and articles written in Portuguese and English and co-author of law reform projects in the field of the legal regime of capacity and mental health. Her main research areas are Family Law, Succession Law and Personal Law, with particular regard to the law relating to vulnerable persons, capacity, elder law, marriage and divorce.

Projecting Images of Families into the Law—the Example of Internet-Related Cases Decided by the German Courts

Thomas Dreier

1 Introduction

Family and Internet may appear to be an "unlikely combination," since technology is generally considered to be neutral and thus not gender-related, even if a clear gender imbalance can be observed among computer science students and professionals who are largely male. From the point of view of the networked structures of the Internet, and hence from the point of view of Internet law, no fundamental distinction is made between family and non-family relationships and connections. Despite this, it may be worthwhile to search legislation and case law for existing rules and decisions that discuss issues of families and their members who use the Internet. In other words, to focus on areas in which the use of the Internet by family members or within the family circle raises legal issues. Of course, such issues are not all that numerous, since intra-family relations are an area of the private sphere which is particularly protected against state regulation and legal interference.

Nevertheless, as scarce as these legal issues—and hence court decisions that deal with them—may be, the present contribution works on the assumption that the way in which conflicts at the interface of family and Internet are described and resolved in the respective argumentation found in court decisions openly or at least implicitly reveals something about the image of the family on which the courts base their decisions.

T. Dreier (✉)
Karlsruhe Institute of Technology (KIT), Karlsruhe, Germany
e-mail: dreier@kit.edu

N. Dethloff et al. (eds.), *Families and New Media*, Juridicum – Schriften zum Medien-, Informations- und Datenrecht,
https://doi.org/10.1007/978-3-658-39664-0_7

Such an approach, however, meets with a major difficulty under German law. The reason is that is a stark contrast to a judge in an Anglo-American-influenced legal system, who—particularly when it comes to decide cases under common law—is accustomed to expressing his or her own views in the judgment at some length. Moreover, the individual personality of the deciding judge, and hence the subjectivity of his or her decision, is highlighted whenever a decision handed down begins with the formulation "I, Judge So-and-so, am of the opinion that [...]". German judges, however, do not decide cases as individuals in their own name. Rather, they speak as an institutional body ("the court") and, even this institutionalized body does not speak for itself, but "in the name of the people" *(Im Namen des Volkes)*. With this self-understanding, it goes hand in hand that German courts are less concerned with the further development of the law by expressing a personal legal opinion than with finding the answer to the legal issue in question—which is already contained in the statutory rules which merely need to be interpreted to be applied to the facts of a given case. In comparison to English judgments, German courts therefore write in a comparatively abstract and less elaborate manner. Hence, other than in English judgments, from which passages close to life can often be quoted verbatim, the pre-legal images German judges have of the family and its members when deciding cases at the interface of family and Internet can only be inferred in an indirect and subjective way from the comparatively scanty sentences of the judgements' reasoning.

Having said these methodological remarks, mainly three groups of cases can be identified which will be examined in more detail in this contribution. The first of these three groups of cases concerns the liability of the owners of a family Internet connection for infringements of third-party rights—mainly copyright—committed by one of the family members. This mainly raises the issue of the scope of the information and control obligations, which the courts impose on the owner of the Internet connection vis-à-vis his or her family members, i.e. vis-à-vis spouse and children (2.). The second group of cases deals with the legal framework for acting as an influencer, who often is still underage at the start of his or her career (3.). Finally, the third group of cases centers around state measures designed to protect the best interests of children in dealing with and being affected by the Internet (4.).

As a final preliminary remark, it should be noted that what follows is not a comprehensive analysis of the subject matter just outlined. Rather, some exemplary court cases and decisions will be selected to demonstrate how the courts are defining family structures and the role of family members when they decide cases that involve actions of family members in connection with the Internet.[1] Likewise, a complete review of legal literature on the subject discussed here, would go beyond the scope of this article. Nevertheless, it is hoped that the following discussion of these exemplary cases may entail both a more comprehensive study of national law and a comparative analysis of different national jurisdictions—and thereby shed additional light on the interplay between non-legal and mostly sociological ideas of families and their members on the one hand, and legal rules on the other.

2 Liability of the Owner of an Internet Connection and Parents' Duty to Supervise their Children

The factual scenario with which the courts are confronted when assessing the liability of the owner of a family Internet connection—either one or both parents—for acts committed by another family member, —usually a child who is often a minor, but also sometimes a partner. The owners of copyright or related rights have learned through an Internet service provider, or through participation in file-sharing networks, that files of their music sound recordings or audiovisual works have been unlawfully offered for file-sharing from a computer via a certain Internet connection.[2] The rights holders then issued a warning to the subscriber,

[1] Additional issues have been before the German Courts; see, e.g., Court of Appeals (Oberlandesgericht, OLG) Frankfurt/M., decision from January 17, 2019 (16 W 54/18), MMR (Multimedia und Recht) 2019, p. 381: Within the closest family circle, there is a space free of dishonor which makes it possible to address each other freely without having to fear legal prosecution; Administrative Court (Verwaltungsgericht, VG) Stuttgart, decision from December 1, 2015 (12 K 5587/15), BeckRS (Beck-Rechtsprechung) 2016, 40553: Repeated gross insults made by a 14-year-old student in WhatsApp comments can justify a 15-day immediate suspension as well as the threat of expulsion from school; Labor Court (Landesarbeitsgericht, LAG) Rheinland-Pfalz, decision from March 23, 2018 (1 Sa 507/17), LSK (Leitsatzkartei) 2018, 44817360: Communication of an older employee to a 17-year-old, spending her voluntary social year in the same firm, that he is willing to have a fling seen as sexual harassment; OLG Hamm, decision from January 14, 2016 (4 RVs 144/15), MMR 2016, p. 425: Sexual conversation of an adult with a 9-year-old child via WhatsApp punishable under Section 174 (4) No. 3 of the German Penal Code (Strafgesetzbuch, StGB) as influencing a child by way information and communication technologies in order to cause the child to perform sexual acts.

[2] Offering protected works for download via a file-sharing platform constitutes "publicly making available" pursuant to Section 19a of the German Copyright Act (Urheberrechtsgesetz, UrhG). See the following decisions by the German Federal Court of Justice

requested a cease-and-desist declaration with a penalty clause, and demanded compensation for the costs incurred for the warning as well as for damages for the unauthorized use of their copyrighted works in the context of the public Internet file-sharing platform.

2.1 Legal Liability Rules

The obligation to pay damages for copyright infringement is established in Section 97 (2) of the German Copyright Act (Urheberrechtsgesetz, UrhG) which provides that "[a]ny person who intentionally or negligently performs such an act shall be obliged to pay the injured party damages for the prejudice suffered as a result of the infringement".[3] If the owner of the connection has committed the infringement him- or herself, he or she is, of course, liable as the infringer. In addition, under German civil law, whoever infringes someone else's copyright must reimburse the infringing party for the cost incurred for sending a private cease-and-desist warning notice (so-called *Abmahnung*).[4] The owner of the connection may also be liable if he or she is aiding or abetting another person's copyright infringement. However, the mere provision of the Internet connection is not enough cause for this sort of liability, since liability, as an instigator or accessory, requires knowledge of the specific infringement(s) which result from the aiding or abetting activity.

(Bundesgerichtshof, BGH) from June 11, 2015 (I ZR 19/14), para. 14, GRUR (Gewerblicher Rechtsschutz und Urheberrecht) 2016, p. 176—Tauschbörse I; BGH, decision from June 11, 2015 (I ZR 7/14), para. 15, GRUR 2016, p. 184—Tauschbörse II; BGH, decision from May 12, 2016 (I ZR 48/15), para 19, GRUR 2016, p. 1280—Everytime we touch.—Section 19a of the German Copyright Act implements Article 3 (1) and (2) of the EU Information Society Directive 2001/29/EC, which in turn implements Articles 8 of the WIPO Copyright Treaty (WCT) as well as 10 and 14 of the WIPO Performances and Phonograms Treaty (WPPT).

[3] Unofficial English translation at https://www.gesetze-im-internet.de/englisch_urhg/index.html.

[4] This claim is based on the duty of the principal to reimburse an agent who, even in the absence of a specific authorization and because avoiding infringement of intellectual property rights, is considered the business of the infringer, legitimately acts on behalf of the principal (Sections 677, 683 1st st. and 670 of the German Civil Code, Bürgerliches Gesetzbuch, BGB).

2.1.1 Liability of the Owner of the Internet Connection

Since in the case of a multi-person household it is regularly not possible to prove which person in the household who has access to the computer connected to the Internet has committed the infringement, the question arises as to who must bear the consequences if proof cannot be provided. The relevant rules of evidence are complicated in German law, since they try to deal with the fact, by way of a kind of ping-pong game, that according to the general principles of the law of evidence, on the one hand, the plaintiff must prove the infringement crime. But the plaintiff cannot provide this proof without information on the part of the defendant, and the defendant is not obligated to provide information according to general principles, even though he or she has or can at least find out the information that the plaintiff urgently needs in order to enforce his or her right.

The courts resolve this conflict as best they can by way of formulating evidentiary presumptions. If the copyright holder has ascertained the IP address from which the infringement occurred, an initial factual presumption exists according to which the connection owner is responsible for the infringement. This presumption exists not only if no other persons could use this Internet connection at the time of the infringement, but also if the Internet connection—as in the case of a family Internet connection—is regularly used by several persons.[5] However, this presumption is rebutted if there is a serious possibility that a third party alone, and not the owner of the Internet connection, used the Internet access for the alleged infringement. According to the German courts, this is particularly the case if the Internet connection was not sufficiently secured at the time of the infringement or was deliberately made available for use by other family members and/or guests.

In such cases, however, case law then imposes a so-called "secondary burden of proof" on the owner of the Internet connection, i.e. the owner of the connection must state whether other persons and, if so, which other persons had independent access to his or her Internet connection and could be considered the perpetrators of the infringement. To this end, the owner of the Internet connection is obligated

[5] On the rules of evidence in this regard, see especially German Federal Court of Justice (Bundesgerichtshof, BGH), decision of May 12, 2010 (I ZR 121/08), GRUR (Gewerblicher Rechtsschutz und Urheberrecht) 2010, p. 633—Sommer unseres Lebens; BGH, decision from January 8, 2014 (I ZR 169/12), para. 15, GRUR 2014, p. 657—BearShare; BGH, decision from June 11, 2015 (I ZR 75/14), paras 37 and 39, GRUR 2016, p. 191—Tauschbörse III; and BGH, decision from May 12, 2016 (I ZR 48/15), para. 34, GRUR 2016, p. 1280—Everytime we touch.

to make reasonable inquiries and to disclose what knowledge he or she has gained about the circumstances of a possible infringement. In this respect, the general assertion of the merely theoretical possibility of access to the Internet connection by third parties living in the household is not regarded as enough. Rather, the owner of an Internet connection must state which persons had—considering their respective user behavior, knowledge, and skills, as well as the time at which the alleged infringement took place—the opportunity to commit the infringing act in question without his or her knowledge or intervention.[6]

2.1.2 Parent's Liability due to Violation of their Duty of Supervision

However, the situation is different in the case of underage children living in the household, who probably commit most of the copyright infringements by way of Peer-to-Peer (P2P) file sharing.[7] This is because parents have a general, independent duty to supervise their children's behavior. The German Civil Code (Bürgerliches Gesetzbuch, BGB) stipulates that parents are responsible for the care of the child as part of their parental custody pursuant to Section 1626 (1) of the German Civil Code, which foremost includes the duty of parents to supervise the child pursuant to Section 1631 (1) of the German Civil Code. And according to Section 832 (1) sentence 1 of the German Civil Code, which lays down the rules for the liability of a person with a duty of supervision, "[a] person who is obliged by operation of law to supervise a person who requires supervision because he is a minor or because of his mental or physical condition is liable to make compensation for the damage that this person unlawfully causes to a third party".[8] If the parents violate this statutory duty of supervision imposed on them by law,[9]

---

[6] German Federal Court of Justice (Bundesgerichtshof, BGH), decision from March 30, 2017 (I ZR 19/16), para. 15, GRUR (Gewerblicher Rechtsschutz und Urheberrecht) 2017, p. 1233—Loud.

[7] Unlike Napster, where the exchange of files was organized around a central address database, peer-to-peer (P2P) file-sharing systems do not require a central node. Rather, the protected works are exchanged via direct contact from computer to computer, with software installed on each connected computer providing the contact.

[8] Unofficial English translation at https://www.gesetze-im-internet.de/englisch_bgb/index.html.

[9] In Germany, an identical duty to supervise results from the so-called interference liability *(Störerhaftung)*. The German form of general secondary liability is for persons who are not tortfeasors or themselves aiding and abetting, but for those who are in any way intentionally and adequately causally contributing to the violation of the protected right. See, e.g., German Federal Court of Justice (Bundesgerichtshof, BGH), decision from November 15,

they are not as such personally liable for the copyright infringement committed by the child. However, they are liable to the copyright holder for the infringement of third-party rights committed by the child, provided they violated their duty of supervision. In this respect, the scope of this supervisory duty is therefore decisive.

2.2 The Family Image of the Courts

It is within the discussion of the scope of the legal liability rules just described that the courts formulate their view of family structures as well as the role of individual family members.

2.2.1 Minors

In the *Morpheus*-case, the most relevant case decided by the German Federal Court of Justice (Bundesgerichtshof, BGH) on the issue of the scope of parents' duty to supervise their children, the parents had provided their children, who were 13, 15, and 19 years old and living in their household at the time, with an Internet connection. For their youngest child's twelfth birthday, the parents gave him the father's used personal computer, which the child in turn used to exchange copyrighted music via the P2P filesharing networks "Morpheus" and "BearShare", offering a total of 1147 audio files and around 11.2 Gigabite of audio and video files for downloading by the others in the P2P filesharing network.[10] The phonogram producers—the copyright owners of the music and the recordings—sued, claiming that although the parents might have sufficiently explained to their son how to properly behave, they certainly had not monitored their son's compliance with these rules of conduct. After all, they argued, the parents had not noticed that their child had downloaded the two P2P filesharing programs, although the icon of the program "BearShare" was visible on the personal computer's desktop.

2012 (I ZR 74/12), para. 41, GRUR (Gewerblicher Rechtsschutz und Urheberrecht) 2013, p. 511—Morpheus. It should be noted that the BGH has referred certain questions regarding the German *Störerhaftung* to the CJEU, which so far had not decided on secondary liability; see cases C-682/18—YouTube and C-683/18—Cyando.

[10] German Federal Court of Justice (Bundesgerichtshof, BGH), decision from November 15, 2012 (I ZR 74/12), GRUR (Gewerblicher Rechtsschutz und Urheberrecht) 2013, p. 511—Morpheus.

Both the Court of First Instance and the Court of Appeals ruled in favor of the plaintiffs and ordered the defendant family father and owner of the Internet connection to pay to the plaintiff damages for illegal use of copyrighted music, and to reimburse the cost incurred by the plaintiff when sending their warning notice.

The BGH, however, held that "parents regularly fulfill their duty to supervise a normally developed 13-year-old child who follows their basic rules and prohibitions by informing the child about the illegality of participating in Internet file-sharing networks and prohibiting the child from doing so. In principle, parents are not obliged to monitor the child's use of the Internet, to check the child's computer or to (partially) block the child's access to the Internet. Parents are only obliged to take such measures if they have concrete indications that the child is violating the prohibition".[11] Without addressing the issue of the scope of the information required in more detail—although the child was quoted as saying he "didn't know it was that bad" and that he "could not imagine being caught at all"—the court only addressed the issue of the scope of the parents' duty to supervise a child whom they had duly informed about what was and what was not allowed when using the Internet.

Explaining this holding, the BGH stated that "[a]ccording to the established case law of the Federal Court of Justice, the degree of supervision required is determined by the age, nature and character of the child and by what can be expected of those responsible for supervision in their respective circumstances".[12] Moreover, other than the Court of Appeals, which had required that the parents review their child's desktop and installed programs on a monthly basis, the German Federal Court of Justice was of the opinion that "the requirements for the duty of supervision, in particular the duty to instruct and supervise children, depend on the foreseeability of the harmful behavior. In this context, the extent to which general instructions and prohibitions are sufficient or their observance must also be monitored depends mainly on the child's characteristics and his or her compliance with educational measures".[13] In general, the Federal Court of Justice went on, although "it cannot be disputed that experience has shown that children and young people occasionally violate prohibitions imposed for educational

[11] Translation by the author.

[12] German Federal Court of Justice (Bundesgerichtshof, BGH), decision from November 15, 2012 (I ZR 74/12), para. 16, GRUR (Gewerblicher Rechtsschutz und Urheberrecht) 2013, p. 511—Morpheus (translation by the author).

[13] Ibid., para. 23.

reasons",[14] this "does not imply an obligation on the part of parents to regularly monitor whether their child is complying with the prohibitions imposed on it when using the computer and the Internet without any specific reason," or "to (partially) block the child's access to the Internet". This is particularly true, the Court continues, if the child is a normally developed, insightful, and behaviorally non-disruptive 13-year-old. Rather, "parents regularly satisfy their duty to supervise a normally developed 13-year-old child who obeys their basic commands and prohibitions by instructing the child about the illegality of participating in Internet file-sharing networks and prohibiting him or her from doing so".[15]

In this way, the BGH implements the fundamental rights' requirements of the German Constitution (Basic Law; Grundgesetz, GG). According to Article 6 (2) sentence 1, the "care and upbringing of children is the natural right of parents and a duty primarily incumbent upon them".[16] With similar wording, Article 7 of the Charter of Fundamental Rights of the European Union declares that "everyone has the right to respect for his or her private and family life, home and communications". In formal terms, the wording, especially of the *German Grundgesetz,* clearly indicates the natural law basis of the fundamental rights. At the same time, the content of parental rights is intended to guarantee the sphere of freedom of parents, in which parents can care for and raise their children according to their own ideas, free from state influence.[17] Furthermore, the provision expresses a general value decision in favor of the child's upbringing in the parental family

[14] See also German Federal Court of Justice (Bundesgerichtshof, BGH), decision from July 12, 2007 (I ZR 18/04), GRUR (Gewerblicher Rechtsschutz und Urheberrecht) 2007, p. 890—Jugendgefährdende Medien bei eBay.

[15] German Federal Court of Justice (Bundesgerichtshof, BGH), decision from November 15, 2012 (I ZR 74/12), para. 16, GRUR (Gewerblicher Rechtsschutz und Urheberrecht) 2013, p. 511—Morpheus. Parents are only obliged to take control measures if they have concrete evidence that the child is violating the prohibition. Moreover, it should be noted that the extent of the danger posed to third parties by the conduct of the supervisor in question also plays a role. However, the Federal Supreme Court held that the "danger posed to third parties by a child's use of copyright-infringing file-sharing networks is significantly less than, for example, the danger posed to third parties by a child's misconduct on the road or when handling fire"; ibid., para. 28.

[16] Unofficial English translation at https://www.gesetze-im-internet.de/englisch_gg/index.html.

[17] Federal Constitutional Court (Bundesverfassungsgericht, BVerfG), decision from July 29, 1968 (1 BvL 20/63, 1 BvL 31/66 and 1 BvL 5/67), NJW (Neue Juristische Wochenschrift) 1968, p. 2233.

circle.[18] Consequently, "parents should take into account the child's growing ability and need to act independently and responsibly when caring for and raising the child".[19] Thus, placing great emphasis on the child's learning curve and respecting the child's personality as expressed by his or her own decisions, the Federal Supreme Court propagates the educational goal of promoting "the child's growing ability and need to act independently in a responsible manner".[20] If the child is allowed to make mistakes, the consequences of which are ultimately borne by the copyright holders, the social costs are ultimately imposed on third parties and thus on society as a whole.

2.2.2 Adult Children and Spouses

In such cases, however, it is not just a question of minors, but also of adult children and spouses of the owner of the Internet connection living in the same household. Unlike in the case of underage children, the question of legal liability is not about the breach of a duty of supervision, but about the circumstances under which the owner of the Internet connection can rebut the presumption that he or she, as the owner of the connection, committed the infringement to escape his or her own liability as the infringer.

As stated above,[21] the owner of an Internet connection must disclose the names of those who, given their user behavior, knowledge, and skills, had the

---

[18] Veit: Commentary on Sect. 1626, note 7.

[19] German Federal Court of Justice (Bundesgerichtshof, BGH), decision from November 15, 2012 (I ZR 74/12), para. 26, GRUR (Gewerblicher Rechtsschutz und Urheberrecht) 2013, p. 511—Morpheus (translation by the author). See also the wording of Sec. 1626 (2) 1st st. BGB. Only recently, the coalition parties of the last Merkel government agreed to place greater emphasis on children's rights by amending the constitution. Provided that the necessary two-thirds majority will agree, the constitution will in future state that "[t]he best interests of the child shall be given due consideration" and that "[t]he primary responsibility of the parents shall remain unaffected", cf. Bundestag printed matter (Bundestag Drucksache; BT-Drs.) 19/28138, p. 5 (translation by the author). This is, of course, a rather symbolic affirmation of children's rights that already apply at present. Moreover, not much is regulated regarding decisions of concrete individual questions such as whether, during the Corona pandemic, schoolchildren have, e.g., a right to be provided with a computer for home schooling at the state's expense.

[20] Ibid. Similarly, in a case not related to the Internet, the German Federal Court of Justice emphasized the right of underage children to unhindered development of their personality and undisturbed development appropriate for children; see German Federal Court of Justice (Bundesgerichtshof, BGH), decision from September 15, 2015 (VI ZR 175/14), NJW (Neue Juristische Wochenschrift) 2016, p. 789.

[21] See above, 2.1.1.

opportunity to commit the infringing act without his knowledge or intervention. Again, the aim is to reconcile the protection of the family with the protection of intellectual property. As likewise stated above,[22] the fundamental rights under Article 7 of the EU Charter of Fundamental Rights and Article 6 (1) of the German Basic Law protect undisturbed marital and family cohabitation from interference by the state. These fundamental rights oblige the state to refrain from interfering with the family and entitle family members to freely shape their community inwardly in family responsibility and respect.[23] The scope of the protection of the family under fundamental rights also covers the relationship between parents and their adult children.[24] This is not only to be observed by the state in the course of its legislation, but also by the courts in the course of interpreting simple statutory law.[25]

In view of this strong protection of the family against state intervention, the German Federal Court of Justice concluded in a recent decision that the protection of intellectual property, which is also protected by fundamental rights both under Article 17 (2) of the EU Charter of Fundamental Rights and Article 14 (1) of the German Basic Law, cannot justify imposing far-reaching obligations to investigate and notify on the owner of a private Internet connection in order to avert his or her liability as a copyright infringer. It is therefore unreasonable, according to the German Federal Court of Justice, to force the Internet connection owner to subject the Internet use of his or her spouse to documentation. It is also unreasonable to require the connection owner to examine his or her spouse's computer and search for file-sharing software.[26] However, the owner of the Internet connection cannot, the court held, contend him- or herself by stating that the adult children had access to the computer in question. Rather, if the owner of the family

[22] See above, 2.2.1.

[23] For this general principle as applied in other contexts see, e.g., Federal Constitutional Court (Bundesverfassungsgericht, BVerfG), decision from January 10, 1984 (1 BvL 5/83), NJW (Neue Juristische Wochenschrift) 1984, p. 1523; BVerfG, decision from October 3, 1989 (1 BvL 78/86 and 1 BvL 79/86), NJW 1990, p. 175.

[24] Federal Constitutional Court (Bundesverfassungsgericht, BVerfG), decision from April 18, 1989 (2 BvR 1169/84), NJW (Neue Juristische Wochenschrift) 1989, p. 2195.

[25] Federal Constitutional Court (Bundesverfassungsgericht, BVerfG), decision from June 23, 1982 (1 BvR 1343/81), NVwZ (Neue Zeitschrift für Verwaltungsrecht) 1983, p. 149.

[26] German Federal Court of Justice (Bundesgerichtshof, BGH), decision from March 30, 2017 (I ZR 19/16), para. 23, GRUR (Gewerblicher Rechtsschutz und Urheberrecht) 2017, p. 1233—Loud; see also BGH, decision from October 6, 2016 (I ZR 154/15), para. 26, GRUR 2017, p. 386—Afterlife.

Internet connection wants to divert his or her own liability, within the framework of the secondary burden of proof, he or she must name the child who admitted the infringement to the owner of the family Internet connection.[27] But, in the absence of concrete indications of an already committed or imminent copyright infringement, the owner of an Internet connection is generally not obligated to inform adult members of his or her shared apartment or his or her adult guests, to whom he or she provides the password for the Internet connection, about the illegality of participating in file-sharing networks or prohibit them from the illegal use of corresponding programs.[28]

3 Influencers

3.1 A Relatively New Phenomenon

Another interesting area where family and the Internet meet in the law are the activities of influencers. The German version of Wikipedia offers the following description of influencers: "since the 2000 s, people who, due to their strong presence and high reputation in social networks, are suitable as carriers for advertising and marketing (so-called influencer marketing)".[29]

The rise and significance of influencers has to do with change in media usage, especially among younger consumers, who are less and less reachable by traditional advertising venues like television and print media.

Whereas at the end of the 2010 s, 42% of over-50-year-olds formed their opinions via television, only 17% of 14 to 29-year-olds did so. The difference in

---

[27] German Federal Court of Justice (Bundesgerichtshof, BGH), decision from March 30, 2017 (I ZR 19/16), para. 24, GRUR (Gewerblicher Rechtsschutz und Urheberrecht) 2017, p. 1233—Loud; see also before, BGH, decision from January 8, 2014 (I ZR 169/12), GRUR 2014, p. 657—BearShare.

[28] German Federal Court of Justice (Bundesgerichtshof, BGH), decision from May 12, 2016 (I ZR 86/15), GRUR (Gewerblicher Rechtsschutz und Urheberrecht) 2016, p. 1289.

[29] https://de.wikipedia.org/wiki/Influencer (translation by the author of [*Personen …, die aufgrund ihrer starken Präsenz und ihres hohen Ansehens in sozialen Netzwerken als Träger für Werbung und Vermarktung in Frage kommen (sogenanntes Influencer-Marketing)*]). It might be noted that the English language version of Wikipedia redirects to the broader notion of "Internet celebrity". For the purposes of the present contribution, the term 'influencer' is used in the somewhat narrower sense of a person engaging, in whole or in part, in an advertising activity.

opinion formation via the Internet was even more pronounced. Here, while it was barely 2.5% among over 50-year-olds, it was almost 55% among 14 to 29-year-olds.[30] Marketing by influencers is particularly promising and consequently used especially in the topic clusters of Beauty, Fashion, Home and Lifestyle, Health and Fitness, and Entertainment.[31] Even if this may appear gender-stereotypical, these are of interest predominantly to female followers—particularly large numbers of young women—both because of the affinity to a particular topic necessary for the success of an influencer and in view of the identification of the followers with the influencers and the para-social interaction between followers and influencers. Because of these interdependencies, influencer marketing raises not only the associated legal issues, but also questions regarding the definition of gender and traditional, outdated role models.[32]

3.2 Influencer and the Courts

It should be noted, however, that for the purposes of the present inquiry, usable statements in court judgments are even sparser than in the cases dealing with the Internet connection owner's liability for copyright infringement by family members. This is due to the fact that, from a legal point of view, the issue raised in the case of influencers is less one of roles or expectations of behavior within the family and its members, but rather a question of whether and if so under what circumstances product recommendations by influencers are to be regarded as mere announcements of personal opinion, or rather as an advertising message, which must be identified as such in accordance with the media law requirement to separate editorial from advertising contributions.[33]

---

[30] Numbers according to Kost/Seeger: Influencer Marketing, p. 8.

[31] Ibid., p. 47.

[32] The issue is not only about objectively ascertainable preferences with regard to certain topics. Rather, at the same time, it is likewise about the maintenance of the construction of traditional role models.

[33] Currently, case law of the German courts of appeals is still inconsistent on this issue; in favor of a labeling requirement even if the influencer was not paid by the producer of the products recommended by the influencer, e.g., Court of Appeals (Oberlandesgericht, OLG) Karlsruhe, decision from September 9, 2020 (6 U 38/19), GRUR (Gewerblicher Rechtsschutz und Urheberrecht) 2021, p. 88; against such a requirement, however, e.g. OLG Munich, decision from June 25, 2020 (29 U 2333/19), GRUR 2020, p. 1096. In the meantime, the question has been referred for decision to the German Federal Court of Justice.

Nevertheless, some indications can be gleaned from the decisions regarding the role attributed to influencers by the courts. Even if it may seem a bit over-interpreted, statements by German courts reveal a certain skepticism of the judges towards the behavior of influencers. For example, a recent decision by the Court of Appeals of Braunschweig refers to an influencer as a "person describing himself/herself as an influencer" as well as to a "so-called influencer".[34] Obviously, the activity of the defendant female influencer is not recognized here as a serious freelance activity. And when it is further stated that the influencers who were sued and convicted for failing to label their recommendations as advertising messages "have themselves paid for being pictured with a certain product", this is somewhat reminiscent of the view of the courts in the imperial era before World War I—that an honorable citizen does not lend him- or herself to advertising a product with his or her personality.[35]

Since, as explained above, in accordance with German legal tradition judgements are handed down as decisions of an institutional panel of judges rather than by individual judges, at least in their published form judgments do not indicate whether they were written by a majority of male or female judges. At any rate, however, such reservations towards the activities of the all female influencers who found themselves before the German courts, are even more surprising since particularly underage, enterprising boy inventors such as Bill Gates, who laid the foundation for his firm in his family garage at the age of 16, are consistently viewed positively in the capitalist hagiography of successful entrepreneurship. Female influencers, on the other hand, who have built up their successful business without further support, seem to be denied a comparable collective appreciation. They seem to be seen all too close to the so-called "it girls", whose fame is not due to special intelligence or achievements that are valuable to society, but rather just to the very fact that they are famous. Apparently, it is not similarly appreciated that in a society where attention is a scarce resource,[36] attracting attention in the form of a great number of followers is certainly an achievement of its own right.

---

[34] Court of Appeals (Oberlandesgericht, OLG) Braunschweig, decision from May 13, 2020 (2 U 78/19), CR (Computer und Recht) 2020, p. 811.

[35] Even as late as 1975, a commentator of a decision handed down by the German Federal Court of Justice warned against a "commercialization of a person's honor"; Neubert: Comment on BGH from July 2, 1974, GRUR (Gewerblicher Rechtsschutz und Urheberrecht) 1975, p. 565.

[36] See Franck: Ökonomie der Aufmerksamkeit; Honneth: Kampf um Anerkennung; Davenport/Beck: The attention economy.

Surprisingly, this view, which is rather committed to a conservative value system, coincides with a more progressive feminist perspective, which tends to see the daily activities of female influencers first and foremost as an uncritical, apolitical perpetuation of traditional female role models. In addition, an anti-capitalist attitude can be identified, according to which—especially underage[37]—female influencers appear to be in need of protection from exploitation by their parents (parent influencers using images of their underage children) and ultimately by themselves (underage influencers); selling merchandise nobody needs and creating unnecessary needs is regarded as an activity that should not be furthered but rather prevented by appropriate legislative measures. Undoubtedly, such arguments resonate reservations that the Frankfurt School in particular harbored about mass culture and the industrially produced world of goods, which was considered superfluous, and about the consumption of goods, which was considered harmful *per se*.[38] Such a view deliberately overlooks both the fact that self-marketing of underage influencers is legally permissible, and the emancipatory self-empowerment of minors who, defying the rules defining the age of majority contained in the German Civil Code, earn their own money and build up their public image. Also, even if only an extremely small number of female influencers is truly successful,[39] their great number of followers proves how highly the activity of influencing is to be valued.

4 Protection of the Child's Best Interests

The third category of legal regulation and court cases in which the image of both children and families play a decisive role are those which deal with government measures to protect the best interests of children in dealing with, as well as being

[37] It should be noted, however, that 31% of influencers creating sponsored posts on Instagram, were between the ages of 18 and 24 (see statista: Distribution of influencers) with underage influencers being a minority. However underage influencers have a particular appeal to underage users of social media (for details of uses, see InfluencerMarketingHub: Influencer Marketing Statistics).

[38] According to Horkheimer and Adorno, the human being as an "eternal consumer" becomes a mere object of industry whose needs are only apparently satisfied; Adorno/Horkheimer: Kulturindustrie—Aufklärung als Massenbetrug, pp. 144 ff.; for a more recent summary, see Ullrich: Alles nur Konsum.

[39] According to Kost/Seeger: Influencer Marketing, p. 40. In 2018, the average engagement rate of influencers with more than one million followers on Instagram was just 0.02%, and of those with 100,000 to 1,000,000 followers just 0.04%.

affected by, the Internet. This is a wide-ranging area, covering both the protection of children against outsiders—i.e., against bullying by their peers as well as against grooming by elders, mostly men, in chatrooms and similar fora—as well as against their own parents who "market" their children in diverse ways online. Although it might well be worth studying and analyzing the legal rules and issues related thereto,[40] their discussion shall be limited here to legal issues surrounding the regular use of smartphones and messenger services, such as WhatsApp, by children in their regular communication.

Two cases decided by a court of first instance particularly merit attention since they highlight some of the difficulties in properly applying existing laws to the changed social uses of digital communication devices. Both these cases deal with the use of WhatsApp by children and the resulting parental obligation of supervision and control, thus reflecting the importance of messenger services in today's digital communication.

In the first of these cases, both of which caused quite a stir in Germany, a court ordered a single father to prohibit his underage daughter from using WhatsApp before she had reached the age of 16.[41] Of course, it is one thing if the EU General Data Protection Regulation (GDPR) provides that whenever an information society service is offered directly to a child, "the processing of the personal data of a child shall be lawful where the child is at least 16 years old" but that if the child is younger, consent may be given or authorized "by the holder of parental responsibility over the child".[42] It is yet another thing to forbid parents to give such consent or authorization unless the child reaches the age of 16 years, and in the case of a developmentally delayed child even until this child's 18th birthday. A judgment which demands the latter as a general rule could hardly be more out of touch with life. A service like WhatsApp has long been an indispensable part of

---

40 See, e.g., Commission of the European Union: Strategy for a more effective fight against child sexual abuse.

41 Local Court (Amtsgericht, AG) Bad Hersfeld, decision from July 22, 2016 (F 361/16 EASO), MMR (Multimedia und Recht) 2016, p. 709.

42 Article 8 (1) subsection 1, 1st and 2nd st. of GDPR. It should be noted, however, that according to Article 8 (1) subsection 2 GDPR, Member States may provide for a lower age for those purposes provided that such lower age is not below 13 years. Likewise, it is worth mentioning that following the enactment of GDPR, WhatsApp set the minimum age requirement for use at 16 years in their general terms and conditions. However, they never proceeded with any effective age verification. For discussion of this failure to monitor legal compliance, see, e.g., Solmecke: WhatsApp jetzt ab 16.

personal communication, not only among adults but also among children who are not of age.[43] Personal messages are sent via WhatsApp, which at the same time serve to construct, insure, and present the sender's own identity to the outside world. At the same time, WhatsApp has become indispensable for planning and organizing collective actions and events even—and perhaps foremost—amongst adolescents. Moreover, from a legal point of view, the ruling mentioned does not sufficiently reconcile the protection of the child's well-being and the protection of his freedom of action, including the child's privacy which conflicts with any monitoring duty imposed upon the parents. It is true that parents have the right of upbringing, which justifies restricting the child's ability to act without the child's consent and, if necessary, even against the child's express will. However, this does not apply without limits. A fundamental core of the child's fundamental rights cannot be affected by the parental right to upbringing, but rather must be respected by the parents. Only if the parents fail, the state has the duty of care for the child which justifies certain restrictions of the parents' right, if necessary, against the will of the parents. However, it should be noted that this judgment was a typical example of the proverbial "bad cases make bad law". The case that led to the judgment was embedded in a custody dispute. The wife of an estranged couple wanted to convince the court that the father was not able to fulfill his responsibility to protect his two underage daughters from lewd and sexually harassing WhatsApp messages sent to the children by the father's friend. In this situation, while upholding the father's custody of the child, the court imposed a heightened duty on the father to prevent his daughter from the manifested negative consequences of using WhatsApp as a communication device.

In the second case, reported here as an example, the strict application of data protection produces a rather strange result regarding the use of WhatsApp by children and adults alike. According to data protection legislation, the processing of personal data requires the consent of the data subjects. If the access of an app such as WhatsApp to the phone directory is considered data processing, the use of this app therefore requires the consent of all those whose numbers are stored in the phone directory of the person who uses the app.[44] In fact, another lower court ordered the mother of a twelve-year-old to do just that, and further required her to

[43] Data Protection Officer of the State of Thüringen: 12. Tätigkeitsbericht zum Datenschutz, p. 403.

[44] This view was also held by the Data Protection Officer of the State of Thüringen; see the Deutsche Presseagentur (dpa): Thüringens Datenschützer—Whatsapp wird meist rechtswidrig genutzt.

first become knowledgeable in both the technology of the phone and the app.[45] If this result is already problematic for adults, it seems most unreasonable for children.

5 Concluding Remarks

Overall, it is clear how complex legal rules have become for issues affecting the family and its members in the digital sphere. This development is, of course, merely a consequence of the technological development and the various business models made possible by and based on digital technology. If this differentiation and complexity already cause problems for lawyers, parents who are not legally trained or educated, and not least the children, are not infrequently confronted with questions and problems that they can hardly solve themselves. Like all social institutions, families are also being sucked into the maelstrom of digitization and networking. Families and their members are making use of digital technology for their internal and external communication, adapting it to their needs and self-images of family life together, which are in turn changing in view of this very adoption and adaptation. In this process, the law also comes into play again, which in turn structures these behaviors adapted by the families to some extent, not least in view of the duty of the state to protect both parents and children from outside interferences.

Of course, from the outset, law does not capture all the relationships that arise from technology, economics, and social behavior. If, following Niklas Luhmann's model of social subsystems,[46] one looks at law in its relationship to technology, the economy, and social norms of conduct (Fig. 1)—leaving aside the subsystems religion and science as well as the autopoietic isolation of the individual systems—it becomes visible that law is by no means involved in all interrelationships between the individual social subsystems of law, social norms, technology, and the market.

According to this admittedly somewhat schematic model, law is intervening only in one half of all possible interrelationships. What is illustrated in Fig. 1 may be demonstrated by just one example. It is only some years ago that technical

[45] Local Court (Amtsgericht; AG) Bad Hersfeld, decision from May 15, 2017 (F 120/17 EASO), BeckRS (Beck-Rechtsprechung) 2017, 112602 = ZD (Zeitschrift für Datenschutz) 2017, 435.

[46] Luhmann: Theory of Society and Law as a Social System.

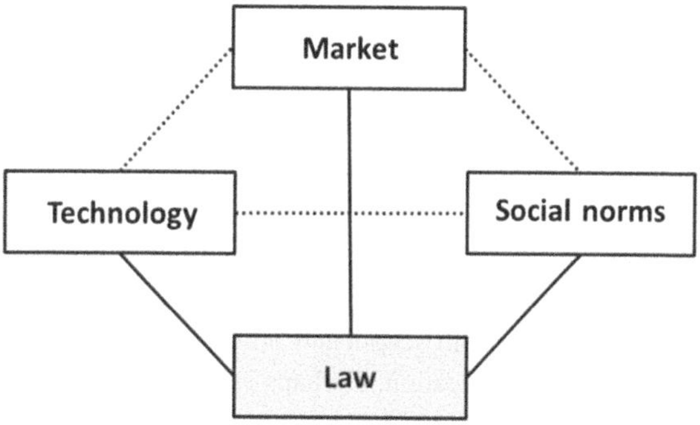

Fig. 1 Law in the context of other social subsystems
(solid lines: interaction with participation of law; dotted lines: interaction without participation of law)

engineers connected a wireless telephone to the Internet and equipped it with a camera. This combination, the demand for which the technicians could only guess at first, has developed into what is known today as the smartphone, something that has had unprecedented success on the market. At the same time, it was leading to new types of images such as "selfies",[47] "party photos", non-professional "fashion photos", and the like. All these developments were as such not regulated, i.e., neither promoted nor hindered by the law. Likewise, legal norms had no influence on the consequences of the playful use the users were making with this new technical device, even though these new uses lastingly changed the social conventions of interpersonal visual communication as well as communication in general. Legal action was only initiated once and to the extent that the technology-induced changes in behavior began to get out of hand and violations of traditional values such as that of privacy (e.g., voyeuristic recordings) and human dignity (e.g., cyberbullying) could be observed.

If one looks back at the examples of case law selected here, one gets the impression that the German Federal Court of Justice is very well able to make decisions with a sense of proportionality, taking due account of the family's constitutionally required self-responsibility. The lower courts, on the other

[47] For a description of the visual properties of selfies, see, e.g., Ullrich: Selfies; for fashion photos, see Weis: Modebilder; for GIFs Baumgärtel: GIFS; and for protest photos Schankweiler: Bildproteste.

hand—and among them, above all, the courts of first instance—are obviously finding it much more difficult to arrive at well-balanced judgments when dealing, for the first time, with new digital technologies. In several cases, the strict application of legal requirements to the letter of the law leads to solutions that are rather, if not completely, out of touch with life. Without further empirical studies, however, the question must remain open of whether—with the exception of the judges of the German Federal Court of Justice—this is possibly due to a gap between an older generation of judges and a younger, more digitally oriented generation, as well as to a certain scepticism on the part of the older generation toward new forms of communication. Perhaps it will still take a while before the born digital natives set the tone in parliament and move into judgeships. Of course, it should not be forgotten that technology and the way it is used within families will have evolved even further by then.

References

Adorno, Theodor/Horkheimer, Max: Kulturindustrie: Aufklärung als Massenbetrug, in: Adorno, Theodor/Horkheimer, Max: Dialektik der Aufklärung, New York 1944, pp. 144–198.

Baumgärtel, Tilman: GIFS. Evergreen aus Versehen, Berlin 2020.

Commission of the European Union: Strategy for a more effective fight against child sexual abuse, Communication to the European Parliament, the Council, The European Economic and Social Committee and the Committee of the regions, Doc. COM(2020) 607 final from July 24, 2020, https://eur-lex.europa.eu/legal-content/EN/TXT/PDF/?uri=CELEX:52020DC0607&from=EN; last accessed May 12, 2021.

Data Protection Officer of the State of Thüringen: 12. Tätigkeitsbericht zum Datenschutz. Öffentlicher Bereich 2016/2017, https://www.tlfdi.de/mam/tlfdi/presse/12._tb_oeffent._webversion_tlfdi_.pdf; last accessed May 12, 2021.

Davenport, Thomas H./Beck, John C.: The attention economy. Understanding the new currency of business, Boston 2001.

Deutsche Presseagentur (dpa): Thüringens Datenschützer—Whatsapp wird meist rechtswidrig genutzt, February 28, 2018, https://www.heise.de/newsticker/meldung/Thueringens-Datenschuetzer-Whatsapp-wird-meist-rechtswidrig-genutzt-3983437.html; last accessed May 12, 2021.

Franck, Georg: Ökonomie der Aufmerksamkeit. Ein Entwurf, Munich 2007.

Honneth, Axel: Kampf um Anerkennung. Zur moralischen Grammatik sozialer Konflikte, Frankfurt/M. 2008.

InfluencerMarketingHub: Influencer Marketing Statistics https://influencermarketinghub.com/influencer-marketing-statistics/; last accessed November 30, 2021.

Kost, Julia F./Seeger, Christof: Influencer Marketing, 2nd ed., Munich 2020.

Luhmann, Niklas: Law as a Social System, Oxford 2004 (German original: Das Recht der Gesellschaft, Frankfurt/M. 1993).

Luhmann, Niklas: Theory of Society, Stanford 2003 (German original: Die Gesellschaft der Gesellschaft, Frankfurt/M. 1997).
Neubert, Bodo: Comment on BGH VI ZR 121/73 from July 2, 1974, GRUR (Gewerblicher Rechtsschutz und Urheberrecht) 1975, pp. 564-565.
Schankweiler, Kerstin: Bildproteste. Widerstand im Netz, Berlin 2019.
Solmecke, Christian: WhatsApp jetzt ab 16—Was droht Nutzern, die ein falsches Alter angeben? May 11, 2018, https://www.wbs-law.de/it-und-internet-recht/whatsapp-bald-erst-ab-16-was-steckt-hinter-der-geplanten-agb-aenderung-ra-christian-solmecke-zur-rechtslage-23592/; last accessed May 12, 2021.
statista: Distribution of influencers creating sponsored posts on Instagram worldwide in 2019, https://www.statista.com/statistics/893733/share-influencers-creating-sponsored-posts-by-age/#statisticContairner; last accessed November 30, 2021.
Ullrich, Wolfgang: Alles nur Konsum: Kritik der warenästhetischen Erziehung, Berlin 2013.
Ullrich, Wolfgang: Selfies. Die Rückkehr des Öffentlichen Lebens, Berlin 2019.
Veit, Barbara: Commentary on Section 1626 of the German Civil Code, in: Hau, Wolfgang/ Poseck, Roman (eds.): Beck'scher Online-Kommentar (BeckOK) BGB, 56th edition, Munich 2019.
Weis, Diana: Modebilder. Abschied vom Real Life, Berlin 2020.

Prof. Dr. Thomas Dreier, M.C.J. (New York University), is Professor of Civil Law and Issues of the Information Society at the Faculty of Computer Science at the Karlsruhe Institute of Technology (KIT), where he is also Director of the Center for Applied Legal Studies, as well as Honorary Professor at the Faculty of Law of the University of Freiburg, Germany. In addition, he was a Senior Fellow at the Käte Hamburger Center for Advanced Study "Law as Culture" in Bonn, Germany. He has published extensively on copyright and digital technologies as well as on art law. Among his recent publications are: Concise European Copyright Law (ed. with P.B. Hugenholtz, Kluwer Law International, 2nd edition 2016); Urheberrecht (ed. with G. Schulze, Verlag C.H. Beck, 7th edition 2022); "Law and Images: Normative Models of Representation and Abstraction" (in: Gephart/Leko (eds.): Law and the Arts: Elective Affinities and Relationships of Tension, Klostermann, 2017, pp. 155–176); Law and Images, Brill Research Papers, Art and Law 3.1 (Brill, 2019); and Digital Ethics: The Issue of Images (ed. with T. Andina, Nomos, 2022).

Civilizing Parents in the Digital Age

Marta Bucholc

After almost half a century of the Internet being a part of everyday life for billions of people, the jury is still out on whether the coming of the digital age is a blessing or a curse for humanity. Even the ongoing Covid-19 pandemic—which has forced whole sectors of social life, including teaching, exercise, religious celebrations, and academic small talk over wine and cheese, into the virtual sphere—did not change the overall ambivalence of our perceptions of the role of digital media in social life. On the one hand, the benefits seem undisputable: They include the wide, if not universal, availability of low-cost communication; global connectivity; retrievability of immense loads of data, which can be processed quickly and efficiently and provide knowledge about societies which would otherwise be out of reach; and the freedom of sharing content, which is harder to control than any kind of media in existence, and thus more equal and less exclusive than any other.[1] On the other hand, the advantages of the Internet

[1] Cf. Castells: The Rise of the Network Society; Bakker/de Vreese: Good News for the Future?, Communication Research, 38(4), 2011, pp. 451–470.

The author acknowledges the support of Polish National Science Centre ("National habitus formation and the process of civilization in Poland after 1989: a figurational approach", 2019/34/E/HS6/00295). I am grateful to Marta Gospodarczyk for her kind assistance in editing the first version of this paper, and to the Editors of this volume for their valuable criticisms.

M. Bucholc (✉)
University of Warsaw, Warsaw, Poland
e-mail: bucholcm@is.uw.edu.p

N. Dethloff et al. (eds.), *Families and New Media*, Juridicum – Schriften zum Medien-, Informations- und Datenrecht,
https://doi.org/10.1007/978-3-658-39664-0_8

invariably turn out to have a dark side: digital exclusion; inequalities in access to digital media and in skills necessary to benefit from them; the overflow of misleading, false, or manipulative content that is hard to discern from the truth; the sinking criteria of quality in communication; the threats to privacy of individuals and secrets of states, enterprises, and families; the vast potential of cyber-criminality; and the latent political control and psychological manipulation seeping right into individual lives in a way that secret police or marketing agencies could not have dreamt of 50 years ago.[2]

Among the dilemmas facing us in the digital age, and one which combines almost all aforementioned concerns, are those related to the new shaping of parenthood and relations between parents and children.[3] The number of studies on the influence of digital media on child and adolescent development is growing quickly,[4] and so is the scholarship in the role of digital technology in parenting[5] and family life[6]. Nonetheless, there is still no theoretical framework that connects the changes in childhood, family, and parenthood with the socio-historical narratives of *longue durée* of the processes of socialization. There are still a number of vital questions which could bear more systematic theorizing: how digital media influence the relationship between parents and children as a part of the broader social setup, how they affect the distribution of power between children and parents, and how shifts in the power balances between them caused by digitalization, if any, are related to the overall direction of social change. These in turn translate directly into specific legal problems: how does the new power differential between parents and children affect the operations of the legal frames shaping these relationships in various legal orders? To what extent is the effect of digitization specific and unique, historically speaking, and thus calling for new

---

[2] Cf. Bonfadelli: The Internet and Knowledge Gaps, European Journal of Communication, 17(1), 2002, pp. 65–84; Krueger: Government Surveillance, Social Science Computer Review, 23(4), 2005, pp. 439–452; Fuchs et al. (eds.): Internet and Surveillance; Prakash/Yadav/Singh: An online cross-sectional study, International Journal of Indian Psychology, 8(3), 2020, pp. 424–432.

[3] See Dethloff: Families and the Law: Taking Account of Children's Evolving Capacities, in this volume.

[4] Cf. Buckingham/Willet (eds.): Digital Generations; Chassiakos et al.: Children and adolescents and digital media, Pediatrics, 138(5), 2016.

[5] Cf. Lupton/Pedersen/Thomas: Parenting and digital media, Sociology Compass, 10(8), 2016, pp. 730–743.

[6] Cf. Devitt/Roker: The Role of Mobile Phones in Family Communication, Children & Society 23(3), 2009, pp. 189–202.

legal-philosophical ideas leading to new regulatory concepts and practices? Does the digitization as a social phenomenon call for more rules or less regulation and policy in the sphere of parent-child relations in order to secure the values which have heretofore determined their legal framing, both on the national and international level? Does the new digital age only challenge us to think about new ways of securing these values, or is the call of the moment rather to reconsider whether these values are still relevant, social, culturally and legally?

In this chapter, I will apply Norbert Elias's process sociology to suggest some tentative answers to these questions. Elias's socio-historical study of what he called "the process of civilization" included socialization as one of its core problems.[7] The process of civilization—a reversible tendency towards the elimination of haphazard violence from social life—had both a psychogenetic and a sociogenetic aspect.[8] On the psychogenetic side, civilization was argued to operate by molding the emotional lives of individuals so as to strengthen their self-restraints and to lease external control exercised in the form of sanctions applied by social institutions: each individual was her or his own guardian, and each was guarded by her or his long-trained habits more than by anything else. As a result, all humans in any given society would be more like each other, and the more complex the society, the stronger the tendency to standardize the individual habitus on which the existence of the social structure ultimately relies. Violence, which is eliminated from social life, is accumulated in specialized institutions, with the nation-state being the most accomplished monopolist of violence thus far. The net beneficiaries of the standardization of habitus and the monopolization of violence are the members of the physically and socially weakest social categories, as the process of civilization reduced the distance between the strongest and the weakest and curbed the abuse of the latter by the former.[9]

Formatting children to make them suited to live in a particular society and in a particular section thereof was of pivotal importance for maintaining a level of self-restraint needed to prevent society from falling victim to the centrifugal forces of human affect. Consequently, Elias sought the key to explaining how an individual and society are interrelated in the modeling of its youngest members by way of manner books, which were one of the main sources of evidence on which his concept of civilization is based.

---

[7] Cf. Elias: On the Process of Civilization.

[8] Cf. Mennell: Sociogenesis and psychogenesis, Comparative Sociology, 14(4), 2015, pp. 548–564.

[9] Cf. Bucholc: A global community of self-defense.

There is a body of scholarship applying Elias's approach to the study of families and the upbringing of children.[10] However, the civilizational consequences of digitalization have not yet been systematically addressed. Therefore, I will first reconstruct the Eliasian view of what he called the "civilizing of parents" over time, and then summarize the effect of this change in late modernity before the digital age, an era which Elias, who died in 1990, neither experienced nor accommodated in his theoretical framework. From there, I will outline the civilizational impact of digitalization, particularly of the Internet, on child-parental relations. In my conclusion, I will elaborate on the notion of a 'civilizing offensive', which was coined in the late 1970 s in the Netherlands and draws on Eliasian sociology. As Ryan Powell wrote:

> "Since then the term has been disseminated widely across Dutch society and penetrated political and popular discourse as a means of describing the deliberate, conscious attempts of powerful groups, including a historically paternalistic state, at altering the behaviour of sections of the population and inculcating lasting, 'civilised' habits."[11]

In regard to the emergence of the Internet and its influence on civilizing parents as a particular form of a civilizing offensive, I point out the ambivalence of the role that digital media play in the process of civilization, in families, and beyond.

1 Civilizing Parents: How it Used to Happen

In 1980, Elias wrote an essay on *The Civilizing of Parents,* the opening statement of which reads: "In the course of the twentieth century we have seen the acceleration of a transformation in the relationship between parents and children that can be traced back to the Middle Ages".[12] Referring to Philippe Ariès's history of childhood, Elias further observed that:

[10] Cf. de Figueiredo Lucena: Elias' Bodies, Educação & Realidade 42(4), October/December 2017; Gabriel: Growing up beside you, History of the Human Sciences, 27(3), 2014, pp. 116–135; Kitchens: The Informalization of the Parent-Child Relationship, Journal of Family History, 32(4), 2007, pp. 459–478; Sarat/Campos: Memories of childhood and education, Educação & Realidade 42 (4), October/December 2017.

[11] Powell: The Theoretical Concept of the 'Civilising Offensive' (Beschavingsoffensief), Human Figurations 2(2), 2013.

[12] Elias: The Civilising of Parents, in: Kilminster/Mennell (eds.): Essays II, pp. 14–40.

> "Despite a growing literature, in many respects we do not completely understand how we can help children enter into such a complex and unchildish society as ours, one which demands a high degree of foresights and self-control: how we can help them survive the inescapable individual civilizing process of becoming adult, without stunting their chances for pleasure and joy. However, this discovery of childhood most certainly concerns not just an advance in knowledge about children and understanding of children, but also something else. We could perhaps characterize it as the necessity for children to live their own lives, a type of life which in many respects is distinct from that of adults, even though the two are interdependent."[13]

The history of childhood is the history of the recognition of children as a particularly vulnerable social category. Children are different from the other wretched of the earth in that they are a dynamically changing group: They are children today, but they will surely no longer be children in 20 years, when they may be expected to have children of their own. Similar to many socially weaker groups in societies around the world, including women, racial and ethnic minorities, migrants, non-heteronormative peoples, the elderly, the poor, the disabled, and the dying, children are dependent on the socially stronger. In the case of children, this dependency is deeper than in most groups: Its basis is biological as well as social. For a significant portion of their lives, children depend on their parents (or other adult caregivers) for their biological survival. In this respect, they are indeed the weakest of the weak. They must rely on the assistance of someone who is infinitely physically stronger than they are, and their means of opposition are extremely scarce. The relationship between children and parents is highly asymmetrical. However, Elias argued that in any social relation, even in the most unbalanced one, the dependence always runs both ways: a slave may be the slaveowner's inferior, but a slaveowner is also dependent on the slave, just much less so than the other way around. But the dependence of children on adults is near absolute and incomparable to the dependence of adults on children, despite all consideration for emotional dependence of parents on tiny babies. "In societies like ours, there is hardly any other form of relationship in which the power differential between interdependent people is as great as that in the parent-child relation".[14]

However, as opposed to other relations of biological dependence, children's dependence ends rather quickly, if we consider the lifespan of an individual. This makes the power differential between children and parents particularly

[13] Cf. ibid., pp. 14–15.

[14] Ibid., p. 20.

problematic: it is an inherently instable one. This is probably one of the reasons why parents' use of physical violence against their children has fought off efforts for external regulation and governance for so long. Now in the twenty-first century, beating up employees, prisoners, beggars, or soldiers is no longer a daily occurrence, but spanking children is still commonplace in some countries, albeit forbidden in many legal orders and no longer a recommended form of educational influence in many cultures, and generally a practice less tolerated than it once was.[15] It is easy to hit a child. Nonetheless, Elias argues that even in places where spanking is still generally accepted, parents can be expected to hit their children less than they used to, and to pay more attention to their children, value them more, and allow them a greater degree of personal, bodily, and mental autonomy than in any previous epoch in human history—even though the scope of the change may differ from society to society, and from one social milieu to another. As parents become more civilized, children become more autonomous, and their power chances grow.

One significant consequence of the gradual civilization of parents is the increasing isolation of an individual, even within the family.[16] The increase in self-restraint routinely takes place through the separation of various bodily functions from the interactional sphere, which is achieved by the individualization of 'use' in housing spaces, such as designating areas as bedrooms, toilets, kitchens, etc., and by the delocalization of various activities, such as work, education, and exercise, which are typically pursued out of the home. Incidentally, the impact of all events preventing this kind of separation—such as the lockdown during the COVID-19 pandemic, which brought all bodily and intellectual functions (back) together into the home space—can thus be expected to cause an increase in domestic violence, a finding also based on the general assumptions of the theory of the process of civilization. Such effects have indeed been observed.[17]

---

[15] On the intercultural comparison of the prevalence and the decrease of spanking by parents, see: Straus: Prevalence, Societal Causes, and Trends in Corporal Punishment by Parents in World Perspective; Gershoff et. al.: Parent Discipline Practices in an International Sample, Child Dev. 2010 Mar, 81(2), pp. 487–502.

[16] Cf. Elias: The The Civilising of Parents, in: Kilminster/Mennell (eds.): Essays II, p. 28.

[17] Cf. Boserup/McKenney/Elkbuli: Alarming trends in US domestic violence during the COVID-19 pandemic, The American Journal of Emergency Medicine, 38(12), 2020, pp. 2753–2755; Campbell: An increasing risk of family violence during the Covid-19 pandemic, Forensic Science International: Reports 2, 2020.

Notwithstanding the variety of forms of civilizing parents in various environments around the world, the increasing autonomy of a child and the recognition of its specific status as a social category were accompanied by extending various forms of external social protection to children. Similar to other socially weaker categories, children have been included under legal protection. Here, Elias mentions the emergence of the international regime of children's rights as a particularly important sign of the civilizing of family relations. State power, which extended its monopoly of violence over parental and domestic relations, contributed to a shift in power between parents and children. By the same token, the power of other adults over children—that of teachers, priests, policemen, shopkeepers, and bona fide strangers—was also limited. In the course of civilizing parents, children became a special social category not only for their parents, but also for other people. This appropriation of children by society in general—the "entry of children into the stadium of history" (and law)—is accompanied by a specialization of various welfare agencies that are mainly there to watch, control, support, and if need be, replace the parents. This may, as has been reported in many countries, lead to bias and to bitter conflicts between parents and welfare agents who do not share the same cultural beliefs about the right standard of child protection, especially in multicultural, multiethnic societies or in the context of recent migration.[18] The "child's best interest", which is certainly a central concept of the state and international regulation of child welfare, is far from inambiguous.[19] Nonetheless, the very fact that such a concept has risen to its current prominent position in global, regional, and national legal orders is in itself proof that a civilizational change has taken place to the benefit of children.

[18] Cf. Crane/Ellisy: Benevolent Intervention or Oppression Perpetuated, Journal of Human Behavior in the Social Environment, 9(1–2), 2004, pp. 19–38; Middel et al.: The effects of migrant backgrounds and parent gender on child-protection decision-making, Child Abuse & Neglect, 104, June 2020, 104479; Sawrikar/Katz: Recommendations for Improving Cultural Competency, Child and Adolescent Social Work Journal, 31, 2014, pp. 393–417.

[19] On "best interest of a child" see e.g. Singer: The Right of the Child to Parents, in: Boele-Woelki/Dethloff/ Gephart (eds.): Family Law and Culture in Europe, pp. 137–150; Skivenes/Sørsdal: The Child's Best Interest Principle across Child Protection Jurisdictions, in: Falch-Eriksen/Backe-Hansen (eds.): Human Rights in Child Protection; for a figurational perspective, see van Krieken: The 'best interests of the child' and parental separation, The Modern Law Review, 68(1), 2005, pp. 25–48.

2 The Figuration of Parents and Children in Late Modernity

What are the general characteristics of the relationship between children and parents in late modernity? The general direction of civilizing parents seems to have been towards less violence, less inequality, less closeness, more distance, more standardization, and less privilege for parents over their own children compared to other humans. A child is far from being a parent's property. Even if the much-mediatized images of parents sacrificing everything for the well-being, education, safety, health, and life prospects of their children need not be indicative of a complete reversal of the relation, a parent in the Global North seems to be much more bound by having children than ever before. Having children is an obligation, a debt—in the case of student loans, a very real debt expressed in monetary terms. Children are, as has been noted for many decades now, increasingly a "value" for their parents. However, they are more of a liability than an asset, at least in economic terms, even though there is evidence that having children may benefit parents' social integration, a vital asset in the late-modern world.[20] Still, the most obvious value of children, the economic one, no longer applies: Children are not permitted to work to an economically significant extent, not even in rural environments where family life and work are often indistinguishable.

Children are being schooled; they are outsourced to specialized institutions. According to Pierre Bourdieu's famous thesis, institutionalized education tends to reproduce class structure by rewarding those with more cultural capital.[21] However, this means that out-of-home schooling does not fulfill the promise of equal opportunity. It does not mean that schooling leads to a simple reproduction of the parents' views, lifestyles, values, etc. Rather, by reproducing inequalities, it reproduces the social distinction that inequalities involve. School is likely to draw children away from their parents, even though it does not happen by moving them upwards in the social structure. The very fact of losing grip of one's child for a few hours a day significantly weakens a parent's power.

According to the 2021 OECD report, "there is nearly universal coverage of basic education for 6–14 year-olds, as enrolment rates for this age group

[20] Cf. Hoffman: The value of children to parents, Proceedings of the American Philosophical Society, 119(6), 1975, pp. 430–438; Nomaguchi/Milkie: Costs and rewards of children, Journal of Marriage and Family, 65(2), 2003, pp. 356–374.

[21] Cf. Bourdieu/Passeron: Reproduction in Education, Society and Culture.

reached or exceeded 95% in all OECD countries. In addition, 84% of the population is enrolled in education between the age of 15 and 19 on average across OECD countries".[22] Effectively, in the OECD countries practically all children are schooled. Globally, UNESCO data as of February 2020 shows over 89% of enrollment in basic education, a rise from 71% in 1970, albeit with vast regional, country and, in many societies, gender differences, with 83% of pupil persisting till the end of the primary school.[23] This would show that, with all reservations for inaccuracy and inequality, in today's world, a big majority of children are schooled on the basic level, typically in public or publicly controlled institutions, even in countries where homeschooling is common. As a result, parents and non-parents have become less differentiated in regard to the scope of power the state exercises over children, be they their own or those of other people. At the same time, the social control of children exercised in a disperse form by all adults seems to have been largely reduced, though no systematic global comparative data can support the thesis. To put it bluntly: 50 years ago, a misbehaving child would have expected to be reprimanded or castigated in some form or another by virtually any grown-up person who felt like it, in most countries of the world. Nowadays, in many countries the parent may expect to be castigated by other adults if her or his reaction to the child's comportment is deemed excessive compared to the social norm.

Reading about more distanced, restrained relations and increasing state control might induce the image of cool, functional family life with little emotional intensity and directness in it. However, with view to the tendencies illustrated above, an additional factor needs to be added that has been characteristic of social relations in the last century: the tendency towards "informalization".

Cas Wouters first described the process of informalization in his studies of Dutch society.[24] He drew on Elias's marginal observation in *On the Process of Civilisation,* regarding the prevalence of very revealing bathing attire on European beaches. Up to a certain point, civilizing seems to work by introducing more complicated, more nuanced, and more energy-consuming behavioral standards, as well as by inducing people to exert themselves in pedantic self-control. Freud's

---

[22] See OECD: Education at a Glance 2021: OECD Indicators.

[23] Cf. The World Bank: School enrollment.

[24] Cf. Wouters: Informalisation and the Civilising Process, in: Gleichmann/Goudsblom/Korte (eds.): Human Figurations, 1977, pp. 437–456; Wouters: Developments in the Behavioural Codes between the Sexes, Theory, Culture & Society, 4(2/3), 1987, pp. 405–427.

men and women are the protagonists of the phase of civilization in which it operates by the formalization of manners: Individuals bound by very detailed prescriptions of social and societal life, which react with various somatic and mental malfunctions, to the unbearable tension between their desires and impulses and the permitted patterns of behavior and thought. Elias was a late Freudian himself, and he shared the basic tenets of Freudian psychology. However, as he observed, the control of impulses in individuals may become so strong and so detailed that it is no longer a burden—it is another nature, interiorized and inalienable, and not to be shattered even in the face of a powerful trigger, such as a woman off her guard and in her bathing suit. The woman need not be formally dressed to be safe, nor does the man need a top hat and a stiff collar to remind him of the rules of proper behavior. Wouters noted, commenting on the sexual revolution of the 1960 s, that this informalization was one of the ways by which civilization works: forms are external restraints that can be dispensed of once internal constraints have become a part of human nature.

In relations between children and parents, the trend towards informalization has been particularly conspicuous over the twentieth century. People who themselves never spoke to their parents unless spoken to, and who were not allowed to sit at the family table until they had learned to 'behave properly', often have nothing against their children calling them by their first names and spitting around happily over everyone's plates when first learning to deal with solid food. There are a number of factors that contributed to shifts in parenting styles between the World War II generation, baby boomers, Generation X, and Millennials, some of which relate to demographic and structural variables (including the percentage of mothers active on the labor market, the fathers' involvement, the number of children, divorce rates, single parents, etc.), and some to purely cultural factors. Even though the changes in parenting styles have not been studied nearly as assiduously beyond the Global North, there is a body of evidence to confirm that a change in parent-child relations is more than a local or regional occurrence.[25] Informalization, though first detected in the Western world, seems to be an element of the whole postwar history of family and parenting. While there may be more self-restraint in parental-child relations, there is also less distance due to a reduction of forms.

---

[25] Cf. Goto/Surkan/Reich: Challenges to Changing the Culture of Parenting in Japan, Journal of Epidemiology, 30(10), 2020, pp. 427–428; Park/Coello/Lau: Child Socialization Goals in East Asian versus Western Nations from 1989 to 2010, Parenting, 14(2), 2014, pp. 69–91.

3 Internet in the Late Modern Figuration of Parents and Children

How does this landscape of civilizing parents in late modernity change with the arrival of digital media? In whose favor does the powerful tool known as the Internet work? Does it serve to further empower children, or does it increase the power differential favorably for parents? And what role does the state play in the process?

At first sight, new media seems to act as an equalizer due to the nature of interactions in the digital space. A child may have gained a large scope of autonomy since the Middle Ages, but until its teen years, it is still unlikely to be taken for an adult in any face-to-face interaction. A child is smaller, and its body, voice, etc. immediately betray its belonging to its special social category. But the Internet, despite all the regulatory measures taken to counteract it, is notorious for its "easy conductivity for anonymous and pseudoanonymous communications".[26] There are still plenty of places on the Internet where everyone could be anyone, including a child playing an adult. Admittedly, this symmetry also works to the advantage of adults who want to—for any licit or illicit reason—pass as a child. But with the Internet, a child is freed from its biological determination by the sheer size of its body, an emancipatory effect similar to that experienced by other categories bearing bodily signs of their belonging, such as racial minorities or transgender persons.[27]

The point of the Internet being a safe space for children pretending to be adults is, of course, a highly controversial one: Being freed from the limitations of bodily recognition comes at the price of being exposed to harmful practices and reactions of other Internet users. Nonetheless, if we consider the civilizing of parents, it can hardly be disputed that children are less controllable once they are able to use digital media. And they are using it extensively. The sphere, which only emerged a few decades ago, and was an adult domain until only recently, has been 'won' by children, including very young children, at a rampant rate.[28] Children and teenagers, as users of content platforms and social media, are a market

---

[26] Frankel/Siang: Ethical and legal aspects of human subjects research on the Internet, p. 7; see also Specht-Riemenschneider/Marko/Wette: Protection of Minors on Video Sharing Platforms, in this volume.

[27] Cf. Austin et al.: It's my safe space, International Journal of Transgender Health, 21(1), 2020, pp. 33–44.

[28] Cf. Holloway/Green/Livingstone: Zero to eight: young children and their internet use.

power, and their impact on their parents' Internet usage is significant.[29] So, both directly and indirectly, children have an additional asset which works in their favor in the family-power balance: They have an additional space where they can move relatively freely. This correlates with the parents' obligation to monitor and control one more sphere of activity (potential or actual) of their own children—not only in the interest of their own liability, but also to protect their children's safety.[30]

Thus, an interesting field emerged where parents have to deal with the unprecedented challenge of raising 'digital natives'. There is no one they can ask for advice; the majority of today's parents did not grow up with constant access to the Internet. The cohorts who are themselves digital natives have now reached the age when they have children of their own: they would be born not earlier than 1980 (in many societies, even in Europe, some years later), with the mean childbearing age in the most digitalized countries systematically increasing, over 29 in the European Union in 2019. As a result, in the scholarship on media use in families it is observed that "children often introduce new media into the family and influence parents' media adoption and use": children are "digital natives" instructing "digital immigrants" not only because they learn the technology earlier, but because they adapt to it faster.[31] From this perspective, the relative technological advantage of children may become a lasting experience even when all cohorts active in the child-rearing will belong to the category of the digital natives. The parents' reactions to the imbalance can vary significantly. They might restrict the use of new media altogether—a solution applied by some statistically marginal groups, despite being highly impracticable, especially in view of the requirements of homeschooling during the pandemic and the resulting awareness of the inevitability of a more digitalized education, even for the youngest. They might impose rules, restrict usage, monitor content, and generally move towards a formalization of the child-parent relationship in the context of Internet usage. However, they might also proceed along the path of informalization.

A number of studies have been conducted to analyze parenting strategies of dealing with digital media at home, and an interesting conclusion is that parents

---

[29] Cf. Correa et al.: Brokering new technologies, New Media & Society, 17(4), 2015, pp. 483–500.

[30] See Dreier: Projecting Images of Families into the Law, in this volume.

[31] Nelissen/Van den Bulck: When digital natives instruct digital immigrants, Information, Communication & Society, 21(3), 2018, pp. 375–387, p. 375.

are applying a style which is very much coherent with the overall idea of civilizing parents: they are, as Sonia Livingstone and her collaborators phrased it, "maximizing opportunities and minimizing risks".[32] The more competent the parents are in the digital world, the more likely they are to guide their children's digital media usage and transfer their knowledge to their children in a relatively equal setting of common experience. There are a number of factors, such as the age and gender of children, which affect the overall picture of equality and cooperation. Nonetheless, restrictive forms of parental mediation in Internet usage seem to be ebbing, at least in high-income countries.

Such informalization can be partly explained by the fact that children and parents share more or less the same resources online, and that learning to use them is a necessary cultural technique, soon to join other 'basics' like writing or counting. While in some countries known for highly digitalized educational systems, like Denmark, digital media literacy is largely assumed by the school, Internet skills are learned outside of the school in many other countries with more analog educational systems, such as Germany. It remains to be seen how much will change in this respect after the COVID-19 pandemic, but there is definitely potential for a rapprochement between children and parents sharing the experience of Internet usage. Moreover, the rapprochement may be sought by the parents, who in many cases may turn out to be less competent users. It would be too simplistic to think of the Internet as a potentially dangerous space where parents know their way around and children do not. While children can get lost and hurt very easily, they are often the ones who have a better and more accurate understanding of digital media operations, even if their critical thinking and discernment skills are not fully developed. Bottom-up technology transmission happens often in families with very young Internet users.[33]

To return to the point about mystery, anonymity, and pseudoanonymity: The Internet is not only a space of personal freedom, but a place for creating and mobilizing group resources. Children, as the socially weaker category, may use digital media to communicate, exchange information, and cooperate with peers, in this case others in a similar position—other children. The extent to which they may be interested in avoiding parental control, participation, and guidance also

---

[32] Livingstone et al.: Maximizing opportunities and minimizing risks for children online, Journal of Communication, 67(1), 2017, pp. 82–105.

[33] Cf. Correa: Bottom-up technology transmission within families, Journal of Communication, 64(1), 2014, pp. 103–124.

highlights the contentious aspect of Internet usage in family life: there is a subversive potential, especially on social media, which connects individual users into communities capable of organized action. "Children of the world, unite!"—this call has been powerfully picked up by the global movement Fridays for Future, forming their collective identity "on Instagram" and apparently beyond the family context.[34]

Fridays for Future may serve as an example of what children's autonomy may mean in the digital age, but it also shows the changing role of the state in light of new forms of social mobilization. Contrary to what many believe, nation-states can be very efficient in controlling the Internet and in exercising overt hidden pressure on Internet service providers. The Internet is, in this sense, far from being completely free. It is being increasingly regulated in some, if not all, regions of the world, and the enforcement of legal rules on the Internet is also developing more dynamically than could have been expected even a few years ago. Still, state control of Internet content and usage, which is frequently motivated by children's well-being (especially in matters of child pornography, child trafficking, and access to violent content), does not reach into the innovative and creative uses of the Internet which allow children and teenagers, as a group, to become not only a psychological or an economic player, but also a considerable political force. Gaining one's own political standing and voice is a great leap in the autonomization of children as a social category. The political voice of children today is still relatively dependent on adult recognition, but if this changes, digital media will surely be instrumental in the process, and the balance of power in families will then shift even more favorably for children.

4 Conclusion: A Digital Civilizing Offensive?

The Internet's arrival in family lives might be perceived as a civilizing offensive, as explained by Ryan Powell in the following way:

> "It is over a third of a century since the term *het burgerlijkbeschavingsoffensief*—the bourgeois civilising offensive—was first coined and the concept subsequently developed. It is, 'of course, derived from Norbert Elias'. Since then the term has been disseminated widely across Dutch society and penetrated political and popular discourse as a means of describing the deliberate, conscious attempts of powerful

[34] Cf. Brünker/Deitelhoff/Mirbabaie: Collective Identity Formation on Instagram.

> groups, including a historically paternalistic state, at altering the behaviour of sections of the population and inculcating lasting, 'civilised' habits."[35]

The civilizing offensive caused by the Internet is a peculiar, authorless one. Even though there is significant content control, manipulation, and fraud on the Internet, it would be naïve to see one single concentrated agency behind it all. Similarly, although there may be many good intentions, high ideals, and sound motives behind the promotion of Internet usage, there is hardly a single benefactor backstage for the World Wide Web. While the Dutch civilizing offensive in the late 1970 s was a deliberate state-made moralizing effort to create a different and more satisfactory society, the digital civilizing offensive does not seem to have a goal. Certainly, it does not aim to create less formal, more equal, and more externally connected families with more autonomous children and less powerful parents. But there are some consequences of the digital age, be they intended or unintended, which seem to work towards the civilizing of parents in an offensive-like manner.

The Internet created the possibility of moving beyond the household space and of lifting the limitations of a child's body. It enables communication with peers beyond one's immediate everyday surroundings, which may be especially important for vulnerable children with statistically rare problems hard to solve in their own circles. The Internet may be instrumental in children's self-defense against threats that they encounter in their young lives. But it seems that in these attempts, adults in general and parents in particular are on the children's side. While parents' restrictive strategies often stem from the desire to protect and guide their children in the digital space, they might result in the reversal of the informalization of family life and the accommodation of new media—and sharing this experience intergenerationally seems to be a prevailing model in high-income countries that have a long history of Internet usage. It seems that the Internet supports the emancipation of children, and that it does away with a few of the last bastions of parental domination, such as privileged knowledge-status and higher operational skills.

One question which must inevitably be posed in the conclusion of a paper on the civilizing of parents by way of digitalization concerns the future of this trend. One hint seems to rest in the functional democratization of families under digital

[35] Powell: The Theoretical Concept of the 'Civilising Offensive' (Beschavingsoffensief), Human Figurations 2(2), 2013 (references contained in the original have been omitted from the citation).

rule: the fundamental fact of children's biological dependence and relative powerlessness might simply be blurred out by the day-to-day efficiency of children in digital communication and by the universal immersion into online interaction. While there is a limit to the empowerment of children by digital means, it might easily be pushed further and further into a shared experience across ages. Trusting digital civilization may turn against both the children and the parents. They may both become oblivious of their interrelatedness because it would matter less and less in their everyday lives. Whether this would be the final step in the civilization of parents as the privileged adults in children's lives is something of a moot point: a creature which is biologically non-self-reliant must rely on someone, and reliance is a source of power. It remains to be seen whether the digital age will undermine this basic inequality inherent in the long and straining course of human socialization by eliminating power despite preserving the family as an environment for socialization. The Internet, which did not live up to the expectations as a universal global equalizer, might yet deliver in the ubiquitous sphere of family relations.

References

Austin, Ashley/Craig, Shelley L./Navega, Nicole/McInroy, Lauren B.: It's my safe space: The life-saving role of the internet in the lives of transgender and gender diverse youth, International Journal of Transgender Health, 21(1), 2020, pp. 33–44, https://doi.org/10.1080/15532739.2019.1700202.

Bakker, Tom P./de Vreese, Claes H.: Good News for the Future? Young People, Internet Use, and Political Participation, Communication Research, 38(4), 2011, pp. 451–470.

Bonfadelli, Heinz: The Internet and Knowledge Gaps: A Theoretical and Empirical Investigation, European Journal of Communication, 17(1), 2002, pp. 65–84, https://doi.org/10.1177/0267323102017001607.

Bourdieu, Pierre/Passeron, Jean-Claude: Reproduction in Education, Society and Culture, Vol. 4, London/Newbury Park/New Delhi 1990.

Boserup, Brad/McKenney, Mark/Elkbuli, Adel: Alarming trends in US domestic violence during the COVID-19 pandemic, The American Journal of Emergency Medicine, 38(12), 2020, pp. 2753–2755, https://doi.org/10.1016/j.ajem.2020.04.077.

Brünker, Felix/Deitelhoff, Fabian/Mirbabaie, Milad: Collective Identity Formation on Instagram—Investigating the Social Movement Fridays for Future, Australasian Conference on Information Systems, 2019, https://acis2019.io/pdfs/ACIS2019_PaperFIN_070.pdf; last accessed May 26, 2021.

Bucholc, Marta: A global community of self-defense: Norbert Elias on normativity, culture and involvement, Frankfurt a. M. 2015.

Buckingham, David/Willet., Rebekah (eds.): Digital Generations: Children, Young People and the New Media, London 2006.

Campbell, Andrew M.: An increasing risk of family violence during the Covid-19 pandemic: Strengthening community collaborations to save lives, Forensic Science International: Reports 2, 2020, https://doi.org/10.1016/j.fsir.2020.100089.

Castells, Manuel: The Rise of the Network Society, Hoboken/NJ 2010.

Chassiakos, Yolanda L.R./Radesky, Jenny/Christakis, Dimitri/Moreno, Megan A./Cross, Corinn: Children and adolescents and digital media, Pediatrics, 138(5), 2016.

Correa, Teresa: Bottom-up technology transmission within families: Exploring how youths influence their parents' digital media use with dyadic data, Journal of Communication, 64(1), 2014, pp. 103–124.

Correa, Teresa/Straubhaar, Joseph D./Chen, Wenhong/Spence, Jeremiah: Brokering new technologies: The role of children in their parents' usage of the internet, New Media & Society, 17(4), 2015, pp. 483–500.

Crane, Kimberly D./Ellisy, Rodney A.: Benevolent Intervention or Oppression Perpetuated. Minority Overrepresentation in Child Services, Journal of Human Behavior in the Social Environment, 9(1–2), 2004, pp. 19–38, https://doi.org/10.1300/J137v09n01_03.

de Figueiredo Lucena, Ricardo: Elias' Bodies: the conception of body and education from three works of Norbert Elias, Educação & Realidade 42 (4), October/December 2017, https://doi.org/10.1590/2175-623664290.

Dethloff, Nina: Families and the Law: Taking Account of Children's Evolving Capacities in Analogue and Digital Contexts, in this volume.

Devitt, Kerry/Roker, Debi: The Role of Mobile Phones in Family Communication, Children & Society 23(3), 2009, pp. 189–202.

Dreier, Thomas: Projecting Images of Families into the Law—The Example of Internet-Related Cases Decided by the German Courts, in this volume.

Elias, Norbert: The Established and the Outsiders: Collected Works of Norbert Elias, Vol. 4, Dublin 2008.

Elias, Norbert: On the Process of Civilization: Collected Works of Norbert Elias, Vol. 3, Dublin 2012.

Elias, Norbert: The Civilising of Parents, in: Kilminster, Richard/Mennell Stephen (eds.): Essays II, Dublin: UCDP 2008, Established and the Outsiders, pp. 14–40.

Frankel, Mark S./Siang, Sanyin: Ethical and legal aspects of human subjects research on the Internet. A Report of a Workshop, Washington, D.C. 1999, https://www.researchgate.net/profile/Sanyin_Siang/publication/268296040_Ethical_and_Legal_Aspects_of_Human_Subjects_Research_on_the_Internet/links/5632302008ae0530378fd404/Ethical-and-Legal-Aspects-of-Human-Subjects-Research-on-the-Internet.pdf; last accessed May 26, 2021.

Fuchs, Christian/Boersma, Kees/Albrechtslund, Anders/Sandoval, Marisol (eds.): Internet and Surveillance. The Challenges of Web 2.0 and Social Media, London 2012.

Gabriel, Norman: Growing up beside you: A relational sociology of early childhood, History of the Human Sciences, 27(3), 2014, pp. 116–135.

Gershoff, Elizabeth T./Grogan-Kaylor, Andrew/Lansford, Jennifer E./Chang, Lei/Zelli, Arnaldo Deater-Deckard, Kirby/Dodge, Kenneth A. et. al.: Parent Discipline Practices in an International Sample: Associations With Child Behaviors and Moderation by Perceived Normativeness, Child Dev. 2010 Mar, 81(2), pp. 487–502.

Goto, Aya/Surkan, Pamela J./Reich, Michael R.: Challenges to Changing the Culture of Parenting in Japan, Journal of Epidemiology, 2020, 30(10), pp. 427–428.

Hoffman, Lois W.: The value of children to parents and the decrease in family size, Proceedings of the American Philosophical Society, 119(6), 1975, pp. 430–438.

Holloway, Donell/Green, Leila/Livingstone, Sonia: Zero to eight: young children and their internet use, London 2013, http://eprints.lse.ac.uk/52630/.

Kitchens, Rachael: The Informalization of the Parent-Child Relationship: An Investigation of Parenting Discourses Produced in Australia in the Inter-War Years, Journal of Family History, 32(4), 2007, pp. 459–478, https://doi.org/10.1177/0363199007304425.

Krueger, Brian S.: Government Surveillance and Political Participation on the Internet, Social Science Computer Review, 23(4), 2005, pp. 439–452.

Livingstone, Sonia/Ólafsson, Kjartan/Helsper, Ellen J./Lupiáñez-Villanueva, Francisco/Veltri, Giuseppe A./Folkvord, Frans: Maximizing opportunities and minimizing risks for children online: The role of digital skills in emerging strategies of parental mediation, Journal of Communication, 67(1), 2017, pp. 82–105.

Lupton, Deborah/Pedersen, Sarah/Thomas, Gareth M.: Parenting and digital media: from the early web to contemporary digital society, Sociology Compass, 10(8), 2016, pp. 730–743.

Mennell, Stephen: Sociogenesis and psychogenesis: Norbert Elias's historical social psychology as a research tradition in comparative sociology, Comparative Sociology, 14(4), 2015, pp. 548–564.

Middel, Floor/Lopez, Mónica/Fluke, John/Grietens, Hans: The effects of migrant backgrounds and parent gender on child-protection decision-making: An intersectional analysis, Child Abuse & Neglect, 104, June 2020, 104479, https://doi.org/10.1016/j.chiabu.2020.104479.

Nelissen, Sara/Van den Bulck, Jan: When digital natives instruct digital immigrants: active guidance of parental media use by children and conflict in the family, Information, Communication & Society, 21(3), 2018, pp. 375–387.

Nomaguchi, Kei M./Milkie, Melissa A.: Costs and rewards of children: The effects of becoming a parent on adults' lives, Journal of Marriage and Family, 65(2), 2003, pp. 356–374.

OECD: Education at a Glance 2021: OECD Indicators, https://www.oecd-ilibrary.org/sites/b35a14e5-en/1/3/3/1/index.html?itemId=/content/publication/b35a14e5-en&_csp_=9689b83a12cab1f95b32a46f4225d1a5&itemIGO=oecd&itemContentType=book#section-d1e1799; last accessed October 6, 2021.

Park, Heejung/Coello, Jordan A./Lau, Anna S.: Child Socialization Goals in East Asian versus Western Nations from 1989 to 2010: Evidence for Social Change in Parenting, Parenting, 14(2), 2014, pp. 69–91.

Powell, Ryan: The Theoretical Concept of the 'Civilising Offensive' (Beschavingsoffensief): Notes on its Origins and Uses, Human Figurations 2(2), 2013, http://hdl.handle.net/2027/spo.11217607.0002.203.

Prakash, Shiv/Yadav, Jai S./Singh, T.B.: An online cross-sectional study to assess the prevalence of internet addiction among people staying at their home during lockdown due to COVID-19, International Journal of Indian Psychology, 8(3), 2020, pp. 424–432.

Sarat, Magda/Campos, Miria I.: Memories of childhood and education: Eliasian approaches on women, Educação & Realidade 42 (4), October/December 2017, https://doi.org/10.1590/2175-623664283.

Sawrikar, Pooja/Katz, Ilan B.: Recommendations for Improving Cultural Competency When Working With Ethnic Minority Families in Child Protection Systems in Australia,

Child and Adolescent Social Work Journal, 31, 2014, pp. 393–417, https://doi.org/10.1007/s10560-014-0334-8.

Singer, Anna: The Right of the Child to Parents, in: Boele-Woelki, Katharina/Dethloff, Nina/Gephart, Werner (eds.): Family Law and Culture in Europe: Developments, Challenges and Opportunities, Cambridge 2014, pp. 137–150.

Skivenes, Marit/Sørsdal, Line Marie: The Child's Best Interest Principle across Child Protection Jurisdictions, in: Falch-Eriksen, Asgeir/Backe-Hansen Elisabeth (eds.): Human Rights in Child Protection, London 2018. https://doi.org/10.1007/978-3-319-94800-3_4.

Specht-Riemenschneider, Louisa/Marko, Alina/Wette, Sascha: Protection of Minors on Video Sharing Platforms, in this volume.

Straus, Murray A.: Prevalence, Societal Causes, and Trends in Corporal Punishment by Parents in World Perspective, 73 Law and Contemporary Problems 1–30 (Spring 2010).

The World Bank: School enrollment, https://data.worldbank.org/indicator/SE.PRM.NENR.MA; last accessed October 6, 2021.

van Krieken, Robert: The 'best interests of the child' and parental separation: On the 'civilizing of parents', The Modern Law Review, 68(1), 2005, pp. 25–48.

Wouters, Cas: Informalisation and the Civilising Process, in: Gleichmann, Peter R./Goudsblom, Johan/Korte, Hermann (eds.): Human Figurations, essays for/Aufsätze für Norbert Elias, Amsterdam 1977, pp. 437–456.

Wouters, Cas: Developments in the Behavioural Codes between the Sexes: The Formalization of Informalization in the Netherlands, 1930–85, Theory, Culture & Society, 4(2/3), 1987, pp. 405–427.

Prof. Dr. Marta Bucholc is Professor of Sociology at the University of Warsaw, Poland, and Associate Researcher at the Centre de recherche en science politique, Université Saint-Louis Bruxelles. She is the Polish PI in the Volkswagen Foundation research project "Towards illiberal Constitutionalism in East Central Europe: Historical Analysis in Comparative and Transnational Perspectives", led by the University of Jena (2021–2025). From 2015 to 2020, she was Research Professor at the Käte Hamburger Center for Advanced Study "Law as Culture".

Regulating Data and Digital Economy, Protecting Children?

Data Collection, Privacy, and Children in the Digital Economy

Olufunmilayo B. Arewa

1 The Collection and Use of Data and Information

Technologies today facilitate widespread dissemination of information, including visual images, and rapid communication to billions of people across the globe. The digital economy highlights the increasing economic importance and value of data, information, and other intangibles for many companies. This in turn underlines a shift in dominant business production and operation models towards approaches that significantly utilize intangibles. Intangibles have thus contributed to a marked yet understudied transformation in business practices and sources of economic value for numerous firms. These trends are only likely to accelerate in an era of big data solutions.

Digital economy firms increasingly shape how we create, disseminate, and access data and information. The activities of such firms have contributed to a growing value of information in recent years. Prominent digital economy firms have strongly embraced Facebook founder Mark Zuckerberg's motto of "moving fast and breaking things".[1] However, this ethos of disruption has posed significant challenges for existing policies, laws, and regulations, especially those that relate

[1] Taplin: Move Fast and Break Things.

O. B. Arewa (✉)
Temple University, Philadelphia, USA
e-mail: oarewa@temple.edu

N. Dethloff et al. (eds.), *Families and New Media*, Juridicum – Schriften zum Medien-, Informations- und Datenrecht,
https://doi.org/10.1007/978-3-658-39664-0_9

to the collection of consumer data and the usage and dissemination of data and information.

Data is the raw material that has come to be an essential and valuable feature of a broad range of digital economy activities. As Julie Cohen notes, "data extracted from individuals plays an increasingly important role as *raw material* in the political economy of informational capitalism".[2] Information is often presented as data that is in some way organized, structured, or otherwise processed. The processing of data is thought to render it relevant for a "specific purpose or context, and thereby makes it meaningful, valuable, useful and relevant".[3] In the digital economy era, data has become a significant driver of economic and business growth.[4] This is reflected, for example, in the market valuations of technology companies in the data technology business, including Alphabet, Amazon, Apple, Facebook, and Microsoft. In August 2020, the combined market capitalization of these five companies constituted more than 20% of the S&P 500, one of the most influential equity indices. That same month, Apple reached a market valuation of $2 trillion, and the market capitalization of the United States technology sector was said to be worth more than the entire European stock market, which was four times larger than the United States technology sector in 2007.[5]

Several data technology companies use business models that derive significant value from targeted advertising driven by such companies' uses of user data. These models involve the collection, aggregation, management, and organization of data in ways that enable these companies to sell targeted advertisements that may look like organic content.[6] For example, in 2019, Alphabet, Google's parent company, derived more than 83% of its total revenues from online ads,[7] while Facebook received nearly all of its revenue from third-parties advertising

[2] Cohen: Law for the Platform Economy, University of California Davis Law Review 51, 2017, pp. 133–204, at p. 157.

[3] Rowley: The wisdom hierarchy, Journal of Information Science 33(2), 2007, pp. 163–180, at p. 171.

[4] Mueller/Grindal: Data flows and the digital economy, Digital Policy, Regulation and Governance 21(1), 2018, pp. 71–87.

[5] Pound: U.S. tech stocks are now worth more than the entire European stock market.

[6] Metz: How Facebook's Ad System Works; Edelman: Why Don't We Just Ban Targeted Advertising.

[7] Alphabet Inc. Annual Report on Form 10-K for the fiscal year ended December 31, 2019, at p. 9.

on Facebook and Instagram.[8] Data technology companies' collection of data has an impact on the ecology of digital spaces.[9]

Data has been described as the new oil, which has contributed to the widespread implementation of data-driven business models: "[c]apitalizing on this data explosion is increasingly becoming a necessity in order for a business to remain competitive".[10] The potential recognized by companies embracing data technology business models has become a beacon call to others who seek to harness value from the collection and exploitation of data and information.

Data-driven business models raise significant issues about the effectiveness of consent for all users and particularly for children. Collectors of data may not be transparent about uses of the data, and users may not be fully aware of the implications of consent. In some jurisdictions with less stringent data protection requirements, including many states in the United States, consumers may not effectively be given a choice about collection and uses of their data. The proliferation of mobile devices may give those collecting user data extensive information about users' location and activities.

The 2021 adoption iOS 14.5 by Apple gives a strong indication of the importance of effective consumer consent. Apple's iOS 14.5 includes App Tracking Transparency (ATT), which gives users of Apple devices greater awareness of which applications are tracking them and more control over such tracking.[11] More specifically, ATT requires that applications ask permission to track activity across other applications and websites.[12] Apple's ATT was strongly opposed by Facebook, which is a leading company embracing an advertising data technology model. Facebook undertook a campaign opposing Apple's ATT, publishing full page advertisements in leading newspapers in the United States: "titled 'We are standing up to Apple for small businesses everywhere', and 'Apple vs. Free internet.' Both the ads call the new iOS 14 privacy update harmful for small businesses because, without targetted ads, their sales will drop by 60%".[13] Initial data about consumer consent suggests that many consumers will not consent to

[8] Facebook, Inc. Annual Report on Form 10-K for the fiscal year ended December 31, 2019, at p. 11.

[9] Graham: Google and advertising, Palgrave Communications 3, 45, 2017.

[10] Brownlow et al.: Data and Analytics.

[11] Apple Inc.: Data Privacy Day at Apple: Improving Transparency and Empowering Users.

[12] Cross: What is App Tracking Transparency and how do you block app tracking?

[13] Imran: EFF calls Facebook's opposition of Apple's new ATT privacy feature 'laughable'.

tracking if they are given the opportunity to block tracking. According to Flurry Analytics statistics, only 15% of iOS 14.5 users in the United States opted-in to ad tracking four months after the software was released, which is noticeably lower than the 21% of users who opted-in worldwide.[14]

Consumer consent in contexts of extensive data collection may also be ineffective because consumers and even the companies themselves may not actually know the value of the information being given. Consumers may also not be aware of the risks of the data that they give such companies, particularly because the aggregation of such data and creation of profiles are part of what renders such data and information valuable. The harm imposed by breaches of such data are thus difficult to determine, even after breaches have occurred, because companies creating such models are not the only actors creating profiles of consumers. Hackers, for example, are actively scraping data from these collections of consumer data.

Once collected, data and information may rest in the hands of private companies that build business models derived from exploitation. The monetization of data has become pervasive among businesses. A 2017 survey by McKinsey found that, although data monetization as a means of growth was in its early stages of development, "an increasing share of companies is using data and analytics to generate growth... [and] are adding new services to existing offerings, developing new business models, and even directly selling data based products or utilities".[15]

The growth of data technology companies has led to a proliferation of business models that seek to monetize data, which has given many companies incentive to collect as much data as they possibly can. Edward Snowden, a former U.S. National Security Agency (NSA) contractor who in 2013 became a whistleblower by leaking classified documents that detailed NSA global surveillance programs, has persistently drawn attention to digital era intelligence collection and monitoring. In 2018, Snowden discussed data collection and data privacy, noting that the collection of data entrenches "a system that makes the population vulnerable for the benefit of the privileged".[16] He also noted that the NSA and Facebook have similar data models.

[14] Fuchs: The Impact of Apple iOS 14.5 on Facebook Ad Campaigns.

[15] McKinsey & Company: Fueling growth through data monetization.

[16] Browne: Edward Snowden says "the most powerful institutions in society have become the least accountable".

The proliferation of data technology companies has contributed to changing cultural practices with respect to expectations of privacy and views about surveillance.[17] This has significant implications for a broad range of legal frameworks, including copyright law and privacy law. Broad data collection also raises questions about the accountability of those who gather, process, or use data. The rapid growth of business models that focus on the collection and use of information has contributed to the widespread retention of personal data and personally identifiable information by companies, governments, and others in varied contexts.

The collection and use of data have a particular impact on children. As the Office of the Children's Commissioner for England (CCO) noted in a 2018 report, more data about children is collected today than ever before; further, the availability of such data may have significant consequences for children.[18] This data may stem from various activities and sources, including parents and children sharing information on social media, smart toys, speakers, and other connected Internet of Things (IoT) devices, which are increasingly present in homes. Data may also come from monitoring equipment like pedometers and location-tracking watches, and information given away when children use essential public services. As the CCO report states, "[c]hildren are being 'datafied' – not just via social media, but in many aspects of their lives".[19] Access to information about children may pose both short-term and long-term threats.

In addition, children, unlike adults, may not have control over decisions related to their data, which must be taken into account in any attempt to regulate data and information about children. The proliferation of data is not just an issue for children. In a world of connected devices, many create data in the course of everyday activities and transactions. Many who use IoT devices, including smart speakers like Amazon's Alexa and smart cameras like Amazon's Ring camera, may not be aware of who might have access to their devices or how data generated by their devices is handled.[20]

Companies and governments are not alone in accessing and collecting personal information. As a result, once private data has been collected, other parties may seek to access and exploit it for their benefit. A number of business models

---

[17] Zuboff: The Age of Surveillance Capitalism.

[18] Children's Commissioner: Who Knows What About Me?, p. 3.

[19] Ibid.

[20] Brown: Amazon's Ring Fires Four Employees; Kelly/Statt: Amazon Confirms it holds on to Alexa data.

are being built around the theft and capture of private data and information, which is now so widely collected and retained.[21] Private data and information may not be well secured by those collecting and retaining it. The rise of data technology business models has been a factor in increased legal and regulatory attention to questions related to data privacy, data protection, and data security. This scrutiny is necessary because the data being collected has a potentially long lifespan and is not really disposable:

> "The data we are all collecting around people has this same really odd property [as nuclear waste]... information about people retains its power as long as those people are alive, and sometimes as long as their children are alive. No one knows what will become of sites like Twitter in five years or ten. But the data those sites own will retain the power to hurt for decades."[22]

Data collected from children has potential to be long-lived, and it is prone to be "dangerous long after it has been created and forgotten because the massive amounts of data collected about people are not disposable; they could be useful at some point, particularly when consumer data are used in national security intelligence".[23]

Personal data is one of the most important targets for participants in markets for stolen data. In 2017, some 17 million Americans had personal data stolen and became victims of identity theft.[24] Data leaks have become pervasive. Concerns about data privacy and security have led to the adoption of data protection legal frameworks throughout the world, including the European Union's General Data Protection Regulation ("GDPR"),[25] which has become a worldwide model for data protection. In his 2018 remarks, Snowden suggested that attention to data privacy and data protection "misplaces the problem" by not sufficiently focusing on the business of data collection itself: "[t]he problem isn't data protection, the problem is data collection... [r]egulation and protection of data presumes that the

[21] Ablon: Data Thieves.

[22] Ceglowski: Haunted by Data.

[23] Mackenzie: The Afterlife of Data, Transgender Studies Quarterly 4(1), 2017, pp. 45–60, at p. 46–47.

[24] Pascual/Marchini/Miller: 2018 Identity Fraud.

[25] Regulation (EU) 2016/679 of the European Parliament and of the Council of 27 April 2016 on the protection of natural persons with regard to the processing of personal data and on the free movement of such data, and repealing Directive 95/46/EC. Official Journal of the European Union, L 119/1, May 5, 2016.

collection of data in the first place was proper, that it is appropriate, that it doesn't represent a threat or a danger".[26]

The extent to which businesses are effectively penalized may play a significant role in determining incentives. GDPR fines may give some indication of incentives. In 2018, the GDPR began being enforced by various European Union data protection agencies. By August 2020, one calculation suggested that GDPR fines assessed collectively surpassed €500 million.[27] The effectiveness of these fines will depend on several factors, including whether those penalized are actually the ones who pay them and what behavioral incentives are induced by fines. These penalties should also likely be evaluated in light of the enormous benefits that flow from uses of data in a wide range of business models today. In October 2020, in one of the largest GDPR fines to date, the Hamburg Commissioner for Data Protection and Freedom of Information fined H&M €35.3 million for excessive monitoring of employees at an H&M German subsidiary.[28] As of mid-September 2021, Google and Facebook led the list of those fined. Google received a penalty of €50 million by the French data regulator CNIL for "lack of transparency, inadequate information and lack of valid consent regarding ads personalization".[29] WhatsApp, owned by Facebook, received a fine of €225 million in September 2021 for failure to fully disclose how it collected and shared user data.[30] Notably, although €50 million is a substantial amount of money by most measures, it is likely not a substantial amount for Google, which had almost $162 billion in revenue and earned $34.3 billion in net income in 2019.[31] Similarly, the €225 million fine imposed on Facebook is a fraction of Facebook's close to $86

---

[26] Browne: Edward Snowden says "the most powerful institutions in society have become the least accountable"; Lyon: Surveillance, Snowden, and Big Data, Big Data & Society, July 2014, pp. 1–13.

[27] CoreView: Major GDPR Fine Tracker.

[28] The Hamburg Commissioner for Data Protection and Freedom of Information: 35.3 Million Euro Fine for Data Protection Violations in H&M's Service Center.

[29] CNIL: The CNIL's restricted committee imposes a financial penalty of 50 Million euros against Google LLC.

[30] Data Protection Commission: Data Protection Commission announces decision in WhatsApp inquiry; European Data Protection Board, Binding decision 1/2021 on the dispute arisen on the draft decision of the Irish Supervisory Authority regarding WhatsApp Ireland under Article 65(1)(a) GDPR.

[31] Alphabet Inc. Annual Report on Form 10-K for the fiscal year ended December 31, 2019, at p. 51 (Consolidated Statements of Income).

billion in revenue and $29 billion in net income in 2020.[32] Google's €50 million GDPR fine is also substantially less than fines imposed on Google by the European Commission's Directorate General for Competition, which totaled close to €10 billion by 2019.[33]

2 Changing Business Models, Cultural Practices, and Regulation

Data technology business models pose constant challenges for regulation in part because they are varied, relatively new, and are often continuously under development. Data technology models enable companies to derive significant value from the collection, aggregation, control, and use of information. Companies and governments today collect a significant amount of data:

> "'These companies take enormous, enormous amounts of data about us' [Senator Mark] Warner told Axios. 'If you're an avid Facebook user, chances are Facebook knows more about you than the US government knows about you. People don't realize one, how much data is being collected; and two, they don't realize how much that data is worth.'"[34]

Google, for example, records every search performed and every YouTube video watched.[35] For users with smartphones, including iPhones and Android phones, Google Maps "logs everywhere you go, the route you use to get there and how long you stay – even if you never open the app".[36] Google will now automatically delete private data after 18 months by default, but only for new users. For the 1.5 billion people on Gmail and 2.5 billion people already using Android, default account settings permit Google to retain private data forever unless the user

[32] Facebook, Inc.: Annual Report on Form 10-K for the fiscal year ended December 31, 2020, at p. 50 (Consolidated Statements of Income).

[33] All of these fines are under appeal, ibid. at pp. 78–79 (Note 10. Commitments and Contingencies).

[34] Kanter: Facebook and Google Could be Forced to Tell You How Much Your Data is Worth under new US Legislation.

[35] Smith: Google Collects a Frightening Amount of Data About You.

[36] Ibid.

changes this setting.[37] Users of IoT devices may authorize devices that enable them to be under surveillance. Although many of these devices are purchased for personal security, the data generated by them may be available to others, which may include employees of companies selling IoT devices, who may have access to such devices, and hackers.

The collection and retention of vast amounts of data, which consumers have in many cases given away for free, has led to problems. Data made available to Facebook has in turn been made available to others, often without the user's consent. For example, Cambridge Analytica, a political data firm hired by the 2016 Trump campaign, "gained access to private information on more than 50 million Facebook users. The firm offered tools that could identify the personalities of American voters and influence their behavior".[38] Cambridge Analytica was also involved in other campaigns, including those of Kenyan President Uhuru Kenyatta in 2013 and 2017 and the Brexit referendum.[39]

Data breaches have become commonplace today and may not be reported in a timely fashion in the United States. The 2017 Equifax data breach revealed personal information about approximately 148 million people in the United States, 8000 people in Canada, and almost 700,000 citizens of the United Kingdom.[40] This data breach occurred between March and late July 2017. Equifax became aware of suspicious network activity in late July 2017 but did not make a public announcement about the breach until early September 2017. Notably, GDPR requires disclosure of certain types of data breaches.[41] Breaches at Equifax and other companies highlight ways in which data may not be properly secured. Companies in possession of such data may underinvest in security, for example, by not encrypting data. IoT and other devices may be compromised or lack basic security features. Companies may engage in improper or illegal data collection, including from children. In 2019, for example, Google and YouTube paid $170 million to the United States Federal Trade Commission and the State of New York for violating the Children's Online Privacy Protection Act (COPPA) of 1998.[42]

---

[37] Ibid.

[38] Granville: Facebook and Cambridge Analytica.

[39] Moore: Cambridge Analytica Had a Role in Kenya Election, Too; Cadwalladr: The Great British Brexit Robbery.

[40] Electronic Privacy Information Center: Equifax Data Breach.

[41] GDPR, Art. 34.

[42] 15 U.S.C. §§6501–6505 (1998); Federal Trade Commission: Google and YouTube Will Pay Record $170 Million for Alleged Violations of Children's Privacy Law.

Changing digital economy business models that focus on data as raw material underscore fundamental changes in cultural practices. Many people generate content on YouTube, Facebook, Instagram, and more recently TikTok, as well as numerous other websites and applications that have become essential digital era tools. Content on these platforms have become important vehicles for expressing creativity, conveying knowledge, and forming and maintaining relationships. It has become commonplace for people to carry devices, including smartphones, that enable others to track them, at times with incomplete or inaccurate knowledge about the capabilities of such devices. People may install other applications that enable others to surveil them. In 2019, news reports emerged from Tennessee, where a stranger hacked a family's Ring camera home security device and was able to watch and speak to young girls, the parents of whom had ostensibly purchased the device and placed it in their daughters' bedroom to enable better security.[43]

Many people voluntarily provide data to sources that they authorize without a full understanding of the potential uses of their data or how data has become a core raw material for varied digital economy business models, including in black-market ecosystems.[44] These and a myriad of other activities and behaviors underscore significant changes in cultural practices that have seemingly shifted views about surveillance and privacy for many, perhaps at times unknowingly because people may not always fully apprehend what their devices actually do or what happens to data they provide.

The applications and devices that have become a part of daily life are key conduits through which many access "the digital". These applications and devices highlight the importance of networks in the digital era, the complexity and transparency that may come with using things we insufficiently understand, and the asymmetries of power and information that have become pervasive features of the digital era landscape.

This ongoing shift in business models and cultural practices poses significant regulatory challenges because we may not yet have an adequate understanding of the incentives driving business practices or the activities and motivations of users of apps and devices. As Professor Lawrence Lessig noted in his seminal discussion of cyberspace, digital economy spaces demand:

[43] 8 News NOW Las Vegas: Man scares, harasses 8-year old after hacking into ring camera in a child's room.

[44] Deloitte: Black-market ecosystem.

> "a new understanding of how regulation works. It compels us to look beyond the traditional lawyer's scope—beyond laws, or even norms. It requires a broader account of 'regulation,' and most importantly, the recognition of a newly salient regulator".

This likely means more flexible approaches to regulation that can adjust with changing technologies, business models, and cultural practices.

3 Privacy and Children's Data

Children's data, just like adults', is subject to the risks of unauthorized disclosure. Data breaches at Equifax and other companies thus affect children. Children, however, potentially have different and perhaps even greater risks because unlike adults, their relationships with digital spaces may be mediated by family relationships and the activities of other people who may have the authority to disclose their data. Child identity theft is a growing problem, and it may occur within the family context when persons related to children or authorized to disclose children's data may engage in identity theft. In 2017, estimates suggest that more than one million children were victim of identity theft in the United States.[45] Two-thirds of the victims were under seven years of age, and 60% of child victims knew the perpetrator. In contrast, only seven percent of impacted adults have personal knowledge of their perpetrator.

Although older children may be more technologically competent than adult family members, young children may not be able to adequately monitor data disclosures about them. Approaches to privacy in the United States at the federal level do not sufficiently reflect the current topography of risks relating to data collection and to the protection of data once collected. The Children's Online Privacy Protection Act (COPPA), as well as regulatory rules adopted by the Federal Trade Commission (FTC) pursuant to COPPA, create a framework of fair information practices to collect, access, and use personal information by websites directed at children under 13 years of age, certain general audience websites, and services whose operators have actual knowledge that they are collecting personal information online from children under 13 years of age.

FTC COPPA rules require operators to provide notice of what information is collected from children, uses of such information, and disclosure practices for

[45] Grant: Identity Theft Isn't Just an Adult Problem.

such information.[46] Operators are required to obtain verifiable parental consent prior to collection, use, and/or disclosure of personal information from children and to provide a reasonable means for a parent to review personal information collected from a child and refuse to permit further use or maintenance of such data.[47] Operators may not condition a child's participation in activities on the collection of more personal information than is reasonably necessary to participate in such activities.[48] Operators must also establish and maintain reasonable procedures to protect the confidentiality, security, and integrity of personal information collected from children.[49] FTC COPPA rules also contain a "safe harbor" provision that enables industry groups or others to submit self-regulatory guidelines that would implement COPPA rule protections to the FTC for approval.[50]

The collection and use of data may also be regulated at the state level in the United States. The California Consumer Privacy Act of 2018 ("CCPA"),[51] which became effective on January 1, 2020, gives California consumers greater control over personal information collected by businesses.[52] The CCPA has been amended and expanded by the California Privacy Rights Act ("CPRA"),[53] a ballot measure (Proposition 24) approved by California voters on Nov. 3, 2020, which will become fully effective on January 1, 2023. The CPRA establishes the California Privacy Protection Agency ("CPPA"), which it grants investigative, enforcement, and rulemaking powers.[54]

Effective enforcement of the CCPA was delayed pending the effectiveness of final CCPA regulations by the California Attorney General's Office.[55] The CCPA applies to actors that satisfy one of the following three conditions: The subject must have a (1) gross annual revenue in excess of $25 million,[56] (2) indepen-

---

[46] 16 e-CFR § 312.3(a) (September 24, 2020).

[47] 16 e-CFR § 312.3(b–c) (September 24, 2020).

[48] 16 e-CFR § 312.3(d) (September 24, 2020).

[49] 16 e-CFR § 312.3(e) (September 24, 2020).

[50] 16 e-CFR § 312.11 (September 24, 2020).

[51] California Consumer Privacy Act of 2018 ("CCPA"), California Civil Code § 1798.100–199 (2018).

[52] California Consumer Privacy Act (CCPA), https://oag.ca.gov/privacy/ccpa.

[53] California Consumer Privacy Rights Act of 2020.

[54] Reilly/Lashway: Client Alert: The California Privacy Rights Act Has Passed: What's in It?

[55] Goldman: A Review of the "Final" CCPA Regulations.

[56] CCPA § 1798.140(c)(1)(A).

dently or jointly annually buy, receive for commercial purposes, sell, or share for commercial purposes, alone or in combination, personal information of 50,000 or more consumers, households, or devices,[57] or (3) derive 50% or more of its annual revenue from selling consumers' personal information.[58] Personal information subject to CCPA includes a broad range of information that identifies, relates to, describes, is reasonably capable of being associated with, or could be reasonably linked, directly or indirectly, with a particular consumer or household.[59] Under CCPA, personal information encompasses information that is not publicly available, such as (1) identifiers like names, aliases, addresses, and IP addresses; (2) characteristics of protected classifications under California or federal law; (3) commercial information, including records of personal property, products or services purchased, or consuming histories or tendencies; (4) biometric information; (5) internet or other electronic network activity information, such as browsing history; (6) geolocation data; (7) audio, electronic, visual, thermal, olfactory, or similar information; (8) professional or employment-related information; (9) education information; and (10) inferences drawn from any other information identified in the CCPA to create a profile about a consumer.[60]

The CCPA gives California consumers five categories of data privacy rights in their personal information, including the right to know, the right of access, the right to deletion, the right to opt out, and the right to equal service. The right to know requires businesses subject to CCPA to make affirmative disclosures to all consumers and respond to verifiable consumer requests with individualized disclosures about the business's collection, sale, or disclosure of that particular consumer's personal information.[61] The right of access gives consumers the right to access a copy of the "specific pieces of personal information" that it has collected about the consumer and receive a copy by mail or electronically.[62] The right of deletion enables consumers to request that a business delete any personal information about the consumer that the business has collected from the consumer.[63] Consumers have a right to opt out of the sale of their personal information to

---

[57] CCPA § 1798.140(c)(1)(B).

[58] CCPA § 1798.140(c)(1)(C).

[59] CCPA § 1798.140(o)(1)(A).

[60] CCPA § 1798.140(o)(1).

[61] CCPA § 1798.100(a).

[62] CCPA § 1798.110.

[63] CCPA § 1798.105(a).

third parties under the CCPA,[64] which also grants a right of equal service that prohibits discrimination against consumers who exercise their rights under the CCPA.[65] The CCPA prohibits selling personal information of consumers under age 16 without consent, which establishes an "opt-in" system for minors. Children aged 13–15 can provide such consent but consumers under age 13 require parental consent.[66]

Although the CCPA bears certain similarities to the GDPR, the core principles of the CCPA differ significantly from the GDPR. The CCPA does not reflect the fundamental principle of the GDPR of a "legal basis" for all processing of personal data.[67] The CCPA requires businesses to allow consumers to "opt-out" of having their information sold (other than in the case of minors, who must opt-in), unlike the GDPR, which requires businesses to implement an "opt-in" system to obtain consumer consent prior to their data being processed.[68] Notably, the CPRA adopts concepts of data minimization, purpose limitation, and storage limitation found in the GDPR.[69] These principles and the creation of the CPPA bring data privacy law in California closer to the GDPR.[70]

The GDPR includes specific provisions that protect children,[71] reflecting the underlying belief that

> "children merit specific protection with regard to their personal data, as they may be less aware of the risks, consequences and safeguards concerned and their rights in relation to the processing of personal data . . . specific protection should, in particular, apply to the use of personal data of children for the purposes of marketing or creating personality or user profiles and the collection of personal data with regard to children when using services offered directly to a child."[72]

---

[64] CCPA § 1798.120(a).

[65] CCPA § 1798.125(a)(1).

[66] CCPA § 1798.120(c)(d).

[67] Future of Privacy Forum: Comparing Privacy Laws: GDPR v. CCPA, p. 5.

[68] GDPR, Art. 6(1)(a) and 7.

[69] Reilly/Lashway: Client Alert: The California Privacy Rights Act Has Passed: What's in It?

[70] This article is based on the CCPA and does not analyze the impact of the CPRA or CPPA.

[71] GDPR, Art. 6, 8, 12, 40, 57.

[72] GDPR, Recital 38; also see Recitals 58 and 75.

Article 8 of the GDPR imposes conditions applicable to a child's consent in relation to information society services. The CCPA and the GDPR both provide for monetary penalties for non-compliance, with different approaches to determinations of liability. The CCPA provides for a limited private cause of action that permits statutory damages for data breaches in the amount of $100-$750 per violation per consumer or actual damages.[73] All other causes of action not involving data breaches must be enforced by the California Attorney General. Penalties for violations subject to enforcement actions by the California Attorney General are up to $2,500 for each violation and $7500 for each intentional violation.[74] Under the GDPR, administrative fines may be imposed up to 1) the higher of two percent of global annual turnover or €10 million or 2) the higher of four percent of global annual turnover or €20 million, depending on the nature of the GDPR violation.[75]

The CCPA excludes certain categories of data such as medical data, which is covered by other legal frameworks[76] like the Health Insurance Portability and Accountability Act of 1996 (HIPAA),[77] and personal information processed by credit reporting agencies.[78] The legal landscape for privacy laws is fragmented to a greater extent in the United States than in the European Union.

4 Conclusion

Failure to secure personal data and information has a particular impact on children. This also implicates the role of parents as decision makers about disclosures of children's data, including images. It also reflects the realities of family dynamics and relationships that may impact the use and protection of children's data. Children may not be able to monitor disclosure or use of their data for varied reasons. Children may not have access to their data, which may be controlled by their parents, or may not have the ability to monitor data disclosure. Given that a significant percentage of children's identity theft comes from persons known

[73] CCPA § 1798.150(a).

[74] CCPA § 1798.155(b).

[75] GDPR, Art. 83(4-6).

[76] CCPA § 1798.145(c-h).

[77] HIPAA, Public Law 104–191 (1996).

[78] Future of Privacy Forum: Comparing Privacy Laws: GDPR v. CCPA, p. 5.

to them, such as family members, regulation of their data implicates family relationships in ways that are potentially difficult and complex. Existing legal and regulatory approaches may focus on data privacy after it has been collected, with insufficient attention to the effectiveness of consent in light of widespread data technology business models, as well as to extensive data collection and aggregation. While this may harm both adults and children, it places a particular burden on children.

References

8 News NOW Las Vegas: Man scares, harasses 8-year old after hacking into ring camera in a child's room, 8 News NOW Las Vegas, December 12, 2019, https://www.youtube.com/watch?v=CpfFF8dK2jM; last accessed April 21, 2021.

Ablon, Lillian: Data Thieves: The Motivations of Cyber Threat Actors and Their Use and Monetization of Stolen Data, Santa Monica/CA 2018, https://www.rand.org/pubs/testimonies/CT490.html; last accessed April 21, 2021.

Alphabet Inc.: Annual Report on Form 10-K for the fiscal year ended December 31, 2019, https://www.sec.gov/ix?doc=/Archives/edgar/data/1652044/000165204420000008/goog10-k2019.htm; last accessed April 21, 2021.

Apple Inc.: Data Privacy Day at Apple: Improving Transparency and Empowering Users, January 27, 2021, https://www.apple.com/newsroom/2021/01/data-privacy-day-at-apple-improving-transparency-and-empowering-users/; last accessed September 21, 2021.

Brown, Dalvin: Amazon's Ring Fires Four Employees for Snooping on Customers' Doorbell Camera Video Feeds, USA Today, January 10, 2020, https://www.usatoday.com/story/tech/2020/01/10/amazons-ring-fired-employees-snooping-customers-camera-feeds/4429399002/; last accessed April 21, 2021.

Browne, Ryan: Edward Snowden says "the most powerful institutions in society have become the least accountable", CNBC.com, November 4, 2019, https://www.cnbc.com/2019/11/04/edward-snowden-warns-about-data-collection-surveillance-at-web-summit.html; last accessed April 21, 2021.

Brownlow, Josh/Zaki, Mohamed/Neely, Andy/Urmetzer, Florian: Data and Analytics – Data Driven Business Models: A Blueprint for Innovation. Working Paper, February 2015, https://cambridgeservicealliance.eng.cam.ac.uk/resources/Downloads/Monthly%20Papers/2015MarchPaperTheDDBMInnovationBlueprint.pdf; last accessed April 21, 2021.

Cadwalladr, Carole: The Great British Brexit Robbery: How Our Democracy Was Hijacked, The Guardian, May 7, 2017, https://www.theguardian.com/technology/2017/may/07/the-great-british-brexit-robbery-hijacked-democracy; last accessed April 21, 2021.

California Consumer Privacy Rights Act of 2020, https://www.oag.ca.gov/system/files/initiatives/pdfs/19-0021A1%20%28Consumer%20Privacy%20-%20Version%203%29_1.pdf; last accessed September 21, 2021.

Ceglowski, Maciej: Haunted by Data, 2015, idlewords.com/talks/haunted_by_data.htm; last accessed April 21, 2021.

Children's Commissioner: Who Knows What About Me?, November 2018, https://www.internetmatters.org/wp-content/uploads/2018/11/Childrens-commissioner-Who-Knows-What-About-Me-i-internet-matters.pdf; last accessed April 21, 2021.

CNIL: The CNIL's restricted committee imposes a financial penalty of 50 Million euros against Google LLC, January 21, 2019, https://www.cnil.fr/en/cnils-restricted-committee-imposes-financial-penalty-50-million-euros-against-google-llc; last accessed April 21, 2021.

Cohen, Julie E.: Law for the Platform Economy, University of California Davis Law Review 51, 2017, pp. 133-204.

CoreView: Major GDPR Fine Tracker—An Ongoing Always-Up-To-Date List of Enforcement Actions, August 24, 2020, https://www.coreview.com/blog/alpin-gdpr-fines-list/; last accessed April 21, 2021.

Cross, Jason: What is App Tracking Transparency and how do you block app tracking? MacWorld, April 29, 2021, https://www.macworld.com/article/344420/app-tracking-transparency-privacy-ad-tracking-iphone-ipad-how-to-change-settings.html; last accessed September 21, 2021.

Data Protection Commission: Data Protection Commission announces decision in WhatsApp inquiry, September 2, 2021, https://www.dataprotection.ie/en/news-media/press-releases/data-protection-commission-announces-decision-whatsapp-inquiry; last accessed September 21, 2021.

Deloitte: Black-market ecosystem: Estimating the cost of "Pwnership", December 2018, https://www2.deloitte.com/content/dam/Deloitte/us/Documents/risk/us-risk-black-market-ecosystem.pdf; last accessed April 21, 2021.

Edelman, Gilad: Why Don't We Just Ban Targeted Advertising, Wired, March 22, 2020, https://www.wired.com/story/why-dont-we-just-ban-targeted-advertising/; last accessed April 21, 2021.

Electronic Privacy Information Center: Equifax Data Breach, https://www.epic.org/privacy/data-breach/equifax/; last accessed April 21, 2021.

European Data Protection Board: Binding decision 1/2021 on the dispute arisen on the draft decision of the Irish Supervisory Authority regarding WhatsApp Ireland under Article 65(1)(a) GDPR, adopted July 28, 2021, https://edpb.europa.eu/system/files/2021-09/edpb_bindingdecision_202101_ie_sa_whatsapp_redacted_en.pdf; last accessed September 21, 2021.

Facebook, Inc.: Annual Report on Form 10-K for the fiscal year ended December 31, 2020, at p. 50 (Consolidated Statements of Income), https://www.sec.gov/ix?doc=/Archives/edgar/data/1326801/000132680121000014/fb-20201231.htm#i5d2898d61ccf450cbccb20a5c73005f3_43; last accessed September 21, 2021.

Facebook, Inc.: Annual Report on Form 10-K for the fiscal year ended December 31, 2019, https://www.sec.gov/ix?doc=/Archives/edgar/data/1326801/000132680120000013/fb-12312019x10k.htm; last accessed April 21, 2021.

Federal Trade Commission: Google and YouTube Will Pay Record $170 Million for Alleged Violations of Children's Privacy Law, September 4, 2019, https://www.ftc.gov/news-events/press-releases/2019/09/google-youtube-will-pay-record-170-million-alleged-violations; last accessed April 21, 2021.

Fuchs, Andrew: The Impact of Apple iOS 14.5 on Facebook Ad Campaigns, August 26, 2021, https://www.silverbackstrategies.com/blog/data-privacy/the-impact-of-apple-ios-145-on-facebook-ad-campaigns/; last accessed September 21, 2021.

Future of Privacy Forum: Comparing Privacy Laws: GDPR v. CCPA, 2018, https://fpf.org/wp-content/uploads/2018/11/GDPR_CCPA_Comparison-Guide.pdf; last accessed April 21, 2021.

Goldman, Eric: A Review of the "Final" CCPA Regulations from the CA Attorney General, Technology & Marketing Law Blog, June 29, 2020, https://blog.ericgoldman.org/archives/2020/06/a-review-of-the-final-ccpa-regulations-from-the-ca-attorney-general.htm; last accessed April 21, 2021.

Graham, Richard: Google and advertising: digital capitalism in the context of Post-Fordism, the reification of language, and the rise of fake news, Palgrave Communications 3, 45, 2017.

Grant, Kelli B.: Identity Theft Isn't Just an Adult Problem. Kids are Victims, Too, CNBC.com, April 24, 2018, https://www.cnbc.com/2018/04/24/child-identity-theft-is-a-growing-and-expensive-problem.html; last accessed April 21, 2021.

Granville, Kevin: Facebook and Cambridge Analytica: What You Need to Know as Fallout Widens, New York Times, March 19, 2018, https://www.nytimes.com/2018/03/19/technology/facebook-cambridge-analytica-explained.html; last accessed April 21, 2021.

Imran, Rida: EFF calls Facebook's opposition of Apple's new ATT privacy feature 'laughable'. iThinkDifferent.com, December 22, 2020, https://www.ithinkdiff.com/eff-facebook-attack-laughable-att-privacy/; last accessed September 21, 2021.

Kanter, Jake: Facebook and Google Could be Forced to Tell You How Much Your Data is Worth under new US Legislation, Business Insider, June 24, 2019, https://www.businessinsider.com/facebook-and-google-could-reveal-value-of-data-2019-6; last accessed April 21, 2021.

Kelly, Makena/Statt, Nick: Amazon Confirms it holds on to Alexa data even if you delete audio files, theverge.com, July 3, 2019, https://www.theverge.com/2019/7/3/20681423/amazon-alexa-echo-chris-coons-data-transcripts-recording-privacy; last accessed April 21, 2021.

Lyon, David: Surveillance, Snowden, and Big Data: Capacities, Consequences, Critique, Big Data & Society, July 2014, pp. 1–13.

Mackenzie, Lars Z.: The Afterlife of Data: Identity, Surveillance, and Capitalism in Trans Credit Reporting, Transgender Studies Quarterly 4(1), 2017, pp. 45–60.

McKinsey & Company: Fueling growth through data monetization, 2017, https://www.mckinsey.com/~/media/McKinsey/Business%20Functions/McKinsey%20Analytics/Our%20Insights/Fueling%20growth%20through%20data%20monetization/Fueling-growth-through-data-monetization.pdf; last accessed April 21, 2021.

Metz, Cade: How Facebook's Ad System Works, The New York Times, October 12, 2017, https://www.nytimes.com/2017/10/12/technology/how-facebook-ads-work.html; last accessed April 21, 2021.

Moore, Jina: Cambridge Analytica Had a Role in Kenya Election, Too, New York Times, March 20, 2018, https://www.nytimes.com/2018/03/20/world/africa/kenya-cambridge-analytica-election.html; last accessed April 21, 2021.

Mueller, Milton/Grindal, Karl: Data flows and the digital economy: information as a mobile factor of production, Digital Policy, Regulation and Governance 21(1), 2018, pp. 71–87.

Pascual, Al/Marchini, Kyle/Miller, Sarah: 2018 Identity Fraud: Fraud Enters New Era of Complexity, Javelin Strategy, February 6, 2018, https://www.javelinstrategy.com/print-pdf/58296; last accessed April 21, 2021.

Pound, Jesse: U.S. tech stocks are now worth more than the entire European stock market, CNBC.com, August 28, 2020, https://www.cnbc.com/2020/08/28/us-tech-stocks-are-now-worth-more-than-the-entire-european-stock-market.html; last accessed April 21, 2021.

Reilly, Brandon P./Lashway, Scott T.: Client Alert: The California Privacy Rights Act Has Passed: What's in It?, November 11, 2020, Manatt, https://www.manatt.com/insights/newsletters/client-alert/the-california-privacy-rights-act-has-passed; last accessed September 21, 2021.

Rowley, Jennifer: The wisdom hierarchy: representations of the DIKW hierarchy, Journal of Information Science 33(2), 2007, pp. 163–180.

Smith, Dale: Google Collects a Frightening Amount of Data About You. You Can Find and Delete It Now, CNet.com, June 28, 2020, https://www.cnet.com/how-to/google-collects-a-frightening-amount-of-data-about-you-you-can-find-and-delete-it-now/; last accessed April 21, 2021.

Taplin, Jonathan: Move Fast and Break Things: How Facebook, Google, and Amazon Cornered Culture and Undermined Democracy, New York 2017.

The Hamburg Commissioner for Data Protection and Freedom of Information: 35.3 Million Euro Fine for Data Protection Violations in H&M''s Service Center, Press Release, October 1, 2020, https://datenschutz-hamburg.de/assets/pdf/2020-10-01-press-release-h+m-fine.pdf; last accessed April 21, 2021.

Zuboff, Shoshana: The Age of Surveillance Capitalism: The Fight for a Human Future at the New Frontier of Power, New York 2019.

Prof. Dr. Olufunmilayo B. Arewa is Murray H. Shusterman Professor of Business and Transactional Law at Temple University Beasley School of Law in Philadelphia, PA, USA. Her research focuses on technology, music, film, business, and Africana studies. She is the author of "Disrupting Africa: Technology, Law, and Development" (Cambridge University Press, 2021), which received the International Studies Association Science, Technology and Art in International Relations (STAIR) 2022 best book award. Prior to becoming a law professor, she practiced law for nearly a decade, working in legal and business positions in the entrepreneurial and technology startup arena, including law firms and companies in Silicon Valley, New York, and Boston.

The Rise of the Algorithmic Child: Protecting Children in Smart Homes

Victoria Nash

We usually think of children's contact with the Internet through the lens of popular entertainment activities such as scrolling through social media, playing games, or watching videos, typically undertaken on personal devices. While these activities shape our perception of children's online engagement, especially because their enjoyment is visible and their usage easily measurable, these are not the only ways in which children interact with online services. In fact, there are at least three key ways in which children now routinely engage with digital service providers online[1]:

1. Actively, and most frequently consciously, via digital apps, services, or content on their own devices, or devices shared with other family members;
2. Passively or unconsciously via screenless devices employed around the home;

[1] This typology expands on a distinction drawn by the UK Children's Commissioner. Cf. UK Children's Commissioner: Who knows what about me?

This research summary draws on findings from a project funded by the Oak Foundation (OCAY-16-667): Child Safety on the Internet: Looking Beyond ICT Actors. I am very grateful to Dr. Huw C. Davies and Dr. Allison Mishkin for their research assistance on this project.

V. Nash (✉)
Oxford Internet Institute, University of Oxford, Oxford, UK
e-mail: victoria.nash@oii.ox.ac.uk

N. Dethloff et al. (eds.), *Families and New Media*, Juridicum – Schriften zum Medien-, Informations- und Datenrecht,
https://doi.org/10.1007/978-3-658-39664-0_10

3. Actively or passively via services set up by third parties and used outside of the home, such as educational tools or services in schools, or on public WiFi networks.

The first of these is well documented in survey-based literature, which provides solid evidence-based research that details which activities are most popular with different age groups across countries, as well as which risks and opportunities children face in their daily use.

The third might seem an unfamiliar focus, but in the years before personal mobile devices became ubiquitous, political battles were fought over how best to keep children safe from adult content when using computers in public spaces such as libraries or schools. In the United States, for example, early efforts to introduce federal-level legislation to protect minors from indecent or offensive communications resulted in the Children's Internet Protection Act (2000) which established compulsory Internet filtering for schools and libraries in receipt of public funding. In the current context of ubiquitous mobile access, attention to welfare in the digital public realm has turned instead to the possible risks associated with connecting personal devices to public WiFi networks, not just in libraries or schools, but in shops, cafes and public transport systems.[2] Similar concerns about access to harmful content have played out on this stage too, resulting in the provision of services such as the United Kingdom's 'friendly' WiFi certification,[3] whereby public providers offer filtered Internet access that would prevent access to adult content such as pornography or illegal content such as child abuse imagery. Security and privacy concerns relating to children's use of public Internet services or networks have yet to receive significant policy attention, but the growing array of academic literature analysing possible risks of data-driven services in contexts such as education suggests this may yet change.[4]

Thus whilst active personal Internet use of devices and apps, and public use outside the home are familiar subjects for both research and policy-making, the second form of Internet access is less well-understood, limiting the potential for providing appropriate safety guidance or policy oversight. It is this topic that forms the basis of the discussion that follows.

---

[2] Cf. Spacey et al.: Filtering Wireless (WiFi) Internet Access in Public Places, Journal of Librarianship and Information Science 49 (1), 2017, pp. 15–25.

[3] Cf. Friendly Wifi: Website.

[4] Cf. Hakimi/Eynon/Murphy: The ethics of digital trace data in education, Review of Educational Research 91(5), 2021, pp. 671–717.

First we need to clarify what we mean by passive or unconscious interaction with screenless devices around the home. The focus on devices without screens is deliberate, as this both alters the mode of interaction (no text, images or videos) and also occludes the digital connectivity of the device—smart devices don't look like familiar phones or computers, potentially making it harder for both adults and children to 'read' their capabilities or risks. Similarly, the focus on passive or unconscious use is also important. Whereas children, even young toddlers can quickly become aware of the enjoyment brought by direct engagement with simple games or videos on a phone or a tablet device, many of the screenless devices in focus here are either a hidden part of the digital landscape of the home and family life or are disguised as analogue toys, with additional functionality potentially hidden from view. Both of these factors make it more challenging for users to understand the digital risks and opportunities of engaging with such devices.

To further clarify these points, it is worth specifying the types of product or service that would fall into this category. Children now have access to a range of Internet-connected devices at home that extend beyond the familiar screen-based smartphones, tablets, or computers, to include many of the following:

- Connected or smart toys that use Internet connectivity to provide interactive features such as the ability to respond to a child's questions or touch[5];
- Smart home assistants, such as Amazon's Alexa or Google Home, which provide a voice-based interface connected directly to the Internet, enabling users to access an array of functions such as playing music, ordering products, providing information or even telling jokes, simply by voicing a command[6];
- Surveillance or tracking technologies, such as smartwatches, that enable parents to monitor their child's location or Internet-connected cameras to remotely monitor babies, children, or childcare workers whilst parents are away from the house[7]; and
- 'Babytech' products that include quasi-medical devices, such as smart socks, to measure heartrate and blood oxygenation, as well as fertility trackers or Bluetooth enabled products like nappies or baby bottles that notify parents when to intervene.[8]

5 Cf. Holloway/Green: The Internet of toys, Communication Research and Practice, 2(4), 2016, pp. 506–519; Chaudron et al.: Kaleidoscope on the Internet of Toys.

6 Cf. Mascheroni: Datafied childhoods, Current Sociology, 68(6), 2020, pp. 798–813.

7 Cf. Mascheroni: Datafied childhoods, Current Sociology, 68(6), 2020, pp. 798–813.

8 Cf. Leaver: Intimate surveillance, Social Media + Society, 3(2), 2017, pp. 1–10.

Although the products described above are nowhere nearly as ubiquitous as mobile phones or tablets, they are used by a significant number of children. For example, according to industry figures, 78 million smart home assistants were sold worldwide in 2018.[9] Almost 10% of children in the United Kingdom used smart home assistants such as Amazon Echo or Google Home to go online in 2018, and a similar rate was reported for the United States in 2017.[10] In terms of other devices, 8% of British children used Internet-connected toys, and 5% had used wearable devices like smartwatches.[11] In the United States, 15% of two to four year olds were reported to have a connected toy.[12]

So far, research shows little evidence of harm resulting from children's use of these new classes of digital devices. However, a closer look at news reports does reveal numerous instances of security flaws or data breaches. The My Friend Cayla doll was, for example, banned in Germany after the country's telecommunications regulator classified the toy as an 'illegal espionage apparatus' because of its reliance on an unsecured Bluetooth connection which enabled anyone within a certain range to listen in on conversations or even speak to the child through the doll.[13] The same regulator also banned the sale of children's smartwatches for similar reasons.[14] Cloudpets, a brand of stuffed animals, were removed from online stores like Amazon after it emerged that consumer voice recordings (including those of children) were stored in unsecured databases, had been accessed by unauthorized parties, and had even been used to hold people to ransom.[15] Other examples include the VTech data breach, during which servers containing customer information and children's personal data were hacked[16]; numerous incidents of baby monitors being hacked (and in some cases being used to speak to a child or broadcast video feeds on the Internet); and multiple reports from consumer organizations demonstrating security flaws in devices like smartwatches.[17]

[9] Cf. Canalys: Smart speaker market booms in 2018.

[10] Cf. Common Sense Media: The Common Sense Census.

[11] Cf. Livingstone/Blum-Ross/Zhang: What do parents think, and do, about their children's online privacy?

[12] Cf. Common Sense Media: The Common Sense Census.

[13] Cf. Oltermann: German parents told to destroy doll that can spy on children.

[14] Cf. Wakefield: Germany bans children's smartwatches.

[15] Cf. BBC: Children's messages in CloudPets data breach.

[16] Cf. Gibbs: Toy firm VTech hack exposes private data of parents and children.

[17] Cf. Laughlin: Kids' smartwatches vulnerable to hackers; Forbrukerrådet: #WatchOut.

Such reports are undoubtedly concerning, but do they really have implications for child welfare, and do they necessitate a new policy response? Security weaknesses in smart home devices may in turn provide easy access to all other devices on a network, including devices that record images or conversations inside homes, as well as store personal data, videos, photos, and passwords. Once accessed, such data can be sold on the dark web, used to buy goods and services, empty bank accounts, or extort.[18] Sadly, such cyber-crimes are not uncommon; however, as of now, there is little evidence that security weaknesses or data theft have resulted in direct harm to children.

There is rather a more insidious and less tangible type of risk conceptualized in the literature analyzing the societal implications of the data economy: the way that data about children is used to make decisions about their lives.[19] Children's data is increasingly being captured and transmitted by the array of new connected devices appearing in many homes, often without much awareness by parents. This data may be utilized to generate reports, recommendations, or notifications about children as part of the service that is offered. For example, 'baby tech' devices, such as smart baby socks or mattresses, use data including motion, temperature, and even heartrate monitors, to analyze a child's wellbeing and inform parents or caregivers of any concerning changes. While tracking devices let parents know exactly where their children are, they may also offer more detailed analysis that enables them to understand more about their children's play habits or even friendships.

The use of these technological aids is undoubtedly well-intended, but the data generated gives the illusion of objectivity and neutrality while at the same time representing only the aspects of a child's life that a company has chosen to record. These digital glimpses of a child's life are described as 'data assemblages', reflecting the fact that they are assembled from parts of a person's life or behavior as viewed through the lens of a particular technology.[20] The risk that results from such 'data assemblages' is that they come to substitute more holistic, personal, and situated knowledge of a child.[21] Parents using smart baby

[18] See, for example, BBC: Miss Teen USA hacker jailed for 18 months.

[19] Cf. Lupton/Williamson: The datafied child, New Media & Society, 19(5), 2017, pp. 780–794.

[20] Cf. Lupton: How do data come to matter?, Big Data & Society, July-December 2018, pp. 1–11.

[21] Cf. Lupton/Williamson: The datafied child, New Media & Society, 19(5), 2017, pp. 780–794.

technologies may privilege the information provided by those technologies rather than trust their own parental judgement about their children; a teacher or school may base important decisions affecting children's educational welfare on the data gathered through a specific online tool rather than on the harder-to-quantify messier realities of children's lives. In many cases, we might hope that using such technologies would improve our decision-making. The risk, though, is that it comes to replace decision-making, in the sense of active consideration of children's best interests. Further, it reduces children's lives to just a series of ones and zeros while making adults feel as if they are better, more responsible caregivers.

The appeal of such technologies is evident. Exhortations that a monitored child is a safe child abound in advertising and marketing strategies that offer parents "Peace of Mind Through Every Milestone",[22] or make claims about "Revolutionising the cot so you can sleep too".[23] But there are more concrete risks to a growing reliance on childcare technologies, especially if it means abandoning our own better judgement. Many of the new 'baby tech' devices and apps are marketed as providing health data that you would expect to be provided only by regulated healthcare devices. Yet the reality is that few of these new technologies are well-regulated, meaning there is no guarantee that the devices will provide accurate, reliable information. There have yet to be tragedies resulting from inaccurate readings, or failed alerts, but paediatricians have provided explicit warnings about the risks to consumers and their families.[24] Similar concerns have been raised about the legitimacy of decisions made in education that are based on app-generated data.[25] Ultimately, these technologies create what could be called 'an algorithmic child', and the risk is that in trying to satisfy the needs and wellbeing of this partial, datafied 'algorithmic child', we ignore the child's actual individual and self-claimed needs.

How might such risks be mitigated? Across Europe, children's welfare and interests are protected by many different regulatory instruments, at both the national and supranational levels. In the context of the types of product discussed in this chapter, the most significant regulatory frameworks relate to toy safety, data

[22] Owlet: Website.

[23] smart cot: Website.

[24] Cf. Bonafide/Jamison/Foglia: The Emerging Market of Smartphone-Integrated Infant Physiologic Monitors, JAMA., 317(4), 2017, pp. 353–354.

[25] Cf. Jarke/Breiter: Editorial: the datafication of education, Learning, Media and Technology, 44(1), 2019, pp. 1–6.

protection, and consumer protection. However, these leave some obvious gaps in the regulatory framework for children's use of connected devices in the home. Security standards for Internet of Things (IoT) devices have yet to be agreed upon at the international level, and it remains unclear how agreements would be enforced in terms of keeping insecure products away from consumers. Consumer protection laws are largely provided by European Union Member States—and enforced with varying degrees of enthusiasm. Internet safety for children is currently largely governed by self-regulatory measures and has thus far focused primarily on content and contact risks. Individual European Union Member States have national legal frameworks to cover criminal conduct and content, such as child sexual abuse, imagery, or grooming, whilst initiatives to develop media literacy and build resilience amongst young Internet users also receive varying levels of investment in different countries. There are some examples of more wide-ranging measures being introduced which recognise the need for a more holistic approach to regulating online risks and harms. Beyond Europe, Australia passed a Digital Safety Act in 2021,[26] whilst in the United Kingdom, an Online Safety Bill has been published and seems likely to become law in 2022/23. This Bill establishes a wide-ranging regulatory framework targeting a variety of online harms, and vitally, imposes a new 'duty of care' on technology companies to prevent these, particularly in relation to children, albeit still with a focus predominantly on content.[27]

None of these approaches seems adequate in the face of the privacy and security-related risks outlined above. Data protection frameworks instead seem to offer the most obvious protection, and indeed the European Union's General Data Protection Regulation (GDPR) awards children special protection in virtue of their more limited ability to understand the implications of personal data processing for their rights and interests.[28] However, as Lievens and Verdoodt note, there are several points on which even the GDPR fails to provide sufficient clarity in relation to the processing of children's data, including whether direct marketing can constitute a legitimate ground for processing children's data, and whether or not the GDPR provides enough protection against the use of children's data

[26] Cf: Minister for Communications, Urban Infrastructure, Cities and the Arts: Digital Safety Act.

[27] Cf. Minister for State for Digital and Culture: Draft Online Safety Act.

[28] Cf. Lievens/Verdoodt: Looking for needles in a haystack, Computer Law & Security Review, 34(2), 2018, pp. 269–278.

for the creation and use of profiles about them.[29] Neither of these gaps causes problems uniquely for children's engagement with the types of product or service discussed in this article, but rather demonstrate that further clarification is needed from data protection authorities in order to provide full protection for children.[30]

One interesting initiative, which may better protect children's data and privacy interests from devices in the smart home, is the United Kingdom's Age-Appropriate Design Code. Introduced as a result of an amendment to the United Kingdom's Data Protection Act, it is intended to ensure that all companies providing information society services (ISS) "likely to be accessed by children" act in children's best interests in data collection and processing, offering a set of fifteen basic standards to guide such action.[31] These standards require, for example, that such companies maintain high privacy standards by default, map the data gathered from UK children, check the ages of users to ensure appropriate protections are offered, avoid using 'nudge' techniques to encourage children to provide more personal data and switch off geolocation services by default. The types of companies listed include those providing apps, websites, search functions, social media and online messaging, but explicit mention is also made of the types of service discussed here: "Electronic services for controlling connected toys and other connected devices are also ISS."[32]

The Code was implemented in 2020 and companies were given a transitional year in which to adapt to the requirements. As enforcement thus only began in September 2021 it is still too early to ascertain how impactful this Code will prove to be. Remarkably though, and coinciding with the end of the transitional period, Facebook, Instagram, Tik-Tok, Google and YouTube all announced the introduction of changes to their services which purport to offer strengthened privacy protections for younger users. None cited the Code, and the changes will seemingly be global rather than solely UK-based, but as likely early targets for enforcement action, it seems plausible that implementation of the Code has prompted such moves.[33] Such early successes do not necessarily indicate that

[29] Cf. Lievens/Verdoodt: Looking for needles in a haystack, Computer Law & Security Review, 34(2), 2018, pp. 269–278.

[30] Cf. Milkaite/Lievens: The Internet of toys, in: Mascheroni/Holloway (eds.): The Internet of Toys 2019.

[31] Cf. Information Commissioner's Office: Age appropriate design: a code.

[32] Cf. Information Commissioner's Office: Age appropriate design: a code.

[33] Cf. Stokel-Smith: Britain tamed big tech and nobody noticed, Wired Magazine.

there will be widespread changes across the sector however, not least because it is well-understood that the body responsible for enforcing the Code, the UK's Information Commissioner's Office (ICO) lacks the resources to monitor or enforce compliance on a large scale. But complaints have already been filed against these and other big tech companies by children's rights organisations, meaning that it should soon become clear how effective the ICO will be in upholding UK children's privacy rights.

Is this enough? In an economic and technological environment where personal data is a source of private profit, the digital wellbeing of both adults and children are inescapably bound to the willingness of private companies to take their ethical and regulatory responsibilities seriously. To date, self-regulatory initiatives to protect children have largely focused on engaging big tech companies, seeing these stakeholders as the most significant players in the battle to keep children safe and happy online. But with the rise of smart devices, such as connected toys, digital home assistants, and 'baby tech', it is now clear that there is a long trail of companies, both big and small, who must take their responsibilities to protect young users (and their data) seriously. Against this backdrop, children's rights, the ethics of capturing and managing their data, and its potential for commercial exploitation are deservedly but belatedly beginning to receive more attention. We may not be able to challenge the fundamental business models that drive the dataveillance practices outlined above, but there is an urgent need for critical data research that can shed light on the extent and purpose of data collected from children in order to inform future policy-making and public debate. This symposium makes a vital contribution to that mission.

References

BBC: Children's messages in CloudPets data breach, BBC News, February 28, 2017, https://www.bbc.co.uk/news/technology-39115001; last accessed May 26, 2021.

BBC: Miss Teen USA hacker jailed for 18 months, BBC News, March 18, 2014, https://www.bbc.co.uk/news/technology-26616913; last accessed May 26, 2021.

Bonafide, Christopher P./Jamison, David T./Foglia, Elizabeth E.: The Emerging Market of Smartphone-Integrated Infant Physiologic Monitors, JAMA., 317(4), 2017, pp. 353–354.

Canalys: Smart speaker market booms in 2018, driven by Google, Alibaba and Xiaomi, 2019, https://www.canalys.com/newsroom/smart-speaker-market-booms-in-2018-driven-by-google-alibaba-and-xiaomi; last accessed May 26, 2021.

Chaudron, Stéphane/Di Gioia, Rosanna/Gemo, Monica/Holloway, Donell/Marsh, Jackie/Mascheroni, Giovanna/Peter, Jochen/Yamada-Rice, Dylan: Kaleidoscope on the

Internet of Toys—Safety, security, privacy and societal insights, JRC (Joint Research Centre) Technical Reports, Luxembourg 2017, JRC105061, EUR 28397 EN.
Common Sense Media: The Common Sense Census: Media Use by Kids Aged Zero to Eight, 2017, https://www.commonsensemedia.org/sites/default/files/uploads/research/csm_zerotoeight_fullreport_release_2.pdf; last accessed May 26, 2021.
Forbrukerrådet (Norwegian Consumer Council): #WatchOut. Analysis of smartwatches for children, 2017, https://fil.forbrukerradet.no/wp-content/uploads/2017/10/watchout-rapport-october-2017.pdf; last accessed May 26, 2021.
Friendly WiFi: Website, https://www.friendlywifi.com; last accessed November 2, 2021.
Gibbs, Samuel: Toy firm VTech hack exposes private data of parents and children, The Guardian, November 30, 2015, https://www.theguardian.com/technology/2015/nov/30/vtech-toys-hack-private-data-parents-children; last accessed May 26, 2021.
Hakimi, Laura/Eynon, Rebecca/Murphy, Victoria A.: The ethics of digital trace data in education: a thematic review of the research landscape, Review of Educational Research 91(5), 2021, pp. 671–717.
Holloway, Donell/Green, Lelia: The Internet of toys, Communication Research and Practice, 2(4), 2016, pp. 506–519.
Information Commissioner's Office: Age appropriate design: a code of practice for online services, 2020, https://ico.org.uk/media/for-organisations/guide-to-data-protection/key-data-protection-themes/age-appropriate-design-a-code-of-practice-for-online-services-2-1.pdf; last accessed October 19, 2021.
Jarke, Juliane/Breiter, Andreas: Editorial: the datafication of education, Learning, Media and Technology, 44(1), 2019, pp. 1–6.
Laughlin, Andrew: Kids' smartwatches vulnerable to hackers, Which?, October 18, 2017, https://www.which.co.uk/news/2017/10/kids-smartwatches-vulnerable-to-hackers/; last accessed May 26, 2021.
Leaver, Tama: Intimate surveillance: Normalizing parental monitoring and mediation of infants online, Social Media + Society, 3(2), 2017, pp. 1–10.
Lievens, Eva/Verdoodt, Valerie: Looking for needles in a haystack: Key issues affecting children's rights in the General Data Protection Regulation, Computer Law & Security Review: The International Journal of Technology Law and Practice, 34(2), 2018, pp. 269–278.
Livingstone, Sonia/Blum-Ross, Alicia/Zhang, Dongmiao: What do parents think, and do, about their children's online privacy? Parenting for a Digital Future: Survey Report 3, London 2018.
Lupton, Deborah: How do data come to matter? Living and becoming with personal data, Big Data & Society, July-December 2018, pp. 1–11.
Lupton, Deborah/Williamson, Ben: The datafied child: The dataveillance of children and implications for their rights, New Media & Society, 19(5), 2017, pp. 780–794.
Mascheroni, Giovanna: Datafied childhoods: Contextualising datafication in everyday life, Current Sociology, 68(6), 2020, pp. 798–813.
Milkaite, Ingrid/Lievens, Eva: The Internet of toys: playing games with children's data?, in: Mascheroni, Giovanna/Holloway, Donell (eds.): The Internet of Toys. Studies in Childhood and Youth, 2019.
Minister of Communications, Urban Infrastructure, Cities and the Arts: Online Safety Act (Cth), Australia, 2021, https://parlinfo.aph.gov.au/parlInfo/search/display/display.w3p

;query=Id%3A%22legislation%2Fbillhome%2Fr6680%22; last accessed October 19, 2021.
Minister of State for Digital and Culture: Draft Online Safety Bill, https://www.gov.uk/government/publications/draft-online-safety-bill; last accessed November 2, 2021.
Oltermann, Philip: German parents told to destroy doll that can spy on children, The Guardian, February 17, 2017, https://www.theguardian.com/world/2017/feb/17/german-parents-told-to-destroy-my-friend-cayla-doll-spy-on-children; last accessed May 26, 2021.
Owlet: Website, https://owletbabycare.co.uk; last accessed October 19, 2021.
smart cot: Website, https://www.smart-cot.com; last accessed May 26, 2021.
Spacey, Rachel/Muir, Adrienne/Cooke, Louise/Creaser, Claire/Spezi, Valérie: Filtering wireless (Wi-Fi) Internet access in public places, Journal of Librarianship and Information Science, 49 (1), 2017, pp. 15–25.
Stokel-Smith, Chris: Britain tamed big tech and nobody noticed, Wired Magazine, September 2, 2021, https://www.wired.co.uk/article/age-appropriate-design-code-big-tech; last accessed October 19, 2021.
UK Children's Commissioner: Who knows what about me?, London 2018, https://www.childrenscommissioner.gov.uk/digital/who-knows-what-about-me/, last accessed December 2, 2022.
Wakefield, Jane: Germany bans children's smartwatches, BBC News, November 17, 2017, https://www.bbc.co.uk/news/technology-42030109; last accessed May 26, 2021.

Prof. Dr. Victoria Nash is Director of the Oxford Internet Institute (OII), UK, where she is also an Associate Professor and Senior Policy Fellow. Her research interests draw on her background as a political theorist, and concern the normative policy implications of evidence characterizing children's use of Internet technologies. She holds several digital policy advisory roles, including membership of the World Economic Forum Global Coalition for Digital Safety, the UK Government's multi-stakeholder UK Council on Internet Safety (UKCIS) Evidence Group, and serves on the Advisory Board of Internet Matters.

Protection of Minors on Video Sharing Platforms

Louisa Specht-Riemenschneider, Alina Marko and Sascha Wette

1 Introduction

Minors can be exposed to violence-glorifying, sexualized and racist content on video-sharing platforms. They can also be influenced by untrue and polarizing information and experience hate speech. Furthermore, this may lead to the infringement of personality rights guaranteed by the German Constitution.[1] Such infringement occurring on the internet rather than by 'analogue' means are more difficult to prosecute due to the principle of anonymity still in place regarding the internet—see § 13 (6) of the German Telemedia Act (Telemediengesetz; TMG)[2]—making it less likely that perpetrators will be held accountable for

[1] Cf. Müller-Terpitz: Persönlichkeitsrechtliche Aspekte der Social Media, in: Hornung/Müller-Terpitz (eds.): Rechtshandbuch Social Media, pp. 253, 254 ff.

[2] Since enactment of GDPR, the independent significance of § 13 (6) TMG (Telemediengesetz; Telemedia Act) has been in question—for a detailed discussion, see cf. Keppeler: Was bleibt vom TMG-Datenschutz, MMR (Multimedia und Recht) 2015, pp. 779 ff. and Tinnefeld/Buchner, in: BeckOK-Datenschutz, Datenschutz in Medien und Telekommunikation,

L. Specht-Riemenschneider (✉) · A. Marko · S. Wette
University of Bonn, Bonn, Germany
e-mail: louisa.specht@forschungsstelle-datenrecht.de

A. Marko
e-mail: Alina.Marko@freenet.de

S. Wette
e-mail: sascha.wette@uni-bonn.de

N. Dethloff et al. (eds.), *Families and New Media*, Juridicum – Schriften zum Medien-, Informations- und Datenrecht,
https://doi.org/10.1007/978-3-658-39664-0_11

their actions. The German Federal Ministry of Justice currently has no plans to implement 'real name' requirements,[3] and the information-providing obligations of the platforms and portals on which such infringing material is distributed are extremely limited. While information can be requested about stored data on users who have committed certain criminal offenses and/or personal sphere rights infringements pursuant to § 14 (3) TMG,[4] this right of information is useless if the platform does not have the infringer's name but only their IP address. The victim in a given case must involve the public prosecutor's office in the hope that they will be able to determine the identity of the perpetrator(s), but in many instances, such cases are dropped. It is abundantly clear that there is an urgent need for more effective protection of minors on the internet, in view of, for example, increasing press coverage of teen suicides prompted by an infringement of personal sphere rights on the internet.[5]

The Audiovisual Media Services Directive (AVMSD) of November 14, 2018 ((EU) 2018/1808)[6] is aimed at improving the protection of minors on video sharing platforms, partly in recognition of a changed risk situation for minors on the internet. Minors are increasingly exposed to harmful content and must be especially protected from incitement to hatred, violence and terrorism, in particular through misinformation, in their development phase. The principal provisions relevant to the protection of minors are set forth in the Interstate Treaty on the Protection of Minors in the Media (Jugendmedienschutz-Staatsvertrag; JMStV),[7]

---

mn. 57; for a differing opinion, see Roßnagel/Geminn/Jandt/Richter: Datenschutzrecht 2016 "Smart" genug für die Zukunft.

[3] Wissenschaftliche Dienste des Bundestags: Klarnamenpflicht im Internet.

[4] Specifically concerned are those falling under § 1 (3) of the Network Enforcement Act (Netzwerkdurchsetzungsgesetz; NetzDG).

[5] See, for example, Spiegel: Erneut Selbstmord wegen Cyber-Mobbing.

[6] Directive (EU) 2018/1808 of the European Parliament and of the Council of 14 November 2018 amending Directive 2010/13/EU on the coordination of certain provisions laid down by law, regulation or administrative action in Member States concerning the provision of audiovisual media services (Audiovisual Media Services Directive) regarding changing market conditions, ABl. 2018/L 303/69.

[7] As amended in the Interstate Treaty on the Modernized Media Regulation (Staatsvertrag zur Modernisierung der Medienordnung in Deutschland; MoModStV) dated April 14, 2020, enacted November 7, 2020.

the Protection of Minors Act (JuSchG),[8] and the Network Enforcement Act (NetzDG). The chief point is for the platforms, as content intermediaries, to be held more responsible than they traditionally have been. A similar trend is observable in other areas of law, including copyright law, for which platforms will in the future bear liability as perpetrators of infringement rather than as mere contributors.[9] Irrespective thereof, general monitoring obligations are prohibited pursuant to Article 14 of the E-Commerce Directive (transposed in § 10 of the TMG), and this prohibition is to remain in place after the drafting of the Digital Services Act. This paper examines what measures are imposed on platforms under the JMStV, JuSchG, and NetzDG, as well as on how these may be structured going forward. In particular, the consequences for the protection of minors will be addressed.

2 Structure of this Paper

The paper begins with a detailed look at the changes brought about by a revision of the AVMS Directive (Sect. 3) before reviewing the corresponding measures used to implement these in national law (Sect. 4). These measures include amendments to the Interstate Treaty on the Protection of Minors in the Media (Sect. 4.1), the Protection of Minors Act (Sect. 4.2), and the Network Enforcement Act (Sect. 4.3). A summary of conclusions is then provided in the subsequent and final Sect. 5.

3 Amendments to the Audiovisual Media Services Directive

Video sharing platforms are subject to the regulatory regime established in the amended Audiovisual Media Services Directive (AVMSD; (EU) 2018/1808).[10] Requirements under the AVMSD and their implementation are discussed below.

---

[8] In the version of the Second Law amending the Protection of Minors Act; adopted March 26, 2021; announced April 9, 2021; entered into force May 1, 2021.

[9] Ultimately, this classification is less relevant than the specific duty of care obligations that are imposed on the platforms, cf. Specht-Riemenschneider/Hofmann: Verantwortung von Online-Plattformen, pp. 102 f.

[10] Recital 45, Directive (EU) 2018/1808 of the European Parliament and of the Council of 14 November 2018 amending Directive 2010/13/EU on the coordination of certain provisions laid down by law, regulation or administrative action in Member States concerning

3.1 Expanded Scope of Application

Amendments to the AVMSD have always involved expansions of scope. As technologies increasingly converged, the original scope covering classic television—thus the name "Television Directive"—was expanded via amendment to include non-linear services.[11] In the amended AVMSD, the scope of application, which is largely prescribed by the definitions of terms per Art. 1, has again been expanded.[12] An audiovisual media service within the meaning of Art. 1 a) i) AVMSD is now defined as a service whose main purpose or separable element is to provide content via electronic communication networks to the general public for informational, entertainment, or educational purposes under the editorial responsibility of a media service provider. The new part is that the AVMSD now applies to any provider of understandable, discrete video content that lacks direct reference to other content.[13] The scope of application has additionally been expanded to include video sharing platforms. The primary purpose or essential function of video sharing platforms is to make programming or user-generated video content electronically available to the general public, with the video sharing platform provider bearing no editorial responsibility. The operator of a video sharing platform solely determines the organization of the platform, not what content is available on it, see Art. 1 aa) AVMSD. Thus, in addition to major providers like YouTube, AVMSD will now also apply to audiovisual content distributed by users on social media platforms like Facebook, or in separate sections of newspaper websites.[14] The expansion of AVMSD to include video sharing platforms has most recently led to the addition of Chapter IXa with Art. 28a and 28b AVMSD. The geographic scope of application is extended under Art. 28a (1) and

---

the provision of audiovisual media services (Audiovisual Media Services Directive) regarding changing market conditions, ABl. 2018/L 303/57.

[11] Kröber, in: BeckOK-RundfunkR, § 6 RStV mn. 38; Holznagel, in: Spindler/Schuster (eds.): Recht der elektronischen Medien, § 2 RStV mn. 3 ff.; Holznagel/Hartmann, in: Hoeren/Sieber/Holznagel (eds.): Handbuch Multimedia-Recht, Rundfunk und Telemedien, mn. 29 ff.

[12] Jäger: Die Novellierung der AVMD-RL, ZUM (Zeitschrift für Urheber- und Medienrecht) 2019, pp. 477, 478.

[13] Ibid.

[14] Hartmann: Welche Dienste zählen künftig zu den audiovisuellen Mediendiensten?, MMR (Multimedia und Recht) 2018, pp. 790, 792.

(2) AVMSD to include providers which have, or effectively have, a branch operation within the territory of an EU Member State, or when that company has a parent company, subsidiary, or corporate affiliate domiciled in a Member State.[15] Preventive protection measures are required under Art. 28b AVMSD, such as certain requirements for the protection of minors applicable to video sharing platform operators.[16]

3.2 Amendments to Media Laws for the Protection of Minors

The former Art. 12[17] and Art. 27 AVMSD, which provided for separate regulation of television programming and on-demand services with graduated regulation levels for media protection of minors, were eliminated in the amended AVMSD. Art. 6a (1) AVMSD now requires all providers of audiovisual media services to establish media exposure/consumption barriers to content deemed deleterious to development. The law provides that audiovisual services that could harm minors' physical, mental, or moral development may only be provided in a manner that ensures that minors will generally not be exposed to or consume such audio and image/video content. The measures implemented to this end include broadcast scheduling, age verification procedures, and other technical measures.

Platform operators' responsibilities were also specifically regulated to implement protections against content that poses a danger to minors or incites hatred or violence (Art. 28b (1) AVMSD), as well as to comply with advertising requirements as per Art. 28b (2) AVMSD.[18] In particular, Art. 28b (3) AVMSD provides

---

[15] The video platform YouTube provides a spectacular case regarding application of the law, because of which the law was presumably passed. While not domiciled in the EU, the company falls within the scope of Art. 28 a (2) AVMSD due to being a Google Group company, cf. Holznagel/Hartmann, in: Hoeren/Sieber/Holznagel (eds.): Handbuch Multimedia-Recht, Rundfunk und Telemedien, mn. 51.

[16] Liesching: Das Herkunftslandprinzip nach E-Commerce- und AVMD-Richtlinie, MMR-Beil. (Multimedia und Recht) (Appendix) 2020, pp. 3, 10.

[17] Directive 2010/2013/ EU of the European Parliament and of the Council of 10 March 2010 on the coordination of certain provisions laid down by law, regulation or administrative action in Member States concerning the provision of audiovisual media services (Audiovisual Media Services Directive), ABl. 2010/L 95/1.

[18] Gundel: Die Fortentwicklung der europäischen Medienregulierung, ZUM (Zeitschrift für Urheber- und Medienrecht) 2019, pp. 131, 132.

that platforms must enable their users to designate content as unsuitable for minors as per Art. 28b (1) AVMSD. Platforms themselves must have reporting systems in place for unsuitable content in accordance with the aforementioned paragraph 1 and provide systems for parental control enabling parents to keep such content out of their children's accounts. Additionally, the AVMSD provides for the "set-up and operation of age verification systems" in these clauses.[19]

4 Measures Required Under National Law

4.1 The Interstate Treaty on the Protection of Minors in the Media

The amended provisions of the AVMSD have been implemented in the similarly amended Interstate Treaty on the Protection of Minors in the Media (Jugendmedienschutz-Staatsvertrag; JMStV) in special regulations applicable to video sharing services. A key change is the new clause § 5a (1) of the amended JMStV, which now expressly obligates video sharing services to implement adequate measures to protect children and teens from content deleterious to their development irrespective of the obligations per § 4 and § 5 JMStV.[20] While the necessity of this detailed clause has been questioned, it does make clear that platforms can be held liable for non-proprietary content.[21] It must be noted that the obligations per the new § 5a JMStV "apply irrespective of the obligations per § 4 and § 5 JMStV". Thus, these require commentary (under points Sect. 4.1.1 and 4.1.2) before addressing the latest amendments to the JMStV (under point Sect. 4.1.3).

General categorical distinction is made in the JMStV between "harmful content for minors" and "content deleterious to development". The former is fundamentally illegal to distribute in general under § 4 JMStV and, pursuant to § 4 (2) 2nd st. JMStV, can only be made accessible in telemedia to a closed user group with robust mandatory age verification. It is, however, fundamentally legal to

[19] Hilgert/Sümmermann: Technischer Jugendmedienschutz, MMR-Beil. (Multimedia und Recht) (Appendix) 2020, pp. 26, 30.

[20] Under the old Interstate Treaty on the Protection of Minors in the Media (Jugendmedienschutz-Staatsvertrag; JMStV), "broadcasting" and "telemedia" were the terms utilized; "video sharing services" were not mentioned as such.

[21] Hilgert: Novellierung des Jugendmedienschutz-Staatsvertrags.

distribute the latter, although providers are obliged under § 5 JMStV to prevent minors from consuming such content "under normal circumstances".[22]

4.1.1 Protection Against Endangering Content for Minors

The list of "absolutely prohibited content" per § 4 (1) 1st st. JMStV remains unchanged. Such content is generally prohibited in both broadcasting and telemedia. The list is intended to ensure the upholding of human dignity and prevent sexual abuse by banning child pornography and similar or related endangering content. In particular, the list of "absolutely prohibited content" serves to establish that making content public in violation of legal norms for the protection of society constitutes a criminal act under media-specific protection of minors laws.[23] The violations of public order per § 24 (1) no. 1 a–k represent such a violation.[24]

In contrast, the distribution of "content endangering to minors" per § 4 (2) 1st st. JMStV is only illegal under certain circumstances. The distribution of such content in telemedia is permitted, as per the 2nd st., if access is restricted to adult users.[25] Content endangering to minors, such as regular pornography in particular (i.e. pornography without relevance to the sexualization of children or other crime), may therefore be distributed via telemedia in exceptional cases despite the general prohibition.[26] The provider must ensure that such content is only accessible within "closed user groups".[27] The existence of such a user group is ensured by having a reliable age verification system in place that requires personal identification, although under the JMStV there are no officially prescribed recognition rules.[28] There is the possibility, however, of the Commission on the Protection

---

[22] Hilgert/Sümmermann: Technischer Jugendmedienschutz, MMR-Beil. (Multimedia und Recht) (Appendix) 2020, pp. 26 ff.

[23] Müller-Terpitz: Persönlichkeitsrechtliche Aspekte der Social Media, in: Hornung/Müller-Terpitz (eds.): Rechtshandbuch Social Media, pp. 253, 293 f.

[24] Liesching, in: BeckOK JMStV, § 4 mn. 1.

[25] Liesching, in: BeckOK JMStV, § 4 mn. 16.

[26] Some question why the exception to the distribution ban should concern telemedia only, cf. Kaspar, in: Beck RundfunkR, § 4 JMStV mn. 81 a; Liesching: Verfassungskonformer Jugendschutz nach der Medienkonvergenz, MMR 2018, pp. 141 ff.

[27] Erdemir, in: Spindler/Schuster (eds.): Recht der elektronischen Medien, JMStV, § 4 mn. 147; Altenhain, in: Hoeren/Sieber/Holznagel (eds.): Handbuch Multimedia-Recht, Jugendschutz, mn. 64.

[28] Altenhain, in: Hoeren/Sieber/Holznagel (eds.): Handbuch Multimedia-Recht, Jugendschutz, mn. 64.; Kaspar, in: Beck RundfunkR, § 4 JMStV mn. 81 a.

of Minors (Kommission für Jugendmedienschutz; KJM) assessing the merits of a given age verification system with reference to the set of criteria the Commission has outlined.[29] Solution concepts based thereupon primarily utilize video calls for identification purposes or draw upon successful identity verification[30] carried out elsewhere, such as when opening a bank or savings account.[31] In a recent development, age verification providers have even integrated autoident technology into their systems.[32] This technology enables user identification by automatically cross-referencing a photo against biometric and other data stemming from an identifying document.[33]

4.1.2 Protections Against Content Deleterious to Development

Conceptual distinction must be made between content "endangering to minors" and content "deleterious to the development of minors". Fundamentally, the distribution of content deleterious to development is legal, but pursuant to § 5 (1) 1st st. JMStV, providers of such content must ensure that children and youth of the concerned age levels will generally not be exposed to it.[34] Content deleterious to the development of minors is content that can lead to dysfunction through overstimulation or other excessive stressors; lack of socio-ethical orientation, such as by confusing fiction and reality; or impairment of the maturation of children and

[29] The amendments in the new § 11 (3) JMStV (Jugendmedienschutz-Staatsvertrag) now expressly state that the Kommission für Jugendmedienschutz (KJM) defines the suitability criteria for protection of minors software in consultation with the recognized voluntary self-regulation organizations in the form of guidelines—see also Kommission für Jugendmedienschutz: Bewertung von Konzepten für Altersverifikationssysteme.

[30] The German Federal Court of Justice (Bundesgerichtshof; BGH) has largely upheld earlier high court rulings, finding that legal criteria for the protection of minors are not met by pornographic internet content being made available to users after solely having to enter their personal identification or passport number, see BGH, decision from October 18, 2007 (I ZR 102/05), NJW (Neue Juristische Wochenschrift) 2008, pp. 1882, 1884 f.

[31] Hilgert/Sümmermann: Technischer Jugendmedienschutz, MMR-Beil. (Multimedia und Recht) (Appendix) 2020, pp. 26 f.; Altenhain, in: Hoeren/Sieber/Holznagel (eds.): Handbuch Multimedia-Recht, Jugendschutz, mn. 71 ff.

[32] Kommission für Jugendmedienschutz: Neue Methode für Altersverifikation.

[33] Ibid.

[34] Hilgert/Sümmermann: Technischer Jugendmedienschutz, MMR-Beil. (Multimedia und Recht) (Appendix) 2020, p. 26.

youth into responsible adults.[35] In implementing the mandatory controls limiting access to such content, providers must take into account what ages are concerned or would thereby be affected.[36] The provider's obligations extend solely to ensuring that minors of the concerned age levels will "generally not be exposed" to content deleterious to their development. There is no requirement that it must be rendered completely impossible to access such content.[37] The potential accessing of such content does not have to be completely prevented, but rather only made difficult. This is implemented on television by limiting the broadcast to a certain time, e.g. late evening hours. Due to the ubiquitous access to content on video sharing platforms, finding technical solutions is increasingly challenging. Providers of such platforms can fulfill these requirements by marking their content as relevant for the protection of minors for filtering software. Such software can be installed by parents and helps to decide which contents are suitable for which age. The filtering software filters the internet and only shows suitable content.[38] Apart from that providers might specify time limits, and/or implement other technical measures.[39] Accordingly, the requirements per § 5 JMStV are less stringent than the requirement of enforcing a closed user group with age verification procedure as per § 4 (2) 2nd st. JMStV.[40]

4.1.3 Expanded Media Protection for Minors

The increasing popularity of video sharing services, among minors in particular, led to the amendments to § 5a and § 5b JMStV, implementing Article 28b AVMSD,[41] which are the primary changes to the law. Art. 28b AVMSD is the

[35] Geidner, in: Beck RundfunkR, § 5 JMStV mn. 5.

[36] Ibid., mn. 6.

[37] Keller/Liesching, in: Hamburger Kommentar, Pflichten von Anbietern von Rundfunk und Telemedien, mn. 6.

[38] Such software must be recognized by the competent state media authority pursuant to § 11 (2) JMStV (Jugendmedienschutz-Staatsvertrag) through the agency of the Kommission für Jugendmedienschutz; one example for such software is the german JUSPROG, see www.jugendschutzprogramm.de.

[39] Liesching, in: BeckOK JMStV, § 5 mn. 9 ff.; regarding technical media protection measures for minors see Hilgert/Sümmermann: Technischer Jugendmedienschutz, MMR-Beil. (Multimedia und Recht) (Appendix) 2020, pp. 26, 27 ff.

[40] Erdemir, in: Spindler/Schuster (eds.): Recht der elektronischen Medien, JMStV, § 5 mn. 57.

[41] MoModStV dated April 14, 2020, Official Unified Declaration of the German Federal States on the Interstate Treaty on the Modernized Media Regulation (Staatsvertrag zur Modernisierung der Medienordnung in Deutschland), III. Argumentation for Article 3,

central norm to implement protection for minors against harmful content or content that incites hatred or violence (see Sect. 3.2). The overall scope of the JMStV was also expanded, including particularly its geographic scope of application, which is of key importance for platform operators.

4.1.3.1 Applicability to Foreign Providers

The new § 2 (1) 2nd st. of the amended JMStV clarifies that the provisions of the JMStV likewise apply to providers based outside of Germany[42] if they host content intended for use in Germany.[43] This was implemented to enhance regulators' ability to enforce the law against foreign providers, among other objectives.[44] Foreign providers are thus now required to appoint a domestic authorized recipient of correspondence under § 21 (2) of the amended JMStV. However, the expansion of the scope of the JMStV to include foreign providers is subject to the limits of the 'country of origin' principle. This became evident through the amendment of a provision to insert an express reference to compliance with the country of origin principle pursuant to a resolution adopted by the Conference of Minister Presidents (Ministerpräsidentenkonferenz; MPK).[45] The country of origin principle proceeding from Art. 3 of the e-Commerce Directive (ECD), and implemented in Art. 3 (2) of the TMG, means that the free movement of telemedia services that are offered or provided in Germany by service providers domiciled in another state subject to the ECD may not be restricted. The effects of the exceptions per Art. 3 (4)–(6) ECD and Art. 3 (5) and (6) TMG must be specifically considered on a case-by-case basis. But in actual practice, regulatory

---

Amendment to the Interstate Treaty on the Protection of Minors in the Media (Jugendmedienschutz-Staatsvertrag; JMStV), B. regarding point 4.

[42] Whereas the previous version of the Interstate Treaty on the Protection of Minors in the Media (Jugendmedienschutz-Staatsvertrag; JMStV) only asserted applicability to German providers.

[43] Such as those which employ the German language.

[44] MoModStV dated April 14, 2020, Official Unified Declaration of the German Federal States on the Interstate Treaty on the Modernized Media Regulation, III. Argumentation for Article 3, Amendment to the Interstate Treaty on the Protection of Minors in the Media (Jugendmedienschutz-Staatsvertrag; JMStV), B. regarding point 2. The extent is questioned to which there is compatibility with the 'country of origin' principle, cf. Hilgert: Novellierung des Jugendmedienschutz-Staatsvertrags.

[45] See also the detailed discussion in Liesching: Das Herkunftslandprinzip und seine Auswirkung, pp. 88 ff.

measures are only allowed in a few individual cases within the framework of these stringent exceptions, and the JMStV is virtually inapplicable to providers domiciled in other EU countries.[46]

4.1.3.2 Expanded Measures for Video Sharing Service Providers

In addition to the familiar pre-existing methods, the suitable measures for protection against content deleterious to minors' development proposed for providers of video sharing services under § 5a (2) of the amended JMStV[47] include implementing and operating age verification procedures and systems that allow parents to control access to content. Using the term "age verification" when referring to less stringent procedures for content that is only detrimental to development can be confusing, as it is also used to refer to the systems employed to create closed user groups for content endangering to minors as per § 4 (2) 2nd st. JMStV, which are distinct in that they are complex and non-circumventable.[48] The Official Unified Declaration of German States clarifies that the term "age verification procedures" per § 5a JMStV also refers to procedures that establish age group classification as well as to those that create closed user groups.[49] Pursuant to § 5a (2) 2nd st. JMStV as amended, a user feedback/rating system must also be implemented for monitoring the effectiveness of such procedures in place with video sharing services.

4.1.3.3 Codified 'Notice and Take Down' Procedure

The newly inserted § 5b in the amended JMStV serves the determination of the illegality of content as per §§ 10a ff. of the TMG. Pursuant to § 10a (1) TMG, video sharing platform providers are obligated to have reporting procedures in place that enable users to electronically file complaints about illegal content being made available on their respective platform. Whether content is illegal proceeds

---

[46] According at any rate to ibid.

[47] I.e. broadcast time restriction, technical or other means, programming of effective protection of minors software in line with § 5 JMStV (Jugendmedienschutz-Staatsvertrag).

[48] Hilgert: Novellierung des Jugendmedienschutz-Staatsvertrags.

[49] MoModStV dated April 14, 2020, Official Unified Declaration of the German Federal States on the Interstate Treaty on the Modernized Media Regulation, III. Argumentation for Article 3, Amendment to the Interstate Treaty on the Protection of Minors in the Media (Jugendmedienschutz-Staatsvertrag; JMStV), B. regarding point 4.

from § 4 and § 5 JMStV, which establish that content deleterious to development of minors is only illegal if made available to the general public and if the video sharing service provider has not fulfilled the obligations per § 5 (1), (3)–(5) JMStV, see § 5b nos. 1 and 2 JMStV as amended.

These provisions codify a 'notice and take down' procedure[50] for video sharing service providers. Established under § 10 TMG, the fundamental rule is that "host providers",[51] a term that includes video sharing providers like YouTube,[52] are not liable for third-party data which they save on a user's behalf. The prerequisites apply, however, that they must either have no knowledge of the illegal act/data—and further, if damages are claimed, be unaware of any facts or circumstances which render the illegal act/content obvious—or have taken action to remove or restrict access to such content immediately after becoming aware of it. Host providers do not in any case have preventive review obligations, i.e. obligations to monitor or investigate activities, pursuant to § 7 (2) 1st st. TMG. However, under § 10a and § 10b TMG in conjunction with § 5b JMStV as amended, video sharing platform providers are now expressly obligated to set up a reporting procedure which is easily recognizable as such, easy to use, directly accessible, and continuously available, as well as to review user reports to ascertain whether content violates media laws concerning the protection of minors. The competent state media authority is responsible for monitoring compliance with these newly created regulations under § 14 (1) of the amended JMStV.

4.1.3.4 Self-Regulation Mechanisms for Social Media

Self-regulation mechanisms supplement the systems/procedures for the protection of minors required by law. Pursuant to § 7 (1) JMStV, the telemedia provider must appoint a Protection of Minors Officer if the provider's platform is publicly accessible and contains content that is endangering to minors or deleterious to their development. Additionally, voluntary self-regulation panels exist, which are recognized by the KJM in accordance with § 16 2nd st. no. 2 and § 19 JMStV.

[50] See Holznagel: Melde- und Abhilfeverfahren zur Beanstandung rechtswidrig gehosteter Inhalte, GRUR (Gewerblicher Rechtsschutz und Urheberrecht) Int. 2014, p. 105.

[51] A host provider saves third-party data for users on its own servers on a non-temporary basis.

[52] YouTube qualifies as a host provider, see German Federal Court of Justice (Bundesgerichtshof; BGH), decision from September 13, 2018 (I ZR 140/15), GRUR (Gewerblicher Rechtsschutz und Urheberrecht) 2018, p. 1132.

Lastly, the terms of use of social media networks also provide for the protection of minors, such as the Facebook ban on nudity and pornography.[53]

4.2 Protection of Minors Act

Under § 24a of the Protection of Minors Act (Jugendschutzgesetz; JuSchG), service providers which save or provide third-party content for users with a profit motive must take appropriate and effective structural precautionary measures, irrespective of § 10 TMG, to ensure that the protective objectives per § 10a nos. 1–3 JuSchG are upheld. The protective objectives per § 10a nos. 1–3 are as follows: (1) to afford protection from media likely deleterious to the development of minors and/or to their maturation into responsible, socially adequate adults (media deleterious to development); (2) to afford protection from media deleterious to the development of minors and/or to their maturation into responsible, socially adequate adults (media endangering to minors); (3) to protect the personal integrity of minors as media users; and (4) to provide orientation for children, youth, parents/guardians, and educators regarding media usage and literacy.

General monitoring obligations are prohibited per Art. 14 ECD and § 10 TMG, thus "structural precautionary measures" do not concern reviewing the content of media available on the platform. The draft Digital Services Act provides that such reviewing of content on a voluntary basis will not, going forward at any rate, potentially result in platforms which merely make third-party content available losing exemption from liability. In the future, such host providers will only be liable for content made available, even if content is checked in advance, if they become aware of a specific legal violation (see Art. 5 and 6 DSA as proposed).

In the argumentation behind the law, the term "structural precautionary measures" per § 24a JuSchG is outlined to mean:

> "the structuring of a service/offering so as to facilitate the protection of the personal integrity of minors, their protection against exposure to content of a deleterious or endangering nature, and their ability to take steps accordingly on their own behalf."[54]

[53] Cf. Müller-Terpitz: Persönlichkeitsrechtliche Aspekte der Social Media, in: Hornung/Müller-Terpitz (eds.): Rechtshandbuch Social Media, pp. 253, 294 f.

[54] Justification for the Law, BT-Drs. 19/24909, p. 27.

A list is provided specifying a range of measures which may be appropriate given the technical features and the terms of use of the respective service or offering, as well as the content and/or structuring thereof. However, measures cannot be imposed upon platforms that would create excessive hardship, for constitutionality reasons among others. Additionally, the 'regulatory triangle' concept applies to platform regulation, according to which the rights and interests of content providers, platform users (minors in this case), and platforms themselves are to be appropriately weighed.[55] It is thus proper and important that each case be considered individually, as the law prescribes. The listed measures include reporting and complaint systems, classification schemes for user-generated content, age verification procedures, information on where to get advice and assistance from and report issues to an independent non-provider entity, technical means provided to parents and guardians for controlling and monitoring content usage, and terms of use suitable for the protection of minors.

These measures are indicative of a trend toward platform regulation predominantly through design obligations, i.e. requiring the operator to structure and organize the platform in a child-friendly manner ('child protection by design').[56] If it is found in a given case that these requirements are not met, a dialogue with regulators first takes place aimed at improving the content offered and the platform design. Only if the issues remain unresolved will specific prevention measures be ordered. Failure to comply with such orders is punishable by a fine of up to five million euros, see § 28 (3) no. 4 and (5) 1st st. JuSchG. The regulator is the Federal Review Board for Media Harmful to Minors, which is to be reorganized as the Federal Center for Media Protection for Minors. The law applies equally to service providers not domiciled in Germany pursuant to § 24a (4) JuSchG.

4.3 Network Enforcement Act

While the Network Enforcement Act (Netzwerkdurchsetzungsgesetz; NetzDG) is not explicitly focused on the protection of minors, it is intended to afford protections to affected parties, including minors. The regulations it sets forth originally

[55] Specht-Riemenschneider/Hofmann: Nutzerrechte als Baustein einer fairen Plattformökonomie, NJW-aktuell (Neue Juristische Wochenschrift Aktuell) 2021, pp. 15 ff.

[56] Regarding the corresponding design obligations cf. Specht-Riemenschneider et al.: Stellungnahme des SVRV, pp. 67 f., 77 f.; Specht-Riemenschneider/Hofmann: Verantwortung von Online-Plattformen, p. 88.

applied solely to social media networks per § 1 (1) NetzDG, but the scope of the law is being expanded to include video sharing platforms as part of implementation of the AVMSD. An outline of the fundamental provisions of the NetzDG is first provided below before discussing the regulations governing video sharing platforms in regard to their applicability requirements and legal ramifications.

4.3.1 The Regulatory Framework of the Network Enforcement Act[57]

Social media networks per § 1 (1) NetzDG that have more than two million registered users in Germany are subject to specific reporting obligations,§ 2, and erasure obligations, § 3, under penalty of fines, § 4, pursuant to NetzDG.[58] Under § 3 NetzDG, social media network providers are required to have a process in place for filing complaints about illegal content that is "easily recognizable as such, directly accessible, and available at all times."[59] Pursuant to § 3 (1) NetzDG, the content specified under § 1 (1) NetzDG is illegal, including content of an insulting nature per §§ 185 ff. of German Penal Code (StGB), of a threatening nature per § 241 StGB, or of a nature violating an individual's intimate personal sphere per § 201a StGB. Whether an offense is culpably committed is legally irrelevant.[60]

Social media network operators were already required to have complaint management processes in place prior to enactment of the NetzDG for breach of privacy issues by virtue of the blog entry procedure established by the German Federal Court of Justice (BGH).[61] However, not every case in which the criteria

[57] Sects. 4.3.1. and 4.3.2. derive mostly from the views taken in the opinion paper Specht-Riemenschneider et al.: Stellungnahme des SVRV. The corresponding text passage in the opinion paper was written by the primary co-author as well.

[58] Regarding the imposable fines, for a detailed discussion, see Guggenberger: Das Netzwerkdurchsetzungsgesetz, ZRP (Zeitschrift für Rechtspolitik) 2017, pp. 98, 99.

[59] For a detailed discussion, see Guggenberger: Das Netzwerkdurchsetzungsgesetz in der Anwendung, NJW (Neue Juristische Wochenschrift) 2017, pp. 2577, 2578 ff.

[60] BT-Drs. 18/12356, p. 20; thus the critical opinion of eco Verband der Internetwirtschaft e.V.: Stellungnahme zum Referentenentwurf, pp. 4 f.; Spindler: Rechtsdurchsetzung von Persönlichkeitsrechten, GRUR (Gewerblicher Rechtsschutz und Urheberrecht) 2018, pp. 365, 368; Holznagel: Das Compliance-System des Entwurfs des Netzwerkdurchsetzungsgesetzes, ZUM (Zeitschrift für Urheber- und Medienrecht) 2017, pp. 615, 620.

[61] German Federal Court of Justice (Bundesgerichtshof; BGH), decision from October 25, 2011 (VI ZR 93/10), GRUR (Gewerblicher Rechtsschutz und Urheberrecht) 2012, p. 311—blog post.

are met for the above offenses contains a legal breach of privacy, nor is every breach of privacy criminally relevant. Even for the overlap between offenses covered by the NetzDG and illegal breaches of privacy, the process now has to ensure that the social media network provider promptly registers the complaint and reviews whether the content reported in the complaint is illegal and has to be removed or access to it restricted.[62] In some cases, other deadlines apply for breach of privacy incidents. However, § 10 TMG already requires action to be taken promptly upon receiving notification as a fundamental principle, and EU Member States are not able to attach further nuance to that principle.[63] Any illegal content has to be promptly removed or access to it restricted, generally within seven days within receipt of complaint.[64] Furthermore, social media network providers must remove content which is obviously illegal or restrict access to it within 24 h of receiving complaint. Thus, for obviously illegal content, a shorter period of time is given. This is conditional upon the complaint in question stating sufficiently specific information.[65] The applicable deadline is extended accordingly if the social media network provider forwards the matter to a recognized regulated self-regulation panel per § 3 (6)–(8) NetzDG[66] to make a decision regarding illegality, accepting the panel's decision as binding. The legal position of such panels and the requirements they are subject to remain unclear,

[62] For a detailed discussion of the review procedure, see Guggenberger: Das Netzwerkdurchsetzungsgesetz, ZRP (Zeitschrift für Rechtspolitik) 2017, pp. 98, 99.

[63] This being the predominant theory view in any case. For an essentially similar view, see also Wimmers/Heymann: Zum Referentenentwurf eines Netzwerkdurchsetzungsgesetzes, AfP (Zeitschrift für das gesamte Medienrecht) 2017, pp. 93, 95; Liesching: Die Durchsetzung von Verfassungs- und Europarecht gegen das NetzDG, MMR (Multimedia und Recht) 2018, pp. 26, 29; Guggenberger: Das Netzwerkdurchsetzungsgesetz in der Anwendung, NJW (Neue Juristische Wochenschrift) 2017, pp. 2577, 2579; Spindler: Rechtsdurchsetzung von Persönlichkeitsrechten, GRUR (Gewerblicher Rechtsschutz und Urheberrecht) 2018, pp. 365, 369; for a differing view not entirely rejecting strict deadlines cf. Höch: Nachbessern: ja, verteufeln: nein, K&R (Kommunikation und Recht) 2017, pp. 289, 291.

[64] Regarding deadline exceptions cf. Schwartmann: Verantwortlichkeit Sozialer Netzwerke, GRUR-Prax (Gewerblicher Rechtsschutz und Urheberrecht, Praxis) 2017, pp. 317 ff.

[65] BT-Drs. 18/13013, p. 20; also: Liesching, in: Spindler/Schmitz (eds.): Telemediengesetz mit Netzwerkdurchsetzungsgesetz, § 3 NetzDG mn. 5.

[66] The Federal Office of Justice (Bundesamt für Justiz; BfJ) recognized the Association of Multimedia Service Providers for Voluntary Self-regulation (Verein Freiwillige Selbstkontrolle Multimedia-Diensteanbieter e. V.; FSM) as such an panel on January 23, 2020, see: BfJ: Erstmals Selbstregulierung nach dem Netzwerkdurchsetzungsgesetz.

however.[67] Enactment of the NetzDG did not result in significant changes to the complaint management procedure employed by social media network providers. Social media networks still primarily review content with reference to their community standards; the specific review required under NetzDG is implemented as a downstream step.[68] There is still no final clarity on whether community standards that differ from fundamental legal requirements are in any way valid.

Violations of the NetzDG are punishable by fine as per § 4 (1) no. 2. If the fine-imposing authority intends to base its decision on the illegality of content, a court decision on the illegality must be obtained first (see § 4 (5) NetzDG. Per § 68 (1) of the Administrative Offenses Act (Ordnungswidrigkeitengesetz; OWiG)). The competent court is the court of jurisdiction in the district where the administrative authority (the Federal Office of Justice) is based, i.e. Bonn Local Court.[69] While the local court decision is binding and cannot be challenged,[70] the Federal Office of Justice's decision, as fine-imposing authority that draws on the local court's decision, can be contested by filing an objection.[71] Some consider this obligation to obtain a decision from Bonn Local Court regarding the illegality of specific content before a fine can even be imposed to be alien to the legal system.[72] In any event, there would likely be agreement that if Bonn Local Court was demonstrably overloaded, involving other courts in the matter should be considered.[73]

Pursuant to § 2 (1) NetzDG, a semi-annual complaint handling report must be posted on the provider's website and in the Federal Gazette. And pursuant to § 5 NetzDG, a non-temporary contact person in Germany who is easily identifiable as such, as well as an authorized served document recipient to facilitate legal enforcement, must be named.

---

[67] For a critical view, see in particular Spindler: Rechtsdurchsetzung von Persönlichkeitsrechten, GRUR (Gewerblicher Rechtsschutz und Urheberrecht) 2018, pp. 365, 370 f.

[68] Cf. Löber/Roßnagel: Das Netzwerkdurchsetzungsgesetz in der Umsetzung, MMR (Multimedia und Recht) 2019, p. 71.

[69] Cf. also Höld: Das Vorabentscheidungsverfahren nach dem neuen NetzDG, MMR (Multimedia und Recht) 2017, pp. 791, 792 ff.

[70] Cf. also Guggenberger: Das Netzwerkdurchsetzungsgesetz, ZRP (Zeitschrift für Rechtspolitik) 2017, pp. 98, 99.

[71] Höld: Das Vorabentscheidungsverfahren nach dem neuen NetzDG, MMR (Multimedia und Recht) 2017, pp. 791, 794.

[72] Holznagel: Das Compliance-System des Entwurfs des Netzwerkdurchsetzungsgesetzes, ZUM (Zeitschrift für Urheber- und Medienrecht) 2017, pp. 615, 624.

[73] Similarly implicit in ibid.

4.3.2 Amendment of the Network Enforcement Act

The Network Enforcement Act (Netzwerkdurchsetzungsgesetz; NetzDG) is currently being altered in two ways: First, by the April 2021[74] enactment of the Act against Right-Wing Extremism and Hate Crimes[75] as well as by an amendment to the NetzDG itself. The explanations outlined below, which particularly concern heightened obligations for platforms and their impact on platform design, proceed mostly from the latter of the aforementioned legislation.[76]

In addition to heightened reporting obligations, the amendment provides for supplementation of the complaint handling procedure per § 3 NetzDG as follows:

- an obligation to promptly notify users when a complaint is received over content stored for them
- an obligation to retain removed content for a period of ten weeks for evidentiary purposes
- an obligation to inform the complainant and the user concerned of the corresponding decisions made
- a legal basis for forwarding data to a recognized regulated self-regulation organization
- provisions for establishing regulated self-regulation

Platform design is addressed as well, with the social media network provider being obligated, for example, to implement a process for reporting to the Federal

[74] The Federal President declined to prepare the document in view of a decision of the Federal Constitutional Court (BVerfG), decision from May 27, 2020 (1 BvR 1873/13, 1 BvR 2618/13), NJW (Neue Juristische Wochenschrift) 2020, p. 2699—Bestandsdatenauskunft II indicating possible unconstitutionality. The Amendment/Constitutional Emendation Act initiated thereupon to yield conformity with the BVerfG decision was adopted by the Bundestag and Bundesrat on March 26, 2021 as drafted by the Mediation Committee (see: Deutscher Bundestag: Vorgang-Gesetzgebung. Gesetz zur Anpassung der Regelungen über die Bestandsdatenauskunft) so the document was prepared later.

[75] In the adopted version BR-Drs. 339/20 (see also the later Repair Act, see footnote 74); for an overview of the proceedings see: Deutscher Bundestag: Vorgang-Gesetzgebung. Gesetz zur Bekämpfung des Rechtsextremismus und der Hasskriminalität.

[76] The article is based on the government draft of March 31, 2020, BT-Drs. 19/18792; at the time of printing, the bill was being discussed in the first round of deliberation in the Bundestag, thus changes are still possible.

Criminal Police Office, see § 3a NetzDG.[77] The provider must additionally ensure that an easily identifiable procedure is in place for contacting the provider (see § 3b (1) 3rd st. NetzDG). A remonstrance procedure is being introduced that enables users whose content has been deleted to protest its deletion (see § 3b NetzDG). An arbitration procedure is likewise introduced under § 3c NetzDG. There are also rudimentary supplemental provisions regarding fines under § 4 NetzDG, and a supervisory authority is established under § 4a NetzDG. The responsibilities of the named domestic authorized recipient of served documents are supplemented under § 5 NetzDG, and the transition period provisions are supplemented under § 6 NetzDG. Lastly, video sharing platforms are placed within the scope of the NetzDG under § 3d–§ 3f NetzDG, implementing § 28b AVMSD. Except as otherwise provided under § 3e (2) and (3), NetzDG applies to video sharing platforms. The NetzDG does not address minors in particular. Thus, the NetzDG does not state an obligation to design specific minor-friendly procedures. The procedures must only be identifiable for the common user. Still, the amendment of the NetzDG might have positive effects that benefit minors such as the deletion of harmful content and the comprehensive and practical implementation of the procedures mentioned.

4.3.3 Provisions Regulating Video Sharing Platforms

Video sharing platforms fall fundamentally and entirely within the framework of the NetzDG by virtue of § 3e (1) NetzDG, thereby obtaining the same status as social media networks. The term "video sharing platform service" is regulated per definitions under § 3d (1) NetzDG. The conceptual content of this term and of other definitions conforms with requirements under the AVMSD.[78] The scope of application of the NetzDG is thus expanded with regard to the provisions of the AVMSD governing the removal of illegal content.[79] Certain video sharing platforms already met the definition to constitute a social media network as per § 1 (1) NetzDG, as all forms of communication are concerned thereunder.[80] However, the expansion in scope affects cases with video sharing platforms that

[77] This amendment, unlike the others, stems from the former of the two laws mentioned above. Footnote 75.

[78] BT-Drs. 19/18792, p. 50; regarding the requirements under the AVMS Directive, see above, 3.1.

[79] BT-Drs. 19/18792, p. 50.

[80] BT-Drs. 18/12356, p. 18.

specialize in the exclusive distribution of specific content, such as the publication of scenes from a computer game.[81] This content is of specific interest for minors and may be harmful due to potential violence or sexualization in computer games. Thus the content regulated by the NetzDG, both in general as well as after the amendment, is of special relevance to children. Here, it must be kept in mind that a social media network under the definition per § 1 (1) NetzDG is a platform designed for any content, rather than for specific content. Because of its legal orientation around the requirements per AVMSD, the NetzDG does not apply in exactly the same ways to social media networks and video sharing platforms respectively, as there are differences regarding details. Thus, the discussion below focuses first on differences in how the NetzDG applies to social media networks versus video sharing platforms before turning to the legal ramifications in regard to the protection of minors.

4.3.3.1 Applicability of the Network Enforcement Act

Limits are set to the applicability of the NetzDG to video sharing platforms under § 3e (2) and (3). These limitations may apply to smaller video sharing platforms with fewer than two million registered users in Germany (sub-Sect. 4.3.3.1.1.) and video sharing platforms that are domiciled outside Germany in another EU Member State (sub-Sect. 4.3.3.1.2.).

4.3.3.1.1 Limited Applicability to Smaller Video Sharing Platforms in Germany

Pursuant to § 1 (2) NetzDG, social media networks of a certain size, i.e. with fewer than two million registered users in Germany, are exempt from all requirements under § 2–§ 3b NetzDG. Smaller sized platforms are to be relieved of excessive burden that would be imposed by having to comply with the NetzDG.[82] Yet regarding smaller video sharing platforms, in contrast, the requirements per the AVMSD still fundamentally apply,[83] i.e. video sharing platform providers with fewer than two million registered users in Germany that are domiciled in Germany are not exempt from all obligations under the NetzDG, pursuant to § 3e (2) 3rd st.

---

[81] The legal definition of a social media network hinges upon the shareability of "any content"; regarding effects on the area of application, see BT-Drs. 19/18792, p. 50 f.

[82] BMJV: Entwurf eines Gesetzes zur Verbesserung der Rechtsdurchsetzung in sozialen Netzwerken (draft legislation for improved legal enforcement against social media networks), p. 19 f.

[83] BT-Drs. 19/18792, p. 51.

Instead, alleged illegal content on smaller video sharing platforms is viewed in relation to distinct categories. Thus, certain content from the general list per § 1 (3) NetzDG is referenced under § 3e (2) 2nd st. NetzDG—namely user-generated videos and broadcasts that constitute criminal acts under §§ 111, 130 (1) and (2), 131, 140, 166, and 184b in conjunction with § 184d of Criminal Code (Strafgesetzbuch; StGB). These are categories of content already covered by the NetzDG, which are also regulated under the AVMSD. Where such specifically listed illegal content is concerned, requirements under the NetzDG still apply to smaller video sharing platforms as well, though to a lesser extent, being exempt from reporting obligations per § 2 NetzDG and notification obligations per § 3a NetzDG. The complaint procedure per § 3 (1) NetzDG is essentially limited to the deletion of obviously illegal content. There is neither a review deadline for 'regular' illegal content nor an obligation to retain removed content nor any specific requirements regarding in-house monitoring of complaint handling. It is required, however, to have a remonstrance procedure in place pursuant to § 3b NetzDG.

Regarding content not relevant to the criminal offenses specified under § 3e (2) 2nd st. NetzDG, smaller video sharing platforms are likewise exempted from all obligations per § 2–§ 3b NetzDG, in accordance with § 1 (2) NetzDG. Such content, which for small video sharing platforms thus does not trigger any obligations under the NetzDG, includes, for example, content illegal for reasons concerning the preservation of the democratic and constitutional state (§§ 86, 86a StGB), preservation of public order (§§ 126, 129–129b StGB), and protection of personal dignity (§§ 185–187 StGB).

Thus, while smaller video sharing platforms enjoy privileges compared to larger video sharing platforms with respect to liability for illegal content and related obligations, such privileging falls short of the exemption for smaller social media networks.

4.3.3.1.2 Limited Applicability to Video Sharing Platforms in Other EU Countries

Because the requirements per the AVMSD are directly referenced, the geographical scope of applicability of the NetzDG to video sharing platforms is derived differently and with greater specificity. The AVMSD applies the country of origin principle.[84] The NetzDG retains this in § 3e (3), thus there is a fundamental reliance on the degree of protection on the European level being ensured by

[84] For detailed commentary see, 3.1. above.

the Member State in which the video sharing platform provider is domiciled, or is effectively domiciled pursuant to § 3d (2) and (3) NetzDG.[85] Therefore, video sharing platforms that are either actually or effectively domiciled in Germany are fully subject to the NetzDG. Video sharing platforms domiciled in another EU Member State are only obligated to comply with the NetzDG to a limited extent. Here, too, alleged illegal content must be viewed in relation to distinct categories. There is no fundamental obligation under the NetzDG regarding content that falls within the above-referenced list per § 3e (2) 2nd st. NetzDG. Such obligation can only be triggered in specific cases by a special order of the Federal Office of Justice pursuant to § 3e (3) and § 4a NetzDG. In contrast, regarding all other content per § 1 (3) NetzDG, the obligations under the NetzDG apply in full. This concerns a substantial amount of illegal content because criminal breach of preservation of dignity and sphere of privacy protections are a particularly significant focus within the framework of the NetzDG. After all, the most frequent reasons for content removal are violations of personal sphere rights or hate speech under community standards.[86] A breach of preservation of dignity and sphere of privacy protections does not only occur to adults, but is of special relevance to minors due to the dangers of mobbing and hate for their development.

This nuanced view regarding geographical applicability to video sharing platforms is distinct from the geographical scope of application of the NetzDG to social media networks. Social media networks have to fully comply with requirements under the NetzDG even if domiciled in another EU Member State.[87] This deviation from the country-of-origin principle remains a subject of criticism.[88]

Accordingly, the distinction between social media networks and video sharing platforms in the NetzDG is highly important, with special relevance to smaller platforms with fewer than two million registered users in Germany and to those domiciled in other EU countries. Platforms that represent a hybrid between a video sharing platform and a social media network, or feature elements of both,

[85] BT-Drs. 19/18792, p. 51. Pursuant to § 3d (2) and (3), the country of domicile may be imputed if the parent company, subsidiary, or corporate affiliate is domiciled in a Member State, see also 3.1. above.

[86] Such complaints are highly common, see, for example, Facebook: NetzDG Transparenzbericht and YouTube: Transparenzbericht.

[87] Liesching, in: NomosBR-NetzDG, § 1 NetzDG mn. 2.

[88] For further references, cf. Hoven/Gersdorf, in: BeckOK-Informations- und MedienR, § 1 NetzDG mn. 9; for detailed discussion, see again Liesching: Stellungnahme, pp. 1 ff.

will have to evaluate and independently decide whether they need to set up a complaint process per the NetzDG, and for what platform content. There is thus some concern that the differing outlined obligations for social media networks and video sharing platforms respectively may complicate efforts to establish coherent and uniform complaint procedures and mechanisms for users.[89] This differentiation can lead to two types of issues and corresponding legal uncertainty. First, platforms must assess whether specific content relates primarily to the function of a social media network or to a video sharing platform. In the case of YouTube, for example, which is domiciled in Ireland, different conclusions can be reached.[90] In a second step, platforms may have to review whether obligations under the NetzDG apply to the entire list of illegal content or only parts of it. Smaller platforms will have to confront the same considerations.[91]

4.3.3.2 Legal Ramifications

Once the few complicated questions regarding applicability of the NetzDG for video sharing platforms have been resolved, the legal ramifications should be crystal clear. Under the NetzDG, video sharing platforms have the same status as social media networks except for the differences described, whereby they fall within the regulatory framework of the NetzDG (see Sect. 4.3.1.) and have new obligations under the most recent amendment (see 4.3.2.). Being only partially subject to these obligations is only possible for smaller video sharing platforms in exceptional cases (see 4.3.3.1.1.).

Video sharing platforms are further characterized by two particularities. Regarding illegal content per § 3e (2) 2nd st. NetzDG, video sharing platform providers are obligated to have platform users contractually agree not to use the service for the content in question, see § 3e (4) NetzDG and to monitor and ensure compliance with that agreement. This does not, however, represent an obligation to proactively review content, as such mandatory monitoring is prohibited under § 10 TMG.[92] Again, there is no special regulation of a contractual agreement with minors. The question whether and under what conditions minors can con-

---

[89] Cf. Bitkom: Stellungnahme, p. 27 f.; Google: Stellungnahme, p. 19.

[90] See also as an example the Federal Council Position Paper (Stellungnahme des Bundesrates), May 20, 2020, BT-Drs. 19/19367, p. 4 f.

[91] Regarding risks, esp. for smaller platforms, cf. Google: Stellungnahme, pp. 18 f. and HateAid: Stellungnahme, pp. 21 f.; regarding concerns in relation to Article 3 of the German Constitution (GG) and appropriateness cf. Liesching: Stellungnahme, p. 9.

[92] BT-Drs. 19/18792, p. 52.

clude a contract with the video sharing platform provider therefore depends on the contract law of the member state. The second particularity is that video sharing platforms are subject to regulatory arbitration pursuant to § 3f NetzDG. The regulatory arbitration panel exists for the sole purpose of settling disputes with video sharing platform providers out of court. Social media network providers do not have this option for disputes, instead having only non-regulatory arbitration options organized under private law as per § 3c NetzDG. However, regulatory mediation is only an option for disputes with video sharing platform providers if the they do not already participate in private-sector arbitration or the recognized arbitration panel is not a private-sector organization (see § 3f (1) 3rd st. NetzDG). This possibility is thus subsidiary to arbitration disputes organized under private law.

4.3.3.3 Legislative Overlap Between the Network Enforcement Act, the Interstate Treaty on the Protection of Minors in the Media, and the Protection of Minors Act

The discussed amendments mean that a 'notice and takedown' procedure for video sharing platforms will be provided under both the JMStV and the NetzDG. There can be overlap between JMStV and NetzDG regarding much content,[93] such as prohibited content specifically illegal under § 4 (1) JMStV, in particular. For example, the content listed under § 4 (1) 1st st. nos. 1–6 and no. 10 JMStV also falls within the scope of § 1 (3) NetzDG.[94] Content deleterious to the development of minors per § 5 JMStV could also be concerned. Minors suffer particularly from violation of personal sphere rights on the internet, as such negative experiences can be deleterious to their development.[95] Therefore, deletion obligations may exist in parallel under the JMStV, and in conjunction with the TMG and the NetzDG, respectively.

In such cases, the procedure per the NetzDG is seen as fundamentally more specific in nature, thus taking precedence. This is evident from the wording of

---

[93] Referring to overlap areas see also Kreißig: Stellungnahme der Medienanstalten, p. 2.

[94] Liesching, in: BeckOK JMStV, § 4 mn. 2.

[95] Cf. Bitkom: Kinder und Jugendliche in der digitalen Welt, p. 13; Medienpädagogischer Forschungsverband Südwest: JIM-Studie 2019, pp. 49 f.; for a discussion based on specific illegal acts, see cf. Brings-Wiesen: Staatliche Reaktionsmöglichkeiten auf jugendlichen und jugendgefährdenden Hass im Netz, ZJJ (Zeitschrift für Jugendkriminalrecht und Jugendhilfe) 2020, pp. 127 ff.

§ 10a and § 10b TMG.[96] The NetzDG similarly also has precedence in case of overlap with § 24a JuSchG, see § 24a (4) JuSchG, although further requirements under the JuSchG then apply relating to the protective objectives outlined above. Regarding possible overlap, however, especially between the JMStV and the NetzDG, there are concerns that the different administrative structures may lead to intersecting competencies and redundant structures that could undermine efforts to implement practical and effective complaint mechanisms, thereby giving rise to conflict.[97] Additionally, the Federal Office of Justice, as a regulatory authority, could become the subject of constitutional concerns in view of its rapidly growing importance with a view to the principle of separation of state and public media, which requires that media supervision must be relatively independent of government authorities.[98]

5 Conclusions

Legislators have formulated significantly less stringent requirements for telemedia than for broadcasting regarding the protection of minors. In practice, there is no concept in place that is absolutely effective in protecting minors, in part because of ubiquitous access to social media content via smartphones and tablets, which renders technical solutions increasingly difficult.[99] Legislators have now explicitly addressed video sharing service providers for the first time, i.e. platforms where users post videos, specifically with respect to the protection of minors, imposing concrete obligations.

---

[96] The German Federal Government has cited this as well in a reply to a Federal Council statement, see Gegenäußerung der Bundesregierung auf die Stellungnahme des Bundesrates, BT-Drs. 19/19367, regarding number 3 c (p. 7).

[97] Stellungnahme des Bundesrates, 20.5.2020, BT-Drs. 19/19367, p. 2; Kreißig: Stellungnahme der Medienanstalten, p. 2.; Facebook: Stellungnahme, pp. 3 f.

[98] Cf. also Google: Stellungnahme, pp. 8 ff.; similarly Liesching: Stellungnahme, p. 10; in contrast the Federal Government reply: Gegenäußerung der Bundesregierung, BT-Drs. 19/19367, regarding 3 e (p. 8); for a view tolerating overlap (given dialogue between the instances), see HateAid: Stellungnahme, p. 23.

[99] Cf. Müller-Terpitz: Persönlichkeitsrechtliche Aspekte der Social Media, in: Hornung/Müller-Terpitz (eds.): Rechtshandbuch Social Media, pp. 253, 296; Beyerbach: Social Media im Verfassungsrecht und der einfachgesetzlichen Medienregulierung, in: Hornung/Müller-Terpitz (eds.): Rechtshandbuch Social Media, pp. 507, 560.

Laws enacted to implement the AVMSD had largely failed to provide either transparent, user-friendly mechanisms that enable user reporting of illegal content or age verification systems to restrict access to content deleterious to the physical, mental, or moral development of minors.[100] These deficits are now being addressed by implementing separate clauses §§ 5a ff. JMStV in conjunction with §§ 10a ff. TMG. On the one hand, it does seem suboptimal that the term "age verification" is used in § 5a, (2) no. 1 of the amended JMStV. At any rate, its usage does, however, yield a mechanism for creating a detailed catalog of appropriate measures depending on the type of objectionable content, the harm it could cause, the defining characteristics of the category of persons to be protected, and the rights and legitimate interests concerned as required under Art. 6 a (1) AVMSD.

This tendency towards greater platform regulation is reflected in the development of the JuSchG and the planned amendments to the NetzDG. The JuSchG focuses on the creation of structural precautionary measures. As before, these are not to give rise to general review/monitoring obligations for video sharing platforms, with reference to the Digital Services Act among other considerations. Instead, a set of various measures is available that may include the implementation of registration, classification and age verification systems, minor-friendly terms and conditions, and advisories on external sources and contacts for information and advice. The 'child protection by design' obligations to be fulfilled are determined with a view to constitutionality considerations, applying the principle of appropriateness, possibly in coordination with the regulator within the framework of a regulatory dialogue procedure.

In addition to outlining specifics and fleshing out the existing complaint procedure, such as additional notification and retention requirements, the draft amendment of the NetzDG also addresses platform design. For example, platforms must have a remonstrance procedure in place and provide uncomplicated channels for contacting them that are easily identifiable as such. The Federal Office of Justice, which in the past functioned solely as fine-imposing authority, is also to play a greater supervisory role. Video sharing platforms will likewise be compelled to meet these requirements going forward, irrespective of whether any kind of content or only content of a specific nature may be shared on the platform. Smaller video sharing platforms and platforms domiciled in EU countries besides Germany are possible exceptions, and will have to consider in detail what content of theirs falls within the scope of these obligations.

[100] Kommission für Jugendmedienschutz: Stellungnahme Novellierung des Medienstaatsvertrages/Jugendmedienschutz-Staatsvertrages, p. 4.

References

Altenhain, Karsten: Teil 20 Jugendschutz, in: Hoeren, Thomas/Sieber, Ulrich/Holznagel, Bernd (eds.): Handbuch Multimedia-Recht, Munich 54th ed. 2020.

Beyerbach, Hannes: Social Media im Verfassungsrecht und der einfachgesetzlichen Medienregulierung, in: Hornung, Gerrit/Müller-Terpitz, Ralf (eds.): Rechtshandbuch Social Media, Berlin 2nd ed. 2021, pp. 507–593.

BfJ (Bundesamt für Justiz): Erstmals Selbstregulierung nach dem Netzwerkdurchsetzungsgesetz, January 23, 2020, https://www.bundesjustizamt.de/DE/Presse/Archiv/2020/20200123.html; last accessed July 20, 2021.

Bitkom Bundesverband Informationswirtschaft, Telekommunikation und Neue Medien e.V.: Stellungnahme zum Entwurf eines Gesetzes zur Änderung des Netzwerkdurchsetzungsgesetzes, February 17, 2020, https://www.bmjv.de/SharedDocs/Gesetzgebungsverfahren/Stellungnahmen/2020/Downloads/021720_Stellungnahme%20_Bitkom_RefE_NetzDG.pdf;jsessionid=25CB94881F7EA6D227F44CC9A65E5DF0.2_cid297?__blob=publicationFile&v=2; last accessed May 12, 2021.

Bitkom Bundesverband Informationswirtschaft, Telekommunikation und Neue Medien e.V.: Kinder und Jugendliche in der digitalen Welt, May 28, 2019, https://www.bitkom.org/sites/default/files/2019-05/bitkom_pk-charts_kinder_und_jugendliche_2019.pdf; last accessed May 12, 2021.

BMJV (Bundesministerium für Justiz und Verbraucherschutz): Entwurf eines Gesetzes zur Verbesserung der Rechtsdurchsetzung in sozialen Netzwerken, April 5, 2017, https://www.bmjv.de/SharedDocs/Gesetzgebungsverfahren/Dokumente/RegE_NetzDG.pdf; last accessed July 20, 2021.

Brings-Wiesen, Tobias: Staatliche Reaktionsmöglichkeiten auf jugendlichen und jugendgefährdenden Hass im Netz, ZJJ (Zeitschrift für Jugendkriminalrecht und Jugendhilfe), 2020, pp. 127–140.

Deutscher Bundestag: Vorgang-Gesetzgebung. Gesetz zur Anpassung der Regelungen über die Bestandsdatenauskunft an die Vorgaben aus der Entscheidung des Bundesverfassungsgerichts vom 27. Mai 2020, https://dip.bundestag.de/vorgang/gesetz-zur-anpassung-der-regelungen-%C3%BCber-die-bestandsdatenauskunft-an-die/271425; last accessed July 20, 2021.

Deutscher Bundestag: Vorgang-Gesetzgebung. Gesetz zur Bekämpfung des Rechtsextremismus und der Hasskriminalität, http://dipbt.bundestag.de/extrakt/ba/WP19/2599/259975.html; last accessed July 20, 2021.

eco Verband der Internetwirtschaft e. V.: Stellungnahme zum Referentenentwurf eines Gesetzes zur Verbesserung der Rechtsdurchsetzung in sozialen Netzwerken (Netzwerkdurchsetzungsgesetz), March 30, 2017, https://www.bmjv.de/SharedDocs/Gesetzgebungsverfahren/Stellungnahmen/2017/Downloads/03302017_Stellungnahme_eco_RefE_NetzDG.pdf?__blob=publicationFile&v=2; last accessed May 12, 2021.

Erdemir, Murad: § 4 JMStV, § 5 JMStV, in: Spindler, Gerald/Schuster, Fabian (eds.): Recht der elektronischen Medien, Munich 4th ed. 2019.

Facebook: NetzDG Transparenzbericht, 2020, https://about.fb.com/wp-content/uploads/2020/07/facebook_netzdg_July_2020_German.pdf; last accessed May 12, 2021.

Facebook: Stellungnahme zum Referentenentwurf eines Gesetzes zur Änderung des Netzwerkdurchsetzungsgesetzes, February 17, 2020, https://www.bmjv.de/SharedDocs/Gesetzgebungsverfahren/Stellungnahmen/2020/Downloads/021720_Stellungnahme_Facebook_RefE_NetzDG.pdf?__blob=publicationFile&v=2; last accessed May 12, 2021.

Geidner, Silvia: § 5 JMStV, in: Binder, Reinhart/Vesting, Thomas (eds.): Beck'scher Kommentar zum Rundfunkrecht (Beck RundfunkR), Munich 4th ed. 2018.

Google: Stellungnahme zur Anhörung des Ausschusses für Recht und Verbraucherschutz des Deutschen Bundestags am 17. Juni 2020 zum Entwurf eines Gesetzes zur Änderung des Netzwerkdurchsetzungsgesetzes, June 17, 2020, https://www.bundestag.de/resource/blob/701152/0f347aec58fff15d3edbd999628c3bb0/frank_google-data.pdf; last accessed May 12, 2021.

Guggenberger, Nikolaus: Das Netzwerkdurchsetzungsgesetz – schön gedacht, schlecht gemacht, ZRP (Zeitschrift für Rechtspolitik), 2017, pp. 98–101.

Guggenberger, Nikolaus: Das Netzwerkdurchsetzungsgesetz in der Anwendung, NJW (Neue Juristische Wochenschrift), 2017, pp. 2577–2582.

Gundel, Jörg: Die Fortentwicklung der europäischen Medienregulierung: Zur Neufassung der AVMD-Richtlinie, ZUM (Zeitschrift für Urheber- und Medienrecht), 2019, pp. 131–139.

Hartmann, Sarah: Welche Dienste zählen künftig zu den audiovisuellen Mediendiensten? Reform des materiellen Anwendungsbereichs der AVMD-RL und Möglichkeiten der alternativen Ausgestaltung, MMR (Multimedia und Recht), 2018, pp. 790–794.

HateAid gGmbH: Stellungnahme zum Gesetzentwurf zur Änderung des Netzwerkdurchsetzungsgesetzes, June 16, 2020, https://www.bundestag.de/resource/blob/701054/02b45b9aca30a33a56750db25cea404f/ballon_hateaid-data.pdf; last accessed May 12, 2021.

Hilgert, Felix: Novellierung des Jugendmedienschutz-Staatsvertrags, December 6, 2019, https://spielerecht.de/novellierung-des-jugendmedienschutz-staatsvertrags/; last accessed May 11, 2021.

Hilgert, Felix/Sümmermann, Philipp: Technischer Jugendmedienschutz. Maßnahmen der Jugendschutz-Compliance in Rundfunk und Telemedien, MMR-Beil. (Multimedia und Recht – Beilage) (Appendix), 2020 (8), pp. 26–30.

Höch, Dominik: Nachbessern: ja, verteufeln: nein. Das NetzDG ist besser als sein Ruf, K & R (Kommunikation & Recht), 2017, pp. 289–292.

Höld, Florian: Das Vorabentscheidungsverfahren nach dem neuen NetzDG. Rechtliches Neuland bei der Bekämpfung von Kriminalität in sozialen Netzwerken, MMR (Multimedia und Recht), 2017, pp. 791–795.

Holznagel, Bernd: § 2 RStV, in: Spindler, Gerald/Schuster, Fabian (eds.): Recht der elektronischen Medien, Munich 4th ed. 2019.

Holznagel, Bernd: Das Compliance-System des Entwurfs des Netzwerkdurchsetzungsgesetzes, ZUM (Zeitschrift für Urheber- und Medienrecht), 2017, pp. 615–624.

Holznagel, Bernd/Hartmann, Sarah: Teil 3 Rundfunk und Telemedien, in: Hoeren, Thomas/Sieber, Ulrich/Holznagel, Bernd (eds.): Handbuch Multimedia-Recht, Munich 54th ed. 2020.

Holznagel, Daniel: Melde- und Abhilfeverfahren zur Beanstandung rechtswidrig gehosteter Inhalte nach europäischem und deutschem Recht im Vergleich zu gesetzlich geregelten notice and take-down-Verfahren, GRUR Int. (Gewerblicher Rechtsschutz und Urheberrecht Internationaler Teil), 2014, pp. 105–113.

Hoven, Elisa/Gersdorf, Hubertus: § 1 NetzDG, in: Gersdorf, Hubertus/Paal, Boris P. (eds.): Beck'scher Onlinekommentar Informations- und Medienrecht (BeckOK-Informations- und MedienR), Munich 30th ed. 2019.

Jäger, Manuel: Die Novellierung der AVMD-RL—Anwendungsbereich und Werberegulierung—eine erneut vertane Chance?, ZUM (Zeitschrift für Urheber- und Medienrecht), 2019, pp. 477–490.

Kaspar, Marcel: § 4 JMStV, in: Binder, Reinhart/Vesting, Thomas (eds.): Beck'scher Kommentar zum Rundfunkrecht (Beck RundfunkR), Munich 4th ed. 2018.

Keller, Rainer/Liesching, Marc: 82. Abschnitt: Pflichten von Anbietern von Rundfunk und Telemedien, in: Paschke, Marian/Berlit, Wolfgang/Meyer, Klaus/Kröner, Lars (eds.): Hamburger Kommentar Gesamtes Medienrecht (Hamburger Kommentar), Baden-Baden 4th ed. 2021.

Keppeler, Lutz Martin: Was bleibt vom TMG-Datenschutz nach der DS-GVO? Lösung und Schaffung von Abgrenzungsproblemen im Multimedia-Datenschutz, MMR (Multimedia und Recht), 2015, pp. 779–783.

Kommission für Jugendmedienschutz: Kriterien zur Bewertung von Konzepten für Altersverifikationssysteme, December 11, 2019, https://www.kjm-online.de/fileadmin/user_upload/KJM/Aufsicht/Technischer_Jugendmedienschutz/KJM-AVS-Raster.pdf; last accessed May 11, 2021.

Kommission für Jugendmedienschutz: Neue Methode für Altersverifikation im Internet, December 20, 2019, https://www.kjm-online.de/service/pressemitteilungen/meldung/jugendmedienschutz-neue-methode-fuer-altersverifikation-im-internet/; last accessed May 11, 2021.

Kommission für Jugendmedienschutz: Stellungnahme der Kommission für Jugendmedienschutz (KJM) zur Novellierung des Medienstaatsvertrages/Jugendmedienschutz-Staatsvertrages, August 22, 2019, https://www.kjm-online.de/fileadmin/user_upload/KJM/Ueber_uns/Positionen/20190822_KJM-Stellungnahme_MStV.pdf; last accessed May 11, 2021.

Kreißig, Wolfgang: Stellungnahme der Medienanstalten zur Änderung des Netzwerkdurchsetzungsgesetzes (NetzDG), June 15, 2020, https://www.bundestag.de/resource/blob/700782/c3c25a329df06b6b832d7aac69490616/kreissig-data.pdf; last accessed May 12, 2021.

Kröber, Martin: § 6 RStV, in: Binder, Reinhart/Vesting, Thomas (eds.): Beck'scher Kommentar zum Rundfunkrecht (BeckOK-RundfunkR), Munich 4th ed. 2018.

Liesching, Marc: § 1 NetzDG, in: Liesching, Marc (ed.): NomosBundesrecht: Netzwerkdurchsetzungsgesetz (NomosBR-NetzDG), Baden-Baden 1st online ed. 2018.

Liesching, Marc: § 3 NetzDG, in: Spindler, Gerald/Schmitz, Peter (eds.): Telemediengesetz mit Netzwerkdurchsetzungsgesetz, Munich 2nd ed. 2018.

Liesching, Marc: § 4 JMStV, § 5 JMStV, in: Liesching, Marc (ed.): Beck'scher Online-Kommentar JMStV (BeckOK JMStV), Munich 18th ed. 1.1.2020.

Liesching, Marc: Das Herkunftslandprinzip der E-Commerce-Richtlinie und seine Auswirkung auf die aktuelle Mediengesetzgebung in Deutschland, Berlin 2020.

Liesching, Marc: Das Herkunftslandprinzip nach E-Commerce- und AVMD-Richtlinie. Anwendbarkeit von NetzDG, JuSchG, MStV und JMStV auf Soziale Netzwerke mit

Sitz in anderen EU-Mitgliedstaaten, MMR-Beil. (Multimedia und Recht—Beilage) (Appendix), 2020 (6), pp. 3–27.

Liesching, Marc: Die Durchsetzung von Verfassungs- und Europarecht gegen das NetzDG, MMR (Multimedia und Recht), 2018, pp. 26–30.

Liesching, Marc: Stellungnahme zum Entwurf eines Gesetzes zur Änderung des Netzwerkdurchsetzungsgesetzes, June 15, 2020, https://www.bundestag.de/resource/blob/700788/83b06f596a5e729ef69348849777b045/liesching-data.pdf; last accessed May 12, 2021.

Liesching, Marc: Verfassungskonformer Jugendschutz nach der Medienkonvergenz. Anforderungen an ein differenziertes Regelungssystem, Multimedia und Recht (MMR), 2018, pp. 141–143.

Löber, Isabell/Roßnagel, Alexander: Das Netzwerkdurchsetzungsgesetz in der Umsetzung. Bilanz nach den ersten Transparenzberichten, MMR (Multimedia und Recht), 2019, pp. 71–76.

Medienpädagogischer Forschungsverband Südwest (mpfs): JIM-Studie 2019. Jugend, Information, Medien, https://www.mpfs.de/fileadmin/files/Studien/JIM/2019/JIM_2019.pdf; last accessed May 12, 2021.

Müller-Terpitz, Ralf: Persönlichkeitsrechtliche Aspekte der Social Media, in: Hornung, Gerrit/Müller-Terpitz, Ralf (eds.): Rechtshandbuch Social Media, Berlin 2nd ed. 2021, pp. 253–304.

Roßnagel, Alexander/Geminn, Christian L./Jandt, Silke/Richter, Philipp: Datenschutzrecht 2016 "Smart" genug für die Zukunft?, Kassel 2016.

Schwartmann, Rolf: Verantwortlichkeit Sozialer Netzwerke nach dem Netzwerkdurchsetzungsgesetz, GRUR-Prax (Gewerblicher Rechtsschutz und Urheberrecht, Praxis im Immaterialgüter- und Wettbewerbsrecht), 2017, pp. 317–319.

Specht-Riemenschneider, Louisa/Dehmel, Susanne/Kenning, Peter/Liedtke, Christa/Micklitz, Hans W./Scharioth, Sven: Stellungnahme des SVRV – Grundlegung einer verbrauchergerechten Regulierung interaktionsmittelnder Plattformfunktionalitäten, Berlin 2020.

Specht-Riemenschneider, Louisa/Hofmann, Franz: Verantwortung von Online-Plattformen – ein Plädoyer für funktionszentrierte Verkehrspflichten, 2021, https://www.vzbv.de/sites/default/files/downloads/2021/02/04/specht_hofmann_gutachten_plattformverantwortlichkeitdocx.pdf; last accessed May 11, 2021.

Specht-Riemenschneider, Louisa/Hofmann, Franz: Nutzerrechte als Baustein einer fairen Plattformökonomie, NJW-aktuell (Neue Juristische Wochenschrift Aktuell) 2021, pp. 15 ff. (accepted for publication).

Spiegel: Erneut Selbstmord wegen Cyber-Mobbing, September 21, 2009, https://www.spiegel.de/netzwelt/web/grossringen-erneut-selbstmord-wegen-cyber-mobbing-a-650340.html; last accessed March 9, 2021.

Spindler, Gerald: Rechtsdurchsetzung von Persönlichkeitsrechten. Bußgelder gegen Provider als Enforcement?, GRUR (Gewerblicher Rechtsschutz und Urheberrecht), 2018, pp. 365–373.

Tinnefeld, Jutta/Buchner, Benedikt: Syst. I. Datenschutz in Medien und Telekommunikation, in: Wolff, Heinrich Amadeus/Brink, Stefan (eds.): Beck'scher Onlinekommentar DatenschutzR (BeckOK-DatenschutzR), Munich 35th ed. 2019.

Wimmers, Jörg/Heymann, Britta: Zum Referentenentwurf eines Netzwerkdurchsetzungsgesetzes (NetzDG)—eine kritische Stellungnahme, AfP (Zeitschrift für das gesamte Medienrecht), 2017, pp. 93–102.

Wissenschaftliche Dienste des Bundestags: Überblick über den aktuellen Diskussionsstand und rechtliche Grundlagen zum Thema “Klarnamenpflicht im Internet”, 2020, https://www.bundestag.de/resource/blob/691400/10dd5fe59e4dc35885d4752f25126350/WD-10-003-20-pdf-data.pdf; last accessed May 11, 2021.

YouTube: Transparenzbericht. Entfernungen von Inhalten nach dem Netzwerkdurchsetzungsgesetz, https://transparencyreport.google.com/netzdg/youtube?hl=de; last accessed May 12, 2021.

Prof. Dr. Louisa Specht-Riemenschneider is Professor of Law at the Rheinische Friedrich-Wilhelms-University of Bonn, Germany, serving as Chair for Civil Law, Law of the Data Economy, Data Protection, Digitalization and Artificial Intelligence and as Head of the Research Center for Legal Issues of New Technologies and Data Law (ForTech, Forschungsstelle für Rechtsfragen neuer Technologien sowie Datenrecht). In addition, she chairs the Council of Experts on Consumer Issues at the German Federal Ministry for the Environment, Nature Conservation, Nuclear Safety and Consumer Protection. Her research focuses primarily on copyright, the internet, data, and data protection law. Among her recent publications are: Data access rights—A comparative perspective (in: German Federal Ministry of Justice and Consumer Protection/Max Planck Institute for Innovation and Competition (eds.): Data Access, Consumer Interests and Public Welfare, Nomos, 2021, pp. 401–438); Verantwortung von Online-Plattformen—ein Plädoyer für funktionszentrierte Verkehrspflichten (2021) (with Franz Hofmann); and Stuck Half Way: The Limitation of Joint Control after Fashion ID (C-40/17) (in: GRUR International, 69(2), 2020, pp. 159 163) (together with Ruben Schneider).

Alina Marko is a trainee lawyer at the Regional Court of Cologne and has worked in the Departments of Civil Law and Information and Data Law at the Rheinische Friedrich-Wilhelms-University of Bonn.

Sascha Wette is a research assistant in the Departments of Civil Law and Information and Data Law at the Rheinische Friedrich-Wilhelms-University of Bonn.

Lost Between Data and Family? Shortcomings of Current Understandings of the Law

Ayelet Blecher-Prigat

Children's right to privacy is recognized under the laws of various jurisdictions and under international treaties, most notably the United Nations Convention on the Rights of the Child (hereinafter: "CRC"). However, in today's world, there is a growing concern for children's privacy in digital contexts, and when closely examining how children's right to privacy is implemented in practice in various legal systems, doubts arise as to whether legal recognition is indeed accorded to children's interest in privacy.

This paper attempts to explain the gap between the recognition given to children's privacy at the declaratory level and the failure to recognize and protect children's privacy interest in practice. The focus rests on informational privacy, meaning on concerns regarding the collection, storage, processing, usage, and disclosure of information related to children in these different contexts.[1]

[1] Other than informational privacy, the concept of privacy also covers physical privacy, which involves respect for a person's physical integrity, home, and correspondence, and the respect for one's being and surrounding environment. Some jurisdictions also recognize the concept of decisional privacy, which protects against intrusion into intimate decisions, such as whether to use birth control or obtain an abortion. There is a voluminous amount of literature about the different categories and definitions of privacy. See e.g., Westin: Privacy

The origins of this paper stem from the chapter "Children's Right to Privacy", in: Dwyer (ed.): The Oxford Handbook of Children and the Law.

A. Blecher-Prigat (✉)
Academic College of Law and Science, School of Law, Hod HaSharon, Israel
e-mail: ayeletb@mishpat.ac.il

N. Dethloff et al. (eds.), *Families and New Media*, Juridicum – Schriften zum Medien-, Informations- und Datenrecht,
https://doi.org/10.1007/978-3-658-39664-0_12

Suggestions are then made about what can be done to remedy this situation and truly protect children's interests in privacy.

1 Legal Failure to Protect Children's Interest in Privacy

When critically examining different settings and contexts that involve children's privacy, it is questionable whether children's interest in privacy actually receives legal protection. As described in this section, children's supposed right to privacy does not guarantee them a space of their own, not even a virtual one. Children are constantly under increasing surveillance and oversight, be it of parents, state agents, or a different group of adults, and this oversight is often buttressed by the law. This observation is true in a plethora of legal systems, whether in the United States, the United Kingdom, the European Union, or Israel.

1.1 Children's Privacy in the Online World

Let us start with examining children's privacy in the online world, since it has been the rise of the digital age, with the expansion of information technologies and digital networks, which made children's privacy a frontline issue. Children's online privacy arises within a wide range of online spaces and activities. It develops in the context of the relationship between children and public entities, children's interaction with commercial entities, and children's relationship with other individuals.[2]

Public entities today collect and keep data on children from the very moment of birth. This practice raises concerns about the purposes for which such data is gathered, whether and how it is shared, and the uses and implications of its collection.[3] Children's online data has also become a valuable commodity for commercial entities, which today gather more information on children than governments

---

and Freedom; Allen: Constitutional Law and Privacy, in: Patterson (ed): A Companion to Philosophy of Law and Legal Theory; Solove: Understanding Privacy.

[2] Livingstone/Stoilove/Nandagiri: Children's Data and Privacy Online (suggesting to distinguish between "institutional privacy", "commercial privacy", and "interpersonal privacy").

[3] Ibid.

do, or are even able to, collect.[4] Children's online activities often require that they provide a substantial amount of personal data, whether intentionally or unconsciously.[5] Commercial entities employ various tactics to obtain and collect such data, and the means they use to process it evolve and advance constantly.

1.2 Legislative Approach: COPPA and GDPR

In this complex set of relationships and interactions involving children, their privacy is considered not only as an interest worthy of protection in itself, but also as a necessary means to protect against harms like commercial exploitation,[6] harm to reputation, and identity theft.[7] Numerous jurisdictions have recognized these risks and enacted legislation with the purpose of safeguarding children's privacy rights in the digital age. Two notable examples are the Children's Online Privacy Protection Act (COPPA), passed by the United States Congress in 1998,[8] and the General Data Protection Regulation (2016/679) (GDPR), enacted by the European Union.[9] Both of these instruments regulate the collection and processing of personal information from children online.

The GDPR applies to children and adults alike, though it does contain special provisions that apply to children and explicitly states that children's personal data merits specific protection.[10] Commercial entities and public authorities are also both subject to GDPR. Contrastingly, COPPA applies only to children's data and concerns mainly commercial activity.

---

[4] Ibid.

[5] Macenite: From Universal towards Child-Specific Child Protection of the Right to Privacy Online, New Media & Society 19, 2017, pp. 765–779, at p. 765.

[6] Goltz: Analyzing the regulation of children's privacy online in the US and the EU, Journal of International Media and Entertainment Law 6, 2016, pp. 21–42.

[7] Ibid.

[8] See 15 U.S.C. § 6501(1) (2006) (defining a child as "an individual under the age of 13"); § 6502(b)(1)(A) (creating requirements for "operator[s] of any website or online service directed to children that collects personal information from children or the operator of a website or online service that has actual knowledge that it is collecting personal information from a child"); see also Arewa: Data Collection, Privacy, and Children in the Digital Economy, in this volume.

[9] The General Data Protection Regulation (GDPR) was adopted on April 14, 2016, and came into force on May 25, 2018. It updated and replaced Directive 95/46/EC.

[10] Recital 38.

Nonetheless, both the COPPA and the GDPR are less concerned about the appropriate flow of information about children, or whether certain limits should be imposed on the collection or processing of their information. Rather, they similarly adopt a legal mechanism that largely relies on parental consent as the means to protect children's privacy. Parents can consent on behalf of their child, thereby granting permission for the child's data to be collected and processed (until the child reaches a certain age, for example 13 or older). Parents control the information gathered about their children by public entities; they give their consent to commercial entities that wish to process private information about their children online.

It is questionable that this mechanism of parental consent can protect children's informational privacy since existing research suggests that parents seem to have a limited understanding of the effects of online advertising.[11] This reliance on parents also seems to overlook the most vulnerable groups of children, such as children whose legal parents cannot adequately care for them.[12] At the same time, reliance on children's own consent beyond the age of 13, or even 16, to authorize the collection and processing of their data for commercial purposes is also problematic since research also indicates that "commercial privacy is the area where children are least able to comprehend and manage on their own".[13]

1.3 Parents as Gatekeepers

Parents are also often the legal gatekeepers of children's privacy concerning their involvement with the media. Few jurisdictions legislatively address, regulate, or limit the relationship between the media and children when the children's parents have given their consent to the media. Indeed, children increasingly appear at the center of media attention, and they take part in reality shows, documentaries, other television shows, and the like.[14] Absent special circumstances, such as care proceedings or a specific law that requires court approval or prohibits publicity altogether, a child's parents have control over the child's publicity.

---

[11] Livingstone/Stoilove/Nandagiri: Children's Data and Privacy Online, p. 18.

[12] Ibid., p. 28.

[13] Ibid., p. 4.

[14] Cf. Oswald/Nottingham: The Not-So-Secret Life of Five-Year-Olds, Journal of Media Law 8, 2016, pp. 198–228.

This paper does not intend to challenge the law's working premise about the unique role of parents. After all, parents act as proxies for the execution and maintenance of children's rights in almost every other aspect. *If* the issue is who can consent on children's behalf, or who should have control over children's information (when children themselves cannot exercise such control), then there are strong arguments to be made in favor of parents. Nonetheless, this contribution challenges the assumption that privacy laws should mainly be about regulating consent (at least where children are concerned). Thus, one might consider whether there should be a general prohibition, or some non-waivable limitations, on the collection, processing, and certainly transfer of children's personal information. Rather than relying merely on notions of control and consent, limitations should also be considered for reality shows and documentaries that involve children. Additionally, a parent-centered model for protecting children's privacy interests fails to consider children's informational privacy interest *in their relationship with their parents*, which will be discussed in greater details below.

1.4 Supervision by Other Adults

Nearly the only area in which parents are not given control over their children's privacy and information is sexual and reproductive health. Here, children are sometimes permitted to withhold information from their parents and exclude them from their decision-making. Many jurisdictions recognize that medical advice and treatment may be given to minors who are sufficiently mature to understand the nature and implications of the treatment, without parental consent or knowledge. But even in this context, parental oversight is merely replaced by medical professionals' and occasionally state agents' supervision.

Indeed, when the law does not support parent's control over children's privacy, it supports supervision by other adults. Thus, schools have increasingly become a site of extensive surveillance, and they have begun to more heavily employ varied surveillance tactics, such as inspecting schoolbags, using sniffer dogs, and filming with surveillance cameras (CCTVs), which are one of the most commonly used school surveillance technologies. Children cannot find legal recourse in their jurisdiction's privacy laws against this "rise of the surveillance school",[15]

[15] Taylor: The Rise of the Surveillance School, in: Lyon/Ball/Haggerty (eds): Routledge Handbook of Surveillance Studies, pp. 225–231.

and legal attempts to challenge these practices based on children's right to privacy have mostly failed.[16]

1.5 Parental Surveillance and Sharenting

To complete the legal picture, let us consider children's right to privacy in the home, as well as their right to privacy vis-à-vis their parents. In these contexts, law plays a more tacit role, as it rarely regulates intra-familial relationships directly. However, no regulation or legal disregard in fact ratifies and endorses existing practices.

Parents today are under increasing pressure to monitor their children, especially online.[17] They are encouraged to safeguard their children using a plethora of apps and services that allow them to block certain websites; listen in to their children's (offline) conversations by remotely activating their smartphone's microphone; and track their online activity, interactions, and location. Monitoring has become associated with good, loving, and responsible parenting, and the surveillance of children has been framed in the language of safety, protection, and care.[18] Parental surveillance is increasing with children's age. As children grow older and become more independent, parents resort more to monitoring and surveillance.[19] Thus, even when legal regulations seem to recognize older children's independent interests by sanctioning their online activity without requiring parental consent, children remain under constant parental supervision. It is not surprising, therefore, that studies on children's experience and conceptions of privacy reveal that many children (mostly teenagers) do not regard the home as a private place.[20]

The phenomenon of "sharenting" (a portmanteau of "sharing" and "parenting"), which refers to the ways that parents use social media to distribute pictures, videos, and other updates about their children, further complicates the protection

---

[16] Blecher-Prigat: Children's Right to Privacy, pp. 363–392, at p. 369.

[17] Steeves: Surveillance of young people on the internet, in: Lyon/Ball/Haggerty (eds): Routledge Handbook of Surveillance Studies, pp. 352–359, at p. 356.

[18] Ibid.

[19] Livingstone/Stoilove/Nandagiri: Children's Data and Privacy Online, p. 25.

[20] Cf. Boyd/Marwick: Social Privacy in Networked Publics.

of children's informational privacy.[21] Various researchers have shown the widespread popularity of parents' posting stories about and photos of their children online.[22] Nonetheless, social science research on sharenting paints a complicated picture. When deciding what to share online, parents do consider the possible implications for their children and, in particular, their children's privacy.[23] For example, parents take some responsibility when deciding what to publish, sometimes deciding against sharing photos that might later embarrass their children.[24] Still, the question of decision-making remains contested between parents and children. Children and parents disagree on the permission-seeking process with regards to posting information and photographs online, with children thinking parents need to ask their permission more often than parents think they should.[25] These findings suggest that parents seem to have internalized the message that they control their children's privacy. They show responsibility and care when making decisions about posting information and photos of their children online; however, they often think the decision is (solely) theirs.

Disputes and disagreements between children and parents regarding the posting of information and pictures online almost never reach the courtroom, and the rare exceptions usually arise in the context of divorce. More importantly, current legal conceptions of privacy seem inadequate to address the complexity inherent to sharenting, since parental sharing is often not just about children; it is about the parents, too, and existing conceptions of the right to privacy provide neither the terminology nor a normative framework to address such complex dilemmas.

2 Possible Explanations for Failure of Existing Laws to Protect Children's Privacy

As demonstrated in the previous section, existing legal policies and rules fail to adequately acknowledge and respect children's privacy interests in the various contexts in which they arise. I argue that four main reasons underlie these failures

[21] See also Autenrieth: The Case of "Sharenting", in this volume; Kutscher: Positionings, Challenges, and Ambivalences in Children's and Parents' Perspectives in Digitalized Familial Contexts, in this volume; Thimm: Mediatized Families, in this volume.

[22] Blum-Ross/Livingstone: "Sharenting", Popular Communication 15(2), 2017, pp. 110–125.

[23] Cf. Ibid.

[24] Kumar/Schoenebeck: The Modern Day Baby Book.

[25] Moser/Chen/Schoenebeck: Parents' and Children's Preferences about Parents Sharing about Children on Social Media.

of the law. First, there is insufficient research and knowledge about children's needs and interests in privacy, and where research does exist, lawmakers fail to take notice of its findings. Second, privacy theories are mainly adult-centered and cannot adequately be applied to children. Third, family law conceptions still focus on parental authority, and lastly, the ideal of "the family" as a unit seems incompatible with children's individual right to privacy. I briefly elaborate on each of these reasons below.

2.1 Limited Knowledge About children's Interest in Privacy and Disconnect Between Research and Legal Policy

Current policies and laws about children's privacy rest upon certain assumptions about children such as what need, if any, they have for privacy, as well as what risks privacy might have for them and how they can be protected. Thus, for example, common assumptions suggest that young children simply do not need privacy, that teenagers today neither care nor value privacy,[26] or that privacy is simply dangerous for children. Nonetheless, it is questionable whether there is evidence to support such assumptions. The research on children's privacy is relatively new, and substantial gaps still exist in current knowledge about the various dimensions related to children's interests in privacy.[27]

More importantly, even when research exists, policymakers seem to pay little attention, if any, to its findings. As noted by Sonia Livingstone and her colleagues, even the GDPR, which allegedly makes children's privacy a central issue, was drafted with limited input about and consideration of research regarding children's privacy.[28]

2.2 Privacy Theories and Conceptions are Adult-Centered

The meaning of the right to privacy is far from clear, even if we limit the discussion to informational privacy, which addresses concerns about the collection,

[26] See e.g., Marwick/Boyd: Networked Privacy, New Media & Society, 16(7), 2014, pp. 1051–1067, at p. 1052.

[27] Livingstone/Stoilove/Nandagiri: Children's Data and Privacy Online.

[28] Ibid at p. 7.

storage, use, and disclosure of personal information. Indeed, for several decades, scholars from various disciplines have tried to define both privacy and the right to privacy. However, children have been excluded from the extensive scholarly engagement with theorizing privacy, which has been written almost entirely with adult right-bearers in mind.[29] As a result, prevailing conceptions of privacy apply only awkwardly, if at all, to children.

Predominant approaches to privacy include Warren and Brandeis' famous formulation of the "right to be let alone",[30] privacy as access,[31] and privacy as autonomy or control.[32] Children, however, are inherently dependent upon and connected to others, thereby rendering a privacy right aimed at drawing a boundary between the right holder and others unapplicable to them. Children likewise do not fit the autonomy basis for existing conceptions of privacy. Perceptions of privacy as access or control assume a possibility, whether cognitive or psychological, of individual control, which young children generally lack. These observations are not merely theoretical; they underlie and explain the aforementioned lack of protection given to children's privacy under the law. If privacy is about drawing boundaries and setting individuals apart, then applying it to children might be no more than „abandoning children to their rights".[33] If privacy is mainly about control, then finding the most adequate proxy for exercising children's control should indeed be the legal goal (and, as such, parents would appear to be the most adequate candidates).

2.3 Prevalent Conceptions of the Parent–child Relationship

The legal approach, which resigns to a mechanism of parental control and consent as the means to protect children's privacy, can be explained by well-established views about the role of parents. As Article 16 of the CRC, which

---

[29] Shmueli/Blecher-Prigat: Privacy for Children, Columbia Human Rights Law Review 42, 2011, pp. 759–795.

[30] Warren/Brandeis: The Right to Privacy, Harvard Law Review 4, 1890, pp. 193–220.

[31] Gavison: Privacy and the Limits of Law.

[32] Nissenbaum: Privacy in Context, pp. 69–71.

[33] Cf. Hafen: Children's Liberation and the New Egalitarianism, Brigham Young University Law Review 1976, pp. 605–658.

incorporates children's right to privacy, was being drafted concerns arose in the Working Group regarding the role of parents.[34] These concerns were ultimately resolved by including Article 5, which requires respect for "the responsibilities, rights and duties of parents ... in the exercise by the child of the rights recognized in the present Convention".[35] Thus, while trumpeting the rights of the child, the CRC, like other international documents on human rights, also acknowledges that the family is the most fundamental, basic, and important unit of society. It also emphasizes the importance of preserving families' autonomy, harmony, and privacy wherever possible.

Nonetheless, various states have issued declarations or reservations about the relationship between parents and their children's rights, mentioning specifically children's right to privacy under Article 16.[36] In fact, in many legal systems, parental rights, particularly their rights to direct the upbringing of their children, are constitutionally protected while children's rights are not.[37]

2.4 Theories About "the Family" as a Relational Unit

Children's right to privacy in the home and especially in their relationship with their parents, which arises in the context of parental surveillance and sharenting, also raises concerns regarding the ideal of the family as a relational entity. Recognizing children's individual right to privacy in their relationship with their parents seems to threaten the intimacy and loving relationships that are (or should be) integral to every family.[38] It also seems to contradict the sense of collectivity family members are believed to share—a sense "that 'we' exist as something beyond 'you' and 'me'".[39] These concerns seem particularly relevant if the right to privacy is understood in a hyper-individualistic way, which emphasizes boundaries and depicts individuals as separated rather than connected.

[34] UNICEF: The Implementation Handbook for the Convention on the Rights of the Child.

[35] Ibid.

[36] Ibid.

[37] See e.g., Dwyer: Parents' Religion and Children's Welfare: Debunking the Doctrine of Parents' Rights, California Law Review, 82, 1994, p. 1371.

[38] Shmueli/Blecher-Prigat: Privacy for Children, Columbia Human Rights Law Review 42, 2011, pp. 759–795, at p. 775.

[39] Karst: The Freedom of Intimate Association, Yale Law Journal 89, 1980, pp. 624–692, at p. 629.

While it is certainly true that the family is more than a mere collection of individuals, we should also remember that the treatment of the family as a unit has been heavily criticized for causing systematic harm to the most vulnerable family members, usually women and children.[40] In recent decades, much feminist research has been devoted to exposing how the family, as a "unit" or an "entity", is no more than a social construction, a fiction that "has hidden a multitude of wrongs".[41] This is particularly true of the concept of "the family's privacy", which has served as an ideological tool to shield the stronger members of the family (usually men, in their role as husbands and fathers) in cases of abuse of the weak (usually women and children).[42] It should also be remembered that the struggle to have children's own interests, needs, and most of all personhood recognized and protected has been long and difficult.

3 How can we Better Protect Children's Privacy Interests in Today's World?

Achieving better recognition and protection of children's right to privacy requires several steps. First, we need more child-focused privacy research to address the existing gaps in our knowledge regarding children's interests, needs, perceptions, and value of privacy. Second, policy should be based on findings from research that does exist, which clearly indicates that children need privacy, and its availability is necessary for their welfare. Children's privacy needs include a space of their own where they can be free from adult supervision, and surveillance is especially harmful for them. When it concerns the collection, processing, usage, and disclosure of information about them, children's needs and interests cannot be adequately guaranteed through a mechanism of consent, even regarding older children, and reliance on parental control is also insufficient. Children need privacy at home and in their relationship with their parents as well. These findings must be taken into account by lawmakers, for the law is to adequately safeguard children's privacy interests.

Third, children and their interests should be brought into the general theoretical engagement with privacy. Theorizing privacy cannot be an exclusively adult-centered project whose end results are merely applied to children. Thus, a new

[40] Woodhouse: The Dark Side of Family Privacy, George Washington Law Review 67, 1999, pp. 1247–1262, at pp. 1251–59.

[41] Ibid., p.1252.

[42] Ibid., p. 1254.

theoretical understanding of privacy, which doesn't focus on boundaries and control, should be developed to incorporate and express children's interest in privacy.

Last, we need to rethink our conceptions of the family and the parent–child relationship and move beyond the dichotomous perceptions of the family as either an "entity" or a mere collection of individuals. Individual rights shape and create relationships, including familial relationships.[43] The individual right to privacy, in particular, plays an important role in enabling, creating, and shaping intimate familial relationships. Understanding children's privacy as a relational *individual* right (alongside the protection of privacy of the relationship) can assist in better defining and shaping the parent–child relationship.

References

Allen, Anita L.: Constitutional Law and Privacy, in: Patterson, Dennis (ed): A Companion to Philosophy of Law and Legal Theory, Oxford 1996, pp. 139–155.

Arewa, Olufunmilayo B.: Data Collection, Privacy, and Children in the Digital Economy, in this volume.

Autenrieth, Ulla: The Case of "Sharenting"—Parental Action Strategies in the Contested Field of Visualizing Children in Online Environments, in this volume.

Blecher-Prigat, Ayelet: Children's Right to Privacy, in: Dwyer, James G. (ed.): The Oxford Handbook of Children and the Law, New York 2020, pp. 363–392.

Blum-Ross, Alicia/Livingstone, Sonia: "Sharenting," Parent Blogging, and the Boundaries of the Digital Self, Popular Communication 15(2), 2017, pp. 110-125.

Boyd, Danah/Marwick, Alice: Social Privacy in Networked Publics: Teens' Attitudes, Practices, and Strategies, 2011, https://papers.ssrn.com/sol3/papers.cfm?abstract_id=1925128; last accessed December 27, 2020.

Dwyer, James G.: Parents' Religion and Children's Welfare: Debunking the Doctrine of Parents' Rights, California Law Review, 82, 1994, pp. 1371-1447.

Goltz, Nachshon: Is There Anybody Out There? Analyzing the Regulation of Children's Privacy Online in the United States of America and the European Union According to the TBGI Analytical Framework by Eberlein et al., Journal of International Media and Entertainment Law 6, 2016, pp. 21–42.

Hafen, Bruce C.: Children's Liberation and the New Egalitarianism: Some Reservations about Abandoning Children to Their 'Rights', Brigham Young University Law Review 1976, pp. 605–658.

Karst, Kenneth L.: The Freedom of Intimate Association, Yale Law Journal 89, 1980, pp. 624–692.

[43] Shmueli/Blecher-Prigat: Privacy for Children, Columbia Human Rights Law Review 42, 2011, pp. 759–795, at pp. 788–790.

Kumar, Priya/Schoenebeck, Sarita: The Modern Day Baby Book: Enacting Good Mothering and Stewarding Privacy on Facebook, Proceedings of the 18th ACM Conference on Computer-Supported Cooperative Work and Social Computing, February 2015, https://doi.org/10.1145/2675133.2675149; last accessed December 27, 2020.

Kutscher, Nadia: Positionings, Challenges, and Ambivalences in Children's and Parents' Perspectives in Digitalized Familial Contexts, in this volume.

Livingstone, Sonia/Stoilove, Mariya/Nandagiri, Rishita: Children's Data and Privacy Online: Growing Up in A Digital Age: An Evidence Review, January 2019, http://eprints.lse.ac.uk/id/eprint/101283; last accessed December 27, 2020.

Macenite, Milda: From Universal towards Child-Specific Child Protection of the Right to Privacy Online: Dilemmas in the EU General Data Protection Regulation, New Media & Society 19, 2017, pp. 765–779.

Marwick, Alice/Boyd, Danah: Networked Privacy: How Teenagers Negotiate Context in Social Media, New Media & Society, 16(7), 2014, pp. 1051–1067.

Moser, Carol/Chen, Tianying/Schoenebeck, Sarita Y.: Parents' and Children's Preferences about Parents Sharing about Children on Social Media, Proceedings of the CHI Conference on Human Factors in Computing Systems, 2015, https://doi.org/10.1145/3025453.3025587; last accessed December 27, 2020.

Nissenbaum, Helen: Privacy in Context: Technology, Policy, and the Integrity of Social Life, Stanford/CA 2010.

Oswald, Marion/James, Helen/Nottingham, Emma: The Not-So-Secret Life of Five-Year-Olds: Legal and Ethical Issues Relating to Disclosure of Information and the Depiction of Children on Broadcast and Social Media, Journal of Media Law 8, 2016, pp. 198–228.

Shmueli, Benjamin/Blecher-Prigat, Ayelet: Privacy for Children, Columbia Human Rights Law Review 42, 2011, pp. 759–795.

Steeves, Valerie: Hide and Seek: Surveillance of Young People on the Internet, in: Lyon, David/Ball, Kirstie/Haggerty, Kevin D. (eds): Routledge Handbook of Surveillance Studies, London/New York 2012, pp. 352–359.

Solove, Daniel J.: Understanding Privacy, Cambridge/MA 2008.

Taylor, Emmeline: The Rise of the Surveillance School, in: Lyon, David/Ball, Kirstie/Haggerty, Kevin D. (eds): Routledge Handbook of Surveillance Studies, London/New York 2012, pp. 225–231.

Thimm, Caja: Mediatized Families: Digital Parenting on Social Media, in this volume.

UNICEF: The Implementation Handbook for the Convention on the Rights of the Child, Fully Revised Third Edition, 2007, https://www.unicef.org/Implementation_Handbook_for_the_Convention_on_the_Rights_of_the_Child.pdf; last accessed December 27, 2020.

Warren, Samuel D./Brandeis, Louis D.: The Right to Privacy, Harvard Law Review 4, 1890, pp. 193–220.

Westin, Alan F: Privacy and Freedom, New York 1967.

Woodhouse Bennett, Barbara: The Dark Side of Family Privacy, George Washington Law Review 67, 1999, pp. 1247–1262.

Prof. Dr. Ayelet Blecher-Prigat is the Dean of School of Law at the Academic College of Law and Science, Israel. Her research focuses on various aspects of family law, children's rights, inheritance law, and law and religion in Israel. Prior to her appointment as Dean of the School of Law, Professor Blecher-Prigat was co-director of the Center for the Rights of the Child and the Family, as well as co-editor of Family in Law, a peer reviewed interdisciplinary journal published in Hebrew. Her latest publications include Echoes of Nonmarriage (in: 51 ARIZ. ST. L. J. 1213, 2020); Children's Right to Privacy (in: Dwyer (ed.): The Oxford Handbook of Children and the Law, 2019); Privacy Within the Family (in: Law, Privacy, and the Surveillance Society, 2019); and Conceiving Parents (in: 41 HARV. J. L & GENDER 119, 2018).

The manufacturer's authorised representative in the EU is Springer Nature Customer Service Centre GmbH, Europaplatz 3, 69115 Heidelberg, Germany. If you have any concerns regarding our products, please contact ProductSafety@springernature.com

Printed and bound by CPI Group (UK) Ltd, Croydon, CR0 4YY
23/09/2026
02221545-0002